WARS AND SOLDIERS IN THE EARLY REIGN OF LOUIS XIV

Volume 6 – Armies of the Italian States 1660–1690

Part 1

Text and Illustrations by Bruno Mugnai

'This is the Century of the Soldier', Fulvio Testi, Poet, 1641

Helion & Company

Helion & Company Limited
Unit 8 Amherst Business Centre
Budbrooke Road
Warwick
CV34 5WE
England
Tel. 01926 499 619
Email: info@helion.co.uk
Website: www.helion.co.uk
Twitter: @helionbooks
Visit our blog http://blog.helion.co.uk/

Published by Helion & Company 2023
Designed and typeset by Serena Jones
Cover designed by Paul Hewitt, Battlefield Design (www.battlefield-design.co.uk)

Cover: Bruno Mugnai, *Royal Piémont Cavalerie*, 1670–71

ISBN 978-1-915113-57-3

British Library Cataloguing-in-Publication Data.
A catalogue record for this book is available from the British Library.

For details of other military history titles published by Helion & Company Limited, contact the above address, or visit our website: http://www.helion.co.uk

We always welcome receiving book proposals from prospective authors.

Contents

Foreword

It is a great pleasure to write a few words to introduce the volume six of this remarkable series.

The development and impact of war in the Western or European world after 1660 is a topic of great interest and importance, and this book is written in the belief that the investigation is fruitful even if it deals with a local context. This is a period that has often received insufficient attention due to the tendency to focus on the subsequent European conflicts. It must be remembered, with regard to Italy, how the seventeenth century never enjoyed a good reputation among Italian historians until even recent times, starting with the historiography of the *Risorgimento*. Furthermore, it is to be emphasised that the military history of the ancient Italian states and their armies after the Peace of Westphalia are subjects that have so far been very little investigated even in Italy.

Crucially, as Bruno argues, though Italy was no more a major battlefield, the Italians themselves were active participants in the conflicts. Therefore, the chapters in this book provide a comprehensive overview of the land and sea warfare that involved them across the Peninsula and the Mediterranean, throughout a period of momentous political, religious, technological, intellectual, and military change. Bruno not only summarises existing scholarship, but also presents new findings and ideas casting new lights and details, much of it fresh from Italian archives.

As always, the book is written and illustrated with the author's characteristic attention to detail, and deserves our attention as a valuable account that does not add anything new to a known topic, but fills an actual gap.

Ciro Paoletti
Rome, October 2022

Acknowledgements

The fact that a book dealing with the 'military' of the ancient Italian states is written by a native author is too obvious. After previous volumes on the armies of some of the major European powers, dealing with a subject like this seemed an easy task. Not at all true. Apart from the scarcity of systematic studies on this subject, the scenario appears extremely complicated and full of aspects that historiography closer to our times has often distorted or even eluded.

This volume is the result of research that began at least 25 years ago. In particular, it was decisive to have access to the outstanding mine of documents preserved in the Historical Archive of the Italian Army. Apart from the large number of works published in glorious publications such as *Rivista Militare* and *Studi Storici-Militari*, the archive contains several interesting manuscripts and research drafts including subjects relating to the Italian scenario of the seventeenth century.

During the various stages of this volume, I had the opportunity to further benefit from numerous conversations concerning its different aspects. Foremost among those with whom I exchanged views was the 'irreplaceable' Ciro Paoletti. His authority on the matter is out of question, and I am proud to have him as a friend.

My thanks are also due to the people who supported me in the 'territories'. They are Professor Virgilio Ilari from Rome, Paolo Giacomone Piana and Enea Mattia Solari from Genoa, Alberto Menziani from Modena, Pier Filippo Melchiorre from Parma, and Dr Stathis Birtachas from Athens, since the history of his country has intertwined with that of Italy throughout the period covered by this book. Their researches enabled me to dedicate myself to this work, and overall they all helped me overcome various difficulties on the way.

I also thank Dr Éric Luc Guillaume Pinzelli, since his research in the Venetian archives has been fundamental for the writing of this book. The quality of his work has left me full of admiration and gratitude.

Very special thanks to General Bruno Buratti from Venice, who provided to me the valuable acts of the conference celebrating Francesco Morosini's 400th birthday.

Finally, I would like to thank Helion & Company, and especially Charles Singleton, Series Editor of the 'Century of the Soldier', for the cordiality and the careful treatment of my manuscript.

BM
Florence, 24 October 2022

1

The Earthen Pots

He had therefore realised … that he was, in that society, like an earthenware pot, forced to travel in the company of many iron pots.[1]

In the early years of the seventeenth century, Italy was still an active country in commerce, manufacture and banking, which were centred mainly in the major towns. In less than a century, the scenario had changed dramatically. Italy was becoming almost exclusively an agrarian country, whose small and lethargic towns were for the most part administrative centres or places of residence for the landowners. Italian finance had vanished as an international economic factor; trade was mainly a memory of the past since the Italian States played no part in the oceanic colonial trade that was the chief commercial activity of the time, and their ports were in full decline. Among the factors of this appalling decline, there was the collapse of the Spanish Empire. Even Genoa was severely affected by the crisis of the Spanish monarchy, of which it had been one of the traditional economic centres. Livorno in Tuscany remained an active port but mainly as a bridgehead for foreign trade, particularly for the Dutch and English. The competition in the sea trade seriously threatened the interests of Venice, which was forced to fight two bitter wars against the Porte in the eastern Mediterranean, Dalmatia and Albania.

Industry also declined. With some exceptions, the number of factories fell dramatically, while the Florentine silk industry virtually disappeared. The collapse of the economy dragged down three-quarters of Italy, favouring the rise of foreign powers, in particular England and Holland, and the aggressive mercantilism of France. Louis XIV's acts of violence against the Italian States were accompanied by silent economic warfare. For example, in the competition of Marseilles with Genoa and Leghorn, and the manufacture

1 These lines are from the Alessandro Manzoni's novel *I Promessi Sposi* (The Betrothed) set in the Lombardy of the seventeenth century. The 'earthen pot' was the curate don Abbondio, who was forced to travel with stronger and more aggressive men. This scene has been interpreted as an allusion to the condition of the Italian states in the seventeenth century, which were at the mercy of the major European powers.

1. 'Capitan Spaventa', after a series of prints illustrating the characters of the Commedia dell'Arte, 1670–80 (author's archive). See image commentaries for more information.

in France of the mirrors for which Venice was famous.[2] Here was another instance of Louis' failure to create concrete links between France and Italy. The growing rigidity of landed property also tended to discourage technical improvements. More and more land passed into the hands of the Church, and the decline in the Papacy's moral and political prestige was becoming more marked, while the noble estates were increasingly burdened by trusts and entails. Finally, the increasing tendency on the part of the merchant families to abandon their traditional activities and their gradual transformation into a landed nobility led to the disappearance of the habits of economic enterprise, industriousness and parsimony and their replacement by aristocratic habits of economic parasitism, idleness and extravagant show. The reduction in commercial volume and the general tendency towards deflation brought to an end the disorders caused by monetary inflation and the worst forms of pauperism, crime and vagrancy. Italy was turning into 'a country of neglectful, affable gentlemen and resigned, fatalistic peasants'.[3] In the second half of the seventeenth century, Italy, as it is said today, seemed to have stepped out of history.

Consequently, nineteenth-century historians have often stated a negative, *trenchant*, opinion about Italy in the seventeenth century, where 'the ruling houses and their courts putrefied in the futile routine of a pointless existence, a decadence which was physiological as well as political and moral'.[4] By the end of the century

2 *New Cambridge Modern History*, 'The Ascendancy of France, 1648–1688' (Cambridge University Press, 1968), vol. V, p.467. A few figures give the measure of the severity of the Italian economic and industrial collapse in the second half of the century. Before 1645, the wool industry in Venice produced an annual average of over 20,000 cloths; by the end of the century, the average had fallen to just over 2,000. In Tuscany, the annual average production of 13,000–14,000 cloths at the beginning of the century had already decreased to around 6,000 by the middle of the century. The other major Italian textile product of the time, silk, also experienced a similar contraction. Competition from Asian manufactures imported by Dutch companies caused silk production to disappear in many regions of Italy. The loss of industrial production consequently caused a decrease in financial investments in this sector of the economy, and so big capital sought more lucrative business abroad, especially in France and Germany.

3 *Ibid.*, p.468.

4 *Ibid.*

2. The work of an anonymous artist, possibly a portrait of Prince Alessandro Farnese (1635–1689), general commander in the army of the Spanish monarchy (author's archive). See image commentaries for more information.

the families of Este, Gonzaga and Farnese offered a depressing spectacle of halfwits and scoundrels. In the nineteenth century, historians, with very few exceptions, also agree that this was a period of substantial decline. Entire volumes have been written on this subject, except to realise that many of them are full of preconceptions: a problem of no small importance for a century that already suffers plenty of them. In Tuscany and Venice, as well as in other Italian states, a certain administrative and intellectual tradition survived, and the descendants of the great noble merchants, even transformed into a landed patriciate, were not all negligible men. Slowly the generation of Galileo, Campanella, Sarpi, Cassini and Boccalini prepared the ground in which would germinate the Enlightenment of the following century. Venice was still an important publishing centre, and Italian universities could boast a few teachers of European fame, such as Marcello Malpighi (1628–94) of Bologna, one of the founders of modern biology. Galileo's heritage lived on in Tuscany with the foundation of the *Accademia del Cimento* (1657) and the excellent studies of its members, among them the Aretine physician Francesco Redi (1626–97) and other prominent scientists, especially in the field of biology. A survey of the accounts left by seventeenth-century travellers shows a less negative picture than the public normally believes. In their opinion Italy was still the great country for art and for refined pleasures. It was the country of the Baroque masters, Bernini, Borromini, Reni, Giordano and the Juvarra brothers, of painters and architects who swarmed across Europe, influencing profoundly the taste of their time. It was the country that created the melodrama with its virtuoso singers and delightful composers such as Rossi, Cavalli, Stradella and Scarlatti; the country of Baroque Rome, with its gorgeous ceremonies, churches and cardinals' villas, of Florence with its extraordinary collections of art, of Venice, with its enchanted palaces along the Grand Canal and its famous gaieties. It was no longer a country that might be expected to provide political guidance, but in the European courts a journey to Italy began to be indispensable for the education of young noblemen and artists. Even from a social point of view, some regions could boast an enviable level of welfare despite the economic crisis. In late seventeenth-century Tuscany, for instance, there was one physician for every 2,500 inhabitants: a proportion that France and Germany did not reach until the 1850s.[5] Yet although intellectuals,

5 Enrico Stumpo, 'Guerra ed economia: spese e guadagni militari nel Piemonte del Seicento', in *Studi Storici*, XXVII (1986), p.377.

3. **Illustration from the *Esercizio Accademico di picca,* by Antonio Vezzani, printed in 1683 and dedicated to Ranuccio II Farnese, Duke of Parma and Piacenza.** Seventeenth-century Italy was also the country of military treaties. The states of the peninsula were gradually losing their centrality in favour of the great powers, but the humanist tradition of the Renaissance was still lived and inspired this type of work, supported by mathematical as well as philosophical reasoning. Although the treatises on military architecture are better known today, the ones relating to the exercise and use of infantry, cavalry and artillery are just as numerous and show that the 'Italian genius' was still engaged in military matters.

professional men and officials might possess ability, they had no political power and could only hope to exert influence in so far as the machinery of the state allowed them. It is not surprising that they should soon have begun to identify themselves with the cause of enlightened despotism and to give it enthusiastic support.

This fruitful scenario, however, did not produce appreciable results at a political level and, as a result, the Italian 'military' remained very fragmented. Historians have extended the negative assessment to all Italian states, with the notable exception of Savoy-Piedmont. As is well known, this had been a historiographical problem centred on the attempt to analyse Italian military institutions in the long term, a task that is severely limited by the lack of studies and, above all, by a questionable prejudice that sees the Italian 'military' divided between a luminous Renaissance military history and the subsequent events, marked by the foreigners' supremacy. This view has strongly conditioned classical studies dealing with Italian military history, with few exceptions. Furthermore, this condition collided with the ideals of the *Risorgimento*, and therefore, with the exception of the Savoy dynasty, this age coincided with the decline of Italian armies and their oblivion.[6] More generally, according to the authoritative Raimondo Luraghi, this oblivion was due to the modalities of the Italian political unification. According to him the Italian army, which came into being after 1861, was essentially the continuation of the Savoy-Piedmontese army; 'the personnel of the old, dissolved military organisations of the Italian states was individually absorbed into the ranks of the army and navy; the former Bourbon officers were not even spared the humiliation of relegation to the rank immediately below.'[7] This also gave rise to the conviction that the task of military historiography was to enhance the Italian historical heritage in a nationalistic key, contributing to alienate many from the study of the seventeenth and eighteenth centuries, namely a period characterised by the prevalence of 'supranational' ideals.

For a long time, historiography has even eluded episodes such as the double conflict of Castro (1641–44 and 1646–49), which at certain times mobilised in Italy no fewer soldiers than the Thirty Years' War.[8]

6 'Hence the lack of attention paid to military matters, which have only recently found renewed interest among scholars.' Luciano Pezzolo, 'La rivoluzione militare: una prospettiva italiana 1400–1700', in A. Dattero and S. Levati (eds) *Militari in età moderna. La centralità di un tema di confine* (Milan: Cisalpino, 2006), p.44.

7 Raimondo Luraghi, Introduction to Piero Del Negro (ed.), *Guida alla storia militare italiana* (Naples: Edizioni Scientifiche Italiane, 1997), p.3: 'In Germany, for instance, although witnessing the birth of the national army, the differentiations between the old military forces remained emphasised not only by symbols, uniforms and titles, but also by recruitment on the basis of the ancient German states and by the tradition of the single regiments.'

8 Yves-Marie Bercé, 'La guerre dans l'Italie du XVII siécle', in *L'Italie au XVIIe siécle* (Paris: C.D.U.. and S.E.D.E.S., 1989), pp.324–326. Despite the absence of detailed information to the size of the Italian armies, the author has tried to estimate the number of soldiers that the Italian states might have paid for in the given year of 1643. This year saw the mobilisation of virtually the whole

Another historiographical problem has been to consider Italian military history before unification as a homogenous field of investigation. Already in the 1970s, some historians had identified the existence of very different realities, to the point of speaking of 'three different Italies', each characterised by its own economic scenario.[9] According to recent theories in military historiography, the dramatic rise in the size of armies and navies and in the general war expenses of the European States in the early modern era is not to be attributed to exigencies related to the 'military revolution' of the age, but rather to the enhanced capacity of the States themselves to find the necessary financial resources to compete against each other and to improve, both technically and numerically, their destructive potential in a fragmented geopolitical environment.[10] From a financial point of view, the differences between Italy's regions clearly appear after a closer examination, since, as outlined by some historians, every economy constitutes a unique case.[11] As for some Italian states, such as Venice or the Papal States, the public debt mechanism provides interesting elements for understanding Italian military dynamics.[12]

In the 1990s the Italian 'military' had been the subject of a study by the talented historian Gregory Hanlon, which, although aimed at an Anglo-Saxon audience, had the merit of giving a new impetus to historical research on the Italian armies of the seventeenth and eighteenth centuries.[13]

Peninsula and the overall number could be close to 100,000 professional soldiers. He estimates that the Pope normally employed 6,000–7,000 good troops, of which perhaps a fifth were Swiss, and an equal proportion Corsicans. The mobilisation of 1643 raised the number to at least 12,000 infantry and 3,000 cavalry, besides the urban and the rural militia that played a role during the Castro Wars, Bercé estimated with a wide margin of error the Venetian forces in the theatre to about 13,000 infantry, including several thousand of the garrison in the *Terraferma*. The armies of Parma, Modena and Tuscany would have numbered 4,000 to 5,000 professional troops each, and presumably mostly Swiss (German) and French mercenaries. In Lombardy, French and Spanish field forces numbered about 10,000 for each, onto which the 5,000 local militiamen could be aggregated for the Spanish side. Finally there were about 10,000 to 15,000 professional troops in the Spanish garrisons of Naples and Sicily. Bercé gives no figure for Genoa and Savoy-Piedmont.

9 Fernand Braudel, 'L'Italia fuori d'Italia. Due secoli e tre Italie', in *Storia d'Italia, vol. 2. Dalla caduta dell'Impero Romano al XVIII secolo* (Turin: Einaudi, 1973), p.2243. Regarding this feature, Giorgio Ponza, in his *Science de l'homme de qualité* published in 1684, already presented a detailed overview of the Peninsula grouping the Italian States in four large areas: Lombardy, Savoy, Central Italy, Southern Italy.

10 Jeremy Black, *Rethinking Military History* (New York, NY: Routledge, 2004), p.138.

11 Carlo Maria Cipolla (ed.), *The Economic Decline of the Empire* (London: Routledge, 2011), p.12.

12 Enrico Stumpo, 'Guerra ed economia: spese e guadagni militari nel Piemonte del Seicento', in *Studi Storici*, XXVII (1986), pp.371–395, and Luciano Pezzolo, 'Una finanza di guerra, 1645–1669', in G. Ortalli, G. Gullino, E. Ivetic, *L'inestinguibile sogno del dominio. Francesco Morosini* (Venice: Istituto Veneto di Scienze, Lettere e Arti, 2021), pp.65–112.

13 Gregory Hanlon, *The Twilight of a Military Tradition. Italian Aristocrats and European Conflicts, 1560–1800* (London: UCL Press, 1998). The two and a half centuries to which the Canadian scholar dedicated his book represent for the ancient Italian States an epoch that is impossible to consider from a unitary point of view. It is banal to say this when addressing the Italian public, but it is

According to this author, a central argument in the evaluation of the 'Italian military crisis' was the so-called 'Pax Hispanica' (1560–1620), during which a general disaffection to warfare would have started among the aristocracies of the Peninsula.[14] Isolating the 'Piedmontese exception', he tried to date this phenomenon by projecting it to the entire eighteenth century.[15] Clearly this is a chronology that does not lend itself to a reading of Piedmontese events; but neither does it lend itself to drawing a picture of the strategic role still played by states like the Venetian Republic, which, after Lepanto, in addition to defending the borders of its own expansion on the mainland, found itself facing the Ottoman power for a long time.[16]

---

not always taken for granted in the community of foreign scholars dealing with the history of this country. Extremising the terms of the discourse, one could say that each state constituted an 'irreducible' exception to the others, and yet the connective tissue of the ancient regime created analogies, similarities and coincidences. For Hanlon, the drastic decrease of the presence of Italian aristocrats on the battlefields actually started by the beginning of the eighteenth century, but also this statement has to be verified, considering that this statement contrasts with that widespread phenomenon of progressive professionalisation and consolidation of military occupation that recent studies have also highlighted in other states of the Peninsula. See in Claudio Donati, *Eserciti e carriere militari nell'Italia moderna* (Milan: Unicopli, 1998), pp.19–35.

14 According to Claudio Donati, in *Eserciti e carriere militari nell'Italia moderna* (Milan: Unicopli, 1998), p.19. The end of the Italian wars and the Spanish monarchy's mistrust in entrusting the defence of its domains on the Peninsula to indigenous commanders led many unemployed Italian captains and soldiers to join other armies and theatres of war: the Mediterranean, Flanders, France and later Hungary and Germany, where the possibility of employment and glory was combined with the defence of the Catholic faith against Islam and Protestantism.

15 It should be pointed out that Hanlon's target audience was American historians, largely unfamiliar with Italian history, or at least bound to a stereotypical knowledge of the military history of the *Bel Paese*. His starting point was a sort of challenge: to demonstrate to friends and colleagues, who were unaware on this topic, the interest of a subject such as the parable of the Italian military genius between the mid sixteenth century and the end of the eighteenth century. Hanlon's aim was to grasp the roots of the negative or weak image that, over the centuries, had gradually undermined the warrior reputation of the Italian elites. Furthermore, drawing on dictionaries published between the 1930s and 1940s by Luigi Marescotti, Corrado Argegni and Aldo Valori, Hanlon has proposed a statistical and descriptive picture of captains of Italian origin and their respective careers for the period 1560–1720. The data, however, must be taken with great caution and would deserve to be verified through research on archival sources. Hanlon himself states that those data are the result of a cursory investigation and that all three sources are not entirely reliable, nevertheless, the work was very informative. The result is that the largest number of Italian nobles employed in a military career is concentrated between 1620 and 1659. This is a period of pronounced military engagement, including Italy, and including such major conflicts as the Thirty Years' War, the Castro War and the beginning of the Cretan War. Hanlon then establishes a ranking of the states with the most Italian officers, with Spain in first place, followed by the Empire and France. As far as Italian states are concerned, Venice has the most, with the Papacy, followed by Tuscany and Savoy-Piedmont.

16 One of the major limitations of Hanlon's work, however, is the use of unreliable sources such as, in the case of Tuscany, the work of Niccolò Giorgetti, *Le Armi Toscane e le occupazioni straniere*

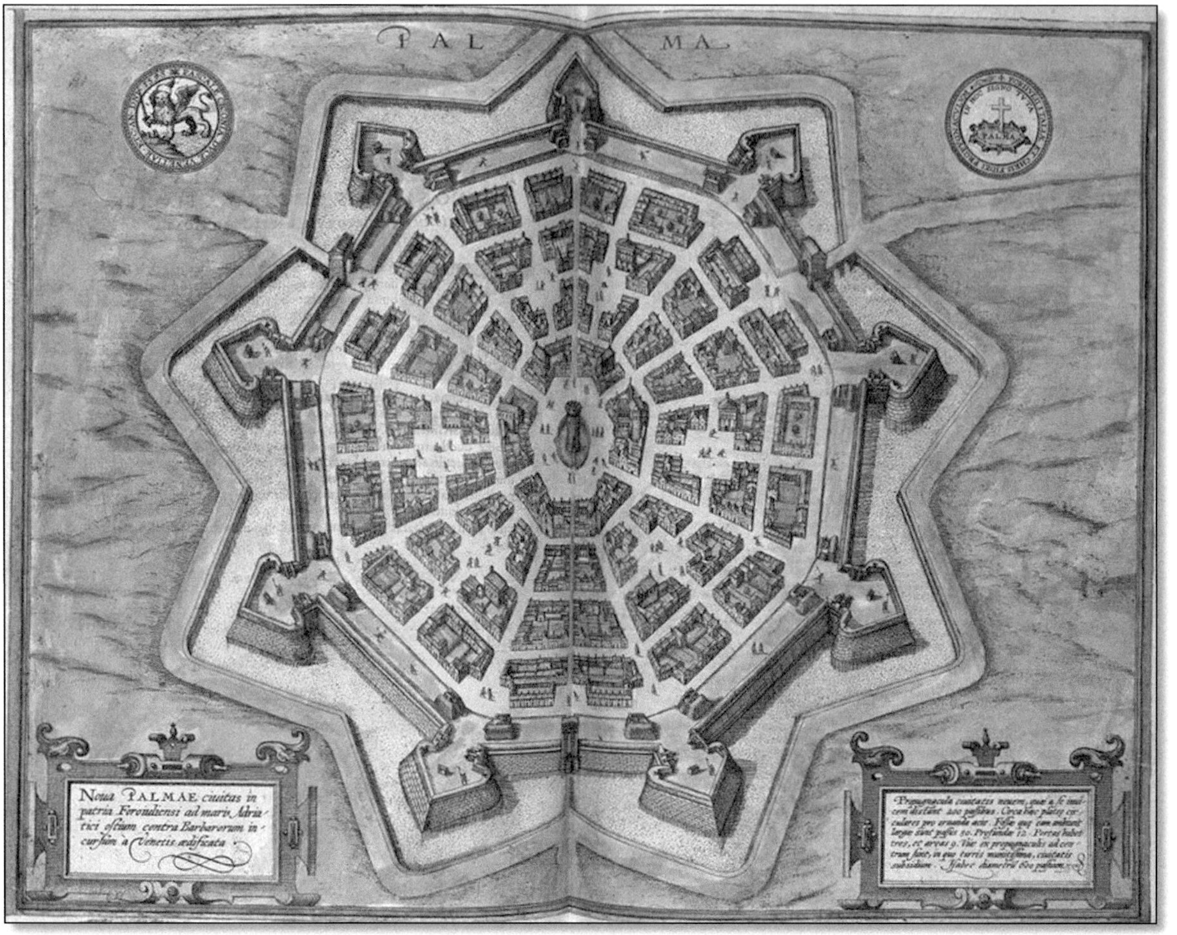

4. The city-fortress of Palmanova, after the *Civitates Orbis Terrarum* of Braun and Hogenberg (1623). See image commentaries for more information.

According to some scholars, the seventeenth century was a kind of golden age for the Italian soldiers serving in the European armies. In Spain, since the creation of the first permanent units raised after the outbreak of hostilities along the Catalan and Portuguese border after 1635 and 1640, Italians were not only a large part of the armies deployed there, but also the stronger core of veteran troops. They distinguished themselves on many occasions, from the rescue of Fuenterrabía (1638), to the siege of Salses (1639), from the Battle of Montijo (1644) and Lérida (1644), to the large operations related to the siege of Barcelona (1651–52), and the final stages of the war against France and during the unfortunate campaigns of 1663–64 launched against Portugal. A presence that continued to be relevant even during the reign of Carlos II until the end of the century along the Catalan border during the wars against the France of Louis XIV.[17] Contemporary commenters had no qualms about

in Toscana, 1537–1860 (Città di Castello, 1916), which contains a large number of inaccuracies and questionable judgements, moreover, conditioned by the ongoing war against Austria.

17 Davide Maffi, *Fieles y leales vasallos del rey. Soldados italianos en los ejércitos de los Austrias hispanos en el siglo XVII*, in J. M. Blanco Núñez (ed.), 'Presencia italiana en la milicia española',

claiming this tradition, as did the Venetian ambassador to Vienna, Marco Foscarini (1696–1763) in 1736. Among the reasons that had determined the unsuccessful conduct of the Imperial armies in Italy during the war of the Polish Succession, the ambassador pointed out the fact that these did not include 'a single Italian soldier', since those regiments had been disbanded because their discipline did not accord with that of the Germans, and that 'such a mixture of peoples was ill-suited to the composition of an effective army'. The skilled and expert diplomat, and future *Doge* of the Republic of Venice, added, 'it cannot be denied by men with little memory of the past, that the Italian nation is very capable of the profession of arms'.[18] Europe was well aware of talented captains like Piccolomini, Galasso, or Montecuccoli, and if the Italian armies seemed to have lost their renown, a lot of skilled officers served in every corner of the old Continent. According to contemporary commenters, Italians had no peers in the technical arms of artillery and fortification, and it is enough to take the number of Italian technicians, such as foundrymen and engineers, in foreign service to understand how the second half of the seventeenth century in Italy was anything but a period of disaffection to military service.[19]

Research focusing on military campaigns in Italy up to 1659 has shown that the awareness that war had become 'universal' and that, above all, there was no end in sight was widespread and well rooted among the population. In the society of those years, there was a more or less widespread conviction that violence, brutality and ferocity were inseparable companions of everyday life, and that the scourge represented by the armies could strike at any time in any place, even those hitherto spared from operations. In the period after 1659, and particularly in the central decades, the most striking phenomena for contemporary observers were the growth of contingents and the increase in military tasks entrusted to the militia, as well as its transformation into an almost permanently armed force in all the Italian states.[20]

International Review of Military History n. 94 (Madrid: International Commission of Military History, 2016), pp.39–40.

18 Luigi Firpo (ed.) *Relazioni di ambasciatori veneti al Senato. Tratte dalle migliori edizioni disponibili e ordinate cronologicamente,* vol. IV, *Germania* (1658–1793) (Turin: Bottega d'Erasmo, 1968), pp.667–668. Among the chroniclers of the period who pleaded the 'Italian cause' were Count Galeazzo Gualdo Priorato from Vicenza (1606–1678), a military man and historiographer, author of numerous studies and treaties; the Neapolitan Dominican friar Raffaele Maria Filamondo (1649–1706), author of *Il genio bellicoso di Napoli* (1694); and Count Giacomo Sanvitale (1668–1753) from Parma, Jesuit and professor of literature and mathematics, who wrote in 1742 *Scelta di azioni egregie operate in guerra da generali, e da soldati Italiani.* Among the authors who instead took up the pen as detractors, the figure of Gregorio Leti (1630–1701) stands out, especially since his predominantly negative judgements on the Italian armies met with considerable success among historians of the *Risorgimento*.

19 Hanlon, *The Twilight of a Military Tradition*, p.74. Between 1554 and 1600, of the 32 published works on fortification today accounted, 26 are Italian, four French, two Spanish, one German, and one Dutch.

20 Claudio Donati (ed.), *Eserciti e carriere militari nell'Italia moderna* (Milan: Unicopli, 1998) p.19.

6. War scene with cavalry, oil painting by Pandolfo Reschi (1643–1699) preserved in a private collection. See image commentaries for more information.

5. Genoese light infantry in an imaginative reconstruction by Italo Cenni (1874–1956). See image commentaries for more information.

7. Illustrations after *Precetti Militari* (Military Precepts) by Francesco Marzioli, printed in Bologna in 1673. Little is known about the author, who was born in Brescia in the first half of the seventeenth century. He also wrote *Regole ed ordini della disciplina militare* (Rules and Orders of Military Discipline), printed in Verona in 1656. The Precetti was dedicated to Ferdinand Maria von Wittelsbach, Prince-Elector of Bavaria, but it is doubtful that those depicted are actually soldiers of some Italian state. Note the musketeers without a bandolier, replaced with an ammunition pouch: a very modern kind of equipment for the period.

Military innovations were well received in Italian military circles, and there was a continuous exchange of information between veterans, princes and military leaders. The actual difference between the major powers of the continent and the independent states of the Peninsula lay in the duration and intensity of the warlike involvement. If it is easy to recognise the pressure exerted by the quasi-continuous state of war in countries such as Castile, the United Provinces, France and, from 1640 onwards, England, it is not so easy to find it in Italy, where war tensions did not assume the same intensity. Yet it is likely that a German or Dutch captain in the mid seventeenth century would not have been completely lost if enlisted in the Venetian or Piedmontese ranks. The circulation of men and treaties led to the formation of a common expertise on the Continent, a broad set of theoretical and technical references that united many soldiers and rulers on both sides of the Alps.[21]

However, with the partial exception of Savoy-Piedmont and Venice, after 1659 military expense began to be a major problem for many other states on the Peninsula. The money needed to build a Genoese galley tripled between the sixteenth and seventeenth centuries, and the price of oak timber increased fourfold. Similar increases affected merchant ships, the price of which doubled.[22] There is no doubt, therefore, that states such as Genoa and Venice faced ever-increasing costs to equip their fleets, while forced to increase the number of units in service to face the external threat. In these contexts, the formation of a permanent force of several thousand men, or a strong war fleet, remained a non-negligible economic and political concern. However, this was not an Italian anomaly, but a characteristic shared by almost all the European states, with the substantial difference that in Italy the economy was stagnating. However, this does not absolve the fact that many Italian governments have made errors of judgement and undertaken unsuccessful military policy choices, as for example happened with the Republic of Venice after the Peace of Carlowitz (1699). Governments, after all, are composed of men and as such are subject to making mistakes, even if everyone expects them to always make the right choices.

Signs that military policy in Italy was changing can be discerned from more than one clue. After 1659 the pillars of any Italian state's defence policy became essentially three: the fortresses; the regular troops; the militia.

21 Italian military treatises, which had flourished impressively in the first half of the seventeenth century, continued unabated in the following decades. Among the treatises that were widely circulated are the works of the Piedmontese Antonio Maurizio Valperga, *Indirizzo del Nuovo Soldato* (1650), and *Esercitio Militare a beneficio del Nuovo Soldato* (1653), the *Difesa e Offesa delle Piazze*, by the Venetian Pietro Paolo Floriani (1654), the *Precetti Militari* by Francesco Marzioli from Bologna (1670), the *Trattato Militare Universale Moderno* by the Venetian Annibale Porroni (1670), *Ars Militiae Pedestris* by Carlo Giovine (1679), and the *Esercitio Accademico di Picca* by the Antonio Vezzani from Parma (1688).

22 Luciano Pezzolo, 'La rivoluzione militare: una prospettiva italiana. 1400–1700, in A. Dattero and S. Levati (eds,) *Militari in età moderna. La centralità di un tema di confine* (Milan: Cisalpino, 2006), p.33.

8. Frontispiece of Antonio Maurizio Valperga's *Indirizzo del Nuovo Soldato* (1650). See image commentaries for more information.

According to some authors,[23] the weakness of the Italian 'military' was not due to the fact that armies were labour-intensive, because, in the second half of the seventeenth century, the prevailing opinion was that 'good fortresses, good artillery, and good navy' were worth more than the small field armies that could be assembled.[24] Moreover, the fact that budgets were set on the number of soldiers rather than on the number of bastions, cannons or galleys depended on other reasons. The first was the absence of a modern type of general staff, capable of planning expenditure. This resolved itself into a mere accounting operation. If there were sufficient resources, the government calculated the forces needed to garrison the fortresses and other strategic locations, and then multiplied the resulting number by the cost of the individual soldier. The more experienced officials would also add the fixed costs for prisons, food, general tenders, annuities and additional expenses, thus obtaining the amount to be demanded from the subjects by means of a war tax or to be borrowed, almost always from the same as in the first case. But more often the solution was to count how much money remained available, subtract the fixed expenses, and divide the result to deduce the balanced strength that the government could afford for that year, and eventually dismiss the soldiers in surplus. This was mostly done by reducing the strength of the companies, or even by decreasing the weight of the bread ration for the troops and the fodder for the horses. The most profitable way was to balance the proportions between the more expensive cavalry and the infantry, which was always much cheaper. All other needs, even if expected and amortisable, were taken into account as extraordinary expenses, or financed from the residue of military budget.

Another reason for Italian weakness was the backwardness of the administrative and logistical organisation of some states. For a practical choice, these matters had remained entrusted to the companies, whose staff had almost always been decreasing. Consequently, the number of officers represented a considerable percentage and consequently the volumeentered

23 Virgilio Ilari, *Storia del servizio militare in Italia (1506–1870)*, vol. I, *Dall'ordinanza fiorentina di Machiavelli alla costituzione dell'esercito italiano*, Collana del Centro Militare di Studi Strategici (Rome: Rivista Militare, 1990), pp.277–282.

24 Raimondo Luraghi, *Le Opere di Raimondo Montecuccoli* (Rome: USSME, 2000), vol. II, p.183.

of salaries increased, and with it the number of those who committed fraud. In this way, increasingly poor services were accompanied by increasing costs in geometric progression. Bad logistics diminished the efficiency of the troops and with it also their importance in comparison to fortresses and artillery. However, by reducing the efficiency of the troops the cost did not always decrease, on the contrary the maintenance of fortifications could be equally expensive. This mechanism naturally affected the smaller states, which although they did not always have a more archaic administrative organisation, were certainly more fragile and had low financial margins. And the weaker they became, the less they were able to centralise services and control the looting of the military budget. The weakness of the Italian states was not so much military, and consequently the reflection of an economic and social crisis, as the result of the political situation of the peninsula, divided between large and small states unable to present a united front.[25]

As for the overall picture, from 1620 to 1659, in a period in which the Peninsula was affected by the presence of foreign armies in Valtellina, Lombardy, Piedmont, Monferrato, Mantua and later also in the central-southern regions, the French historian Ives-Marie Bercé calculated that the total Italian military forces in the Peninsula numbered more than 100,000 men, out of a total population estimated at 12,000,000 inhabitants, and thus approximately one soldier for every 100 inhabitants.[26] In addition to this, the militia figure appears even more significant. According to a demographic estimate updated to the mid seventeenth century, around 200,000–250,000 adult Italian males were enrolled in the militias of the different states.[27]

25 Piero Peri had already expressed these concepts in the 1930s, and they are valid in general terms. Among other things, the talented Italian historian denounced the substantial disengagement of university civil historiography from 'modernist' military history. See Piero Pieri, *La crisi militare italiana nel Rinascimento nelle sue relazioni con la crisi politica ed economica* (Naples, 1934), p.VIII.

26 Bercé, *La guerre dans l'Italie du XVII siécle*, pp.324–326.

27 Luciano Pezzolo: 'Le Arme Proprie in Italia nel Cinque e nel Seicento: Problemi di Ricerca', in: T. Fanfani (ed.), *Saggi di storia economica. Studi in onore di Amelio Tagliaferri* (Pisa: Pacini, 1998), p.56.

2

Italy After 1659

Whoever is in control of Italy is in control of Europe
(Emperor Charles V of Habsburg)

Historians usually consider the Peace of Westphalia and that of the Pyrenees the political acts which maimed Spanish imperialism and halted the Counter-Reformation. As an indirect result, Italy was relegated to the margins of European geopolitics. Thus, the end of the Thirty Years' War was a date of fundamental importance in the history of Italy, although its effects came to be seen only with the passage of time. The Peace of Westphalia did not at once terminate the conflicts in which the Peninsula and its states were involved, since the War of Castro entered its second phase (1646–1649), and the Cretan War (1645–1671) also continued; nor did it substantially change the political map of Italy, the features of which were settled by the Peace of Cateau-Cambrésis (1559). Furthermore, Westphalia did not end the war between France and Spain, which after 1651 extended into Northern Italy and continued until the Treaty of the Pyrenees in 1659.

Conflicts, both local and international, had severely affected the Peninsula. The population of Italy had suffered gravely from the terrible epidemics conveyed by the war, from the devastations and from the resultant poverty. The gaps were only slowly filled during the next 40 years, but epidemics, although less serious, continued until the 1660s while other negative factors, such as the disproportionate growth of a celibate clergy and the general poverty and wretched living conditions of the lower classes, had effects over a longer time. The period of peace after 1659 did eventually bring some improvement, but the cities did not attain their former levels of population. In the late sixteenth century Rome and Venice had had about 120,000 and 200,000 inhabitants respectively. Both were decimated by the epidemics of the early decades of the seventeenth century, and although later both cities made a certain recovery, their populations did not significantly rise if compared to the major European centres.

Though there were years of relative peace, military problems were typical of an insecure post-war period in which the major powers continued to cast their menacing shadow over the states of the Peninsula. After 1659 Italy continued to show a very complicated scenario, where the interests of the major powers reverberated in the geopolitics of individual states in different ways from one region to another. In this sense the literate Giorgio Ponza, in his *Science de l'homme de qualité* published in 1684, presented a detailed overview of the Peninsula grouping the Italian States in four large geostrategic areas: Lombardy, Savoy, Central Italy, Southern Italy. According to a fifteenth-century meaning, Lombardy included Piedmont, Monferrato, Milan, Mantua, Modena, Parma, the Republic of Venice, the Republic of Genoa and small states such as Mirandola, Monaco, Cisterna, Masserano, San Marino, Torriglia and Sabbioneta. Savoy-Piedmont, in the political sense, was divided into lands beyond the Alpine arc and subalpine territories; the latter, from a geographical point of view, was included in Lombardy. Central Italy then started from Tuscany and included Lucca, Massa, and the Papal States. Finally, Lower Italy consisted of the Kingdom of Naples, the Kingdom of Sicily, and the island of Malta. Ponza reserved a few words for the Imperial and Papal fiefs still reigning as independent lordships, which constituted another division with more than 80 states, mostly located in Northern Italy. The author completed his work with a presentation of the reigning dynasties, preserving the largest space for the Spanish domains with their internal articulations.

9. Alessandro II Pico della Mirandola (1631–1691), portrait attributed to Biagio Falcieri, City Museum of Mirandola. See image commentaries for more information.

In 1659 Spain still reigned on almost half of the Peninsula as mistress of Milan, Naples, and Sicily.[1] By means of a series of strategic points, *Los Austrias* retained control of the Tyrrhenian Sea, which was vital to Imperial communications, and of the states along its coast. The Genoese Republic, with its own territories of Liguria and Corsica, continued to be a pawn of Spanish policy; it was watched over by the strategic strongholds of the Marquisate of Finale (on the Ligurian coast and under direct Spanish rule), and the *Estado de los Presidios* in southern Tuscany, an area that included Piombino and the island of Elba, both fiefs of the Buoncompagni-Ludovisi family who were theoretically vassals of the Empire, but in practice dependants of the Spanish governor of the *Estado*. From these enclaves the Spaniards also controlled two very small neighbouring states, the Cybo Principality of Massa and Carrara and the Republic of Lucca, and overlooked the Grand Duchy of Tuscany. Finally, these strongpoints safeguarded the route from Naples to Genoa and indirectly secured the Papal States under Madrid's control.

1 Some historians also include Sardinia, but since the fifteenth century the island had belonged to the Kingdom of Aragon.

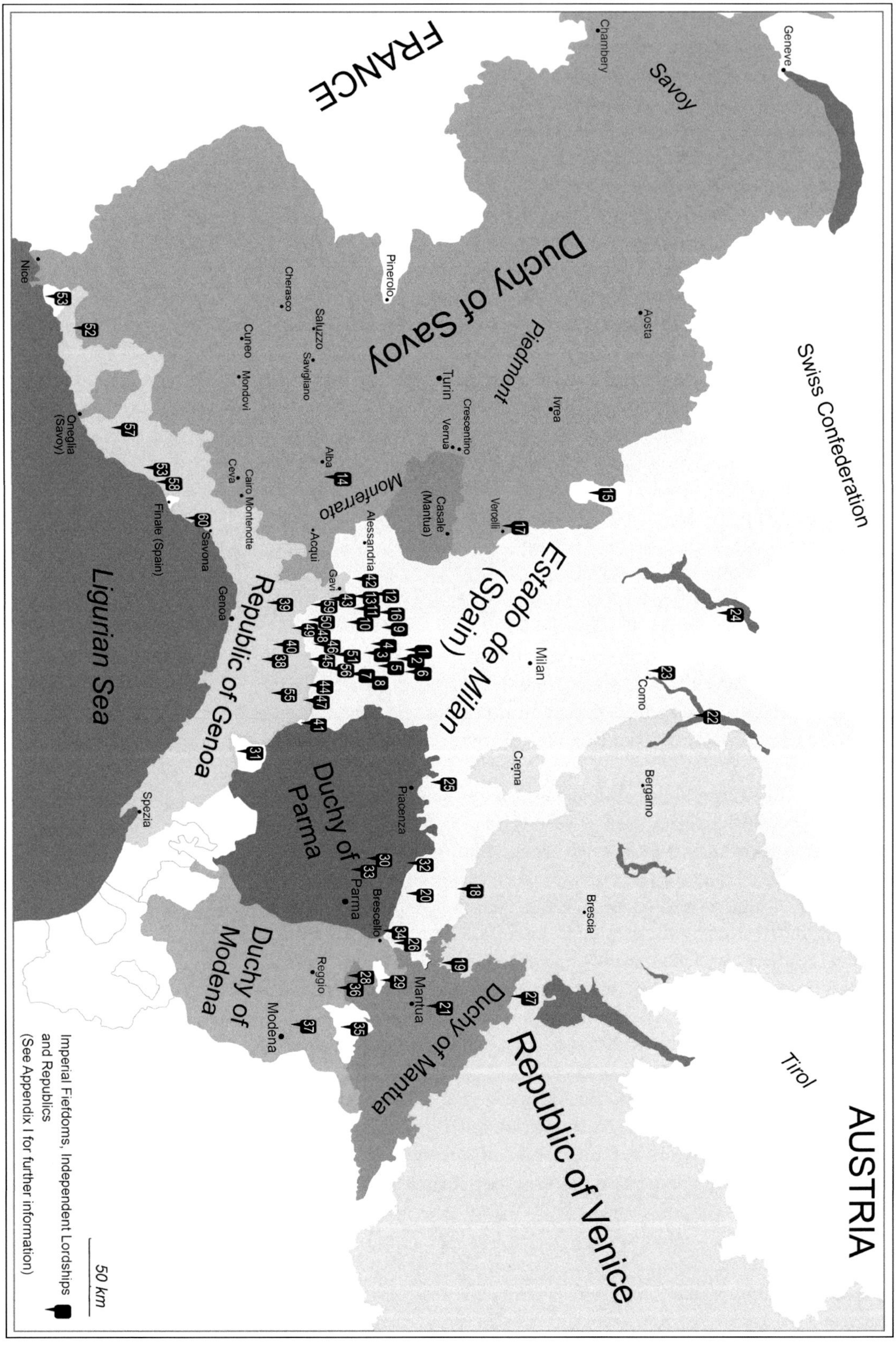

Map 2. Savoy-Piedmont and Northern Italy, 1660–90

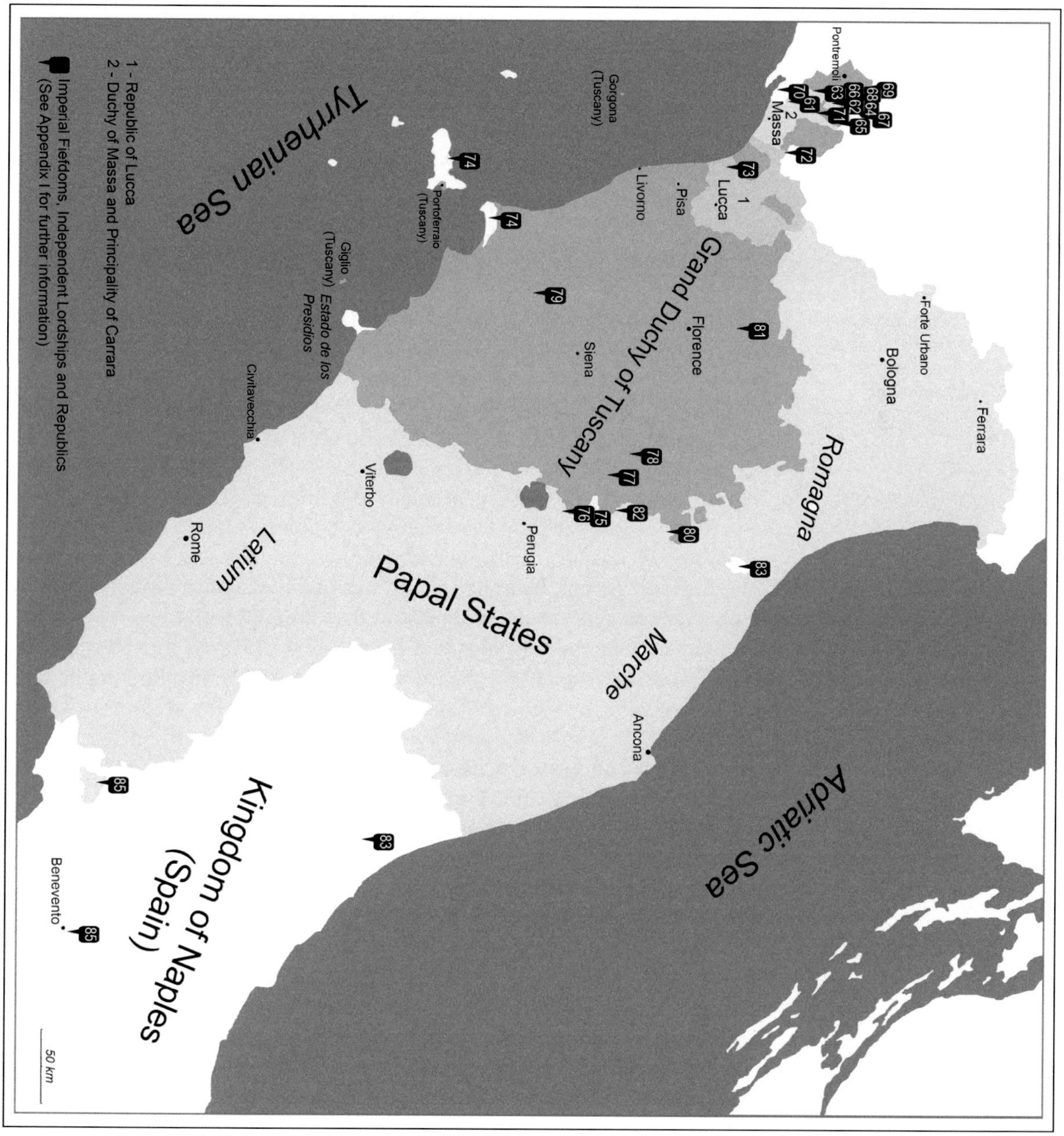

Map 1. The Papal States, 1660

10. A view of Piombino in 1700 (author's archive). See image commentaries for more information.

Spain had other good reasons to control Italy. The main land connection between the Kingdom of Naples, Spain and northern Europe was the so-called *Camino de Flandes* – literally 'the Path of Flanders' – better known in English as 'The Spanish Road'. It was the vital strategic artery of the whole Spanish geostrategy, and this was the objective that France wanted to sever. Although from a geostrategic point of view Spain still appeared as the dominant power in Italy, this supremacy was at its zenith. The pillars of the old Spanish-Catholic regime were silently crumbling, and no new order was forming to take its place. This political void was emphasised by the fact that Venice, the strongest of the Italian states, was involved in the Cretan War and for a quarter of a century it could play no part in Italian affairs.

Popular understanding states that from 1659 to 1690 Italy lived through a time of political immobility during which, apparently, nothing happened. Instead, even after the signing of the Peace of the Pyrenees, there continued in Northern Italy a sort of permanent 'cold war' between the pro-Spanish Duchy of Parma and the Duchy of Modena, which sided with France. The same occurred between Genoa and the House of Savoy, vassals of the French, who at the same time were in dispute with the Gonzaga-Nevers, the ducal family of Mantua and Monferrato, over the latter territory which lay in a strategic position between Lombardy, Piedmont and Liguria. France, by the Treaty of Cherasco (1631),[2] had become the arbiter of this quarrel and

2 It was Richelieu's intention that the Treaty of Cherasco should enable France to follow an ambitious policy of conquest in Italy similar to the one that occurred in the sixteenth century. However in 1648 France lacked the material means needed for such a policy. Both France and Spain were so exhausted by the Thirty Years' War that their struggle in Italy was reduced to an inconclusive exchange of blows. During the first phase, the crisis of the Fronde enabled the Spaniards to drive the French from the key positions of Casale and Piombino and to attach several Italian rulers to their party by satisfying their ambitions. Innocent X was able to gain Castro from the pro-French Farnese (1649), while Ferdinando II de' Medici was freed from the threatening presence of the French at Piombino, and in 1652 purchased Pontremoli from Spain. Madrid allowed Francesco I d'Este, Duke of Modena, who became an ally of Spain, to annex Correggio, and Carlo II of

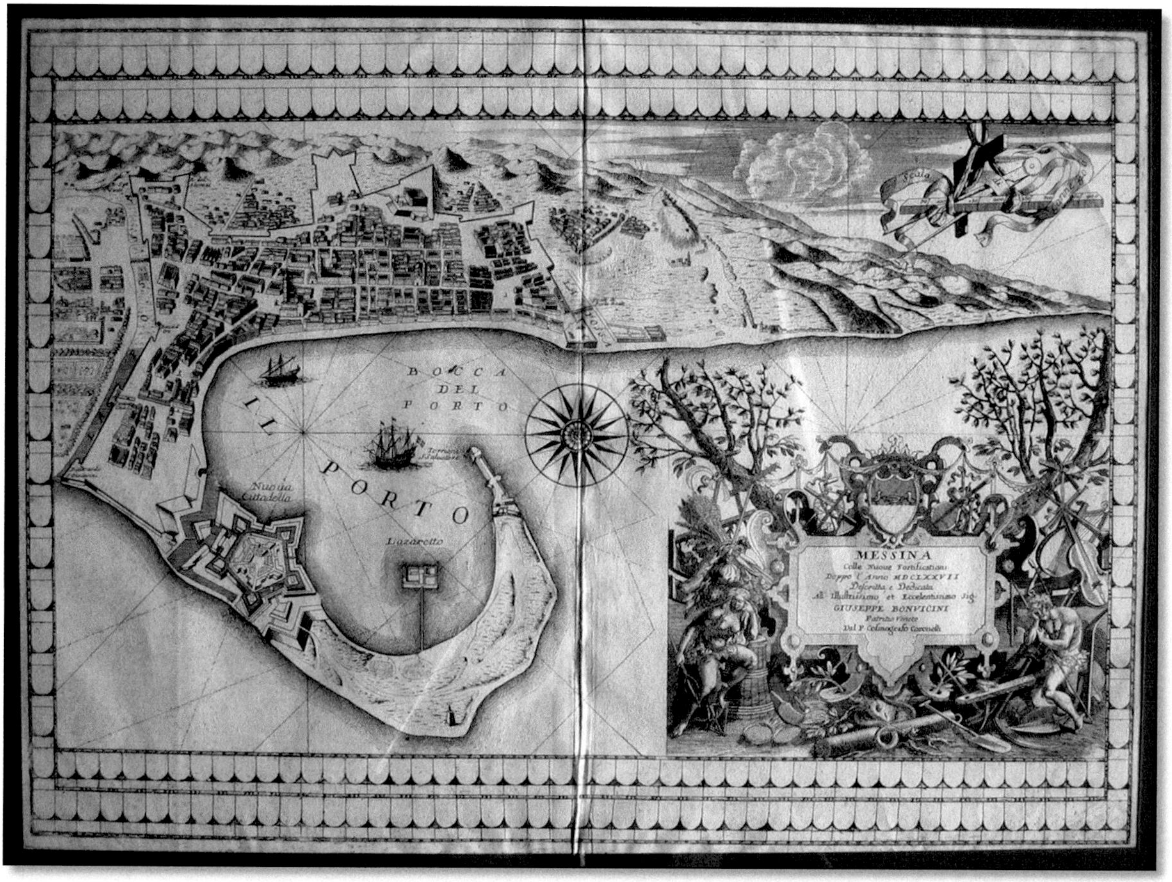

11. The city of Messina, in a print by Vincenzo Maria Coronelli (1690). See image commentaries for more information.

reduced Savoy to vassalage, meanwhile guaranteeing Casale to the Gonzaga-Nevers. The ancient capital of Monferrato became one of the focal points of the French strategy for Italy. Returning under Spanish influence in 1652, Mantua retained possession of Casale thanks to economic support from Spain, which bore the costs of maintaining a Mantuan garrison in the city. At the beginning of the 1680s Madrid's catastrophic financial situation led to an interruption in funding, and consequently led the venal Duke Ferdinando Carlo to cede sovereignty of the insecure enclave to France in 1681.[3]

Gonzaga-Nevers also joined the Spanish side, and in 1652 regained Casale. Immediately after this, however, Mazarin returned to power (1653) and succeeded in neutralising these Spanish successes; but he in his turn failed to persuade the Italian States to form a league sufficiently strong to withstand the Spaniards. This was largely due to the refusal of the Venetians to participate; they were too fully occupied in Crete to be willing to enter into adventures elsewhere. Thus, the Cardinal had to seek decisive diplomatic success elsewhere, and he turned towards an alliance with Cromwellian England. See also *The New Cambridge Modern History* (Cambridge: Cambridge University Press, 1964), vol. V: 'The Ascendancy of France. 1648–1688', p.458.

3 However, the cession was to appear as the result of an action of force. According to the secret agreement between the Duke of Mantua and Louis XIV orchestrated by the pro-French minister Ercole Mattioli, on 30 December 1681 the garrison of Casale surrendered to General

12. Fortifications and citadel of Casale-Monferrato, in a print dating to the 1680s (author's archive). After its acquisition in 1682, the city became another French bridgehead to extend Louis XIV's interference in the geopolitics of Northern Italy.

After 1659 many states looked at French ascendancy as an opportunity to increase their political prestige among the others. The phenomenon was symptomatic and attracted the attention of political commentators of the time. It was now clear that the Italian situation was profoundly changing. The Italian states were less and less in awe of Spain and openly beginning to favour French penetration. There were also those who warned the Italian princes to hand over 'the keys and the gates of Italy' and feared that after Spanish dominance there would follow one with even worse consequences.[4] Over

Nicolas Catinat at the end of a feigned siege. Carlo Botta, *Storia d'Italia continuata da quella del Guicciardini sino al 1789* (Paris, 1832), vol. VIII, p.301.

4 Ambassador Giacomo Corner commenting the cession of Casale to Louis XIV, in *La Storia. Il Seicento e l'età dell'Illuminismo* (Turin: Utet, 2004), p.440: 'princes should only ponder the consequences that the never-believed annexation of Casale may at any moment bring about and produce'.

time, a widespread sense of fear grew in the face of Louis XIV's unscrupulous warlike undertakings. In the climate of economic conjuncture, and with the disappearance of a common defensive policy, the periodically repeated and then empty calls for the formation of an 'Italic League' appeared rhetorical and useless.

However, though Spain's influence continued to decrease in the following decades, France made no serious attempt to drive Spain from Italy before 1674, and take its place in controlling the Peninsula by other means. France remained encamped at Pinerolo and occasionally frightened the states of the peninsula by a display of military strength. It was enough that Italy should remain inert, creating no problems, while French armies pursued more important objectives in other theatres of war. After 1674, during the rebellion of Messina, the Republic of Venice was forced to conduct a cautious and uncertain foreign policy. After denying permission to send reinforcements for the Spanish army in Sicily across the upper Adriatic, the Senate had to face French enticements that promised the return of the ancient possessions in Southern Italy if the Republic adhered to an alliance with France. In 1675 Simon Arnaud de Pomponne, the French Secretary of State for Foreign Affairs, had offered this possibility to the Republic's ambassador in Paris, but the latter had replied evasively. A similar proposal was made to the Venetian ambassador in Rome, but the French agents had received the same reply. In spite of this, on 8 December 1676 Pomponne considered it necessary to renew the offer to the new Venetian ambassador, offering the possibility of raising an independent Kingdom of Sicily under French protection.[5]

A third foreign actor was conducting Italian geopolitics, although he found himself in a situation no better than the Spanish one. The German emperor was still the ruler of the 'Lombard Kingdom' as King of Rome. Imperial Italy included the whole northern part of the Italian peninsula between the Alps and the Papal States, except for the Republic of Venice. It was heritage from Charlemagne's Empire. Once shared among his heirs, Germany and Northern Italy formally composed the Holy Roman-German Empire. Therefore, the small duchies of Modena, Parma and Piacenza, Mirandola and Mantua, the Duchy of Milan, Tuscany, as well as the Republics of Genoa and Lucca, and the Principality of Piedmont, were officially under the Emperor's rule.

Until a few decades ago, scholars represented the Italian states of the seventeenth century as monads for their own sake. Instead, every Italian 'prince', whether he was a monarch or a republic, was fully aware of his interactive role in the geopolitical context of Italy. Each of them knew that Italy's prosperity depended on the safety of the Mediterranean routes. Although the discovery of America had shifted a significant percentage of trade to ocean routes, populous states faced the Mediterranean basin, capable of increasing the demand for products as a simple effect of population growth. In the past, the 'turmoil of Italy' had forced the Italian states to organise themselves to face, if necessary,

5 Émile Laloy, *L'expédition de Sicile et la politique française en Italie (1674–1678)* (Paris, 1929), vol. III, p.95. Pomponne concluded with the advice that it would be time for the Republic to acquire some place in the Kingdom of Naples it had once possessed in the past.

enemy threats with armies strong enough to act as a deterrent. Ultimately this policy had to pay off, especially to face Ottoman expansionism, which essentially aimed to replace the Venetians in the eastern Mediterranean but never assaulted Italy after 1480 by sea and 1499 by land.

The same policy managed to face another dangerous potential enemy in the Mediterranean: France. At least until the age of Louis XIV, the French failed to have a sufficiently large and powerful fleet to enable them to support an eventual invasion of the Peninsula or, as in the case of Orbetello in 1646, to preserve the conquests they had made. But in the 1660s France was becoming a respectable naval power, and its armies the most organised and powerful in the world. Consequently, for the Italian states neutrality was the only solution to prevent them from becoming an arena of confrontation between Spain and France.

One Body and Two Souls

Though from a geopolitical point of view seventeenth-century Italy was a country composed of states that could at best be considered regional powers, the Peninsula contained one superpower: the Papal State. Although with the Peace of Westphalia the influence of the Papacy had been reduced, the network of foreign relations managed by the cardinals was still unique, making the Holy See one of the major diplomatic players of the century. Rome and Venice were the only actual independent states of Italy, and the former had another characteristic that made it unique, namely having 'one body and two souls.'[6] The pontiff was in fact not only the ruler of a state, but the head of all Catholics and head of a feudal order that was the basis of the law of many Italian states. It is therefore no coincidence that Louis XIV found in the Holy See one of the greatest opponents to his hegemonic design. Relations between the Holy See and France had become unfriendly for several years. A particularly serious episode of conflict had occurred with the affair of Cardinal de Retz, Archbishop of Paris, who was persecuted by Mazarin because of his participation in the Fronde. In order to placate the Pope, Mazarin gave his agreement to the Papal condemnation of Jansenism in 1653.[7] However, Jansenist agitation did not come to an end, and the problem of Franco-Papal relations was threatening to become a permanent danger to the popes. On the death of Innocent X (Giovanni Battista Pamphili, r. 1644–1655), the successor elected as Alexander VII was the Sienese Fabio Chigi (r. 1655–1667), who had been the Papal nuncio at the congress of Westphalia. He issued frequent condemnations of Jansenism, and returned his state to a relevant political role

6 Paolo Prodi, *Il sovrano pontefice. Un corpo e due anime: la monarchia papale nella prima età moderna* (Bologna: Il Mulino, 1982).

7 *The New Cambridge Modern History*, vol. V: 'The Ascendancy of France', p.467. 'Contemporaries, however, spoke of the 'Gallican Church' and its 'Liberties' and saw these as contrasted with Papal pretensions and French claims, both suspect to Louis XIV, who feared the hand of Spain behind them.'

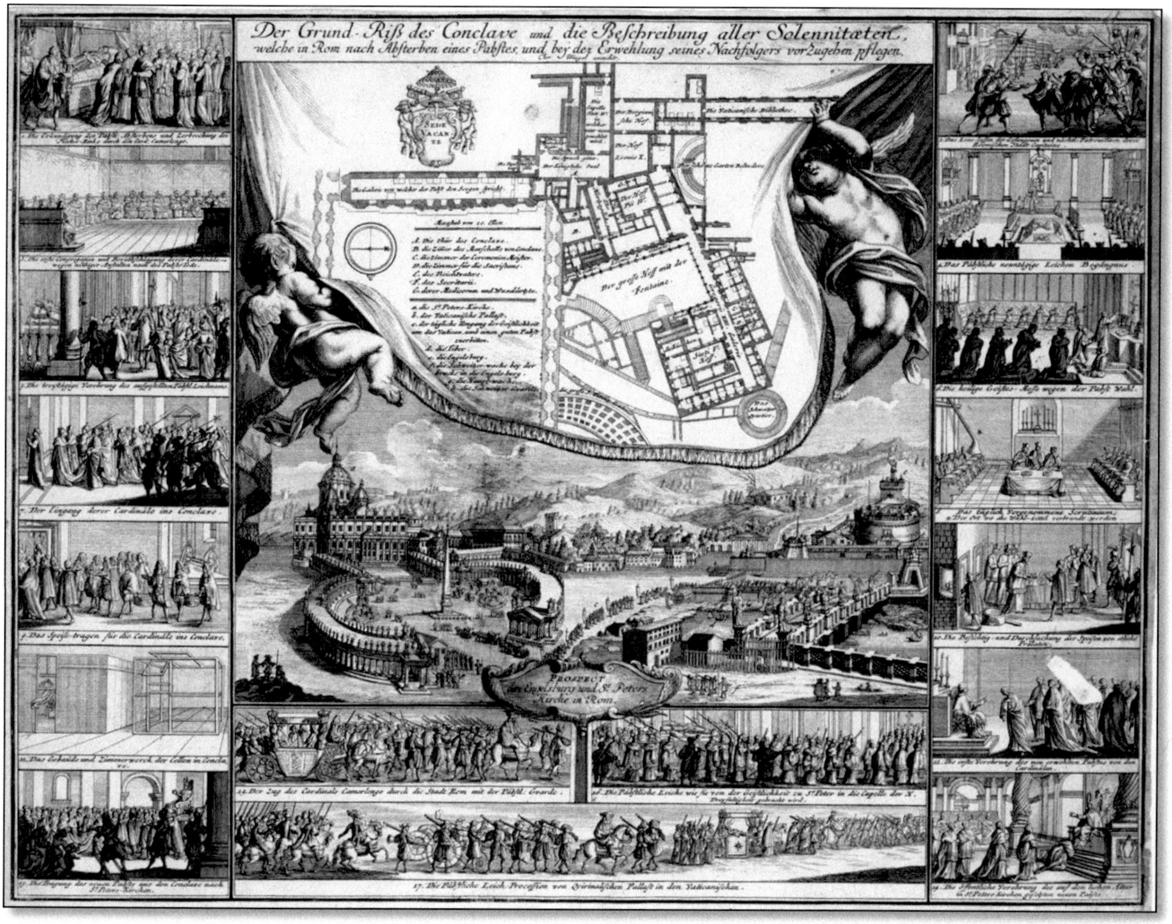

13 Print of Christoph Weigel representing the conclave of 1700, which elected Pope Clement XI (author's archive). Although in the second half of the seventeenth century the influence of the Papacy had been reduced, the network of foreign relations managed by the cardinals was still considerable, making the Holy See one of the major diplomatic player of the century. Since the 1660s, Louis XIV found in the Holy See one of the greatest obstacles to his hegemonic design.

when he received Christina of Sweden with great pomp after her conversion from Protestantism, and secured the return of the Jesuits to Venice. But he fell foul of Mazarin, who was personally hostile to him. Once again, relations between Rome and Paris did not proceed without incident. In 1662 a futile little brawl between some Corsican soldiers in Papal service and servants of the French ambassador to the Holy See, the Marquis of Crequì, was made the pretext for a violent onslaught. Louis XIV occupied Avignon and even threatened to send an army into Italy. So weak was the Pope's position that in 1664, he had to accept an utterly humiliating settlement of this quarrel, and his brother, Mario Chigi, was sent to France to make Louis a formal apology.

In the following years France was the scene of varied and bitter conflicts between Church and State. This is scarcely surprising. In the first place Louis XIV was by far the most ambitious ruler of his time, and his assumption of an overriding authority, based on Divine Right, historical tradition, and *raison d'etat* came into conflict at many points with the Papacy; it was a conflict that resembled an ecclesiastical civil war, since the King could depend on Gallican sectors in the French Church to support his cause against Rome. In the following decades, the Gallican tradition of the French Church

14. Cardinal Francesco Buonvisi (1626–1700). A native of Lucca, he was one of the most eminent diplomats of the Pope. Thanks to his link to Poland, where he had been apostolic nuncio until 1671, Buonvisi favoured the alliance between Emperor Leopold I and Jan III Sobieski. He personally contributed to the payment of the Polish contingents that joined the relief army at Vienna in 1683.

conditioned to a greater or lesser degree all the ecclesiastical controversies of the reign.[8]

Louis XIV's overbearing pressure was felt in the conclave after Alexander VII's death in which another Tuscan was elected, Giulio Rospigliosi, who took the name of Clement IX (1667–1669). He was the last of those Tuscan administrators who had played so great a part in Papal history. Thanks to his diplomatic ability and gentle temperament Clement was able to diminish tension with France, thus to help in the negotiations leading to the Treaty of Aix-la-Chapelle with Spain in 1668, and to secure a temporary settlement of the Jansenist question in 1669. But his attempts to induce Europe to assist Venice against the Turks were completely unsuccessful, and this failure so depressed him that he died soon after.

French pressure, even more shameless in the next conclave, was responsible for the election of the fragile and elderly Roman cardinal Emilio Bonaventura Altieri, who took the name of Clement X (1670–1676). Clement did his best to please Louis XIV and avoid further disputes; but even his willing submissiveness could not shield him from painful humiliations, in particular at the hands of the haughty French ambassador d'Estrees who on more than one occasion publicly insulted the aged pope. In the conclave after Clement X's death, French diplomacy emphasised that the late Pope had fallen into disgrace with Louis XIV by insisting that no cardinal who had been friendly with Clement should be elected. In the end the choice of the Lombard Benedetto Odescalchi as Innocent XI (1676–1689) was permitted only because he was represented as an opponent of his predecessor. A skilful diplomat and statesman, Innocent XI did not cease to oppose Gallicanism. In 1687, in his zeal for reform, he was even willing to face another dispute with the French ambassador Lavardin over the latter's intolerable abuse of diplomatic immunity, and he was not intimidated when Louis XIV again threatened to send an army into Italy.[9]

8 *Ibid.*, pp.130–131. The Faculty of Theology at Paris sought to uphold various maxims, including the defence of the authority of councils against Papal superiority, and of the divine institution of bishops against the claim that the Pope was *episcopus universalis*, and the Church an absolute monarchy under him, from whom all other authority was merely delegated. Far less forceful was the Gallicanism of the bishops who, relying on the King for support against either Papal or secular encroachment, were frequently sacrificed to the dictates of political exigency.

9 *Ibid.*, p.467. Thus ended a period of 40 years during which French policy towards the Holy See consisted exclusively of intimidation and the use of force. This policy gravely damaged Papal prestige in the eyes of the Italian princes and did nothing whatever to link French power with

Difficulties between Venice and the Papacy were endemic throughout the period. Papal support for the Venetians in their fight against the Ottoman Empire led to generous grants from ecclesiastical property and clerical taxes for the expenses of war, for example in 1653, 1657, 1660 and 1667; but constant trouble occurred over jurisdiction, nomination to bishoprics, the curbing of the Inquisition, and until 1657 when they were readmitted, the banishment of the Jesuits. Venice's adherence to the Holy League in 1684 was to some extent a triumph for Innocent XI's crusading policy against the Porte, but in ecclesiastical matters the Venetians were determined to maintain their own traditions of independence and tension did not cease.

Despite Innocent XI Odescalchi's solemn promotion of the Holy League, Rome's aid to Venice in the early years was quite modest. Moreover, pre-existing links between the *Serenissima* and Protestant states such as the United Provinces of the Netherlands or the Hanseatic Republic of Hamburg incited animosity between the Holy See and Venice. For its part, Venice capitalised on every opportunity to demonstrate its dislike for Roman interference in the appointment of bishops. The search for funds to support the war's costs soon caused a new diplomatic crisis. In the summer of 1684 the Pope refused to cede any ecclesiastical revenues from the Venetian state to the Republic. This culminated with the expulsion of Cardinal Marcantonio Barbarigo which caused 'great concern' in Venice.[10] The relationship became easier after 1689 with the new pope: the Venetian Alessandro VIII Ottoboni.

Venice also had an ongoing dispute with England, a confrontation raised as a result of English commercial penetration in the Mediterranean. Although relations with the United Provinces of the Netherlands had weakened, the long-standing friendship between Venice and The Hague had further increased hostility towards England, when the latter had three times started a war against the Dutch Republic. But certainly far more serious in the eyes of Venice had been the support provided by English ships in transporting supplies and ammunition to the besieging Ottoman army at Candia. In 1660, exasperated by the umpteenth case of aid granted to the Ottomans, Venice, through its ambassador Francesco Giavarina, presented a plea to the English government, complaining that 'for the transport of troops and supplies to Candia, the Turks have rent two British merchant ships' and outlining how 'the inconvenience is large and considerable and if such abuses continue, the prejudice would be affected not only the Republic but all Christianity'.[11]

In 1686, when Venice was again in war against the Porte, English merchantmen had repeated these trades.[12] The Venetian government had protested by addressing the complaints to the King, but London preferred

the Catholic cause in the way that the Habsburgs had linked Spain with the cause of the Counter-Reformation.

10 Giacomo Diedo, *Storia della Repubblica di Venezia dalla sua fondazione sino l'anno MDCCXLVII* (Venice, 1751), vol. III, pp.383–389.

11 ASVe, *Senato, Dispacci degli ambasciatori e residenti*, Inghilterra, f. 68, cc. 122–123

12 *Ibid.*, f. 71, cc. 249–250: 'the most serious inconvenience of the scandalous liberty practised by the ships of this (English) nation in transporting provisions to the common enemies of Christianity'.

15 The *Sala del Collegio* of Venice, in the seventeenth century. See image commentaries for more information.

not to intervene in the matter.[13] England and its trading companies were not in favour of the Venetian territorial expansion into Greece and the Balkans, as it hindered British trade with the Ottoman Empire, of which the company concerned retained a monopoly.[14]

Relations between London and Italy as a whole deteriorated further with 'Glorious Revolution' of 1688. In the weeks following the King's first attempt to take refuge in France, popular fury was unleashed against the 'Papists' and the symbols of the Catholic religion. An angry mob poured through the streets of London in search of Catholics, Italians included. The Tuscan representative Francesco Terriesi saved himself by fleeing over the rooftops and taking refuge in a house in Haymarket where a family of friends lived. The diplomat's servants, made to lie on the ground by the attackers, could

13 James II himself, as the Venetian ambassador Paolo Sarotti learned, was involved in the affairs of the trade company. See Alessandro Cont, *Corte Britannica e Stati Italiani, Rapporti politici, diplomatici e culturali (1685–1688)* (Rome: Società Dante Alighieri, 2019), Biblioteca della 'Nuova Rivista Storica' n. 55, pp.114–115.

14 *Ibid.*, 'and thus obliged it to import raisins at any price from the Venetian domains alone, which these (British) peoples could not live without due to the enormous daily consumption of this fruit in almost all food, and even in bread'.

not prevent the looting of the dwelling and the burning, on the public street, of everything that could not be removed. If nothing else, the grand ducal minister managed to save with him the diplomatic correspondence, money and a chest full of gold and jewellery given to him by James II shortly before he fled from London.[15] Subsequently the Venetian resident's home in the City of Westminster was targeted, 'having (the attackers) canes, pitchforks, swords, halberds, spontoons and some also held pistols and harquebuses'. The indomitable Paolo Sarotti barricaded himself in with 100 or so friendly *cavalieri*, their servants, fellow Italians, some soldiers loyal to the King, artisans and others who came to his aid. The fierce resistance against the attacks continued for three days and four nights, but this did not prevent the diplomat from 'the painful loss of many very expensive furnishings, and a gallery of paintings, as well as his rare, cherished books'.[16]

It is remarkable to notice how all these events involved the diplomacies of the Italian states as an effect of decisions and events taken and orchestrated elsewhere. To change the Italian geopolitical order would require a major international event, as would happen in the following century with the War of the Spanish Succession.

Imperial and Independent Fiefdoms

In the course of the Modern Age, different and complex reasons favoured the permanence in certain areas of central-Northern Italy of territories that declared themselves, and were considered, subject to the jurisdiction of the Empire. These were mostly lordships of ancient medieval origin, authentic relics from the time of the Ottonians and Swabians, which by virtue of their marginal position had managed to maintain their own autonomy over the centuries, avoiding being annexed by regional states around them.

The scenario, already intricate, was further complicated by the fact that some of the Italian states continued, at least formally, to derive their authority from as many Imperial concessions. All the major states of North-West and Central Italy were formally Imperial fiefdoms or aggregates of them. These were subject to the jurisdiction of the *Reichshofrat*, the Supreme Court of the Empire, with a special Italian section, but did not have a seat or vote in the Imperial Diet, with the exception of the Duchy of Savoy, which right from the second half of the seventeenth century was in fact no longer exercised. The six largest fiefs were called *Feuda latina* (Latin fiefdoms): the Grand Duchy of Tuscany (formed by the Florentine and Sienese states); the Duchy of Milan, Duchy of Mantua, Republic of Genoa, Duchy of Parma and Piacenza; the Duchy of Savoy. The medium-sized Imperial fiefs included Monferrato, the duchies of Modena and Reggio, the Republic of Lucca, the Principality of

15 Francesco Terriesi to Grand Duke Cosimo III, London 17/27 December 1688, in *Les derniers Stuarts à Saint-Germain en Laye. Documents inédits et authentiques puisés aux archives publiques et privées*, by E. Rowles Campana de Cavelli (Paris and Edinbourgh, 1871), vol. II, p.290.

16 ASVe, *Senato, Dispacci degli ambasciatori e residenti, Inghilterra*, f. 73, cc. 210–213.

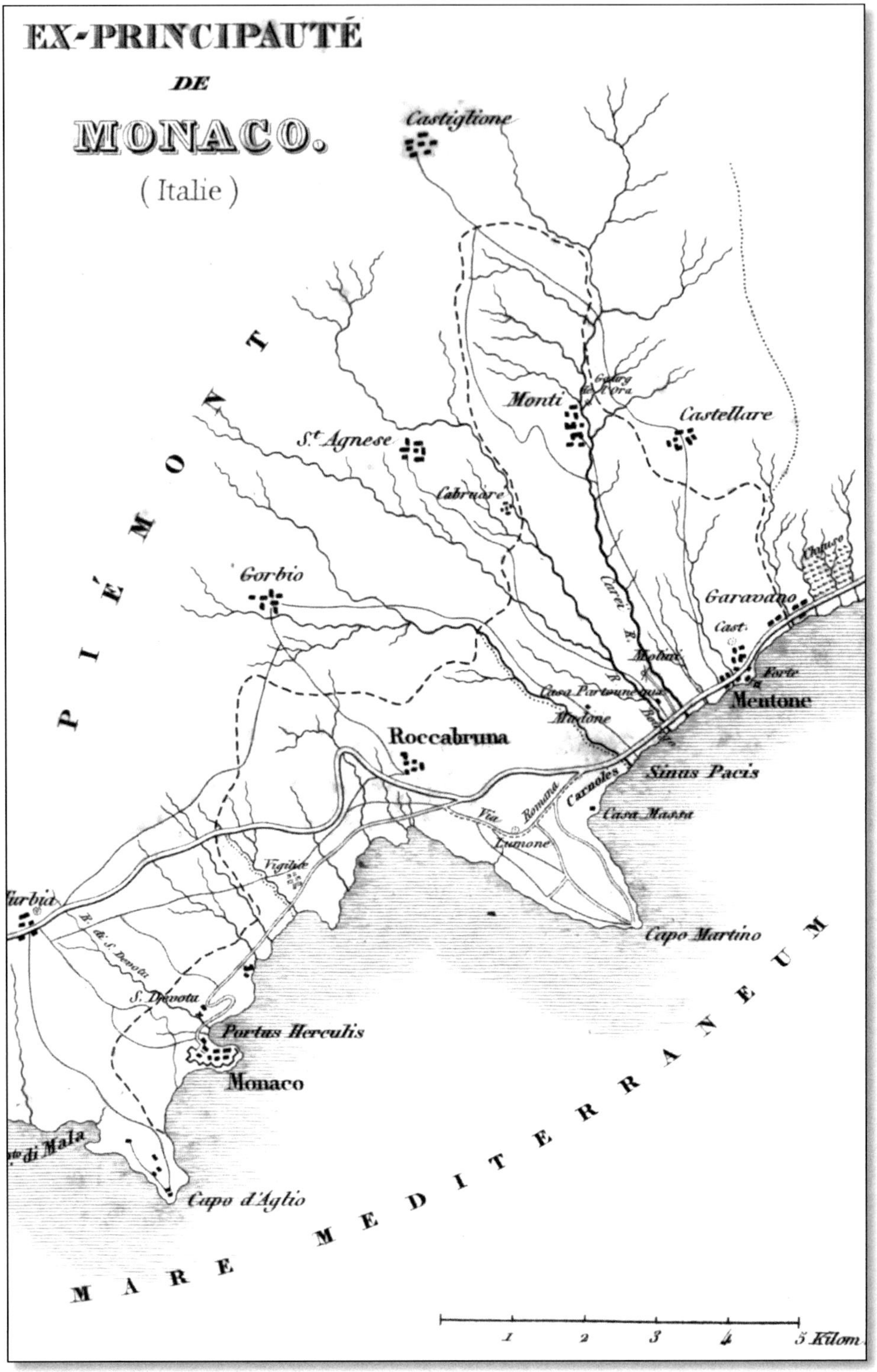

16. The Principality of Monaco with its pre-1848 borders, including the territories of Mentone (Menton) and Roccabruna (Roquebrune). The principality had been ruled since the end of the thirteenth century by a branch of the Genoese Grimaldi family, and by the end of the seventeenth century it gravitated permanently into the orbit of France.

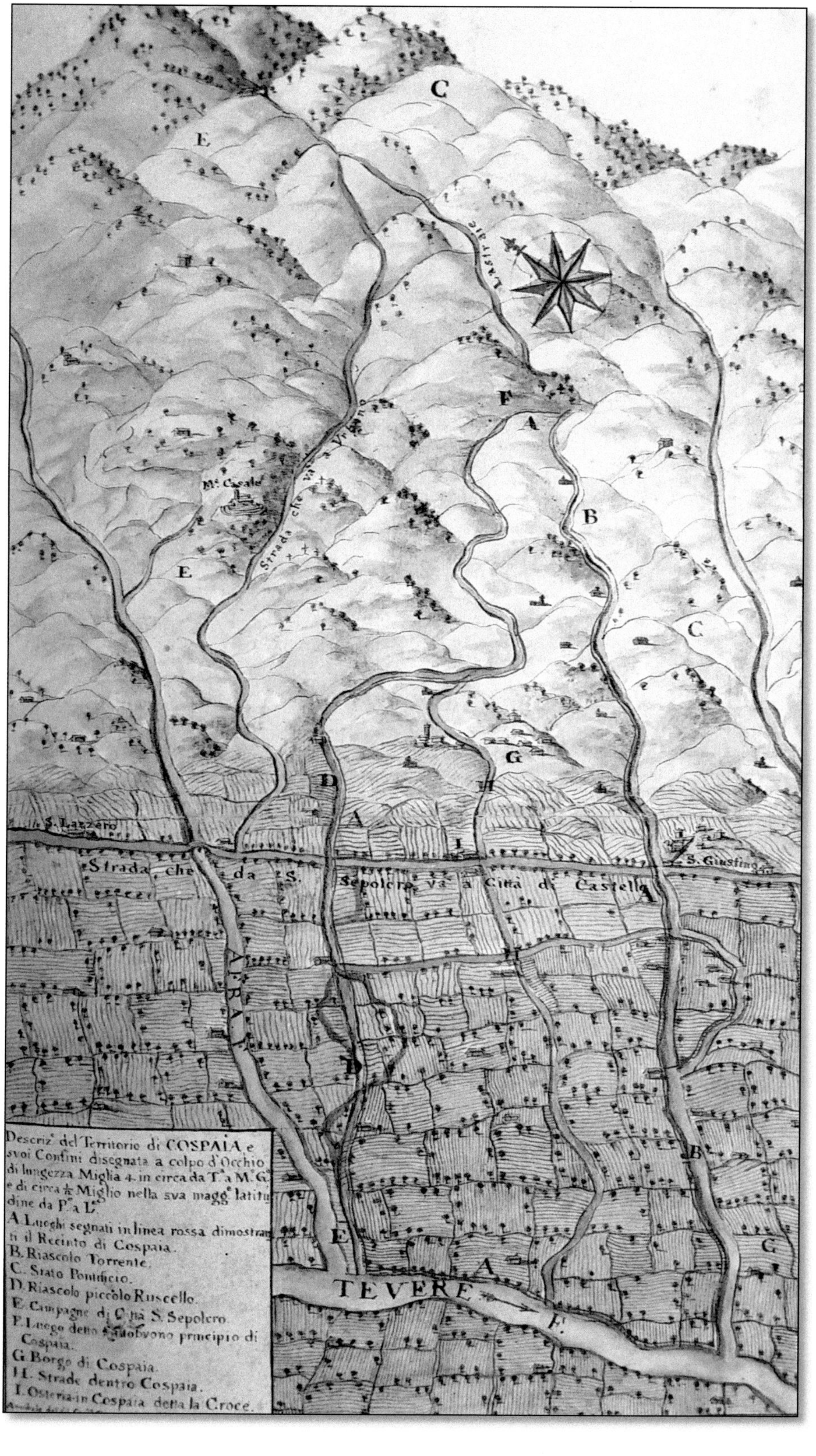

17. The territory of the Republic of Cospaia in a seventeenth-century map (author's archive). See image commentaries for more information.

Above: 18. San Marino in a seventeenth-century print (author's archive). Together with the State of the Church and the Principality of Monaco, the Republic of San Marino is the only ancient Italian state still in existence, but unlike the first two it has retained its original territorial extension of 61.19 square kilometres. In the mid 1600s the total population was estimated at around 5,000. The defence was entrusted to three class of militia, which numbered about 1,000 men. These were the *fanti* (infantrymen), who constituted the elite corps, and were responsible for the effective military defence of the state. They were entrusted with the main guard, control over the arsenals and surveillance of the town gates. Alongside these troops there were the *cerne*, for guard and sentry duties only, and the *lartaleria* (artillery) in charge of the guns defending the fortifications of San Marino. However, the Republic did not have modern fortresses, nor expansionist aims.

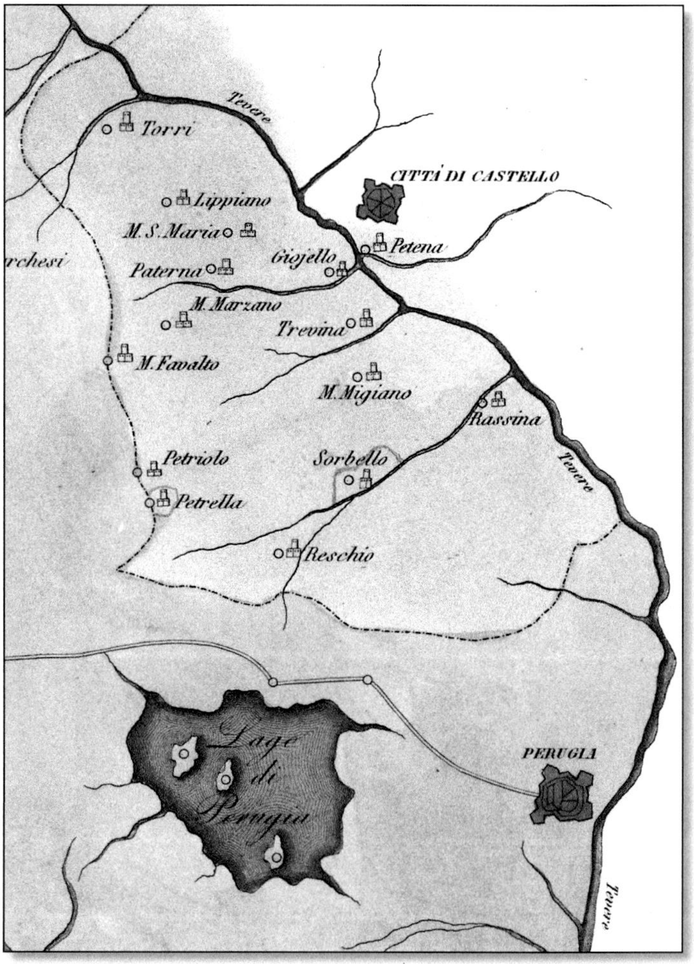

Right: 19. Map of the fiefs of Monte Santa Maria Tiberina, Petrella and Sorbello, after the work of Pompeo Litta, *Famiglie Celebri d'Italia* (Milan, 1842). The fief of central Italy was one of the many small states held by independent vassals under Imperial protection. For these fiefs, investiture was more than a formal matter, as only Imperial protection could guarantee political autonomy and existence as an independent state. The lordship of Santa Maria Tiberina belonged to the marquises Bourbon del Monte, who maintained strict relations with Tuscany and the Papal States. The marquisate offered political asylum for fugitives from other states, a very convenient privilege for small fiefs, and retained the right of *campo franco*, where duels were permitted without fear of Papal excommunication. The marquisate was one of three European states where this kind of permission lasted until 1800.

Massa, and other small states mostly located in the Po Valley. There was also a series of small fiefdoms, denominated *Feuda minora* (minor fiefdoms), especially in the Ligurian mountains and on the hills of lower Piedmont up to the Tuscan-Emilian Apennines, consisting of ancient fiefdoms established after the desegregation of the ancient marquisates. For these fiefs, investiture was more than a formal matter, as only Imperial protection could guarantee political autonomy and existence as an independent state.

Their political role became central again in the seventeenth century, because in the 1650s the court in Vienna pursued a policy of revitalising Imperial power in Italy. The reasons were dictated by a Habsburg programme of a political, strategic and not least an economic nature, since through these territories the Austrian Habsburgs could maintain a remote but strategically extensive control of the Peninsula. Emperor Leopold I intensified this policy in order to politically and economically face the aggressive French expansionism. Between the 1680s and 1690s many local lords hastened to have their possessions recognised as fiefdoms of the Empire, for greater political protection and independence from neighbouring states.[17] As an unexpected result, diplomatic tensions between Vienna and the Holy See escalated after 1690, especially over certain Imperial fiefdoms such as those of Comacchio and Carpegna, in Emilia and Tuscany, which were integrated into the States of the Church. The Papacy, in turn, was lord of fiefdoms outside the juridical borders of the Empire, such as Benevento and Pontecorvo.

The surviving Imperial fiefs in Italy can be divided into two categories: 1) sovereign fiefdoms that enjoyed political autonomy and had a direct formal relationship with the emperor as 'immediate fiefdoms', with the connotation of true sovereign states; 2) fiefdoms placed under the protectorate of other states, semi-sovereigns and 'mediated fiefdoms' that were subject of a prince intermediary between their feudal lord and the emperor, and then with a limited political autonomy.

Belonging to the second group are a multitude of fiefs that, in their relative independence, were politically linked, even in the form of protectorates, to the more powerful states and survived only thanks to the protection of the emperor. Mention must be made of the numerous marquisates of the Malaspina family, the last remnant of the great territorial patrimony of this

17 Cinzia Cremonini and Riccardo Musso (eds), *I feudi imperiali in Italia tra XVI e XVIII secolo* (Rome: Bulzoni, 2010), p.12. 'Perennially in search, one could say, of a 'third way' that could guarantee them both international distinction and the survival of independence in the local area in which their small lordships were inserted, the Italian Imperial feudal lords, while not disdaining relations and contacts with the princely courts of the Peninsula, continued to renew their ties with the Holy Roman Empire conceived as an important way of recognition within the international aristocracy and at the same time as an instrument of differentiation with respect to the nobility of the Italian regional states. For this reason, the Italian vassals of the Empire did not disdain, throughout the Modern Age, to continue to make use of Imperial legitimations as a solid political argument to secure protection against the aggressive policy exercised by the regional states against them in certain micro-areas and at particular junctures, despite the relations they had attempted to establish.'

ancient family that stretched across the Apennine arc from the Apuan Alps to the Piedmontese Langhe.[18] These include, among others, the marquisate of Fosdinovo in Lunigiana, whose sovereigns continued to hold the title of Imperial vicars until 1797. With them, the other branches of the families and lords ruling in Lunigiana, in 1692 met a *congresso* to prevent the emperor from selling the rights of the Imperial fiefs to the Grand Duke of Tuscany. To the same category also belonged territories that enjoyed a certain degree of autonomy and were generally governed by a cadet branch of a reigning family over a major state. This was the case of the Gonzaga of Mantua, who throughout the sixteenth and seventeenth centuries had up to 14 fiefs ruled by a branch of the same family. The history of these small lordships is often interrupted by annexations, but also by further fragmentations.[19]

A further case concerned the numerous feuds located within the Republic of Genoa, where two types of fiefdoms had been established over the centuries. The former were the so-called 'Republic' fiefdoms, namely territories governed by the heirs of the ancient feudal lords and for which Genoa endeavoured to acquire greater shares of property to eliminate the inconvenient presence of these local lords. The latter were the actual Imperial fiefdoms that had been sold in the sixteenth and early seventeenth centuries by the Viennese court, taking advantage of its constant financial needs.

Finally, there was a further category of small states that were formally independent although they were neither Imperial fiefdoms nor domains of collateral branches ruled by princely families. The best known cases are the Republic of San Marino, whose legendary origins date back to 301 AD, the Principality of Piombino, ruled by Buoncompagni-Ludovisi, who were vassals of Spain through the Kingdom of Naples, and the Principality of Monaco, which became a protectorate of France, from 1297 held by the Grimaldi family.[20]

Almost none of these states possessed a military force, with the exception of a local militia and lifeguard, which most often served as a palace corps. In 1650 the prince of Monaco acquired three galleys with the crews from Tuscany, creating his own fleet to protect the coast against the action of corsairs.[21]

18 The Marquises of Malaspina were divided in two major branches: Malaspina Spino Secco and Malaspina Spino Fiorito, with 25 collateral branches still ruling as independent lords in the late seventeenth century.

19 These were Guastalla, Bagnolo in Piano, Bozzolo, Castel Goffredo, Castiglione delle Stiviere, Luzzara, Medole, Novellara, Ostiano, Rivarolo, Sabbioneta, San Martino dall'Argine, Solferino, Vescovato and Viadana.

20 Prince Antonio Grimaldi (born 1661), Duke of Valentinois, received command of the *Soissons* (formerly *Carignan-Saliers*) French infantry regiment in 1688. See Belhomme, *Histoire* de l'Infanterie *en France* (Paris and Limoges, 1893–1902), vol. II, pp.270–272.

21 ASFi, Niccolo Capponi, *L'organizzazione militare del Granducato di Toscana sotto Ferdinando II de' Medici* (Padova, Università degli Studi, 1998), p.13.

3

Savoy-Piedmont

J'atans mon anstre[1]

The Duchy of Savoy was ruled by one of the most ancient dynasties of Europe which, according to tradition, had received the core of its future state in 1003. In the following centuries the House of Savoy secured its domains west to the Alps and gradually gained more territories on the eastern side, moving the geostrategic balance to Northern Italy. In the middle of the seventeenth century Savoy reigned over five duchies: Savoy, Genevois, Chablais, Aosta and Monferrato; three principalities: Piedmont, Oneglia and Barcelonette; four marquisates: Susa, Ivrea, Saluzzo and Ceva; seven counties: Moriana, Tarantasia, Asti, Cocconato, Nice, Tenda and Beuil *vers la mer*; the barony of Faucigny and the lordship of Vercelli. The dukes also claimed a royal title, as heirs of Giacomo III Lusignano King of Cyprus.[2]

The Princedom of Piedmont was the most populous province with about 800,000 Italian-speaking inhabitants.[3] West of the Alps, in the Duchy of Savoy lived a French-speaking population of 250–300,000 inhabitants. Between these two domains, the small Duchy of Aosta had about 50,000 inhabitants speaking a French patois.[4] Almost isolated from the main territories and connected to the other domains only by mountainous roads, the county of Nice had a population of about 70,000 inhabitants, and with Villafranca (today Villefranche in France) formed the main ducal harbours on the Mediterranean. The Ligurian town of Oneglia (today part of the modern Imperia) housed about 16,000 inhabitants, but it was totally cut off by Genoese territory. The weight

1 'I am on my own', motto of the House of Savoy.

2 The same title was also claimed by the Venetian Republic, since Giacomo III's mother, Caterina Cornaro, the widow of Giacomo II Lusignano, had donated Cyprus to her hometown.

3 Enrico Stumpo, 'Guerra ed economia: spese e guadagni militari nel Piemonte del Seicento', in *Studi Storici*, XXVII (1986), p.372.

4 The two regions (Savoy and Valle d'Aosta) were contiguous with the county of Nice, an area that according to some authors was widely bilingual, as were many centres in Savoy, Val di Susa and Cuneo. See B. A. Raviola (ed.) 'Introduzione' in *Lo Spazio Sabaudo. Intersezioni, frontiere e confini in età moderna* (Turin: Franco Angeli, 2007), p.13.

20. Carlo Emanuele II, Duke of Savoy (1634–1675), portrayed by unidentified artist, c. 1660 (private collection). See image commentaries for more information.

of taxation varied considerably from region to region. Piedmont, the most economically advanced region, was also the most heavily taxed.

While Savoy had a well-defined politic geography, its Italian possessions were not homogeneous. In Piedmont, the Marquisate of Casale was a territory that depended on the Duchy of Mantua, which was some 150 miles from Turin on the opposite side of Lombardy. Another foreign enclave in Piedmont was the fortified town of Pinerolo, resolutely held by France. Furthermore, the Duke of Savoy was the natural lord of the Val Pellice, but the effective control of this area was hampered by the fierce Waldensian Reformed communities, and the precarious sovereignty also endangered the communications between Piedmont and Savoy-France through the Monviso pass.

Despite the strong Duke Emanuele Filiberto, the 'Iron Head', refounding the state after the Peace of Cateau-Cambrésis (1559), the duchy remained a strategic mistake. The successors of Emanuele Filiberto had faced decades of devastating conflicts, but gradually the duchy had benefited from the temporary weaknesses of France and Spain by annexing marquisates, counties and other territories, but essentially having no secure borders. Savoy had always been regarded as indefensible in the event of a French invasion, while Piedmont was indeed considered one of the many 'doors of Italy' entered with little difficulty by an enemy coming from the north-west. After half a century of wars, which brought the annexation of 74 *terre* (districts) of the Monferrato, the border with the Duchy of Milan and of the Duchy of Mantua's enclave of Casale had advanced towards the Po Valley, stopping at Valsesia and the Spanish-held territory of Novara.[5] This area was dotted by formally independent Imperial fiefdoms and enclaves that complicated the geostrategic scenario. Further south, the Spanish fortified line formed by Casale, Valenza, Alessandria and Tortona controlled the vital artery of the Po River, and dominated the Piedmontese plain. It should be noted that this border constituted the historic line of collision between France and Spain for the domination of Italy. In all logic, the duchy was a buffer state.[6]

After the conclusion of the Thirty Years' War, Piedmont remained subject to the danger of sudden aggression from the Spaniards. This was the reason why Turin was cleared of French troops only in 1645, called to succour the regent Christine of France (1637–1663) when she moved to Savoy, while a

5 The territories of Monferrato annexed to the Duchy of Savoy included the centres of Trino and Alba, which had eliminated the extensive Gonzaga wedge between Vercelli, Asti and Turin.

6 Stumpo, 'Guerra ed economia', p.376.

French garrison guarded the citadel until 1657. By the middle of the century the duchy had many fortresses, but few of these could be considered as modern, with the exception of Turin and Vercelli. Furthermore, fortresses alone could not guarantee security against threats, since the actual weakness of the duchy stemmed from its location astride the western Alps. The modest walls of Nice and Montmélian, at the confluence of the Isere and Moriana valleys, closed off the approaches to the Col de Tende and Mont Cenis and to France. As the Duke of Savoy never had sufficient forces to conduct a military campaign across the Alps, a besieger only needed to block both places and wait for the end of supplies without having to engage in a regular siege. However, Col de Tende and Mont Cenis were secondary accesses, as the main Alpine pass was Montgenèvre which led directly to Turin, and France could secure the loyalty of Savoy-Piedmont by controlling Pinerolo and Santa Brigida, which effectively barred that strategic access. In this area the Savoy dukes held the fortified place of Saluzzo, but only enough to control the plain between Susa and Avigliana, both on the direct route to Turin. The fortified villages of Bobbio and Luserna enabled the dukes to control the Val Pellice, bordering Pinerolo, and guarding the unquiet Waldensian communities. On the Piedmontese side of the Alps, France also controlled the fortresses of Oulx, Chiomonte, Exilles and Fenestrelle. Further south, the French barred the Monviso pass with the fortified centre of Château-Dauphin (today Casteldelfino in Italy).

21. Youthful portrait of Vittorio Amedeo as Prince of Piedmont, approximately 1675–76, by Pierre Mignard, Museum of Palazzo Madama, Turin. See image commentaries for more information.

The situation on the coast was equally precarious. Here, the dukes held the little harbour of Oneglia, which was almost indefensible in the case of a Genoese assault, also Villafranca was at the mercy of France. The double enclave created problems with France, as Villafranca was a port with blocked development for orographic reasons, and Oneglia needed continuous transit agreements with the Republic of Genoa. The presence of foreign enclaves within the territory of Savoy-Piedmont was a feature that conditioned foreign and military policy, to the point of having consequences for the economy of the state.[7]

A useful way to escape from isolation was the continental route via the Great St Bernard Pass. This road made it possible to exploit a trade route to Central Europe as an alternative to the ones to France and the Spanish State of Milan. The dukes had secured the St Bernard pass thanks to an expensive treaty with the Valais Republic. The latter, like the Swiss cantons, had secured

7 *Ibid.*

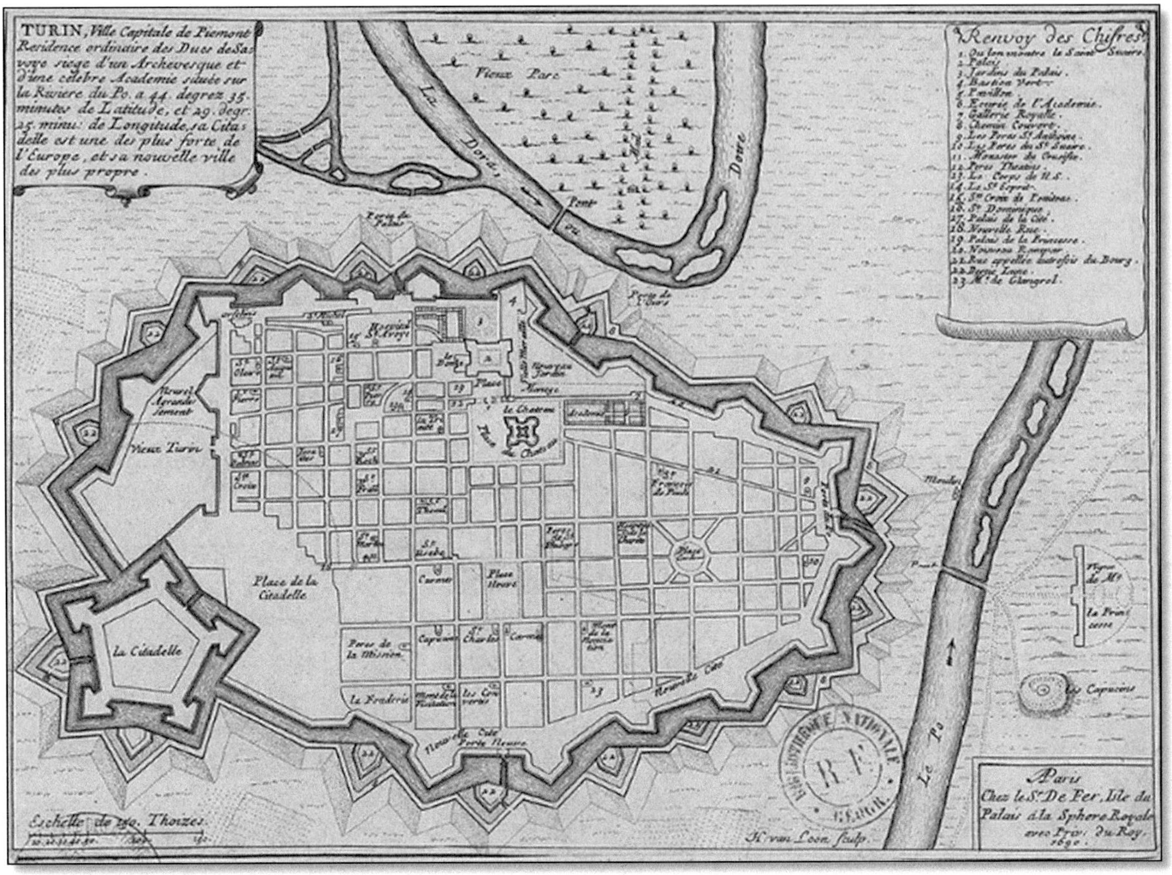

22. The fortification of Turin after the enlargement of the north-west sector in the 1670s, in a French print dated 1690 (Bibliothèque Nationale de France, Paris). See image commentaries for more information.

access to the sea and Mediterranean trade, and at the same time the pass could be a useful route for transferring mercenaries from Germany and Switzerland to Piedmont.

Nevertheless, there were also contested borders. The most significant case was that of Geneva: 'felt as a wound by the dukes of Savoy'.[8] Only after the failure of the escalade and the defeat of the adventurous attempt to seize it by surprise did the situation find greater stability, but without it being truly accepted by Turin. Neither were relations better between Turin and Genoa. The western border between the Republic and the Duchy of Savoy was often a source of mutual disputes. These territories were areas of salt smuggling between Piedmont and Liguria, a criminal activity that threatened one of the most solid revenues of Savoy taxation. Every attempt at settlement was complicated, since after the war of 1625 the Republic lived under constant threat. Genoese fears increased every time the Duke of Savoy entered into an alliance with France.

From a geostrategic point of view, the major problem for the House of Savoy was the French presence in Pinerolo. This fortress posed a number of

8 Giuseppe Ricuperati, 'Frontiere e territori dello stato sabaudo come archetipi di una regione europea: fra storia e storiografia', in B. A. Raviola (ed.), *Lo spazio sabaudo. Intersezioni, frontiere e confini in età moderna* (Milan: Franco Angeli, 2007), p.38.

problems, also linked to the fact that there was in the valleys a continuous passage of officials and troops from France, which in weak moments of the state accentuated the difficulty, while in stronger ones it solicited a climate of challenge in the circles of the Savoy court. It was clear that the problem of communication routes that crossed the territory outside ducal control also meant a religious concern, especially when the dukes had inaugurated a policy of containment and, possibly, confrontation and elimination of the Waldensian heresy. After all, this was the stubborn Savoy point of view, while Pinerolo favoured relations between the Piedmontese Waldensians and the French Huguenots.

After Christine's long regency – inaugurated by the civil war fought by the factions of the *madamisti* and *principisti*, the latter represented by the clientele linked to the two princes Tomaso (1596–1656) and Maurizio (1593–1657) – the reign of her son Carlo Emanuele continued to support the French axis at dynastic level, marrying Christine of Bourbon, also known as *Madama Reale*, and at a political level maintaining the duchy under the protection of France throughout his reign and that of the regent Duchess. However, it is no coincidence that the actions of Carlo Emanuele and Vittorio Amedeo sought to ensure control of the territories, healing both problems that had been exacerbated by the regencies, especially the older ones, such as the possession of Pinerolo by France, held by a ruler like Louis XIV who was anything but conciliatory. From the 1680s, ambiguity, a flair for grasping international changes, and typical Italian improvisation dominated the scene. The qualities of a Machiavellian prince were immediately evident in Vittorio Amedeo. He had not hesitated to denounce the conspiracy in his favour of the court aristocrats to his mother, while with a 'mysterious illness' he had avoided marriage to the Portuguese dynasty. Vittorio Amedeo II ascended the throne in 1681, at the age of 15, as was the custom in the House of Savoy. Three years later, Minister Louvois ordered *Madame Reale* to choose between the citadel of Turin and the marriage of her son to Duchess Anne of Orleans, niece of Louis XIV. Subsequently, Vittorio Amedeo ousted his mother Giovanna Battista of Nemours from power, forcing her into exile in a monastery. But that was not all. In the same year, the unscrupulous Duke had taken advantage of the revocation of the Edict of Nantes to attempt to eliminate the Reformed Waldensians once and for all, acting ruthlessly, expelling them from the territory and forcing thousands of people on a painful march to Switzerland. Vittorio Amedeo had even thought of moving the Waldensian survivors to the Vercelli area, next to the 'indociles of Mondovì', to uproot them by populating the hospices set up in the capital and in the most important cities with neo-converts: a geography of violence and the uprooting of an entire community that was only interrupted when a new international context changed these balances in the 1690s.

However, the Savoy subservience to France should not be seen as a condition to which the dukes had resigned themselves. Savoy, like other Italian dynasties, continued to keep channels open with other powers through the networks of relations they could exploit. Often the architects of these links were the military. Many historians, including contemporary ones, do not highlight the presence of a pro-Austrian party, represented by the cadet branch of the Savoia-Carignano. Although Eugenio Maurizio (1633–1673) had been

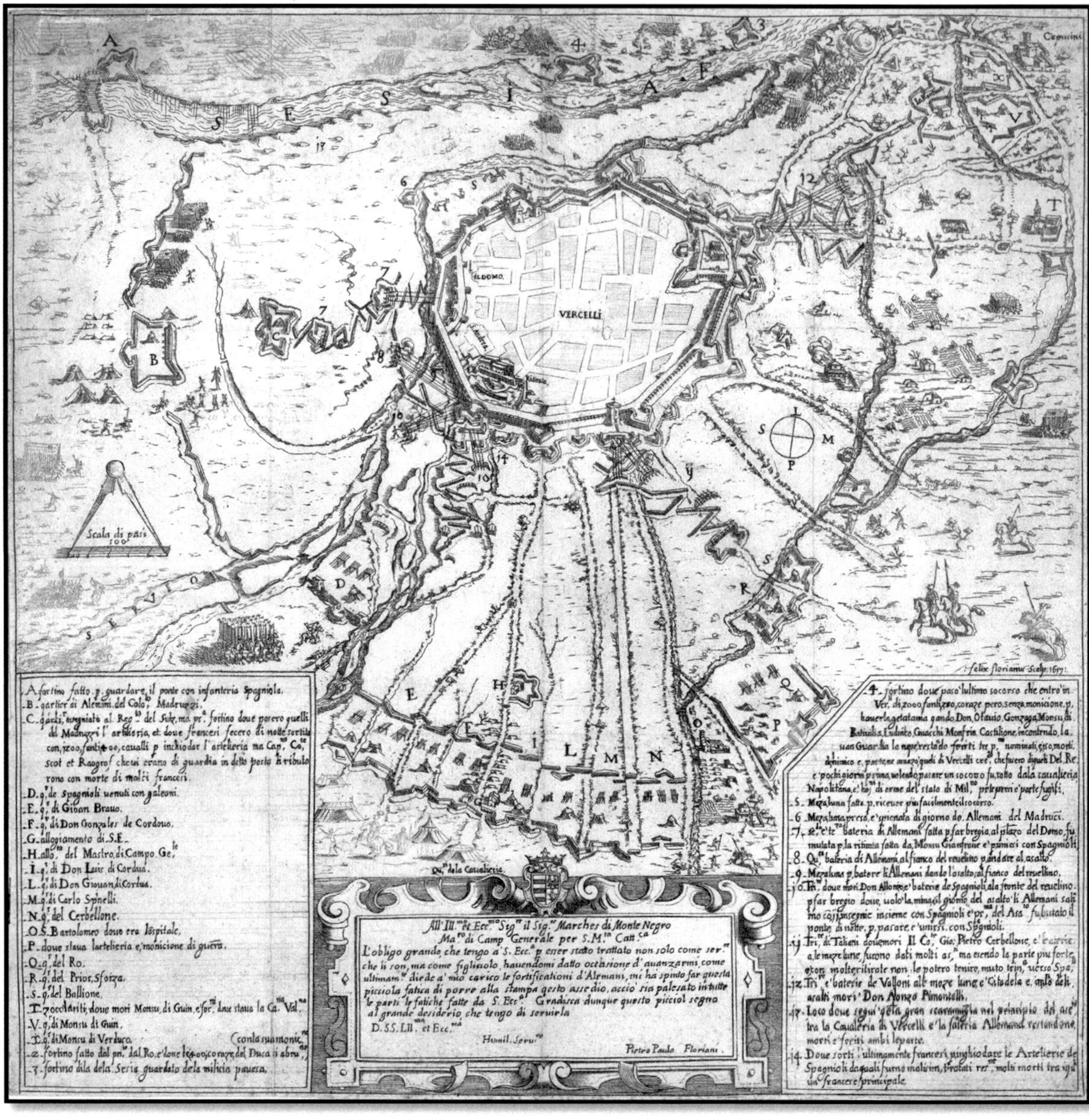

23. Vercelli fortifications, in a print dating to 1629, when the city was besieged by the Spanish Army (author's archive). Vercelli was the second major Piedmontese fortress after Turin, which guarded the border with Spanish Lombardy.

a colonel of the Swiss Guards regiment of Louis XIV, his son ff (1660–1683) entered the service of Emperor Leopold I of Habsburg as a cavalry officer, obtaining the title of colonel-proprietor of a regiment of dragoons in 1682.[9] It was also through this channel that his brother Eugene arrived in Vienna in 1683, an event destined to change not only the history of Austria and Savoy-Piedmont, but that of the whole of Europe.

9 See Bruno Mugnai, *Wars and Soldiers in the Early Reign of Louis XIV, Volume Two – The Imperial Army 1657–1687* (Warwick: Helion & Company, 2019), pp.199–200.

The 'Piedmontese Exception'

A recurring idea in the historiographical context states that the Duchy of Savoy could maintain its autonomy thanks to its modern military policy. Almost no historian questions the special feature of Piedmontese history, yet there is not always agreement on the form of this exception: an exception that, often accepted uncritically, has contributed to marginalising Piedmont in the Italian historiographical debate of recent decades within the framework of the ancient Italian states.[10] For some historians, it is undoubtedly true that Piedmont embodied an idea of power and institutional structure different from those realised in Italy.[11] However, this did not isolate the Savoy territories from Italian affairs. According to some recent works, Savoy has been defined as 'a European dynasty in Italy', namely a dynasty that exercised its government in a way that differed from Italian practices, but also following strategies that were not always antithetical to the rest of the other states of the Peninsula. The military image that has often been associated with the Savoy-Piedmontese domains, including the territories that were gradually annexed by the dukes, has privileged a picture aimed at exalting presumed natural qualities like the vocation for the arms. At the same time, the emergence of a solid pact of loyalty between the reigning dynasty and the local elites prefigured an unexpectedly precocious intention of 'national resurgence'.[12]

The capital itself was perceived as a different place compared to other cities of Italy.

Possibly it is no coincidence that, towards the end of the seventeenth century, Turin and its court had become an internationally recognised training ground for politics and diplomacy by travellers who knew how to value the government's quality.[13] The Piedmontese capital was reputed as an

10 Paola Bianchi, 'Immagine e realtà dell'eccezione militare del Piemonte' in P. Bianchi (ed.), *Il Piemonte come eccezione? Riflessioni sulla 'Piedmontese exception'* (Turin: Centro Studi Piemontesi, 2008), p.57: 'It is common to read about the relations between Florence and Rome, between Naples and Milan, between the duchies of the Po Valley, between the ancient republics and between these republics and the various Italian states, but very little is said about Piedmont in this network of political contacts and circulation of men.'

11 Andrea Merlotti, 'I Savoia: una dinastia europea in Italia', in W. Barberis (ed.), *I Savoia. I secoli d'oro di una dinastia europea* (Turin: Einaudi, 2007), pp.87–133.

12 Paola Bianchi, 'La riorganizzazione militare del Ducato di Savoia e i rapporti del Piemonte con la Francia e la Spagna. Da Emanuele Filiberto a Carlo Emanuele II', in E. García Hernán, and D. Maffi (eds), *Guerra y sociedad en la monarquía hispánica: política, estrategia y cultura en la Europa moderna (1500–1700)* (Madrid: Fundación MAPFRE, Laberinto; Consejo Superior de Investigaciones Científicas, CSIC, 2006), vol. I, p.208: 'In other words, the political-military events of Savoy-Piedmont from the early nineteenth century onwards – not to mention the embarrassing repercussions of twentieth-century history – ended up by flattening within a circumscribed horizon, at most national, a reality that was in fact very permeable to European contacts and connections: the latter being an essential reading key for any investigation into the centuries of the modern age.'

13 Paola Bianchi, 'La corte dei Savoia: disciplinamento del servizio e delle fedeltà' in W. Barberis (ed.), *I Savoia. I secoli d'oro di una dinastia europea* (Turin: Einaudi, 2007), p.137

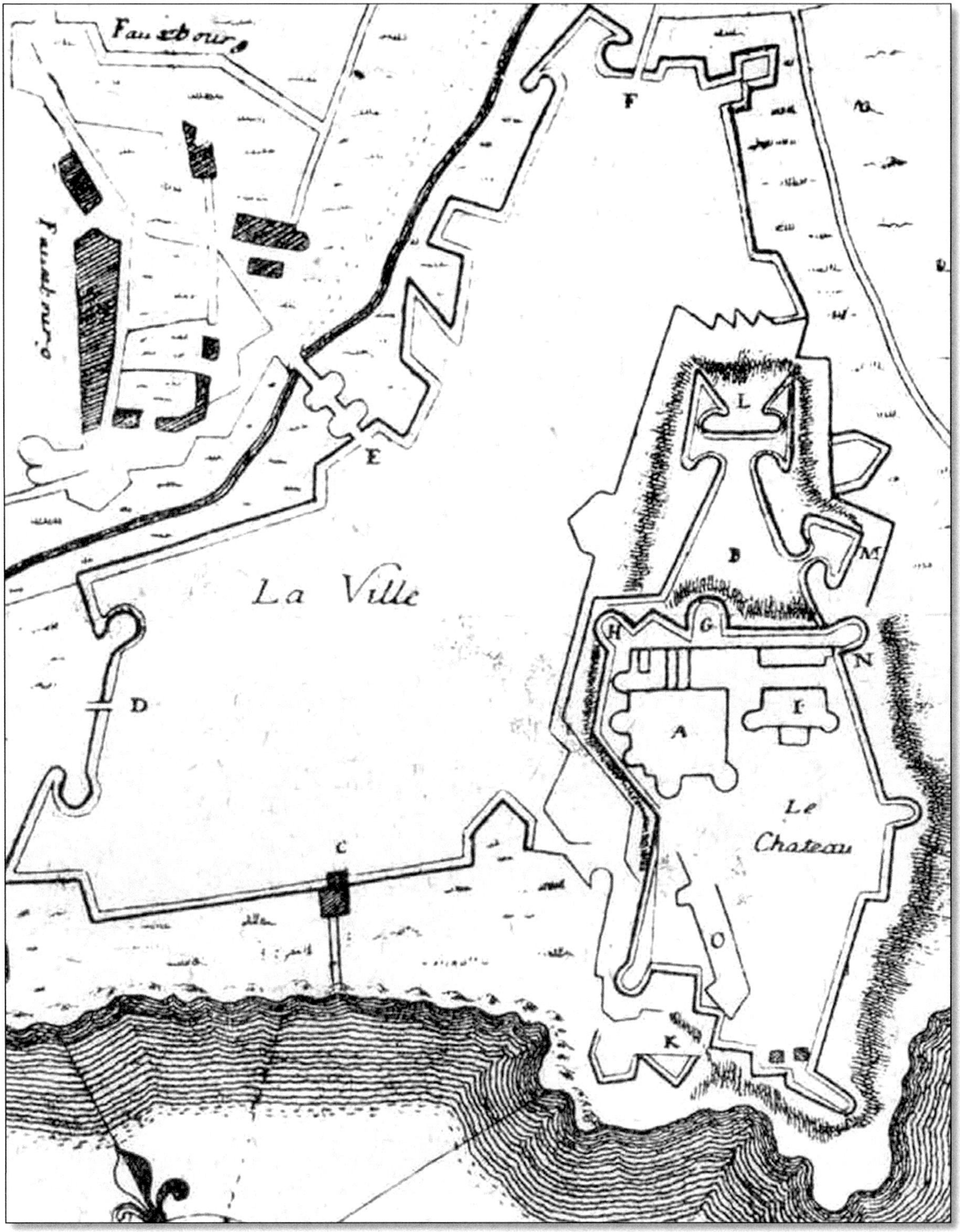

24. Nice and its harbour in the late seventeenth century. (Author's archive)

important destination for many gentlemen of the European aristocracy as an important stage of the 'journey to Italy.'[14] Turin, as the seat of the court, already appeared to have a specific peculiarity that made it different from other Italian capitals.[15] People came to Turin mainly to take up service in the army, for diplomatic delegations or, the younger ones, to perfect their studies. The turning point at the end of the seventeenth century was noticed, among others, by John Dodington, who served as secretary to the English envoy Lord Fauconberg. Dodington wrote in his own handwriting the report of his journey from Lyon to Piedmont, speaking in the third person of the impressions recorded between April and May 1670 by the King of England's Ambassador Extraordinary, who took scrupulous care to have the official speeches given at the court of Turin in English and Italian attached to the text. Commenting on the rituals that had accompanied the English delegation's meetings with the House of Savoy, Dodington pointed out that 'There is the same difference between ambassadors and princes of the blood of this court as is at Paris.'[16] Dodington's impressions were similar to those of a number of French travel journals, which confirmed the excellence of the Savoy court on the Italian scene. One of these journals described the ceremonials in Turin, 'which held a candle to the rules of the more fashionable European monarchy', but unlike the Paris' court, that of Turin appeared 'more military, being a sort of garrison', as the envoy noted, struck by the fact that at the gates of the Duke's palace stood 'a corps of foot guards on permanent duty'.[17]

Historians have argued that one of the consequences of the military revolution was the increase in the administrative apparatus and, ultimately, in the state's ability to control it.[18] Indeed, in some cases, the military administrative

---

14 Bianchi, 'Immagine e realtà dell'eccezione militare del Piemonte', p.59: 'It is no coincidence that, between the seventeenth and eighteenth centuries, with the definition of the military-diplomatic apparatus of the Savoy court and the consequent affirmation of Turin as an important destination for the training of many gentlemen of the European aristocracy, the states of the Savoy were presented as a stage in all respects of the 'journey to Italy'. The travel literature testified to this and the treatises destined to accompany, well beyond the baroque age, the chivalric education of the nobility showed it with learned notes on political geography.'

15 On the consolidation of the military and diplomatic profile of the Turin court see in Paola Bianchi, 'La corte dei Savoia: disciplinamento del servizio e delle fedeltà' in W. Barberis (ed.), *I Savoia. I secoli d'oro di una dinastia europea* (Turin: Einaudi, 2007), pp.135–176.

16 *Ibid.*, p.162.

17 Mirabal, *Voyage d'Italie et de Grèce, avec une dissertation sur la bizarrerie des opinions des hommes* (1691), Guignard, Paris 1698, p.7. The author remarked that Turin was a centre of courtly life far less opulent than the French one and others in Italy, yet extremely elegant, and in this second to none. Turin was a 'city of free and sociable manners' compared to the 'savage customs of the rest of Italy, where there are more statues than men.' Turin was the seat of a court that was anything but boring, indeed one of the most 'easy-going' in Europe, where 'the French language is no less known than Italian'.

18 Luciano Pezzolo, 'La Rivoluzione Militare: una prospettiva italiana 1400–1700', in A. Dattero and S. Levati (eds) *Militari in età moderna. La centralità di un tema di confine* (Milan: Cisalpino, 2006), pp.15–62. According to the author, in the mid seventeenth century, the French military

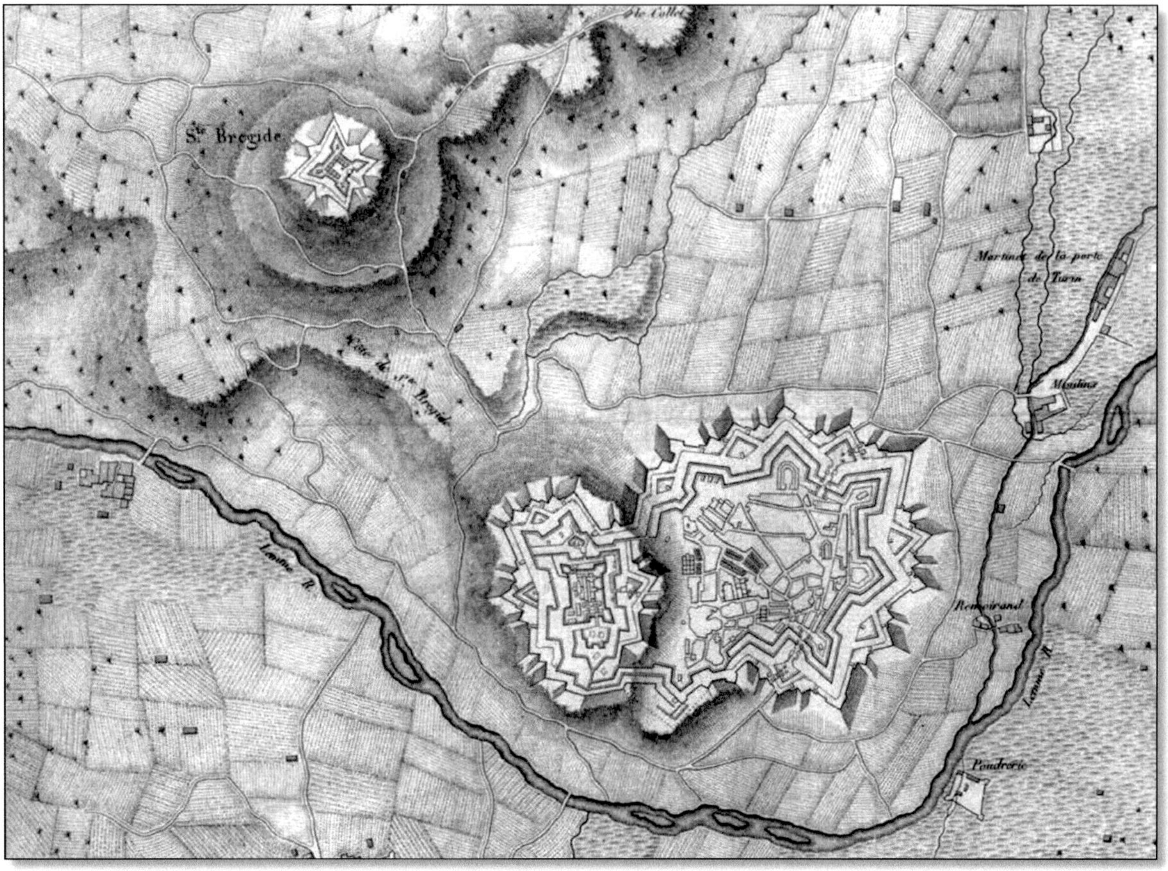

25. The fortress of Pinerolo and the subsidiary fort of Santa Brigida, in a French print of the 1680s. In 1696, after having been France's open gateway to Italy for 66 years, Pinerolo returned to Savoy rule, but its strong fortifications were demolished by Louis XIV beforehand.

structure established as a result of the creation of a permanent war apparatus may have offered the model on which the civil sector could be formed. This relationship only seems to become clear from the end of the seventeenth century and in the middle of the eighteenth century. While it is true that the Duchy of Savoy was not able to hold its own against other states that were better organised militarily and financially, it is also important to note that, from the 1560s onwards, Savoy concentrated its efforts on establishing a solid apparatus on the model of the major monarchies of the time. Consequently, since the beginning of the modern age, long before the need to link the destinies of Piedmont with those of the yet to be completed unified state in a new epic, one of the obsessive thoughts of Italian historiography had been to claim the traditional warlike attitude of the local nobility.[19] Alongside this view,

effort was still the product of improvisation rather than the result of an efficient bureaucratic system. Efficiency of the administrative system and war are found as closely connected elements in Hanoverian England and, later in Prussia; whereas in Italy, the relationship between military necessity and expansion of state administration is found in the Savoy state.

19 On the Piedmontese military exception elaborated in the nineteenth-century works, see also Piero Del Negro, 'Guerra e politica nel Risorgimento. La Storia militare del Piemonte di Ferdinando Augusto Pinelli', in *Rivista Storica Italiana*, XCVIII (1986), pp.221–244, and Paola

the exceptional nature of the Savoy political-military experience constituted an interpretative key that emerged in nineteenth-century historiography and continued in the following century, when even the previous exaltations of the dynastic achievements of the Savoy dukes were joined by a representation that differed during the Risorgimento from those of the subsequent post-unification age.[20] From this scenario emerged a line of thought that identified the Piedmontese exception at three levels. The first level was the social one, represented by a nobility characterised by a resistant 'legitimist' and pro-dynastic feudal class. The second level was the institutional one, with the creation of a firm and centralised state, foreign to contemporary Italian models. Finally the military one, characterised by the strong and lasting militarisation of the state and society, and the raising of a modern permanent army.[21] Unlike the other states of the Peninsula, Savoy-Piedmont did not relinquish its role as a regional military power, and this choice alone was what determined its destiny, becoming 'the peculiar element of Piedmontese history within the framework of the ancient Italian states'.[22]

This representation has been challenged in recent years. On the social level, the hegemony of the ancient feudal nobility was in recent years placed in a complex relationship with the ruling classes that did not exclude the existence of urban patriciate not dissimilar to those prevailing in various territorial realities of the Peninsula. On an institutional level, no one speaks any longer of the linear and progressive centralisation operated by Savoy policy: the model of absolutism as a laboratory that would have been traced first in the footsteps of France and later in Prussia – when Savoy-Piedmont became the 'Brandenburg of Italy' – constitutes a very outdated historiographic image. Equally obsolete is the representation of a militarist Piedmont in the Prussian style, which would have founded its survival almost exclusively on the army and on the spirit of service of the nobility.

However, not everything about the military talent of the Savoy court has to be devalued. The central years of the seventeenth century were marked by the growing influence of officers who had participated in the Spanish campaigns in Lombardy or who had joined the new ducal army as captains of mercenaries and militia officers. The military profile of a court that would

Bianchi, 'Esercito e riforme militari negli Stati Sabaudi del Settecento. Un bilancio storiografico', in *Società Italiana di Storia Militare*, Quaderno 1995 (Roma, 1997), pp.7–38.

20 Bianchi, 'La riorganizzazione militare del Ducato di Savoia', p.189.

21 These three levels were also the basis for the 1990s revival of the concept of 'Piedmontese exception' used by Gregory Hanlon in *The twilight of a military tradition. Italian aristocrats and European conflicts, 1560–1800* (London: UCL Press, 1998). Hanlon reconstructs the 'twilight' of the Italian military tradition, from the post-Tridentine age to the creation of the new model of the Napoleonic army, transversally, in the different states of the Peninsula, in relation to the main phases of international politics, isolating from the common denominator of demilitarisation a single case, namely the Savoy-Piedmont.

22 Bianchi, 'Immagine e realtà dell'eccezione militare del Piemonte', p.57. The author states: 'an exception that, often accepted uncritically, has contributed to marginalise Piedmont from the Italian historiographical debate in the recent decades'.

26. 'The Boar Hunting', by Jean Miel, 1660–61 (Collection of the Venaria Reale, Turin). See image commentaries for more information.

reserve the most prestigious ranks for the exponents of that profession – the soldier – guaranteed the Savoy dominions the possibility of intervening in alliances with the major European powers: first France, then the Austrian and Spanish Habsburg, England and the Dutch Republic.

Described as a semi-military state that would essentially adopt the military structures of France, Savoy-Piedmont actually eludes a comparison with the chronological grid that some authoritative historians have established for France during the early modern era.[23] A greater harmony of the Savoy domains with the European powers from a strategic point of view – first and foremost with the 'French model', but later also with the Habsburg Empire and Prussia – certainly occurred in the eighteenth century, when from the age of Vittorio Amedeo II (1684–1730) onwards the distance from the Italian panorama increased, and the discontinuity and heterogeneity that had characterised the organisation of the troops in the previous two centuries were largely overcome.[24]

As always, it is economic analysis that explains the exceptions at best. Like the rest of Italy, Savoy-Piedmont had an essentially agricultural economy, yet it displayed different characteristics to that of the other states. Internally, the social balance was more stable in comparison to the 'dominant' oligarchic centres such as Venice, Genoa or Florence. Despite the many wars sustained and suffered on its territory, the economy did not suffer the economic collapse of the great crisis of the seventeenth century. In the second half of the century not only did agricultural production increase with the introduction of new crops, but also specialised farming and livestock breeding became widespread. In 1667 the introduction of new silk mills initiated a process of industrialisation that gave rise to good manufacturing within a few years.[25] In other words, sufficient economic solidity favoured more than anything the creation of an efficient standing army.

Furthermore, Savoy-Piedmont also had an indigenous dynasty, entrenched for centuries, who allowed for the imposition of a political absolutism firmly

23 Andrè Corvisier (ed.), *Dictionnaire d'art et d'histoire militaires* (Paris: PUF, 1988), p.485.

24 The debate on the Piedmontese exception was enriched by two texts that were in many ways antithetical. The first of these, Walter Barberis, *Le armi del Principe. La tradizione militare sabauda* (Turin: Einaudi, 1988), aims above all to capture the ambiguities, contradictions, and management difficulties that the Savoy 'tradition' would have developed within itself, with long-term consequences on the character of the 'Piedmontese ruling classes'. The military organisation was interpreted by Barberis not so much as an instrument of defence and offence, but as a form of relationship between the elites and the court and as a 'field of exhibition' of a military honour not always corresponding to an effective exercise of the craft of arms. A different perspective was taken, in the same years as the publication of Barberis' book, by a scholar with a historical-economic background: Enrico Stumpo, 'Guerra ed economia: spese e guadagni militari nel Piemonte del Seicento', in *Studi Storici*, XXVII (1986), pp.371–395, who read the Savoy exception, as early as the seventeenth century, substantially as the ability to exploit a war market destined to mark a turnover of personnel among the elites and to initiate a precise custom in the management of contracts and 'extraordinary finance' of the court of Turin.

25 Stumpo, 'Guerra ed economia', pp.376–377.

rooted in the feudal nobility, and this facilitated the employment of mercenary troops in the service of the Duke, and the establishment of an efficient military organisation.

Savoy-Piedmont Geostrategy

From a purely military point of view, the experience in which Savoy-Piedmont matured its geostrategy was mainly the Italian one, which relied essentially on three components: fortresses, mercenaries, and peasant militias. After all, in its structure, the army did not differ much from the armies of the other Italian states at least until the majority of Carlo Emanuele II, lacking as it did forms of professional and permanent recruitment, and modern field organisation. The geostrategy of the duchy had been already established in the sixteenth century. Since Savoy was indefensible against a French attack, the concentration of forces was to be deployed for protecting Turin. The city and the territories around it represented the core of the state and the one that generated the most revenue. Duke Emanuele Filiberto had moved the capital from Chambéry to Turin in 1563, and by the seventeenth century the population had doubled to 43,000, including one of the largest Jewish communities in Northern Italy. The city was then at the centre of the international market with banks and wholesale markets, a luxury manufacturing sector, and a well-established silk spinning industry exporting raw textile to France for further manufacture in Lyon. The abundant availability of water power had enabled the development of a wide variety of manufactures, as well as a metallurgical industry supported by military needs. The city managed valuable water reserves, storage and a modern arsenal enlarged in 1659. Since 1540 it had a strong curtain which by 1669 had been modernised. In 1671 Carlo Emanuele II demolished the first extension of the city, and on 23 October 1673 storages laid the foundation for the second extension. The new city boundaries provided for expansion eastwards and southwards.[26] Turin and its citadel were considered two independent fortresses with their own administration and garrisons.

After 1676 the Duchy strengthened the defence of the capital with an ambitious plan for improving the fortresses within a radius of 60 km. The goal was the creation of a perimeter of fortified places for supporting a field army that could easily manoeuvre by internal lines. The southern side of the border was guarded by a line of fortresses that comprised the aforementioned Saluzzo, with Asti, Cherasco, Savigliano, Cuneo, Mondovì and Alba as the main strongholds. The first step of this plan had occurred in 1664, when the ducal treasury financed the restoration of the fortification of Verrua and the improvement of the defence of Vercelli, which continued until 1676. All these fortified centres controlled a territory of approximately 3,500 square kilometres. Although defended more by militiamen than by modern infantry

26 In 1700 the government completed the last providential improvement of Turin's defence, just before the French–Spanish siege six years later.

and artillery, this area was considered an important logistical reserve for the Duchy in the case of invasion. For this reason, in the last 20 years of the century the defences were improved and strengthened by new fortifications, such as Alba and Cairo Montenotte. To a lesser extent, strengthening works also involved the places on the northern area for protecting the road to the Grand St Bernard pass. The fortified town of Ivrea guarded the left flank, while further north the fort of Bard secured the road to the other side. After Turin, the best fortresses of the Duchy were the ones guarding the eastern border. Here, Vercelli was the second major fortress of the Duchy, and had a modern citadel designed by Francesco Paciotto. The fortress of Asti would have needed further modernisation, but after Vercelli there were two lines of well-built strongholds to guard the roads heading to Turin. The main places were Crescentino and Verrua, three kilometres apart, but connected by a gallery. Further west, and located just 20 km from Turin, there were the forts of Chivasso and Castagneto, and both were a replica of the former couple. Ceva, which guarded the border with the Republic of Genoa, was improved with a modern curtain in 1672. In the 1660s further improvements were made concerning two forts located on another 'sensitive border', the Val Pellice, where the threat represented by the French enclave of Pinerolo doubled the troubles coming from the restless Waldensian communities. In this area the forts of Luserna and Bobbio were the major strongholds, to which a third, the fort of Santa Maria of Torre Pellice, was added in 1664.

This defensive structure had been challenged on more than one occasion, but resisted against, perhaps, all odds. Foreign occupations and a civil war between *principisti* and *madamisti* in 1639–1642 did not alter the state structure, and not even the much mistreated government of the regent widows Christine of France and Maria Giovanna Battista of Savoie-Nemours could cause the collapse of the state.[27] The first regency in particular succeeded in rebuilding relations with the German princes. Christine moved closer to the major family of the Empire, using marriage policy wisely. In 1650 she married her daughter Adelaide Enrichetta to Ferdinand Maria von Wittelsbach, the Duke of Bavaria, and in 1653 her niece Louise Christine to the Margrave Hermann of Baden. Years later, she also tried, but without success, to arrange the marriage of Carlo Emanuele with a princess of Saxony. The alliances thus established were important when in 1657 Emperor Ferdinand III appointed the Duke of Mantua as Imperial vicar and commissioner in Italy. The support

27 The encounter between *principisti* and *madamisti* had been interpreted by the most significant historians of the *Risorgimento* as a struggle between the former, who represented independence, against Christine's party, who would enslave the Duchy to France. In reality this reading, repeated by Christine with her daughter-in-law Giovanna Battista, must be strongly redimensioned if only because the Regents showed they had a strong sense of state and power and succeeded in any case not only in keeping the territory firm, but also in suppressing the centrifugal impulses of the classes, which, in strict adherence to Salic law, were unleashed when faced with a recognised weaker power. See Giuseppe Ricuperati, 'Frontiere e territori dello stato sabaudo come archetipi di una regione europea: fra storia e storiografia', in A. Raviola-Blythe (ed.), *Lo Spazio Sabaudo. Intersezioni, frontiere e confini in età moderna* (Turin: Franco Angeli, 2007), p.36.

of the electors, led by the Duke of Bavaria, was decisive in preventing Gonzaga's vicariate from becoming perpetual, thus undermining the rights of the House of Savoy in Casale and the Monferrato.

The policy towards the clergy was also important. Like every court of a princely state of the Old Regime, Savoy-Piedmont also used the relationship with the Church in a strategic and symbolic sense, maintaining however some long-lasting basic lines. The elements of peculiarity were intertwined, also in this case, with certain affinities in respect of the European framework. Compared to other Italian dynasties such as the Medici, the Farnese, the Este, the Savoy did not bind themselves to the Church State through the acquisition of cardinals' seats and Papal tiaras, while in their choices of ecclesiastical policy they certainly allowed themselves to be influenced by the alliances established now with the Spanish and now with the French monarchy. In the seventeenth century only one Savoy obtained the purple: Prince Maurice, who in 1642, after 30 years as a cardinal, was to put down the *beretta* to marry his very young niece Ludovica, thus putting an end to the civil war.

The State and its 'Military'

The organisation of Savoy's states was modelled on that of its powerful French neighbour. The duke embodied the centre of power: he was the chief of the dynasty, the commander-in-chief of the army, and all the offices were appointed by him. However, as absolute as his power was, the duke had to delegate certain tasks to his officials and dealt with the state's representatives. The three senates of Turin, Chambéry and Nice had function very similar to the French *Parlements*. Each acted under the direction of the *cancelliere* (chancellor), and represented the supreme civil authority save in the cases where the decision could be appealed to the duke. The main task of the senate was the administration of the justice, entrusted to provincial judges, the *prefetti* (prefect), whose tasks were redefined in 1620.[28] Together with the *Chambre des Comptes* at Chambéry and the *Camera dei Conti* at Turin, which dealt with fiscal matters, the senates exercised a wide variety of administrative powers, including matters concerning the army and the militia. The history of relations between these institutions and the sovereign is not without episodes of bitter disputes, however, the senates and the courts loyally supported the duke's policy.[29]

28 Geoffrey Symcox, *Victor Amadeus II. Absolutism in the Savoyard State*, 1675–1730 (Los Angeles, CA: University of California Press, 1983), p.55.

29 *Ibid.*, p.57. The *Chambre des Comptes* was more openly hostile to the Duke, probably because it felt more threatened by encroachments on its jurisdiction. The Duke's intendant appointed to Savoy in 1686 took over the chamber's traditional functions of supervising road, bridges, military lodgings and a wide range of economic matters. Faced with the loss of its fiscal jurisdiction, the Chamber made common cause with the disaffected nobles and constantly skirmished with Turin, refusing to approve a new land survey – which threatened noble tax exemption – and opposing new customs tariffs.

Savoy-Piedmont Chain of Command

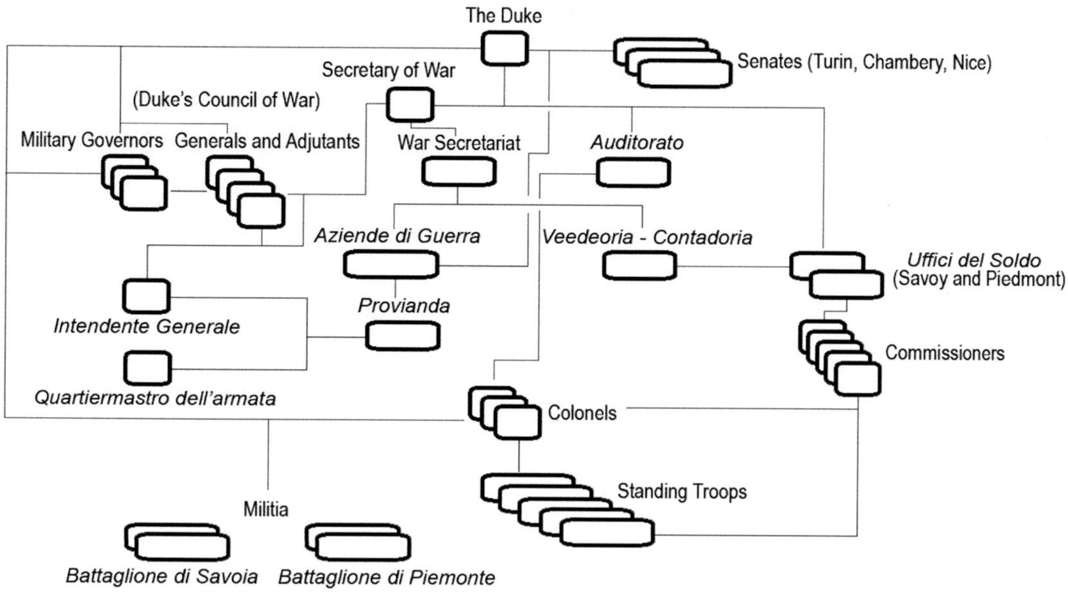

27. The Savoy-Piedmont army chain of command

Government posts also appear to mirror those in France. The high magistrates and the chancellor, who usually was a minister and presided over the duke's council of advisers, had always held the dominant position in the hierarchy of state officials. During the seventeenth century the traditional order of rank began to change. Prestige passed increasingly to the financial agencies, which grew in size and importance after the reforms undertaken by Vittorio Amedeo II and his finance minister Giambattista Gropello in the late 1690s.

Before this age, the most serious obstacle to efficient financial administration lay in the lack of central funds through which all revenues had to pass. As occurred in many other countries, different sources of revenue were earmarked for different purposes, and paid to different treasurers and receivers, or sometimes to several government agencies at once. There was a treasurer-general for the whole of Piedmont, who represented the closest approximation to a central fund, but a good deal of tax revenue never passed through his hands. He supervised the work of the *referendari*, replaced in the 1680s by the *intendenti*, who assumed the delicate task of extracting revenue in the provinces. There were other provincial treasurers for Savoy, Nice, Aosta and Oneglia, along with various subsidiary treasurers and receivers of minor revenues from these regions.

After several years of submission to his mother's directives, in 1663 Carlo Emanuele II received a state that had been painstakingly returned to a period of peace. However, if modernising factors in the political-military plans must be identified during his reign, as the historiography of recent years has amply demonstrated, these began to take shape in the period immediately following the Peace of the Pyrenees. It was in 1659 that the regency intervened to reorganise the finances and in the same year introduced a new tax to finance defence, called the *sussidio militare*.

As for the pre-existing funds for the army, these came from the taxes paid to various provincial treasurers, especially from Piedmont, which included the *quartieri d'inverno* (winter quarters), replaced in 1659 by the aforementioned *sussidio militare* (military subsidy) collected by a particular military treasurer, and from other sources levied from its own receiver.[30] In 1659 the transformation of the subsidy from an extraordinary tax into an ordinary contribution was the subject of intense, almost obsessive legislative activity, which would soon produce positive effects.[31] Formally, at the apex of the Savoy-Piedmontese administration, was the Secretariat of State. However, its importance was severely conditioned by the fact that it was a hereditary office, acquired from 1625 by the Carron family, later Marquises of San Tommaso, and held until 1696. The planning criterion of the *Ancien Régime* does not allow for a sufficiently exact calculation of the military expenditure for personnel, operational and investment. In fact, the expenses for the army did not only include the salaries actually paid, but also the cost of primary logistical services and equipment, as well as the expenditure of remounting horses. This was the typical case for Savoy-Piedmont, where these items of expenditure were charged on the budgets of several *Aziende* (agencies) dealing with the army. These affairs were managed by the *Ufficio del Soldo*, one for Piedmont and another for Savoy, which handled most military expenditure, and directed the officials in charge of paying the troops in the garrisons.[32] More complications arose from the number of different government agencies that actually spent the revenues: the households of the Duke and the regent Duchess; the director of the mint; the separate bureau for the artillery and fortifications, and so on.[33]

Between 1631 and 1660, military expenditure averaged around 1,090,000 *lire*, rising again between 1661 and 1689 to 2,123,000 *lire* and reached 3,400,000 *lire* at the end of the century.[34] Premising that there is not much data on military expenditure for the period 1660–1680, the Savoy-Piedmont army

---

30 Felice Amato Duboin, *Raccolta per ordine di materie delle leggi cioè editti, patenti, manifesti, ecc. emanate negli stati di terraferma sino all'8 dicembre 1798 dai sovrani della Real Casa di Savoja* (Turin, 1848), vol. XXI, pp.405–407, 409–413. The *quartieri d'inverno*, established as early as 1642, was collected until the Peace of the Pyrenees (1659); then reintroduced by Vittorio Amedeo II during the War of the League of Augsburg and in the War of the Spanish Succession; by the 1730s it was no longer applied. See also ASTo, *Materie militari, Ordini e regolamenti*, mz. 2, n. 22. *Ordini militari dell'Altezza Reale di Carlo Emanuele II dall'anno 1648 sin all'anno 1674.*

31 Stumpo, 'Guerra ed economia', p.386.

32 The direction of the Piedmontese *Ufficio del Soldo* was continually held by Giuseppe Ferrero Count of Lavriano from 1629 to 1674, replaced by Count Michelangelo Lodi, who remained in charge until 1691. See Brancaccio, Nicola, *L'esercito del vecchio Piemonte. Sunti storici* (Rome: 1922), p.273.

33 Stumpo, 'Guerra ed economia', p.387.

34 Enrico Stumpo, *Finanza e Stato moderno nel Piemonte del Seicento* (Rome: Istituto storico italiano per l'età moderna e contemporanea, 1979), pp.153–154.

historian of the 1920s, Nicola Brancaccio, shows a picture of progressively increasing military expenditure:[35]

1660: 1,200,482 Piedmontese lire
1665: 1,077,943 Piedmontese lire
1670: 1,224,665 Piedmontese lire
1675: 1,508,673 Piedmontese lire

These figures, however, do not consider the variations that occurred in these years. For instance, from 1664, the *Ufficio del Soldo* no longer administered the salaries of officers, nor the cost of other related services such as the rent of barracks, and the procurement of military hospitals and transport.[36] However it is possible to estimate, albeit only broadly, the incidence of infantry, cavalry and artillery by calculating some parameters. The value of the troops remained constant throughout the second half of the century, equal to 91.5 lire per year for each infantryman, 183 for the artilleryman and 419.75 for the cavalryman. The sum of the salaries of the companies' officers amounted to a further 1,750 lire in the infantry, and 3,868 in the cavalry. In addition, the captains were paid an annual premium of 40 lire for service in the arsenals and another two lire for health expenses.[37] Finally, it is necessary to calculate the cost of bread, equal to 2,737.5 lire per year for each ration. The total cost of an infantry company of 50 men and officers was therefore 9,400 lire per year, therefore identical to an artillery company of 35 men and half of what 32 cavalry troopers cost. In relation to general expenses, military expenses were a considerable sum, amounting to almost 40 percent of the Duchy's total expenditure during some periods. On the other hand, the idea that support for the defence of the state should be demanded from almost all subjects had become more widespread, thanks to the gradual introduction of an 'extraordinary finance', namely a mass of indirect taxes and occasional donations, the collection of which was entrusted to often short-lived bodies, on which a large class of contractors, suppliers and capital lenders built their fortunes.[38]

The classical historiography of the Italian army attributes the administrative and accounting regulations introduced under Carlo Emanuele II on 8 January 1671 and subsequently on 17 September 1673, as

35 Nicola Brancaccio, *L'esercito del vecchio Piemonte. Gli Ordinamenti. Parte I (1560–1814)* (Rome, 1923), p.154.

36 For further comparison, it should be considered that throughout the second half of the seventeenth century the cost of the bread ration was budgeted, whereas from 1705 onwards only the bread ration was calculated, because the grain was no longer purchased by the military agencies, but by the civil administration. See also Stumpo, *Finanza e Stato moderno*, pp.127–128.

37 It is also necessary to take into account the engagement bonuses: at the end of the century they were 15 *lire*, plus another nine for recruitment costs. Calculating the strength of a company of 50 men, and a rotation of soldiers of a quarter of the force, another 288 *lire* must be added for each company. See Stumpo, 'Guerra ed economia', pp.391–392.

38 Bianchi, 'La riorganizzazione militare del Ducato di Savoia', p.202.

28. Carlo Emanuele Giacinto di Simiana, Marquis of Pianezza (1608–1677) in a print after Gualdo Priorato's Historia di Leopoldo Cesare (1670). See image commentaries for more information.

the origin of the modern military administration in Italy.[39] Only at the end of the seventeenth century, with the brief interval of peace that preceded the War of the Spanish Succession, did the state further reform these mechanisms in order to improve the functioning of state and army. The complexity of the system for collecting revenue was thus matched by an almost equal degree of complexity in the instructions for spending it, and this scenario did not change until 1717, when Gropello and Vittorio Amedeo remedied the defects with their last reforms.

The secretariats and economic magistracies exercised control in the provincial centre, while in the peripheries there was a different system of power that divided the tasks of court representation. The best way to connect the centre and the periphery was therefore to centralise activities such as social control, public order and defence, under a specific official: the magistrate, the intendant, or, as for the army, the secretary of war. In 1671, Duke Carlo Emanuele transformed the pre-existing war secretariat into an office headed by a minister appointed by him. This was Carlo Emanuele Giacinto di Simiana, Marquis of Pianezza (1608–1677), one of the personalities who more than any other dominated the political and military scenario until his death, when he was replaced by his son, Carlo Giovanni Battista, Marquis of Livorno di Piemonte (1634–1706). Within a few months the latter was suspended and replaced by Donato Chapel de Saint Laurent, who held the office of *segretario di Guerra e di Milizia*. In 1682 the Dowager Duchess –the regent – re-established Carlo Giovanni Battista, but two years later Vittorio Amedeo dismissed him again and inaugurated a new era in military affairs with the appointment of the skilled Filiberto Sallier de la Tour, an abbot, who later held the office of the Duke's representative to the Dutch Republic.[40]

Before 1684 the function of the secretariat ministry of war lay somewhere between a major staff and a council of war, rather than an actual department in charge of the administration of the army, and mainly dealt with general affairs, correspondence with the sovereigns and transmission of orders. The economic budget and the funds for the troops were in fact managed by the State Treasury, which dealt with the military through administrative

39 Brancaccio, *L'esercito del vecchio Piemonte. Gli ordinamenti*, p.155.

40 Duboin, *Raccolta per ordine di materie delle leggi*, vol. VIII, pp.331–332. Duke Vittorio Amedeo II reformed the 'Secretariat of State and War', and gave it a structure comprising a first secretary dealing with all affairs of war on land and sea, and all economic affairs concerning the standing army. Under him there were three secretaries with as many subordinate under-secretaries: the first of these was entrusted with war and naval affairs, the second with troop and marches affairs, the third with economic affairs and the archives.

offices, the most important being the aforementioned *Ufficio del Soldo* and the *Veedoria Generale*, which acted like modern accountants. Each office was directed by an official, respectively the *contadore generale*, in charge of administering the roles of the regular troops, and the *veedore generale*, who controlled economic matters, especially those regarding the militia. The Minister of War also exercised limited control over the personnel responsible for controlling the compliance of payments in relation to troop numbers. These officials were in fact subordinate to the central treasury, and only secondarily acted with the war minister. The management and planning of the forces was the responsibility of the four *grand commis*: the Secretary, later Minister of War, and the chiefs of the autonomous administrations, which included the *Azienda di Guerra* (War Agency) with the *Azienda dei Grani* (foodstuff), the *Azienda delle Fabbriche e Fortificazioni* (arsenals and fortifications) and the *Azienda d'Artiglieria* (artillery).

In 1688, responsibility for economic planning and budget proposals concerning the army was transferred to the *contadore generale*, who in the same year took over all the functions of the *veedore generale* in military matters.[41] Under him depended the enlistment of troops, general payments, including the inspection control of troops, extraordinary payments, and all logistical services, united under the name *provianda*. These were generally assigned to private procurements, managed by contractors, whose name, *assente*, sounds similar to its Spanish counterpart *asientista*. These expenses, which formed the complex of military administrative affairs, constituted the *Azienda di guerra*, again analogous to the Spanish *Hacienda*.[42] The *contadore generale* only managed the expenditure for Piedmont, while in Savoy, where there was an autonomous office, the same task was carried out by a *commissaire* with four intendants. Both the officials were connected to the General Treasurer, chief of ducal finance, and to the *commissari di guerra* (war commissioners), five in number until 1696. These latter were in constant communication with the *ufficiali del soldo*.[43]

Disciplinary and judicial affairs were examined by the *Auditorato di Guerra*, one for Piedmont and another for Savoy, established between 1559 and 1562. Directing the office was the *auditore generale*, who had mixed civil and penal authority concerning only the army. He was the supreme military judge, entrusted with duties of various kinds: from drafting edicts for the

41 From 1641 to 1676 the *Veedoria Generale* was directed by Count Renato Roero della Val d'Andona, replaced by Count Giovanni Michele di Monasterolo until 1680, and then by Marquis Vittorio Amedeo de Mainard de Tournon-San Damiano. Nicola Brancaccio, *L'esercito del vecchio Piemonte. Sunti storici*, p.271.

42 If many of the institutions were organised according to a French scheme, those relating to the military appeared to be of a typically Spanish origin, being introduced by Duke Emanuele Filiberto, commander-in-chief of the Spanish army from 1553 to 1557. For instance when the office of the *contadore generale* was established in 1560, the choice was made of a Spaniard, Diego Hortiz de Pros, already in the service of the court of Madrid, whom the Duke had met in Flanders. See Bianchi, 'La riorganizzazione militare del Ducato di Savoia', p.205.

43 Brancaccio, *L'esercito del vecchio Piemonte. Gli ordinamenti*, p.181.

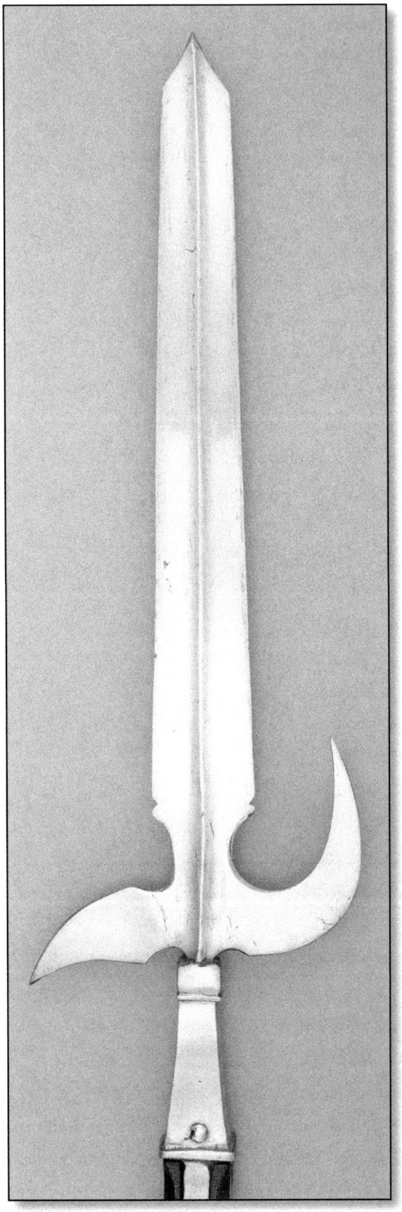

Left: 30. Halberd, Piedmontese manufacture, 1680–1690 (Metropolitan Museum of Art, New York). This type of weapon belonged to the Savoy's Compagnia Guardie della Porta. Overall length 233.8 cm; blade and base measure 75.8 cm.

Below: 31. NCO's halberd, Italian manufacture, 1680s (private collection); possibly belonging to infantry regiment Crocebianca.

Below Right: 32. Matchlock musket, Savoy-Piedmont, 1680–90, overall length 149.5 cm. (Private collection, Turin)

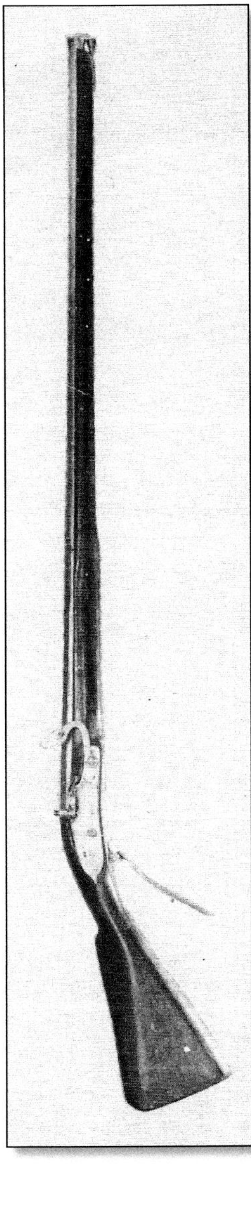

raising of troops to administering statutes, from intervening in artillery affairs to monitoring the fulfilment of laws against desertion and other crimes involving professional soldiers. In 1663 the Piedmontese auditor added the title of *sovrintendente generale di guerra*, a responsibility held until 1675 by the authoritative Carlo Antonio Blancardi.[44] Each titular officer had a subordinate official known as *luogotenente auditore generale*. The work on the ground was entrusted to the *vice-auditori*, who were to instruct the processes within the corps. In the 1690s, each infantry regiment had its own officer to hear the examination of disciplinary and criminal matters. This regulation only applied to the Duke's subjects, while for foreign soldiers all disciplinary matters were carried out by the respective commander.[45] However, in the absence of a real homogeneous discipline regulation for permanent troops, justice was marked by paternalism and arbitrariness, and punishments were executed within the regiments according to the decisions of the officers. Not only these latter, but also sergeant-brigadiers and corporals had coercive power, with the possibility of beating soldiers.

In each province the dukes appointed an official with the rank *governatore* (military governor). He dealt with the troops quartered in his province or fortress, and in wartime extended his authority over the militia. He managed military matters in strict relation with the civil powers, especially the local senate and the intendants. The secretary-minister and governors were the pivotal actors of the Savoyard military policy. They and other officers formed the council of war when requested by the sovereign as commander-in-chief. This group of officers was joined by others such as aides-de-camp and the generals of the infantry and cavalry, following a scheme inherited from the Hispanic army. Until 1668 the post of general of the infantry was held by the Marquis of Pianezza, secretary of war, who was replaced by the Marquis Ghiron Francesco Villa, who in turn handed over the post of general of the cavalry to the Duke's half-brother, Don Gabriele of Savoy. On Villa's death in 1670, Don Gabriele assumed both offices. In 1672 a third rank of general was established for the artillery. Each general had a *luogotenente generale* (lieutenant general) and a *maresciallo di campo* (field marshal) under his orders.

These officers formed a kind of major staff, but the most important, qualified as *primo rango*, was the general of cavalry, although the ducal army had a very modest cavalry force. Under Duke Vittorio Amedeo II this group of senior commanders formed the general staff of the army, and all cavalry officers took precedence over their counterparts of infantry and artillery. However, they were not expressly required to direct troops on campaign, which in this case was assumed by the most senior colonel, who in the 1690s assumed the title of *brigadiere*, and held the direction of corps formed by

44 Carlo Antonio Blancardi (1623–1676), native of Nice. After a career spent entirely in the service of the sovereign, in 1666 he was appointed as member of the presidency of the accounts' chamber of Piedmont. He became member of the Senate in 1672. Rivalry intrigues, as well as the aversion of the military aristocracy, led to his death sentence. Further reading: Dionisotti, *Storia della magistratura piemontese* (Turin, 1881), vol. II, p.274 and pp.325–328.

45 *Ibid.*, p.156.

a variable number of battalions or squadrons. Next to this group of senior officers there was one *commissario generale* of infantry and another of cavalry, established on the French model.

Apart from the *consilium* convened on an optional basis by the duke, in peacetime the senior commanders had no duties. However, under Carlo Emanuele II the highest generals held disciplinary authority over the troops, which they exercised through their subordinates. Also subordinate to the Duke for military matters, there were the holders of permanent offices such as the aforementioned *commissario generale* of cavalry, the *elemosiniere generale* (almoner-general, the Archbishop of Turin) and from 1692 the *primo ingegnere* (first engineer). This corps of officers and specialists could be augmented in the event of war by other military figures.

In wartime the sphere of command also included other officers with temporary assignments, such as the *generale del cannone* (artillery general) until 1660, the chief physician, the chief surgeon, and the *ingegnere*. In addition to these, each senior commander appointed his aides-de-camp. The most important tasks were those entrusted to the *intendente generale* and the *quartiermastro dell'armata*, with the equivalent *commissario maggiore* and *foriero maggiore* for the cavalry alone. The first two officers supervised supplies, including requisitions and general accounting; *quartiermastro* and *foriero* dealt with marching, camps, and transport, and extended their disciplinary authority over the personnel in charge of these services. For this task, the quartermaster also had at his order the *gran prevosto* with his *arcieri* (guards). The *capitano del bagaglio* (captain of baggage) and the *capitano delle guide* (captain of guides) with 12 horsemen with knowledge of the territory, also depended from the *quartiermastro dell'armata*.

The formation of a standing army had also generated characteristic effects in Savoy-Piedmont. The main one was the increase in command and control positions, but the number of officers in the basic administrative units – the companies – was still the same as in the previous century.[46] In the first half of the seventeenth century, tactical units averaged between 400 and 600 men and normally consisted of two or three companies. The mutation that occurred in the second half of the century had transformed the companies into units of 40–50 soldiers and the company required to lead a regular battalion on the battlefield had simultaneously increased the number of officers, since this could comprise 18 to 30 officers. Colonels soon realised that the proliferation of officers did not always produce greater efficiency. The causes were many, and the solution adopted in Savoy-Piedmont was the periodic discharge of officers when the army was in winter quarters. Rotating the officers though the companies, the Duke intended as a result that many of them accumulated experience and would be ready to train and lead a larger army when the next war came along.

However, this does not mean that all officers benefited from the ability to serve for limited periods. In 1673 the obligatory presence of officers in units

46 Brancaccio, *L'esercito del vecchio Piemonte. Gli ordinamenti*, p.129. In the Savoy army, the rank of second lieutenant was introduced in the 1690s and exclusively in the infantry.

or garrisons had been established: at least nine months for captains, six for lieutenant colonels and four for majors and colonels,[47] then for the latter the period was reduced to three months.[48] The officers of the Guards regiment enjoyed greater privileges that allowed them longer absence. In 1675 the regency granted the captains up to four months of license per year. Two years later the colonel was granted the same period of license, while those of the *ordinanze* regiments were granted only three.[49] However, it seems that the presence of senior officers and captains was poorly respected. The drawback was not exclusively negative since at least it served to reduce the cost for quartering the officers and the consumption of fodder. No other solution was possible, considering that the formation of larger companies would have forced the Duke to dismiss a considerable number of officers. If this did not happen, it was because the officers, belonging to the aristocracy at all levels, were able to impose their interests and be maintained in service. After 1660 the officers' lobby continued to hold a considerable political power, and on the other hand, in the absolutist state the profession of arms performed the function of public employment found in modern welfare states, namely redistribution of public wealth, but for the benefit of the privileged classes.[50]

Though the aristocracy was predominant in the officer class, it is not correct to state that the whole officer corps was composed of nobles. Certainly in the cavalry the officer post required nobility, but gradually, in the artillery and navy, the bourgeois became the majority by the end of the century. Historians attribute this phenomenon to Vittorio Amedeo II, who encouraged the new bourgeois or newly entitled elites to take up employment in the army.[51] There are currently no statistical records for the second half of the seventeenth century, but a sample from the early eighteenth century shows that for the nobility, 15.5 percent chose a military career, while in first place was ecclesiastical employment, over 30 percent. In the cavalry, non-noble officers were only seven percent, grouped mainly in the less ancient and prestigious units, so that none served in the regiment *Dragoni di Sua Atezza Reale* (SD-1). Unfortunately, in this field of investigation it is only possible to proceed by analogy, and furthermore the status of nobility differed from case to case. However, the data allow us to state that the nobility choosing a career in the army was not a consequence of its cultural backwardness or a forced choice, as occurred in France and especially in Spain, but rather a process of redefining the social role of the aristocratic class.[52]

47 *Ibid.*, p.131.

48 Guerrini, Domenico, *La Brigata dei Granatieri di Sardegna. Memorie storiche* (Turin, 1902), p.29.

49 *Ibid.*

50 Barberis *Le Armi del Principe*, pp.166–167.

51 Loriga, Sabrina, *L'istituzione militare nel Piemonte del Settecento* (Venice: Marsilio, 1992), p.66.

52 *Ibid.*, pp.188–189. At a time in which birth privileges and aristocratic identity were the subject of constant claim, a military career acquired a distinctive value over the rest of the aristocracy and bureaucracy. Far from being a second-best solution, therefore, according to the author, the profession of arms was an 'excellent investment' that gave access to prestigious positions in the machinery of state and power at court.

33. Detail of the view of the Valentino castle, c. 1670, attributed to Giovanni Battista Abret (1643?–1705), preserved in Palazzo Madama – the City Museum of Ancient Art, Turin. The artist produced a series of paintings illustrating the Duke's residences and today it is a useful source for the first uniforms of the Savoy-Piedmont army. In the painting, the picket guarding the entrance is formed by a musketeer wearing in grey with blue stockings, and a non-commissioned officer dressed in blue.

The position of officer was certainly a prestigious one, but for access to positions at court, membership of the *Gardes du Corps* (Horse Lifeguards) was certainly the one that gave the most guarantees, as it allowed for a quicker ascent up the hierarchy without waiting for the usual process. Furthermore, unlike the powers already mentioned, the inheritance and venality of military offices did not exist in Savoy-Piedmont. The assignment of military corps recruitment to each province helped turn military service into a family business. As always, the artillery and the navy remained the exceptions, but only because in this case the family monopoly was facilitated by the profession.[53] This system had its merits, but it discouraged the military vocation of the volunteers. However, these had other channels of access available, especially through employment in the corps of specialists, especially engineers.

Another basis of ascent for the officers' corps was the *Accademia Reale*, inaugurated on 1 September 1677 by Regent Christine of France, in the palace especially built in Turin for this purpose. The academy did not produce a large number of officers, as it was not a training institute for military cadres, as it became in the following century. With attendance on courses the students did not receive official licenses but received an education above all in the humanities, necessary for the training of the cadets of the nobility. The Turin

53 Brancaccio, *L'esercito del vecchio Piemonte. Gli Ordinamenti*, p.84.

34. Vittorio Amedeo visits the port of Nice, 1689; oil painting of unknown artist (Umberto II and Maria José of Savoy Foundation, Geneva). See image commentaries for more information.

academy was an imitation of the *Académie Royale de la Noblesse*, created by Richelieu, and aimed at training the cadets of the nobility. It was a secondary consequence that some of the pupils embarked on their own military career in the service of the duke.

All appointments were conferred by the duke and the candidates were normally selected by the colonels. Generally, each regiment of cavalry and infantry, and the artillery corps, had a list of aspirant officers, often employed for years as adjutants or substitutes of their titular officer (he who owned the regiment) in case of need. Naturally, ample space was left for the officers' sons, brothers and cousins, each regiment being monopolised by a small number of families from the province in which the regiment recruited the soldiers. Access had no age limit, considering that eight-year-olds were also on the lists.[54] Naturally the most prestigious corps, such as the *Guardie* regiment, attracted many aspirants. As early as the late 1660s many aristocrats excluded from inheritance by the *maggiorascato* offered to serve in the regiment as volunteers, even as simple soldiers. The Duke issued the order to register these volunteers in a separate role, to whom were granted pay and privileges as the other private guards. In 1672, at the beginning of the war against Genoa, Colonel Carlo Ludovico Emilio Marquis of Parella was ordered by the Duke to mobilise all aspiring volunteers to join the regiment. Although the exact number for 1672 is not known, three years later it was established that 10 *anspessades* (demi lances) volunteers were to be assigned in each company, for a total of 200.

54 *Ibid.*

They were to be ready to serve the sovereign 'whenever they are called upon'.[55] They did not perform as sentinels and were excluded from the corvée, but they were obliged to preserve clothing, weapons and equipment. The matter was examined again in 1676, when regent Duchess Marie-Jeanne-Baptiste of Savoy-Nemours (1644–1724) established a list that introduced 200 new aspirants, and at the same time dismissed all those present until then: one way to create a loyal clientele in the regiment in charge of guarding the sovereign.[56] The volunteers had 15 days to join the regiment, but it was necessary to extend the deadline twice due to the low turnout of applicants. The operation must not have had the desired effect, because two years later these 200 were also dismissed. After this episode, the volunteers disappear from the chronicles.

Two types of conscription existed in the Duchy of Savoy. The earliest was the *capitolazioni*, which remained in force until 1680 for foreign regiments commanded by a colonel-proprietor. The amount of the capitulations varied according to the corps, but normally an equal monthly payment was established for all. With this system, the sums paid to the colonels were equal to the number of soldiers in the regiments they owned. In 1618, with the creation of the first *reggimenti di Sua Altezza* (regiments of His Highness), paid directly by the sovereign, the less risky system of individual salary was introduced. This method reduced the income of the colonels, as it was more difficult to make gains on vacant posts, but at the same time a prize and other privileges were introduced as compensation, in favour of the most diligent and efficient officers. In order to limit abuses, these compensations were also extended to the captains. The House of Savoy had acted strongly to limit the frauds that physically afflicted the army, being the most common abuse of the actual number of soldiers in the corps. The most-used method to limit fraud was to resort to periodic inspections of regiments and companies, the so-called *mostre*.[57] In 1620 Carlo Emanuele I had introduced the death penalty by hanging for fictitious recruits, or *passavolante*, discovered in the musters. The colonel or officer who had hired the false soldier risked the suspension of his salary for a month if at the next muster the established strength was less than one fifth, while the confiscation of command was applied only if the real strength was below 40 percent. These punishments remained in force for the rest of the century, and it was only in 1671 that Carlo Emanuele II granted the right of supplication to officers caught *in flagrante*.

As in other Italian states, the search for recruits was subject to the treatment received by the soldiers, and this was often a source of discontent and the main cause of desertions or dismissal. In 1667 Charles Emmanuel established a reward for all soldiers in the Guard Regiment who had served more than six months. This measure bore the desired fruit, as the regiment

55 Duboin, *Raccolta per ordine di materie delle leggi*, vol. XXVIII, p.73

56 Guerrini, *La Brigata dei Granatieri di Sardegna*, pp.41–42.

57 *Brancaccio, L'esercito del vecchio Piemonte*, p.196. The war treasury had the right to deduct two percent on all soldiers' salaries to pay the commissioners of the *Ufficio del Soldo*.

had many long-serving soldiers within it.[58] With regard to the minimum length of service, in 1675 it was set at two years 'without interruption' for all infantry recruits. Three years later, the term of service was increased to four years, but after two years the soldier had the possibility of asking for a discharge if he presented a replacement.[59] During the regency of Duchess Maria Giovanna Battista, the regiments found it more difficult to find recruits. The commissioners also reported that many times some soldiers passed from one regiment to another without due leave, 'at the instigation of some officer who wanted to keep his own company in the established number to the detriment of those of others'.[60]

It became clear to everyone that officers were the key element in the functioning of a permanent army. Since 1671 Duke Carlo Emanuele II expressly asked the colonels and lieutenant colonels to supervise the service of the captains in the garrisons, demanding that each of them be 'a good father and guardian' of the soldiers, and prescribing that captains and lieutenants should go every day to inspect the quarters, check the cleanliness of the rooms and visit the sick in the infirmary to ensure that they receive the appropriate medicines to cure their illness.[61] In 1674 the Duke ordered that no more than two officers in each company should be on license at the same time and for no longer than eight days.

In garrison, the soldier received only bread. With the edict of 17 September 1673, Carlo Emanuele prescribed that captains should establish *camerate* (rooms) of four soldiers, one of whom was in charge of buying food for all. This method served to prevent soldiers from squandering all their salary with the officers' retailers, where prices were normally higher. This method, common to all armies of the time, was also a way to prevent soldiers from buying cheap food to save their salary, often in order to pay debts.

Each regiment established its own internal service regulations for the quarter and encampment. The earliest regulation of this kind that has come down to the present day is a manuscript 'dictated' in 1701 by an officer of the Guards regiment. The document contains rules that include discipline, drill and ordinary service, and describe the life and training of common soldiers of a seventeenth-century army.[62] We learn that each recruit received a nickname from the sergeant that would accompany him throughout his life in the regiment. Each soldier was required to know all officers and those of other units if he was in garrison; to all of them he owed respect and obedience. The same obedience was to be observed with sergeants and corporals, and in the event of violent action or even threats, the soldier could be punished even by death. The soldier had to be brave, precise and disciplined in service, and 'jealous of his honour'. He was requested to be 'religious and pious' and

58 Guerrini, *La Brigata dei Granatieri di Sardegna*, p.39.

59 *Ibid.*, p.40.

60 *Ibid.*, p.41

61 Brancaccio, *L'esercito del vecchio Piemonte. Gli ordinamenti*, p.131.

62 *Evolutions et exercice militaire que l'on pratique dans le regiment des Gardes de S.A.R., dictées par Mr. De Blagnac du dit Regiment en l'année 1701, le 20 mai.*

35. A view of Piazza della SS. Annunziata with the *Reggia* of the Venaria Reale in the background; Turin, 1682 (author's archive). The ducal carriage is escorted by a picket of halberdiers, while in the square there are some Swiss Guards. Since the *Compagnia Guardie della Porta* did not leave the guard of the Ducal residence, the escort is probably formed by the *Gardes du Corps* on foot. Note the Swiss Guards wearing tall plumed headgear.

be terrified of blasphemy, refrain from drunkenness, a libertine life and theft. It was a severe obligation to report for duty in good order and clean, so every week he had to change his underwear, shave his beard but not his moustache, and at least once a month cut his hair. In his quarters he had to hang his coat, hat and sword on the nails given to him by the steward. If he had a work permit, he performed it without wearing his uniform, and the same in the *corvée* services, on pain of punishment on the wooden horse. The same care and cleanliness was reserved for his armament, which had to be polished at all times, and ammunition stored in a dry place. Every soldier was naturally required to learn to perfection all the motions required for the handling of weapons, and the manoeuvres of the battalion, and above all to shoot by aiming carefully 'and at the right time', reloading the weapon without wasting time, always maintaining silence and heeding the orders of the officers and sergeants. The soldier had to learn the concept that the company flag was 'the symbol of honour' of the whole unit, and the main rallying sign if the company had to regroup after a retreat, and that above all it was preferable to die than to leave the flag to the enemy. Furthermore, every soldier had to learn the drum signals. There were 12 different signals in all: *generale* (call of arms); *assemblea* (exit from the tent or the barracks); *bandiera* (rally); *al campo* (greeting a prince or general); *carica* (assault); *appello* (call for a muster); *ritirata* (return to the tent or barracks by night, or join the drummer by day); *diana* (waking up); *bando* (notification of orders); *chiamata* (for the surrender of a fortress); *fascinata* (to assemble soldiers for a corvée); *ricevimento* (to introduce a new officer); *preghiera* (religious service).

The regulations specified how pickets were to be formed, patrols in the quarters and in encampments, the formulation of watchwords, sentinels, as well as the duties of corporals and non-commissioned officers. A chapter included regulations governing relations with civilians, especially matters concerning provision of food, beds, straw, wood and candles.

On campaign, winter quarters were supplied by the community hosting the troops. The local authorities were therefore obliged to provide accommodation, utensils and every day two *libbre* of bread (736 g) a pound and a half of meat (552 g), and a pint and a half of wine (1.5 litre), as established in 1664. Cavalry also received hay and fodder. This method continued under Carlo Emanuele II, and only with Vittorio Amedeo II, facing the increased size of the army on campaign, did the service of *provianda* supply the troops during the winter. The officers had to provide food and fodder for themselves. As for concerns about military accommodation during winter quarters, in the 1670s Carlo Emanuele introduced a new regulation. For this purpose, buildings were rented or requisitioned to house troops on campaign.

The Duke also established the first medical service for the troops, limited, however, to garrisons only. These first regulations followed those introduced in 1644, when the 'infirmaries of the garrisons' were created, where sick soldiers were cared for by military physicians appointed with a ducal licence. In 1666, physicians and surgeons entered as permanent members of the garrisons. Sick soldiers kept their pay, but had to provide for any burial expenses.[63]

The Army of Savoy-Piedmont

The Savoy state showed a singular tendency to stabilise itself on an armed force with few variations: in 1625 there were 25,000 infantry and 1,200 horsemen; and at the end of the century the former were 21,000 and the latter 2,500.[64] In the Regency period Savoy-Piedmont developed a standing army of approximately 6,700 men in 1664, which constantly increased to 26,178 men in 1672 for the war against Genoa. In 1675 the new regent Christine of France, a second *Madama Reale* in the history of the duchy, inherited from her husband Carlo Emanuele II a professional army that had been reduced to 6,000 infantrymen, 1,500 selected cavalry militiamen plus another 3,000 trained militiamen on foot. This force looked much

63 *Ibid.*, p.156.

64 Luciano Pezzolo, 'La "rivoluzione militare": una prospettiva italiana 1400–1700', in A. Dattero and S. Levati (eds), *Militari in età moderna. La centralità di un tema di confine* (Milan: Cisalpino, 2006), p.48.

discredited following its defeat in the war against Genoa three years earlier. Moreover, the peace conditions imposed had forced the Duke to reduce the fleet to a few units for coastal surveillance. In winter 1676–77, Louis XIV made overtures to the Regency for a joint invasion of Lombardy. Spain was so deeply involved repressing the Messina rebellion that its forces in Northern Italy were now minimal. The plan failed, though, for the French King would not permit significant expansion of Savoy-Piedmont, and simply intended the negotiations to induce Spain to agree the peace. After 1659 the state remained under heavy French tutelage. Louis XIV maintained a garrison of 3,000 men in Pinerolo. In 1681, when Vittorio Amedeo was 15 years old, an alarming turning point came: Louis XIV purchased Casale from the Duke of Mantua increasing the subjection of the duchy. The French now had not only free passage across the Alps, watched by Pinerolo, but also direct control of the western flank of the Spanish Road. Piedmont was locked in as never before.

However, the impulse for a rearmament of the state came from France, when in 1682, the Sun King decided to finance the strengthening of the ducal army and reduce the garrison of Casale by a third. Through the treaty of 24 November 1682, France granted aid of 300,000 French *livres* to increase the infantry from 6,700 to 7,200 men; the cavalry was to be organised in stable units totalling 600 gendarmes and 1,200 dragoons. The loan was to be paid in six annual instalments, to be repaid after 1688. According to Article 5 of the treaty, Vittorio Amedeo had to enrol and keep on active duty a further 1,000 light cavalrymen, or dragoons, regardless of the 800 he already had, and a further 500 infantrymen, not considering the 6,700 he already had. Louis promised to pay an annual 300,000 *livres tournoises* subsidy, in monthly shares. As soon as these new troops were ready to march, Louis would withdraw one third of the troops he had in Piedmont. Therefore, Vittorio Amedeo was compelled to increase his troops by 20 percent, who had to remain scattered in their garrisons, while he had to host in his country a foreign, centralised, and not exactly friendly military force, not under his command and ready to intervene against any enemy of France, including him. Moreover, the increased force of his army would depend on French money, and in case that money was lacking, as happened just before the Grand Alliance, the situation would become difficult whenever the Duke's policy differed from the French one. Lastly, in the case of war, the French promised to give a yearly 1.2 million *livres* funding, and this funding had to be spent to increase the Duke's army to 4,000 cavalry – dragoons included – and 8,500 foot. On their own side, the French promised to commit 3,000 cavalry and 14,000 foot more than the soldiers already in Piedmont, to be supported by an artillery train of no less than 15 and no more than 30 field guns. The command had to be entrusted to a French general whenever the two armies operated jointly and their commanders' rank equalled.[65]

65 *Traité d'alliance défensive entre Victor Amedé Duc de Savoie et le Roi de France*, signed in Turin on 24 November 1682, in Solaro della Margarita, Clemente, *Traités publics de la Royale Maison*

In 1686 Vittorio Amedeo made an agreement with Louis XIV to repay the debt of 1682 by sending his bastard uncle Don Gabriele of Savoy with 4,500 soldiers and as many militiamen to join the 4,000 French troops under Catinat in the Val Pellice in the ruthless *dragonnade* against the Waldensians. It was on this occasion that the Duke decided to modernise his infantry by replacing pikes and matchlock muskets with flintlocks and bayonets. This upgrade alerted the court of France, which interpreted this decision as an express wish of the young duke to create a modern infantry oriented towards offensive tactics: an approach that contrasted with the predominantly defensive orientation that had been established by France, and was therefore judged as a desire to emancipate himself from French tutelage. In 1688 confirmation came from spies, who informed Louis XIV of secret negotiations with the League of Augsburg. In February 1688, in an attempt to avert the duchy's passage to the side of the allies, the Sun King ordered a third of the ducal troops to be taken hostage and ordered Vittorio Amedeo to send 2,000 infantrymen to Flanders under the orders of his generals. The Duke could not refuse to obey, but in 1690, when the French demanded the surrender of some fortresses and participation with the rest of the army in the invasion of the State of Milan, he responded by stipulating a defensive and offensive alliance with Spain and Austria. The status of minor ally turned out to be very advantageous for Vittorio Amedeo. In fact, the Duke was able to maximise his political income thanks to the high strategic value of his state. Furthermore, he could achieve more success than he would have had by remaining on the French side. However, the geostrategy in which his state found itself allowed the Duke limited room for manoeuvre, but by skilfully managing to move between the two camps, he continued to deal secretly with Louis XIV, and was able to escape the defeats suffered during the war by limiting the political damage.

Vittorio Amedeo continued his father's work of modernising the army, and in many fields went even further by introducing reforms and new regulations ahead of his time. With the edict of 2 April 1685 the corps of invalids was established, financed by a deduction from the wages of all regular soldiers, including officers. The fortress of Vercelli was the chosen location for quartering elderly soldiers or those no longer able to serve.[66]

The Duke also ordered the army train. He followed the French system, which included up to three carts and up to 40 pack animals available to each general and colonel. Further pack animals and two four-horse carts for the supplies and food providers were assigned to each infantry regiment on campaign.

de Savoie avec les puissances étrangères depuis la paix de Château-Cambresis jusqu'à nos jours, 6 vols (Turin, 1836), vol. II. pp.103–104.

66 Brancaccio, *L'esercito del vecchio Piemonte. Sunti storici*, p.289.

36. Gardes du Corps, 1685–89. See image commentaries for more information.

Left: 37. Private musketeer of the *Guardie* regiment, after the album of Galateri di Genola, *Armata Sarda. Uniformi antichi e moderni* (Turin, 1844). The illustration is the result of superficial reconstructions of the first military uniforms attempted in the nineteenth century.

Right: 38. Musketeer of the *Guardie* regiment, after the *Manoscritto Militare* preserved in the Royal Library of Turin, wearing the uniform of 1659. Apart from the headgear, the style of the dress is closer to 1758, the year when the figures were painted. However, the archival sources of the 1680s confirm, with few exceptions, the reliability of the manuscript concening the uniform colours.

39. Grenadier, *Guardie* regiment 1684, wearing the berretta slouch cap of red cloth. (Author's illustration for Ciro Paoletti's *William III's Italian Ally. Piedmont and the War of the League of Augsburg*, Helion & Company, 2019)

40. The drum major, drummers and fifers of all foot regiments, Guards included, wore a red coat with Savoy's livery – the so-called *biscia* (snake) – in azure and white edgings, blue or red cuffs, blue lining, breeches and stockings. In the 1690s some regiments drummers wore breeches and stockings like the private soldiers of their unit. (Author's illustration for Ciro Paoletti's *William III's Italian Ally. Piedmont and the War of the League of Augsburg*, Helion & Company, 2019)

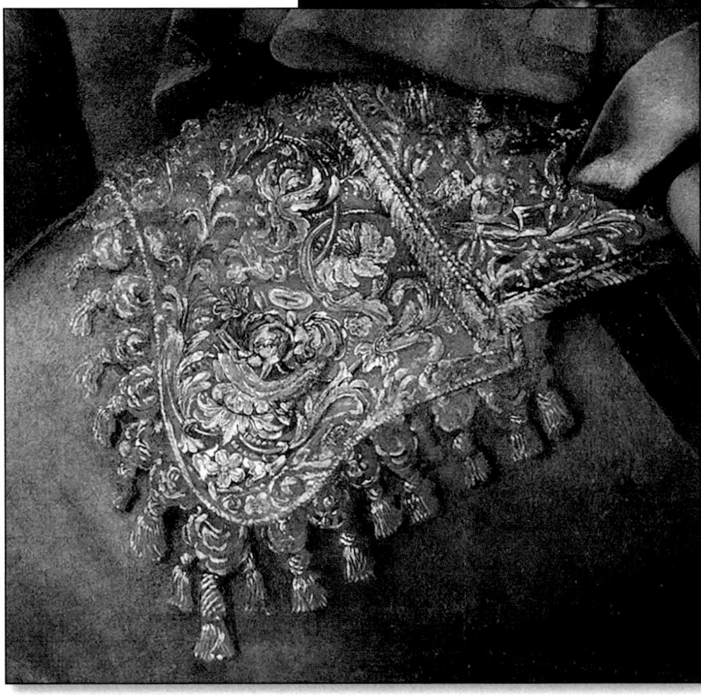

41. Equestrian portrait of Duke Carlo Emanuele II and Prince Vittorio Amedeo, and a detail of the saddle cover of the Prince's horse, in red with silver embroidery and tassels, by Charles Dauphin, 1674–75 (Collection of the Venaria Reale, Turin). Note on the left, the page-boy wearing Savoy's livery with the *biscia* (snake) lace of blue and white.

The *Maison Savoie*

The dukes of Savoy established the first standing unit of lifeguard in 1560, when they raised the company of the *Archibugieri a piedi* (foot arquebusiers) followed the year after by another company of *Archibugieri a cavallo* (mounted arquebusiers). In 1566, the company on foot was joined with the palace guard of the *alabardieri* (halberdiers), becoming a single unit also including the cavalry company of life guards. Then in 1607 Duke Vittorio Amedeo I joined the horsemen in the *Compagnia dei Gentluomini Archieri della Guardia*, composed of nobles and by 'the most selected bourgeois of Savoy'.[67] The infantrymen assumed the denomination of *Archibugieri Guardia della Porta,* or *Compagnia Guardie della Porta* (arquebusiers or company gate guards). This company formed the corps in charge of guarding the Duke's residences in Turin, providing services of honour and representation at official ceremonies and receptions of foreign diplomats. They maintained the usual strength of 40 men also enlisting the aged veteran NCOs as a prize for their loyal service.

The *Archibugieri* shared palace duties with the company of the *Cent-Suisses*, created in 1650 as *Gardes Suisses*.[68] The unit had a strength of 100 men in title only, as its strength consisted of three officers and 70 guards. The succession of commanding captains shows that the majority of the guards came from the cantons of Lucerne, Uri, Zug and Unterwalden, in practice from those which, together with Schwyz and Freiburg, had signed the agreement with Duke Emanuele Filiberto in 1577 to enlist a contingent of 6,000 mercenaries. The captain of the Swiss Guard held the rank of General of the Swiss Infantry.[69]

In 1609 the mounted company became the *compagnia archibugieri a cavallo di Sua Altezza Reale.* This company provided the mounted escort to the Duke until 1638, when a new company was established for the same task: the *Corazze di Sua Altezza Reale.* In 1677, this latter and the *Archibugieri* received the denomination of *Guardie del Corpo* (or more exactly *Gardes du Corps*). A third company was added in 1684 for the Dowager Duchess and finally a fourth in 1685. In 1690, the companies were established according their seniority receiving a new denomination:[70]

1a Compagnia Guardie del Corpo, former *Archibugieri a cavallo di Sua Altezza Reale*
2a Compagnia Guardie del Corpo, former *Corazze di Sua Altezza Reale*
3a Compagnia Guardie del Corpo, former *Corazze di Madama Reale*
4a Compagnia Guardie del Corpo, former *Archibugieri di Madama Reale*

The transformation from the Duke's escort to an elite unit was inspired by the coeval French *Gardes du Corps* of Louis XIV's *Maison du Roi*, and the

67 Camussi, Eugenio, *Dizionario analitico delle circolari dell'Azienda Generale di Guerra* (Turin, 1853), *Guardie del Corpo di SM.*

68 Nicola Brancaccio, *L'esercito del vecchio Piemonte. Sunti storici dei principali corpi, 1560–1859* (Rome, 1922), p.6.

69 Brancaccio, *L'esercito del vecchio Piemonte. Gli Ordinamenti*, p.181.

70 Brancaccio, *L'esercito del vecchio Piemonte. Sunti storici*, p.3.

number of companies, four, was also a sign that resembled the original model. The organisation also imitated the French model, since each company had one *capitano tenente*, one *tenente*, one *alfiere*, one *maresciallo*, two *brigadieri*, four corporals but only 40 guards. Like their transalpine counterpart, the Savoy-Piedmontese lifeguards accompanied the sovereign every time he took part in a military campaign, as they did in the second war against the Waldensians (1686–1689). In 1692 the overall strength of the four companies increased to 250 guards, officers included.[71]

Infantry

In 1660, after the war against Spain, the Regency reformed the infantry by establishing 10 regiments, including the *Régiment aux Gardes*.[72] This unit went through a complex organisational phase that had begun in the previous year. According to the sources, some companies from the disbanded regiments were joined with the regiment under the Count Françoise de Mesmes-Marolles (SI-2).[73] This regiment was one of the oldest still in service and is conventionally considered the forerunner of the Guards. In April 1659 the Duke ordered that the regiment had to deploy 12 companies for 1,200 men in total. In January 1660 the soldiers received new equipment and weapons, which included 714 muskets and 315 pikes.[74] In August the regiment deployed just six companies, but before the end of the year new companies were added. At this point, however, there are some incongruities. The company of Captain Blanc Rocher was under the regular force status, established at 50 men, but the muster of the company of Captain Villacardet de Fleury shows a force of 164 men in the same month.[75] Another relevant difference appears in October, when the regiment is now formed by 13 companies. In 1663 two new companies increased the total to 15; then four years later the companies became 20, but decreased to 19 in 1668. In 1671 the companies were reduced to 18, but one year later the regiment newly increases to 20 companies and maintains this number on paper until 1701.[76] As for the number of men, in 1664 the Duke reduced the company strength to 60 soldiers, except the first company which numbered 112 soldiers, and the second which numbered

71 ASV, *Segreteria di Stato Savoia*, 17 July 1692.

72 All the nineteenth-century texts dealing with the origins of the Savoy-Piedmont army in the 1660s set the number of infantry regiments at six. However, this number does not take into account the regiments raised for the relief of Venice for the war against the Ottoman Empire, and also excludes other units temporarily formed between 1658 and 1660. Even the authoritative *L'esercito del vecchio Piemonte*, by Cesare Brancaccio, does not include these and other regiments raised in 1672 for the war against Genoa.

73 ASTo, *Sezione III, Conti delle Milizie*, a. 1659, c. 321 and *Sezione III, Registri delle Livranze*, vol. VIII, c. 41.

74 ASTo, *Sezione III, Registri delle Livranze*, vl. VIII, 1660.

75 The archival documents relating to this company do not agree with each other and report different data for the same dates without explanation.

76 Guerrini, *La Brigata dei Granatieri di Sardegna*, p.27.

80.[77] In early 1672, shortly before the war against Genoa, the Duke ordered the companies increased to 90 men.

As a lifeguard of the sovereign, the regiment enjoyed special status and prerogatives. The colonel ranked as *maresciallo di campo*. Captains exercised authority over the infantry lieutenant colonels of the other regiments, while lieutenants had the same right over captains, and ensigns over lieutenants.[78]

Each company of the Guards numbered 101 men, with:

1 *capitano* (captain)
1 *tenente* (lieutenant)
1 *alfiere* (ensign)
2 *sergenti* (sergeants)
1 *scrivano del ruolo* (clerk/accountant)
1 *furiere* (quartermaster)
3 *caporali* (corporals)
1 drummer
90 private guards

The other regiments consisted of a variable number of companies, which varied considerably in 1660. According to Brancaccio's *L'esercito del vecchio Piemonte*, regiment *Savoie* (SI-3) had 25 companies, while *Piemonte* (SI-4) was formed by 22 companies in 1659, and *Aosta* numbered 23 companies in the same year.[79] In 1664 all the regiments were reorganised into 10 companies, each with an established strength of 56 men. They were:

1 *capitano* (captain)
1 *tenente* (lieutenant)
1 *alfiere* (ensign)
2 *sergenti* (sergeants)
1 *scrivano del ruolo* (clerk/accountant)
1 *furiere* (quartermaster)
2 *caporali* (corporals)
32 *moschettieri* (musketeers)
15 *picchieri* (pikemen)

Each company also included a couple of musicians recruited by the captain, while other personnel such as servants or surgeons could be enlisted by the officers. The first three companies belonged to the regiment's senior officers, and then replaced the captains with three *capitani-luogotenenti*, directly paid by the titular officer, who in fact received a double salary. The actual number rarely corresponded to the established strength, and while

77 *Ibid.*

78 ASTo, *Sezione II, Materie Militari, Ordini e Regolamenti*, m. 2, n. 11.

79 Brancaccio, *L'esercito del vecchio Piemonte. Sunti storici*, p.28, p.37, and p.45.

the guards were kept at the expected strength, the other regiments deployed between 70 and 75 percent of the regular force.[80]

Each regiment, Guards included, had its own staff, which followed the French system and comprised the following ranks:

1 *colonello* (colonel)
1 *luogotenente-colonnello* (lieutenant colonel)
1 *capitano maggiore* (major)
1 *capitano aggiunto* (deputy captain)
1 *aiutante maggiore* (major adjutant)[81]
1 *maresciallo d'alloggio* (maréchal de logis)
1 *prete* (priest)
1 *chirurgo* (surgeon)

Until 1666 some regiments had also one *medico* (physician), but after this year all the physicians were permanently assigned to the garrisons.[82] As occurred in the French infantry, the *capitano aggiunto* was in charge of the administration, instructions and discipline, while the *aiutante maggiore* was selected among the lieutenants with better knowledge of the drill, and usually he was promoted to the rank of captain after some years of service. The *maresciallo* was selected from the sergeants of the companies and ranked as a lieutenant.

Usually in wartime Savoy-Piedmont recruited foreign mercenaries, and then after the peace of 1659, according to the nineteenth-century authors, all the foreign regiments were licensed, and only a part of the French officers and soldiers would have been incorporated into the Savoyard regiments *de Challes* (SI-3) and *Senantes* (SI-5). However, the assertion that all foreign regiments had been dismissed in 1659 is not fully supported by the archival sources, since the Valais regiment of Colonel Kalbermatten was disbanded only in 1660, while *de Challes* (SI-3), in 1662 is still referred to as 'our French regiment'.[83] In 1660 further foreign troops retained in ducal service were two Swiss companies of Captains Müller (Schmid in 1675) and Ghidt, and three from the Valais Republic under Captains Quartery and Kalbermatten, and Stocalper (Berthod in 1674).[84] They served principally as garrison troops in the remote Alpine fortresses, but during the war against Genoa three companies joined the field army, participating in August at the unsuccessful defence of Oneglia.

---

80 *Ibid.*, p.28. In 1660 the regiment *Savoie* (SI-3) numbered 20 sergeants, 10 drummers, 30 corporals, and 400 private soldiers divided into 10 companies.

81 The *capitano maggiore* meaning the 'most important captain', shortened to *maggiore* (major) commanded the 'major's company'. All the remaining companies were commanded by captains.

82 Brancaccio, *L'esercito del vecchio Piemonte. Gli ordinamenti*, p.156.

83 ASTo, *Sezione IV, Patenti*, letter dated 23 March 1662. One year later, another letter mentions regiment *de Challes* as 'foreign regiment'.

84 Brancaccio, *L'esercito del vecchio Piemonte. Gli ordinamenti*, p.149.

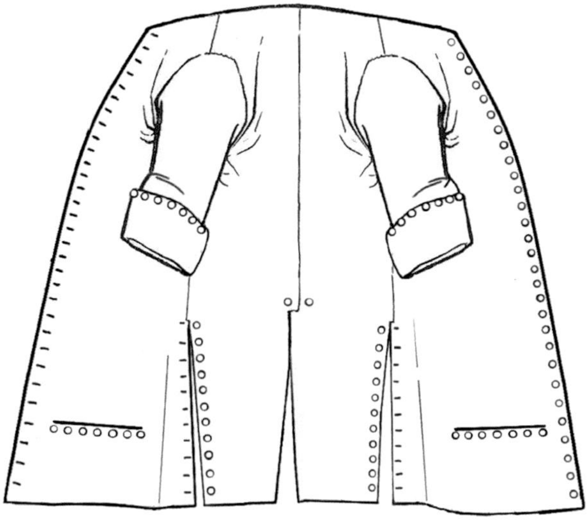

44. Coat pattern for the Guardie Regiment, 1671

Until 1664 the infantry regiments were identified by the name of the colonels who administered them on behalf of the sovereign by means of a specific capitulation, and allowed them to propose the officers of the companies. One year after, Duke Carlo Emanuele II declared six infantry units to be regiments of *ordinanza*, namely 'standing' regiments, identified by this term because they had to form the main order of battle, or the army's core on campaign. Historians have established in these regiments the birth of the House of Savoy's standing army and consequently the beginning of the history of the modern Italian army, but actually the Duchy had standing units long before. In 1689 at least 12 regiments raised before 1664 were still in service. In 1619 the Savoyard regiment *du Cheynez* had been raised, which later evolved into the *Monferrato* infantry regiment (SI-1). The *Savoie* Infantry regiment (SI-3) was originally raised in 1624,[85] followed in 1636 by the regiment of foot *Catalano Alfieri*, after its commander's name, which became *Piemonte* in 1664 (SI-4).[86] Prior to 1659 more units were organised, including the *Guardie* (SI-2), *Aosta* (SI-5), and *Nice* (SI-7) infantry regiments. Almost certainly the seniority of the Guards was established in 1659 because the only related document was found in the archives in the nineteenth century and dated to that year, but this could have generated a mistake: probably the document refers to the re-establishment of the regiment's strength at the end of winter quartering, and there is in fact much direct evidence of the existence of the regiment before this date. An unequivocal testimony is provided by Anne-Marie-Louise d'Orléans, the *grande Mademoiselle*, daughter of Gaston d'Orléans, younger brother of Louis XIII – *Monsieur* – who mentions the regiment in her memoirs of a meeting between her father and Carlo Emanuele II in Lyon in 1658. Anne-Marie wrote:

> It was said that the Prince of Savoy had complained that Monsieur, one day in the king's carriage, had asked him 'is your regiment of guards on foot?' He answered 'yes'. Later Monsieur asked him if there was not a royal square in Turin and he answered the same. Then 'Did you have a palace built that they call a royal palace?' He answered again 'yes'. Knowing Monsieur, I found that he asked all these questions to the Prince of Savoy in order to mock him, but as there was no

85 According to Guerrini, *La Brigata dei Granatieri di Sardegna*, p.23, many inaccuracies are due to the work of Saluzzo, *Histoire Militaire du Piémont* (Turin, 1818) who allegedly confused the history of different regiments. The most obvious case concerns the regiment *Savoie* (SI-3), confused with that of *Chablais* (SI-24).

86 Later, 1st and 2nd *Savoia* Infantry Regiments in the Royal Sardinian army, and then *Re* ('King') Infantry Regiment in the Royal Italian army.

> reason to do so, I do not think he noticed. Even if he were not a great sovereign, as he is, treated as Royal Highness, there have been enough daughters of kings married in that house to have royal squares and a royal palace. As for the regiment of guards, it is efficient and very fine, according to what I have heard from officers who have served in that country there; so I was annoyed that Monsieur had said it, and even more annoyed that the Prince of Savoy had remarked on it, because this speech had a somewhat childish air.[87]

Therefore the 1664 ordinance established a new seniority of the regiments, promoting the *Régiment des Gardes* (SI-2) to the first position, moving to second place the regiment *Savoie* (SI-3), while the most ancient regiment, *Coudray-Monferrato* (SI-1), raised in 1619, became number four.[88] In the same year, regiments *Ayazza* (SI-14) and *Mezerac* (SI-15), both raised in 1660, became the seventh and eighth in the *ordinanza*.[89]

The reform of 1664 introduced another substantial novelty, establishing the six regiments of *Sua Altezza Reale*, namely belonging to the House of Savoy, which assumed a territorial designation coinciding with the recruiting province or city. It was another measure that followed the direction taken by Louis XIV when the King assumed the post of Colonel General of Infantry for himself in 1661. Of the first eight regiments five were recruited in Piedmont, and three in Savoy, Nice and the Val d'Aosta. Between 1667 and 1668 three new infantry regiments were raised but entrusted to colonel-proprietors. Among these, the regiment of Colonel Cesare Badat, a knight of the Maltese Order of St John, in 1674 assumed the denomination *Crocebianca* (SI-17),

87 *Mémoires de Mademoiselle de Montpensier, petite-fille d'Henri IV, collationés sur le manuscript autographe* (Paris, 1858), vol. IV, p.325. There is another, even older testimony, preserved in the Turin State Archives, where it appears that on 22 April 1617 Duke Carlo Emanuele I ordered the raising of the regiment for the imminent campaign against the Spaniards, in ASTo, *Materie Militari, Ordini e Regolamenti*, m. 2, n. 11: *Ordine del Duca Carlo Emanuele I per la levata delle Compagnie di Soldatesca ivi espresse per il suo Reggimento delle Guardie.* In all likelihood this is the same unit that the *grande Mademoiselle* refers to. However, the regiment disappears from the battle orders to reappear in 1621, and then disappears again. The fact that it was an elite regiment may have meant it took longer than usual to enter service, and subsequently might have assumed the colonel's name, as was the practice. Thanks to Ciro Paoletti for noticing this. Another proof about the existence of the regiment before 1659 comes from the chronicles of the war against the Waldensians. According to the sources Count François de Mesmes, lord of Marolles in 1655, is already qualified as colonel of the *Régiment á pied de la Garde.* Although he does not completely deny the date of 1659, Guerrini, in *La Brigata dei Granatieri di Sardegna*, pp.14–19, suggests that the creation of the regiment took place before this date, as he mentions acts and documents concerning it dating back to 1657.

88 Regiment *Aosta* became the third of *ordinanza*, *Piemonte* took the fifth position, and *Nice* the sixth. See Brancaccio, *L'Esercito del vecchio Piemonte*, p.164. This sequence gave rise to a dispute between the Guards and *Savoie*, who both claimed the first position. According to tradition (or legend), Duke Carlo Emanuele settled the matter by transferring the *Savoie* to the citadel of Turin, disbanding the regiment and then reconstituting it the next day.

89 Practically, the ordinance reset the precedence of all units back to 1659. This caused the misunderstanding that the *Régiment des Gardes* was raised in that year.

because the Colonel and all the officers were knights of the Order. In 1680 the regiment became the property of the House of Savoy, alongside *Saluzzo* (SI-21), increasing the number of the Duke's regiments to eight.

For budgetary reasons, at the end of the 'cold war' on the borders with the State of Milan during the War of Devolution, Carlo Emanuele II reduced the infantry regiments to nine. The decrease was even more noticeable considering that the number of companies was also reduced to half and each regiment retained just five or six companies.

The war against Genoa soon required an increase of the infantry with new regiments, while the companies were strengthened with 20 men, and the regiments increased to a war-strength of 10 companies. The newly raised units included a regiment called *La Marina* (SI-20) formed for service on the fleet. In November 1672, after the failure of the campaign against Genoa, and faced with the prospect of a new reduction of strength, the Duke ceded the newly raised regiment *La Marina* to his patron Louis XIV for the war against the Dutch Republic. The regiment had been completed including 100 soldiers from the *Gardes*.[90] Rather than disband the army Carlo Emanuele followed the practice common in Germany where small states maintained the cadres for a considerable military force, renting his soldiers to other countries. This was a legitimate way of keeping the regiments intact but not on payroll. The next year another regiment, *Piemonte* (SI-4), entered the French army in Flanders and this time the Guards ceded 70 men. The only condition placed on their use was that they were not to be used directly against the Imperial army, since the Duke was still a prince of the Empire.[91] The regiment returned to the Duke in 1678, after the Peace of Nijmegen.

The unsatisfactory outcome of the first campaign against the Genoese made the need to find troops for the continuation of the war urgent. No longer able to turn to the traditional reservoirs of mercenaries in France and Switzerland, the Duke sought troops in Germany. In July 1672 Carl Emmanuel II obtained from his brother-in-law Ferdinand Maria von Wittelsbach, Prince-Elector of Bavaria, the rent of a 1,700 men strong infantry regiment under *Obrist* Beltin, to which a battalion of 500 infantrymen under lieutenant colonel Bertrand de la Perousse was later joined.[92] In September the Bavarians arrived in Piedmont by marching through Switzerland, to join the Savoyard troops for the campaign against Ovada. They participated in the operation until the armistice agreed in the meantime, which was followed by a peace in January 1673.[93]

During the regency period, the infantry regiments were kept on a peacetime strength, corresponding to 360–400 men divided into eight or 10 companies. In 1683, with the money from the French loan, a new *della*

90 ASTo, *Sezione IV, Regolamenti Militari*, a. 1671. The regiment was later incorporated in the French army.

91 *Ibid.*

92 Brancaccio, *L'esercito del vecchio Piemonte. Gli ordinamenti.* p.150

93 Anonymous, *Carlo Emanuele II e la guerra del Piemonte contro Genova. L'anno 1672* (without place and date, USSME Archive), p.119.

Marina regiment was also raised, intended as landing infantry for the war fleet that was to be reconstituted, since the navy included only three galleys based in Villafranca.[94] The regiment was raised joining the companies of marine infantry quartered in Nice, Villafranca and Sant'Ospizio.[95] With the majority of Vittorio Amedeo II in 1684, the infantry regiments increased to 12–14 companies of 40 men each, which was also the strength of the Guards companies. This more or less coincided with the ordinary tactical strength of the single battalion, except for the Guard which formed two battalions. In wartime the numbers of companies of the ordinary regiments had to increase to 16 always with the 'regular' 40 private soldiers, including corporals and now also one or two drummers, alongside the customary sergeants, quartermaster, accountant and three company officers. From 1684 the regiment's staff of the Guards also comprised the *arciere* (Provost) and his men, who acted as military police in the regiment, and a musical band of eight oboists.

The proportion of pikes to muskets did not change, but the experience of the war on the mountains and the relatively low number of troops persuaded the Duke of Savoy to provide his infantry with firearms only as early as 1688–1690. In 1685, simultaneously with the disappearance of the pikemen, Vittorio Amedeo introduced grenadiers into his infantry regiments, imitating the French who had introduced them in the 1670s. The new infantry speciality was introduced only in the *ordinanze* regiments, excluding the Guards, as also practised in France. Between April and October 1685 six grenadiers were established in each company,[96] then in 1686 each regiment formed a whole grenadier company of 72 men. Before the end of the year the Guards also introduced grenadiers, always six per company, an arrangement that remained unchanged until 1696.[97]

Cavalry and Dragoons

In the aftermath of the Peace of the Pyrenees the regency had a mounted force divided into companies of cuirassiers and mounted arquebusiers (dragoons), which on campaign were joined to form larger tactical corps. Overall this was a very modest force, both for reasons of containing military expenditure and because of the eminently defensive role of the ducal army. Moreover, up until then, the French cavalry had largely compensated for the tactical tasks required of the mounted units. In 1667 the companies of *corazze* formed a regiment that was, however, very short-lived, as in November of the following year the Duke disbanded it alongside two companies of the mounted arquebusiers. The only cavalry in permanent service were the four companies of cuirassiers that formed the lifeguard assigned to the senior cavalry commander, in imitation of the similar units existing in Spain and

---

94 Ciro Paoletti, *William III's Italian Ally. Piedmont and the War of the League of Augsburg 1683–1697* (Warwick: Helion & Company, 2019), p.51.

95 Brancaccio, *L'esercito del vecchio Piemonte. Sunti storici*, p.60.

96 *Ibid.*, pp.71–79.

97 Guerrini, in *La Brigata dei Granatieri di Sardegna*, pp.48–49.

Austria. In 1683 these companies were joined in the regiment of *Corazze Piemonte* under the command of Don Gabriele of Savoy, which was another short-lived unit disbanded two years later.[98]

The lack of a line cavalry was compensated for by resorting to the practice of the feudal age that required the nobility to serve in arms on horseback, recruiting other volunteers from their vassals to form a company of *gendarmes*. In wartime the cavalry companies formed a field corps called a *squadron* in both Savoy and Piedmont. The Savoy squadron was under the orders of its own general, whose companies varied between four and nine in the period 1660–1690 and was usually denominated as *Savoie Cavalerie*. In Piedmont too the *gendarmes* formed their companies, but the difference between the two squadrons was the greater availability of recruits in Savoy, where large fiefdoms still existed, whereas these were disappearing in Piedmont, and it was therefore more difficult to form the squadron in this part of the ducal domains.[99] In order for Piedmont to field its own cavalry squadron it was necessary to resort to the *cavalleria paesana* (country cavalry, namely the mounted militia). Thus in 1668 the Duke could deploy 1,000 horsemen or *gendarmes* on paper, who four years later formed 20 companies. These mounted troops, also known as *cavalleria dello stato* (state cavalry) were a semi-permanent cavalry, since the rank and file served only from April to October.[100]

42. Ensign of Piemonte Dragoni regiment (later *Nizza Cavalleria*), 1690, by Italo Cenni. Apart from some minor detail, the uniform is correctly represented: yellow coat with black facing, red cloak, white metal buttons.

Generally the gendarmes were enlisted for two years while maintaining their residence at home, periodically meeting in the residence of the commander, and where the other officers had their homes, to carry out reviews and training. Each company was to serve two months in the capital, serving as cavalry escort for the duke and duchess when they moved to other localities.[101] The first four companies belonged to the members of the ducal family, being *Sua Altezza Reale, Madama Reale, Principe di Carignano* and *Conte di Soissons*. Each company had a variable strength of 30–40 men, and included one captain-lieutenant, one lieutenant, one ensign and one brigadier. In 1677 the company of *Sua Altezza Reale* was licensed,[102] but further companies were formed in the

98 Brancaccio, *L'esercito del vecchio Piemonte. Gli ordinamenti*, p.236.

99 *Ibid*., p.147. This was the same regiment offered to Venice for the war against the Porte. See the following chapter, p.187

100 *Ibid.*

101 *Ibid*., p.148.

102 Brancaccio, *L'esercito del vecchio Piemonte. Sunti storici*, p.231.

following years, although their actual numbers varied considerably. However, at least a couple of these assembled enough horsemen to form the nucleus of the new mounted regiments in the early 1690s. These were the *Gendarmes* of None and the regiment of Cavaglià.[103]

In the late 1670s the *squadrone di Piemonte* was organised on a war establishment formed by four companies of gendarmes, as well as the squadron of Savoy. In the early 1680s two companies of mounted arquebusiers were raised. These were the company of Princess Ludovica and that of Don Gabriele of Savoy, who was General of Cavalry. In 1684 the Piedmontese squadron was reorganised as *Gendarmerie* by increasing the eight companies to a strength of 100 men each. All the companies were joined into three brigades assigning each the name of one of the provinces of the Duchy, with the exception of the first brigade which maintained the name *Gendarmi di Sua Altezza Reale.*

The companies were as follows:

Gendarmi di S.A.R., Captain Count of Ozegna
Gendarmi del Genevois, Captain Marquis de Balbiano
Gendarmi di Chablais, Captain Count of Agliano
Gendarmi di Piemonte, Captain Count of None
Gendarmi del Monferrato, Captain Marquis de Garessio
Gendarmi del Faucigny, Captain Count of Pertengo
Gendarmi di Saluzzo, Captain Count of Sales
Gendarmi di Savoia, Captain Marquis de Cavaglià

The *squadrone* also included the two companies of *Corazze* (cuirassiers) still in service, the company of *Archibugieri di Sua Altezza Reale* (Arquebusiers of His Royal Highness), and the *Archibugieri di Madama Reale*, both incorporated into the *Guards du Corps* between 1684 and 1685.

Previously, in early 1671, another regiment of horse was formed by joining volunteers from the Piedmontese gendarmes, which took the denomination *Prince de Piémont* (SC-1). The genesis of this regiment is not always consistently related by nineteenth-century historiography. The fact that a few months later the regiment was ceded to Louis XIV has been interpreted in different ways. Certainly, the benefits of serving in a great foreign army were useful for the formation of a well-trained officer corps instructed according to modern theories, and this was probably one of the reasons that convinced Carlo Emanuele to raise this cavalry regiment. And all this, by the way, occurred just before the war against Genoa, which was fought on a terrain where cavalry was of poor utility. In August 1671 the regiment was ceded to France to join the cavalry engaged in the war against the United Provinces of the Netherlands. Although the French ordinance of 4 February 1672 stipulated that all cavalry regiments had to be based on six companies of 54 horsemen, the *Prince de Piémont* regiment – now denominated *Royal*

103 In 1692, None gendarmes originated *Savoie* cavalry regiment, and Cavaglià formed the core of *Piemonte* cavalry regiment.

43. Exhibition of the Holy Shroud in Piazza Castello, Turin 1684, by Pieter Bolckmann (Collection of the Castello di Racconigi, Cuneo). See image commentaries for more information.

Piémont – had only four.[104] The agreements stipulated that all officers had to be subjects of the Duke of Savoy and the regiment retained its original name. The regiment had a command staff comprising three field officers, one *maréchal*, one *brigadier* and three corporals for each company. The Prince of Piedmont, Vittorio Amedeo, was formally the regiment's colonel-proprietor, but on campaign he was replaced by the Savoyard Count Prosper de Lusinge, who in 1677 succeeded the Baron of Saint-Joire, former lieutenant colonel, and in 1678 Joseph-Philippe de Saint-Martin d'Aglié, Marquis of Rivarola, who was the last Duke's subject to hold the post.[105] According to the French sources, the regiment was completed with rank and file including Catholic English exiled in France.[106]

The turning point in cavalry matters came with Vittorio Amedeo's rise to power. In January 1683 two regiments of dragoons were created, the regiment of *Sua Altezza Reale* (SD-1) and the regiment of *Madama Reale* (SD-2) financed by the French loan. Both regiments had a field strength of

104 Quincy, *Histoire Militaire du Regne de Louis le Grand, Roy de France, où l'on trouve un détail de tous le Batailles, Sieges, Compat particuliers ...* (Paris, 1726), vol. I, p.384.

105 Général Suzanne, *Histoire de la Cavalerie de France* (Paris, 1874), vol. II, p.95.

106 *Ibid.* The regiment participated in the siege of Maastricht in 1673 and the Battle of Seneffe in 1674.

six companies with approximately 300 men.[107] In April, in order to muster and train all the dragoons, a *champ volant* quarter was established close to the Duke's residence of Venaria Reale, to which all the mounted troops were transferred.

Count Gaspare Roussillon of Bernezzo was appointed as colonel of *Madama Reale* dragoons, while the Count of Verrua received the command of *Sua Altezza Reale*. However, the latter left ducal service shortly afterwards to enter the French army, the abrupt defection occurring because Verrua's wife had become the mistress of Vittorio Amedeo. On the other hand, the history of the second regiment was thwarted by the change of policy at court, which brought the disbanding of regiment *Madama Reale* after just two years of existence.[108] Nonetheless, the precedent had been set, since new units of dragoons were raised in subsequent years. The regiment *Genevois Dragons* (SD-3) – known also as *Dragons Verts* – was formed on 7 October 1689, with Colonel Louis Deschamps, Marquis de Chaumont, already captain of *Sua Altezza Reale* dragoons, as first colonel. The regiment was established at eight companies. In August 1690 the dragoon regiments increased to three with *Piemonte* (SD-4), or *Dragons Jaunes*, under colonel Bonifacio Antonio Solaro, Count of Macello. Both regiments would have a strength of six companies with 300 men in all, while *Sua Altezza Reale* would increase to eight companies.[109] From a strategic point of view the formation of dragoon regiments was a fair compromise for a regional power such as Savoy-Piedmont, especially from a defensive perspective. Although cavalry continued to be represented by autonomous companies, the formation of dragoon regiments anticipated the first cavalry regiments by eight years.

At the beginning of 1691, Waldensians and especially French Huguenot refugees were enlisted in Balthazar's Dragoon Regiment, recruited with England's war loans, which finally passed into the service of the Dutch Republic in 1695.

Artillery

The edict of 15 January 1603 marked the definitive entry of the Piedmontese artillery into the military institutions. With this act, the Duke granted the *bombardieri* and their officers the privileges granted to the militia.[110] In subsequent years the artillery personnel were divided into three sections: Piedmont, Savoy and the County of Nice. The command of the first section was established in Turin and included:

---

107 ASTo *Camerale Piemonte* Misc. Art. 305–320 Reg. II *Cavalleria*, 1681–1684, dated 26 January 1683.

108 Colonel Bernezzo was appointed as captain of the *Archibugieri Guardie della Porta*.

109 In 1691 the Count of Verrua was replaced in command of *Sua Altezza Reale* dragoons by the Count of Macello, former colonel of the *Piemonte* dragoons, replaced in turn by Felix Emanuel Maillard, Marquis d'Alby.

110 Brancaccio, *L'esercito del vecchio Piemonte. Gli ordinamenti*, p.184.

29. Model of a 12 lb bronze gun with carriage painted red and black; late seventeenth century, collection of the Venaria Reale, Turin. See image commentaries for more information.

1 *capitano generale* (captain commander)
1 *commissario* (commissioner)
1 *controllore delle munizioni* (ammunition controller)
1 *munizioniere* (ammunition custodian)
1 *primo ingegnere* (first engineer)[111]
1 *polverista* (gunpowder maker)
1 *capo petardiere* (chief artificer)

With them, there was a variable number of *gentiluomini* (gentleman volunteers), *sergenti del cannone* (constables) and arquebusiers. In Savoy there were the *generale del cannone* – commander-in-chief – commissioner, and ammunition custodian; in Nice operated one captain, one commissioner, one ammunition controller and one ammunition custodian.[112] The edict of 1635 established a strength of 200 artillerymen divided among the main garrisons of Turin, Nice, Montmélian and Vercelli.[113]

With a specific edict signed by Duke Carlo Emanuele II on 9 April 1667, the *Consiglio d'artiglieria e munizioni da guerra* (council of artillery and munitions of war) was established under the direction of the artillery commander, or *generale del cannone*. The council supervised the administration service, the arsenals, the factories, and promoted the study and deliberation of all technical matters concerning guns, mortars, ammunition, and trains. The execution of decisions was entrusted to an *Azienda* entrusted to the *Intendente e Provveditore Generale* of the artillery.[114]

In 1650 the service of miners for the army was also introduced with the appointment of a captain miner. With the *viglietto* of 20 May 1657, the Regency prescribed that no candidate should enter the corps of miners without having passed the selection examination by an artillery captain assigned to the mine service, and appointed to that post by the General of Artillery. In 1660 the newly formed corps of miners came under the authority of the artillery commander, forming a corps divided into garrisons

111 This was not a fortification technician, but he was in charge of cannon casting.

112 Brancaccio, *L'esercito del vecchio Piemonte. Gli ordinamenti*, p.85.

113 Stumpo, *Finanza e Stato moderno nel Piemonte del Seicento*, p.188.

114 Brancaccio, *L'esercito del vecchio Piemonte. Gli ordinamenti*, p.157.

with officers and commons evenly distributed. Volunteers and ammunition custodians remained in Turin with some officers for the direction of the garrison services. In that year the artillery corps assigned to the garrisons of Piedmont, Savoy and Nice numbered six captains, eight gentlemen, 12 constables and 71 *bombardieri*. Duke Carlo Emanuele II realised the importance of technical weapons, and in 1667 tried to encourage the development of artillery by establishing an 'artillery school' in Turin. The first attempt to establish a technical training centre was unsuccessful, but in 1672 the school was reconstituted with its seat in the citadel of Turin.[115]

In April 1677 the Marquis del Borgo, who had been in office as General of Artillery for five years, resigned his post under pressure from the Regency, which rewarded him with a generous pension. The Count Filiberto of Piossasco was appointed to this office.

Militia

Historians of the *Risorgimento* tend to extol the role of the militia of the Duchy of Savoy, which, from the beginning, would have embodied the values of loyalty to the sovereign and state. Over the years, the evolution and transformation of the militia into semi-permanent territorial units reinforced the myth. Consequently, in recent times there are many authors who point out that the Savoy-Piedmont militia was better equipped and better trained than those of other Italian States. Though from an organisational point of view the Savoy-Piedmont militia introduced modern features, its military role was initially no better or worse than that performed by the other Italian militias. All considered, as was the case in other Italian states, the dukes of Savoy sought to assemble a territorial force capable of supporting the regular army on campaign, and to constitute a strategic reserve for defence in the event of invasion. However, what should not be underplayed is that as early as 1672, the ducal militia formed a reserve of recruits for the professional infantry, which proved very useful to remedy the failure of the campaign against Genoa in the spring of 1672.

The introduction of peasant militia in Savoy-Piedmont, established in 1560 but only organised in 1564, was issued by limiting the obligations of the *descritti* (male subjects registered in the roles) aged between 18 and 50, to a few days of annual training in peacetime and an active presence, although never complete, in times of war.[116] These burdens were compensated by exemptions and privileges of some importance such as 'personal servitude', the right not to pay tribute to communities and guilds, the right to bear arms, albeit with certain limitations, and to enjoy a special tribunal, both criminal and civil. In organisational terms, the militiamen were a burden on the communities, albeit under the duke's orders, and furthermore they did not provide continuous service in the territory. The guarding of the sovereign's

115 *Ibid.*, p.148.

116 Bianchi, 'La riorganizzazione militare del Ducato di Savoia', p.204: 'The militia was therefore not a permanent corps, even with all the ambiguity that has been assigned to the meaning of this expression.'

person, the control of the fortifications, the surveillance of the borders remained assigned to professional soldiers, including foreigners, paid by the treasury because of the needs of the state.

In December 1564, as *sergente maggiore generale*, Giovanni Levo from Piacenza drew up the first militia regulations, which formed the basis for all subsequent literature on this matter.[117] The new militia was divided into four subalpine *colonnellati*: Ivrea, Asti, Piedmont and Nice, and three others in Savoy. Each *colonnellato* numbered 2,400 foot divided into six companies, in turn divided in *centurie*. Five companies comprised 150 pikemen, and 250 musketeers, while the sixth was formed by 360 musketeers and 40 halberdiers. In 1566 the number of *colonnellati* in Piedmont was doubled from four to eight. Alongside the infantry, a number of companies of cavalry militia were formed in 1569, the *celate* (sallets), recruited from the families that could maintain at least one horse. The *elezione* (selection) and *descrizione* (registration) of recruits was conducted by the colonels and captains, or by *castellani* and governors, depending on the size of the location. According to the sources, which provide a large number of complaints, these officials often used arbitrary criteria, which involved the negotiation of quotas and recruits with the municipal magistracies.[118] All weapons and ammunition were paid for by the communities, which is a first clue about the origin of the protests. Furthermore, it must have been very difficult to field such a large number of musketeers in the absence of any standardisation of calibre.[119]

The idea of turning the militia into a quasi-permanent military force began to take hold at the beginning of the seventeenth century, when the Duke's councillors proposed to distinguish between an ordinary and an 'elected' (elite) militia. According to this plan, local officials were to constitute a quota of foot soldiers by selecting the strongest and best trained militiamen. These recruits, for whom a 15-year service in the militia was established, were nevertheless left with the open possibility of being replaced. It was assumed that in Piedmont alone, a force of 8,000 militiamen would be recruited by placing them under 20 captains and five provincial colonels. The government introduced some restrictions to face the constant spread of the exemptions. The roles of these contingents were to be forwarded to the *generale della fanteria*, who together with the *veedore* was responsible for authorising redundancies and exchanges of candidates proposed by colonels and captains. Subsequent attempts at reorganisation show that the weakest link in the reform remained the role assigned to the mayors of the communities. In fact, they were unable to submit replacements of expatriate

117 *Discorso dell'ordine et modo di armare, compartire et esercitare la milizia del Serenissimo duca di Savoia* (Turin, 1566).

118 Bianchi, 'La riorganizzazione militare del Ducato di Savoia', p.205.

119 *Ibid.*, 'Also disproportionate was the frequency of the exercises recommended in the *Discorso*. These occurred every public holiday or at least every Sunday, fortnightly or monthly for the *centurie*, monthly or bi-monthly for the companies, in addition to four annual muster of colonels and two general battles' at Pentecost and San Martino, a rhythm that was certainly incompatible with the needs of agricultural work.

or dead militiamen, while potential candidates presented all kinds of excuses for refusing service.[120] The plan was temporarily abandoned, but a few years later a ducal edict revived the project in a different way. With the reform of the militia in 1618, still relating to Piedmont alone, the Duke ordered the recruitment of companies of 300 men, raised by 'fireplaces' and subdivided into *centurie* numbering, on paper, one quarter wealthy people, one quarter artisans, and half peasants. The expenses for quartering and supplying these contingents were still paid by the municipalities, grouped into 12 districts, which would be reconfirmed in 1622. The communities, in return for the money spent for the militia, obtained discounts on certain taxes. The call to arms distinguished between one-month turns for the general militia and a full year's service for the elected militia.[121]

A new reform was issued in 1649, diminishing the turn to 40 days and moving the age limits from 16 to 55 years. A special tax was issued to the people who were exempted. However, the new arrangements did not produce good results. Indiscipline and malversation were compounded by typical cases of embezzlement. Officers were inclined to bargain with soldiers by exempting them from service against payment of a fee, but collecting wages as if they had been present. The inspections carried out were not sufficient to restrain abuses. Moreover, service in the militia attracted 'criminal people' who took advantage of the right to bear arms to commit abuses and even revenge.[122] Thus, the government resorted to the expedient of decreasing the quota of men for each province by a third, in order to increase the pay of the militiamen engaged and trying to decrease the possibility of fraud. It was also ordered that officers should serve for 160 days a year and keep at least 40 men per company in active service in rotation every 40 days.[123] Abuse, however, did not disappear, but the failures did not diminish the government's determination to field a conveniently trained territorial militia.

Besides the size of the militia, which over the course of the century came to involve a large number of people, and their organisation and employment, there is the fact that these units were still firmly community based, each company being composed of elements belonging to the same territory. It is also noticeable that, contrary to what the government might expect, it was not only the poorer class of the population which formed these contingents, but also members of families belonging to the local elites. Consequently, this situation reproduced the same power dynamics within the militia as existed in civil society, and with it, other abuses.

Regarding the caution on the use of militia, there is an important element to consider, namely the fact that the militiamen were still armed men, who if pushed to the extreme could use firearms against its officers or its regular troops. The authorities were well aware of this, so much so that on the occasion of popular uprisings, for example, they advised the local governors

120 *Ibid.*, p.211.

121 Duboin, *Raccolta per ordine di materie delle leggi*, vol. XXI, p.685; vol. XXVI, pp.22–23, 832, 834.

122 *Ibid.*, p.835.

123 Brancaccio, *L'esercito del vecchio Piemonte. Gli Ordinamenti*, pp.144–145.

not to make use of militiamen such as happened during the rebellion of Mondovì of 1681–82, for fear that they would join the rioters.

The 1669 reform was the decisive militia reform, marking an intermediate step between the peasant militia introduced in the sixteenth century and the provincial regiments of Vittorio Amedeo II in the next century. In order to reorganise the militia, the Duke established the formation of the Piedmontese *battaglione* divided into 12 territorial regiments identified by the names of the *colonnellati*.[124] These were Vercelli, Biella, Ivrea, Susa, Pinerolo, Torino, Chieri, Asti, Savigliano, Cuneo, Mondovì and Saluzzo. These regiments were formed by six percent of selected *descritti* of each community aged from 18 to 30 years, who received special training, complete military equipment, and salary. The Duke estimated that he could muster at least 6,000 men, not including the mounted force. These militiamen were no mere commoners. The members of the battalion were paid directly by the *Ufficio del Soldo*, and above all joined on a voluntary basis, which brought them closer to the infantry of the *ordinanze*. They were graced with the privileges long granted to the duke's subjects, such as permission to bear arms, exemption from participating in certain tax obligations, and legal advantages in the event of debts to the community.[125] Mounted militiamen, who still provided their own horses, enjoyed the right to hunt with dogs, like *seigneurs*; furthermore, after five years of service they could legally fight duels with nobles to defend their honour if they received offence. Troopers and their wives could wear silk, and hats with golden trim and feathers like any aristocrat.[126] According to historians of the 1920s, the offer was enthusiastically accepted and volunteers rushed forward in large numbers.[127]

To command the companies, the duke appointed trusted noblemen. He could confer on retainers and notables to whom he owed favours of all kinds the title of captain, which carried serious responsibility. However, the unfortunate outcome of the war against Genoa went far beyond the dismay of having to incur an expense that was as fruitless as it was exaggerated. The challenge remained open, of creating a semi-professional corps to be used in defensive as well as offensive campaigns, and above all the accusation of treason that had involved some high-ranking officers, with the effect of damaging relations between the sovereign and the nobility for a long time.[128]

Although the available data is not complete, the 1669 reform of the militia, if it was not a military success, certainly proved to be a successful attempt to integrate the nobles of the provinces into a central state institution,

124 *Ibid.* The author states that the regiments were also identified by the names of the colonels.

125 Bianchi, 'La riorganizzazione militare del Ducato di Savoia', p.215.

126 Hanlon, *The Twilight of a Military Tradition*, p.277.

127 Brancaccio, *L'esercito del vecchio Piemonte. Gli Ordinamenti*, p.145.

128 In July 1672 the Duke complained that the battalion's rising had not been as prompt as the urgency of the moment would have required, and then he had instructed the officers to apply the traditional pecuniary penalties of 10 *scudi* for each men missing, and to the local authorities to precept the *descritti* and send them to the companies. Duboin, *Raccolta per ordine di materie delle leggi*, vol. XXVI, pp.884–885.

creating a bond of direct service and mutual recognition with the sovereign. The problem faced by the Duke was substantially of this nature. On the one hand the militia was a military necessity, and he was to constitute a semi-professional force of subordinate soldiers and officers, to flank an army commanded and reinforced by mercenary soldiers and senior officers from the nobility with military experience in European conflicts. For this, the senior officers of the militia were always chosen, where possible, from among the available experienced officers. On the other hand, finding subordinate officers from their own territory who combined service with a reasonable skill in the craft of arms was the central problem for Carlo Emanuele since the very beginning of the reform. This difficulty stemmed from the method of selection of the intermediate officers. As a rule, in fact, they proceeded according to patronage criteria, which depleted the military potential of the corps, as commands often ended up with people lacking in resources, often involved in petty conflicts and rivalries between the communities of the state.

The war against Genoa also emphasised the difficulty of joining regular force and militia together in the absence of common regulations and discipline. This aspect was well synthesised by the auditor and *sovrintendente generale di guerra* Carlo Antonio Blancardi in 1673, whose concern was the risk of weakening the highest military court, the *Auditorato*, with a consequent fracture between regular troops and militia. In this regard, he wrote:

> Military privileges are much more assisted by the reason of the people than feudal customs. There are two qualities of soldiers: infantry and cavalry. Infantry is either in the garrisons or in the field, in which case it is for the Auditor General to know the privileges of all, not just vassals. Cavalry in peacetime consists for the most part of the companies of the guards, at most staying with the person of the ruler, in time of war either at the mark or in the field or in the garrisons, in which cases the cognitione pertains, as above, to the Auditor General. As for the officers of the militia, in the whole state they shall not exceed 300, most of them vassals or living in immediate places … In the patents of 2 November last year, His Royal Highness greatly enlarged the jurisdiction of vassals, depriving the Auditor General of the jurisdiction of militiamen who numbered five thousand and more.[129]

Subsequent reforms, undertaken by Vittorio Amedeo after 1683, did not deviate from the purpose designed by his father and continued with the creation of a semi-permanent trained and disciplined force capable of supporting the standing army. On the other hand, he continued his father's policy by establishing a militia *bataillon* in Savoy, despite all the problems coming from a territory that was almost impossible to defend.

129 Bianchi, 'La riorganizzazione militare del Ducato di Savoia', pp.213–214.

Piedmontese Conflicts

Before being used against external enemies, the army and militia, so carefully organised and trained, were employed to suppress revolts in the Duchy. This happened in 1680, when the Regency revoked the exemption of the salt tax to the community of Mondovì. The province's population had been enjoying this privilege since the fourteenth century and the government's sudden decision was also accompanied by a request of a donative for the Prince's wedding. The local authorities responded that the imposition was a violation of prerogatives and summoned the population for a popular demonstration on the evening of 4 August.

The response of the ducal governor, the Marquis de Bagnasco, angered the population even more and in a short time, unrest spread throughout the province. The government sent in the army and for a while the situation was brought back under control, also due to the promise not to suspend the privileges enjoyed by the population of Mondovì until then. On 25 May 1681 the Regency sent Don Gabriele of Savoy with 2,000 infantrymen and 500 mounted gendarmes with the order to restore the law and announce the introduction of the salt tax. This immediately met with resistance from the population of Montalto, who said they would rather die than pay the tax and prepared to defend themselves.[130] Don Gabriele also called the militia from Ceva and marched against the rebels on 23 June. The Savoyard commander prepared an elaborate plan involving diversionary and main assaults from five different directions. Key to the rebels' defence were the two access bridges to the village, manned by 200 armed inhabitants. The resistance was fierce, but after an hour Don Gabriele's troops entered Montalto, sacking the houses and setting fire to the village. The rebels had taken refuge on the heights, and when the ducal troops came out of the village they began targeting them again. At the end of the day, Don Gabriele claimed to have lost almost 200 men. However, when the rebels realised the extent of the damage suffered by the village their resolve began to falter, and many laid down their weapons and asked for a pardon. Don Gabriele granted them one, and in the following days he issued the Regency's proclamation ordering all inhabitants of the province to surrender their weapons. But soon, other disturbances occurred in Mondovì and Vico, where the construction site of the fortress was set on fire. Governor Bagnaso called the militia to arms and headed for Vico, but in the open countryside a strong handful of rebels ambushed and routed them in a short time. Encouraged by this success, the rebels headed for Mondovì, and they would probably have conquered it if a downpour had not stopped them, and they were finally dissuaded by the friars of the local convent. At that point the riots spread to the countryside around Carassone, where they set fire to the government mills. News of these events reached Don Gabriele, who marched with troops to Mondovì. Here he replaced Bagnasco by appointing the Marquis of Senantes as the new governor. On 20

130 Ciro Paoletti, *Dal Ducato all'Unità. Tre secoli e mezzo di storia militare piemontese* (Rome: USSME, 2011), p.169.

August, Don Gabriele's troops set fire to the villages of Breo and Carassone, obtained the submission of the population and occupied the entire territory, setting up camp with the Aosta and Piedmont regiments in Breo, Savoy and Crocebianca regiments in Carassone and a company of Swiss in Vico. The troops left for winter quarters, at which point the incidents began again. Riots and encounters occurred in the villages of Braglia, Roburento, Pra, Frabosa, Monastero and again in Montalto, the village that had triggered the rebellion.

After almost two years, the issue of the salt tax had not been resolved. From Mondovì, the governor wrote to the Regency that at that point, there were only two solutions: revoke the salt tax, or send troops back into the province. Meanwhile the rebels had laid siege to Vico, and the Regency's uncertainty made the situation worse. Finally the news of the French occupation of Casale diverted the court's attention to bigger problems. The government tried to appease the rebels by opening negotiations that continued until the spring of 1682, while the complications of the international scenario continued to weaken the duchy's position. On 5 April the Regency accepted the rebels' demands and closed the matter with a general amnesty, the abolition of the salt tax and the cancellation of unpaid taxes. The peace was a defeat for Savoy, but at least it removed the pretext for France to send troops to Piedmont, postponing, at least for now, the imposition of the alliance in 1684.

Uniforms, Equipment and Ensigns

Conventionally, the introduction of uniforms in the Savoy-Piedmont army is made to coincide with the order of Duke Carlo Emanuele II issued in 1671, with which he authorised the captains to deduct seven *denari* a day from soldiers' salaries to pay for the cost of clothing distributed annually on campaign and every two years in the garrison.[131] This order followed the same issued in 1670 concerning the Guard regiment.[132] However, reading the full text of the documents, it is possible to understand that the troops had already been uniformly dressed for several years, at least as far as coats and headgear were concerned. The ordinance of 1671 confirms, among other things, that the distribution of the coats was the responsibility of the colonels, who delegated administrative matters to the captains. The formation of permanent regiments under a colonel therefore suggests that all companies were already more or less uniformly dressed in the previous decade. Furthermore, the attribution to the Duke in 1664 concerning the property of the regiments, confirms that uniform in Savoy-Piedmont was a non-improvised matter, since the presence of a central administration is a crucial prerequisite for the uniformity in the clothing issued to the troops.

131 ASTo, *Materie Militari, Ordini militari dell'Altezza Reale di Carlo Emanuele II dall'anno 1648 sin all'anno 1674*, m. 3, 8–1671.

132 *Ibid.*, 6–1670.

Unfortunately there is little iconographic evidence about the clothing of Savoy-Piedmont soldiers before the 1670s.[133] On the contrary, there are many images produced in the eighteenth and nineteenth centuries relating to the uniforms of the ancient regiments. It would seem that poor iconography acts like bad money, namely, it makes the good one disappear. Among the iconography, that concerning the regiment of the Guards is undoubtedly the most abundant. Some nineteenth-century prints show this regiment in 1659 wearing a blue French-style *justaucorps* with cuffs, breeches and stockings of red. In one of these images the soldier also wears an anachronistic red waistcoat tightened at the waist by a belt from which his sword hangs. His coat carries lapels in Swedish style and the stockings are blue.[134] As in many other cases, the reliability of these sources is very poor. Even in modern re-enactments curated by the Italian army, the uniform of the guards in 1659 is based on this kind of iconography, depicting them with the conventional blue coat with red facings. At an intermediate place between the nineteenth-century reconstructions and the original appearance there is a collection of drawings dating to 1758, which was painted on behalf of King Carlo Emanuele III to collect the history of all the regiments since their foundation.[135] The style of the uniforms is more similar to the mid eighteenth century than to the late seventeenth century, and only the headgear appears more or less in line with seventeenth-century patterns, but the fact that the collection was produced only 100 years later is a fact to be taken into consideration. Firstly there was a recent memory of the uniforms worn by the Savoy-Piedmontese soldiers in the second half of the seventeenth century. In 1758 there may still have been a few veterans alive who had served in the army when they were very young, and retained memories of their uniforms. Furthermore, the collection may have been made on the basis of documents that have not survived to this day, but were still available in 1758. Ultimately, this collection is a source to be taken into account in forming a coherent picture of the first uniforms of the Savoy-Piedmont army, since the archival sources of the 1680s substantially confirm the colours of coats, facings and buttons.

Regarding the contemporary iconography, the few pieces identified today are all of excellent quality. Among these, the excellent series of paintings by Jean Miel dating from the years 1660–64 is certainly the most remarkable. The Flemish painter painted seven court scenes during his stay in Turin, and everything suggests that he portrayed the figures from life. In some of these, gentlemen, pages and servants of the ducal house are dressed in blue coats with red facings. This suggests that the two colours, coinciding with the dynastic colour of the ducal house, and the main one of the Savoy heraldry, had long since become part of the livery clothing. Therefore it might be

133 In this regard Enrico Ricchiardi, in *Il costume militare Sabaudo*, vol. I, Carlo Emanuele III (1730–1773) (Turin: Lucchetti, 1989), p.47, states that before 1736 the military iconography of the Sardinian army is practically nonexistent.

134 The image is published in the album of Galateri di Genola, *Armata Sarda. Uniformi antichi e moderni* (Turin, 1844).

135 BRT, *Manoscritto Militare*, Ms. 134.

45. Savoyard cavalry, 1670–1690, in a painting of an anonymous artist (the Italian Army's Cavalry Museum of Pinerolo). See image commentaries for more information.

reasonable to suppose that for his own guards the Duke chose these colours to manufacture their uniform. Another good clue regarding the blue and red uniform of the Duke's foot guard is supplied by some figures portrayed in the series of paintings at his residence. These paintings are attributed to Giovanni Battista Abret (1643?–1705),[136] and in the one entitled the *Veduta della Vigna* some figures wearing blue and red coats could be soldiers, NCOs and drummer of the *Guardie* regiment. Another painting, exactly illustrating Valentino castle in the early 1670s, shows a soldier wearing grey with blue stockings, and a non-commissioned officer dressed in blue. The figures are not very detailed, but everything suggests that they could belong to the infantry regiment *Savoie*, since the uniform of 1671 essentially consisted of a *justaucorps* of grey cloth for all the *ordinanze* regiments, long up to the knees and widening from the waist. The tin or brass buttons, 16 to 20 distributed on a single row, were flat. The sleeves have their cuffs flaps turned back from the elbow, showing the lining colour. A canvas cravat, after a double round on the neck, was knotted on the front with the two flaps falling on the breast. The guards wore a cravat of white canvas, while the *ordinanze* had it in red. The headgear, a broad-brimmed hat called a *caudebec*, was manufactured of black felt and fitted with a strip of coloured cloth around the cup. The distribution of clothing also included two shirts of linen, while the waistcoat was introduced after 1690. From 1675 the clothing distributed to the troops also included breeches and stockings.

136 Otherwise, the paintings are attributed to the Maestro of the Savoy's residences. The series is preserved in La Venaria palace.

The appearance of the Savoyard-Piedmontese soldiers must have been very similar to the one of their French colleagues, since until the end of the 1680s, the uniforms were manufactured in France, especially in Lyon, as confirmed by the documentation preserved in the archives.[137] The baldric and bandolier were of brown leather while the sword scabbard was generally in black leather with brass accessories. At the current state of research, there is no mention of metal shields for pikemen, which were probably *picche secche* ('just pikes', namely without armour), as they were called in contemporary documents. The pike, however, disappeared quite soon in the ducal army compared to other European armies, the low usefulness of these weapons on the terrain of Liguria or the Val Pellice being realised. Grenadiers, introduced in 1685, replaced the broad-brimmed hat with a wool cap, probably in the colour of the facings, and only in the 1690s was it trimmed with dark brown dyed lamb fur.

Sergeants were dressed with cloth of a fine quality, and usually wore coats laced with silver instead of the white fabric reserved to the corporals. The drum major, drummers and fifers of all *ordinanze* regiments, the Guards included, were dressed in the ducal livery which was a red coat with blue cuffs and lining, blue breeches and stockings. The drum belt was covered with a blue or red cloth, piped with a blue and white or silver lace: the duke's livery lace known as the *biscia* (snake). This lace was usually sewn on the coat at the seams, cuffs and pocket flaps. Drums were made of wood and painted in blue or red with the duke's or regiment's coat of arms with small white crosses scattered at regular intervals on the drum.

As for the officers' clothing, there were no specific prescriptions before 1683 and the only military attribute was the sash of azure silk, worn over the shoulder or around the waist. In 1683 Duke Vittorio Amedeo II introduced the first regulation of the uniform of the officers of the Guard regiment and *Gardes du Corps*. According to a description supplied by the Apostolic Nuncio in Torino, all officers on active service were to wear a *justaucorps* of crimson velvet for the infantry and red for the mounted guards, laced with golden-yellow. Exceptionally, the order contained also some detail concerning the cloth and the lace of the different ranks:[138]

> S.A.R. [His Royal Highness] has therefore ordered that velvet produced in this city [Turin] be taken, and the form regarding the quantity of the lace has been prescribed for all, so that the subordinates can be identified by their superiors.

In 1685 the Duke returned to the subject, prescribing that all infantry officers should dress in the same colours as the troops. In the 1690s this

137 ASTo, *Camerale Piemonte, contratti, Reggimento Aosta*; contact stipulated with Pietro Oliviero (Pierre Olivier) in Lyon, dated 14 une 1687. Between 1687 and 1688, the same supplier signed contracts for manufacturing the uniforms of the regiments *Savoie, Piemonte, La Marina, Crocebianca* and *Saluzzo*. In 1689 Olivier signed new contracts for the uniforms supplied to five infantry regiments.

138 ASVe, *Nunziatura di Savoia, Lettere 1683*, 28, March.

disposition was also extended to officers of the Foot Guard, and only NCOs and corporals continued to wear the coat of reversed colours.

It is only from 1684 onwards that the Turin archives have preserved contracts for the supply of military clothing. It is difficult to speculate why no contracts or other documents concerning these supplies existed before that date. Although the first regulations date back 14 years, no contract has been traced so far. Probably, as was also the case in other countries, contracts were concluded by notaries and only they preserved the official act, releasing only a summary note which unfortunately has not come down to us.

The clothing contracts are very useful documents, giving many details of the first military uniforms of Savoy-Piedmont of the seventeenth century, since they mention colours and other details very probably introduced in the previous decade. From this documentation it is possible to know that the buttons were of white metal for the Guards, *Piemonte*, *Aosta*, *Nice*, *Crocebianca*, *Saluzzo* and *La Marina* regiments, and brass for *Savoie* and *Monferrato*. NCOs and corporals were dressed in reversed colours and the latter were identified by straps on the right shoulder.

Thanks, once again, to the Apostolic Nuncio in Turin, it is possible to learn that a cavalry regiment was also dressed in blue. It was on the occasion of the arrival in Turin in 1671 of the Bishop of Laon that two squadrons of the *Gardes du Corps* and two others of the Regiment *Piémont* were deployed in his honour in the Piazza Reale. According to the nuncio, the mounted soldiers of this regiment wore turquoise jackets and new hats, 'and at the head of them stood the *sig. Principino* with the pike'.[139]

Research has shown a close connection between uniforms and the heraldry of the ducal domains. In 1689 the coat of arms of the *Piemonte* dragoon regiment (1st Cavalry Regiment, *Nizza Cavalleria*, of the modern Italian army) was that of the city of Susa and coincided with one of the numerous domains that Vittorio Amedeo extracted from his own great coat of arms to assign to each regiment. An observation, perhaps more interesting as it is complementary to the issue of the coat of arms, relates to the colours of the regiment's first uniform; the *Dragons Jaunes* were so called because of their yellow coat, lined and faced with black, as stated in the *capitolazione* dating 4 July 1690.[140] A red cloak and a pair of breeches, the latter presumably also red, completed the uniform. It should be noted that the indication of the colours yellow and black for the coat and red for the cloak can be found in the second part of the act of capitulation of 4 July 1690, concerning the duties to be carried out by the colonel and captains; these are the conditions added to the document at the behest of Vittorio Amedeo. It was divided into 12 chapters and presented to the Duke by the Count of Macello in June 1690,

139 *Ibid.*, *Lettere 1671*, 28, March.

140 ASTo, *Camerale Piemonte, Memoriale a capi con risposte di S.A.R. per la levata di un reggimento di Dragoni, proposto dal Conte di Macello*, and Duboin, *Raccolta di Leggi ed Editti*, Vol. XXVIII, Tomo 26, pp.111–113.

still evidently lacking the sovereign's approved formulas.[141] It is plausible that the Duke of Savoy, in agreement with the first designated colonel, had chosen these colours. In addition to the appellation of *Dragons Jaunes* (SD-4), the dragoons also bore the appellation of *Dragons de Masel*, at least for the first few years. The reason why it was decided, in that year, to dress a regiment of dragoons precisely in these colours is probably linked to the fact that a centre of importance such as Susa had to be adequately represented in military heraldry as well. However, a further reason could be found in the existing link between the Solaro family of Macello and the city of Susa. A first clue can be found, bearing in mind that Count Antonio Bonifacio Solaro di Macello, founder of the *Dragons Jaunes*, belonged to a secondary branch of the Solaro di Moretta family, whose feudal lands were located on the Susa–Novalesa route.

In conclusion it is likely that, when Count Solaro di Macello took command of the regiment of dragoons, he wished to evoke the city of Susa. On the other hand, it was to the Principality of Piedmont that the name of the regiment was dedicated, and Susa was considered the gateway to Piedmont and the crossroads to Savoy.[142]

There are other links between the heraldry of the ducal domains and the various army units, which began before the reign of Vittorio Amedeo II. According to the classic author of the Savoy army, in 1674 the gendarmes of Piedmont received a standard with the white Westphalian horse, which was part of the duke's coat of arms.[143] In 1689 the standard of the dragoon regiment *Sua Altezza Reale* (SD-1) also carried the cross of the kingdom of Jerusalem on its ensigns. These figures continued to be used as symbols of these regiments until the next century.

Unfortunately no ensigns or standards prior to the end of the seventeenth century have survived to the present day, but due to the fact that most of the units that make up the Italian army are descended from the ancient Savoyard regiments, there are many studies on the subject. Some of these works have been conducted with scientific criteria that have sometimes brought new

141 As for the red colour of the cloak, it is mentioned in Chapter 10 of the *atto di capitolazione*: 'a cloak of red cloth'. Roberto Sconfienza, 'Sulla prima uniforme e lo stemma del Reggimento Dragoni di Piemonte', in *Armi Antiche. Bollettino dell'Accademia di San Marciano*, 1995 (1998), p.7. Regarding the uniform of this regiment, the author adds: 'In the same document, there is no mention of the colour of the breeches, called *calze*, but it is specified that they were "at the discretion of the Colonel", namely the colour could be chosen by the Count of Macello and probably he opted for red in keeping with the cloak and the heraldry of the city of Susa.'

142 *Ibid.* While being aware that these are conjectures loosely connected to the foundation of the regiment, and far from being probative arguments, the author hypothesises that the founding colonel wanted to tie the new regiment to the ancient city of origin of his family, closely linked to the city of Susa.

143 Brancaccio, *L'esercito del vecchio Piemonte. Sunti storici*, p.231.

knowledge on the subject, or have demonstrated the inconsistency of some traditions introduced in later centuries.[144]

When the first ducal infantry regiments were formed in 1664, it was established that the colonel's ensign was to be on a *turchino* (medium blue) background with the reigning duke's coat of arms, while the insignia of the other companies were on backgrounds of different colours, but all carried by the white cross of Savoy. These latter insignias were commonly called *ordinanze*. All the infantry ensigns were generally square, measuring more than two metres per side. In 1690, to better identify the Savoyard ensigns from those of the French infantry, a cravat of blue fabric was added.

144 Among the most remarkable work on this subject, see Stefano Ales, *Insegne militari preunitarie italiane* (Rome: USSME, 2001).

4

The *Serenissima* Republic of Venice

With a population of around 2.1 million, in the late seventeenth century the Republic of Saint Mark was the most populous state in Italy after the Kingdom of Naples. The *Serenissima* extended its dominions in northeastern Italy and along the eastern Adriatic as far as the Ionian Islands and Aegean Greece. This 'Venetian Empire' had developed following the route of trading ports with the East, drastically reduced by the loss of Crete in 1669. The land–sea dichotomy was at the basis of the constitution of the Venetian state. The original nucleus comprising Venice and the surrounding area proudly retained the denomination *Dogado* (Duchy), to which were added the territories corresponding to modern Veneto and Friuli (except Gorizia and Trieste), Istria, and the provinces of Brescia and Bergamo with the enclave of Crema in Lombardy; all together also known as *Terraferma* (mainland). *Dogado* and *Terraferma* in turn constituted the *Stato da Terra* (Land State), while the domains in Dalmatia, Albania and Greece were the *Stato da Mar* (Sea State).

The economic crisis of the seventeenth century had heavily affected the Republic, but the Venetian economy had reacted positively and by mid century Venice was one of the most prosperous states in Italy. This wealth had enabled Venice to sustain the long war for Crete, but the conflict had been a bloodbath that had consumed huge material and human resources. To complicate this scenario, in the last quarter of the century the Venetian aristocracy suffered a significant demographic decline. It was aggravated by growing political disputes between rich and poor, new and old nobles, oligarchic temptations and democratic demands.[1] Notwithstanding these difficulties, the Republic pursued an 'imperial projection' in the Mediterranean, marking a strong difference from the policy of all Italian states, and even managed to set aside the obvious difficulties of a critical

1 Piero Del Negro, 'La Milizia', in *Storia di Venezia*, Vol. VII (Rome: Istituto dell'Enciclopedia Italiana, 1997), p.511.

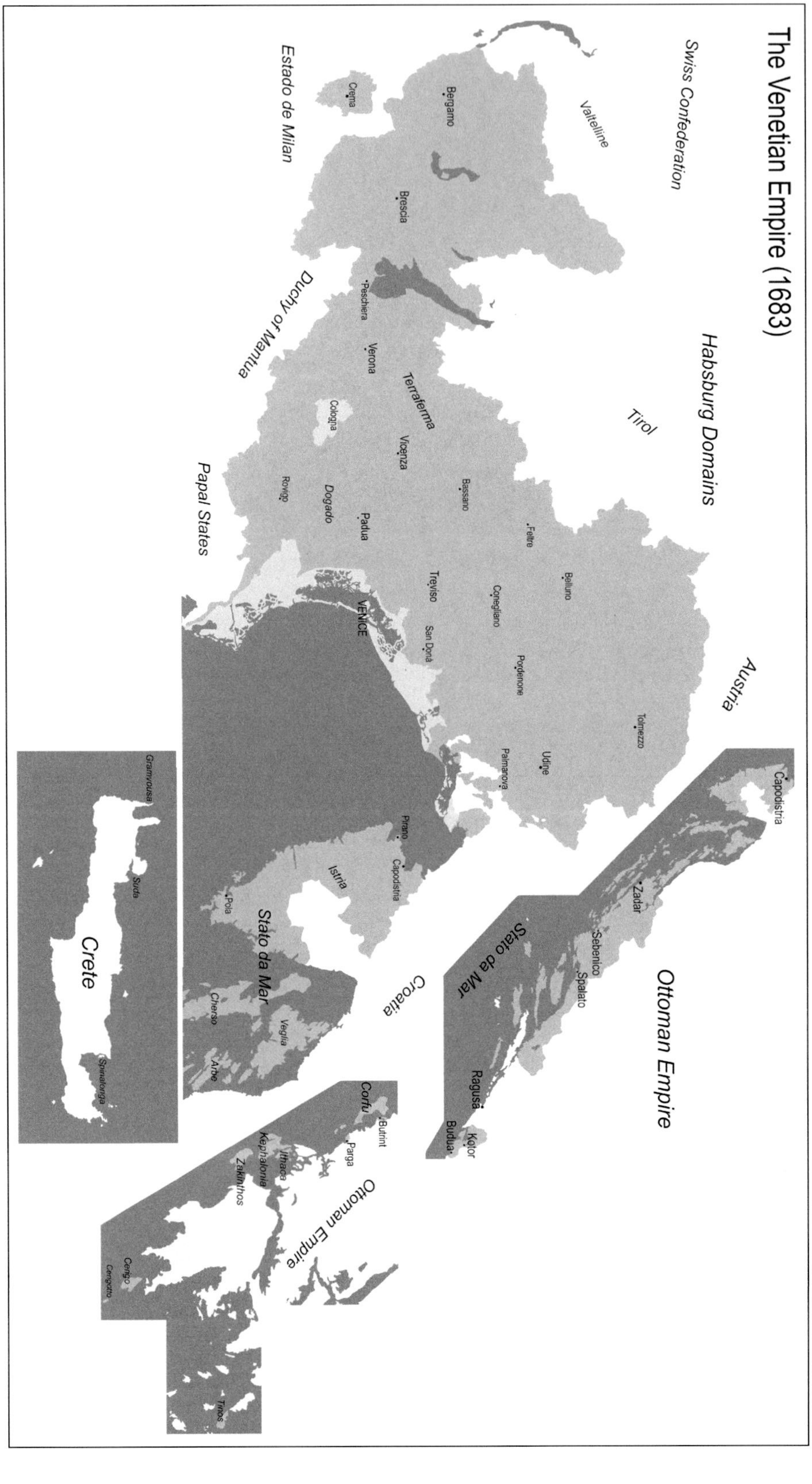

Map 3. The 'Venetian Empire,' 1660–99

financial situation.[2] Another extraordinary fact was that the Venetian Republic continued to be the only multiethnic state of Italy, where different languages and religious beliefs coexisted until its dissolution in 1797.

Historians outline the attitude of the Venetian leading class to perpetuate the anachronistic myth of the *Stato da Mar*, since the resistance against the modernisation of the 'military' was nourished by the 'city-state ideology'.[3] In Venice, the government continued to pursue the goal of managing the mosaic of peoples and military corps in a rather conservative way. These military choices seem to suggest what a historian has called 'the double paradox of Venice': unable to free themselves from the city-state's role to become the capital of a territorial state; but also to rule its territories beyond the traditional schemes of domain.[4] In 1684 the Holy League War could be a reversal in this trend thanks to the reforms introduced by Francesco Morosini in the 1680s, interrupted, however, by his death in 1694.[5] Historians have long considered the Venetian military trajectory as an unsuccessful parable, neglecting the innovative tactics and weaponry introduced in the Peloponnesian campaigns. Even when they investigated the naval strategy focusing on tactical and technical improvements, they assumed some not completely correct common views,[6] or considered

---

2 Mario Infelise, 'L'ultima crociata', in M. Infelise and A. Stouraiti (eds), in *Venezia e la guerra di Morea. Guerra, politica e cultura alla fine del '600* (Milan: Franco Angeli, 2005), p.10. The author remarks that 'rather than face the difficult situation with coolness and rationality, the Venetians preferred to find an alibi in dreams and mystical constructions, confusing the memory of a glorious past ... with a present that the "gentle Venetian rule" would restore to its former power.'

3 Piero Del Negro, 'Il Leone in Campo: Venezia e gli Oltramarini nelle Guerre di Candia e di Morea', in *Mito e Antimito di Venezia nel Bacino Adriatico (secoli XV–XIX)* (Rome: Il Calamo, 2001), p.332.

4 Jean Claude Hocquet, cited in Tamburrini, Pier Luigi, *L'organizzazione militare di Venezia nella prima metà del Settecento* (Collana SISM, 2014), p.9.

5 The first 'modern' reform of the army occurred in 1708 under the German *generale delle armi* Heinrich von Steinau.

6 It is remarkable to observe how the military history of Venice in the modern age is known especially by outdated stereotypes. The works of John Hale and Michael Mallett opened a window to investigate the Venetian military structure, but unfortunately their contributions have been confined to the sixteenth century. The accurate works of Jeremy Black, *Warfare: Renaissance to Revolution 1492–1792* (Cambridge 1995), and John Childs, *Warfare in the Seventeenth Century* (London, 2001), have both neglected the Venetian wars. The same oversight occurred in the excellent book of John Glete, *Warfare at Sea* (London 2000), closing his study just before the Cretan War and the development of sea warfare in the Mediterranean. Therefore the military history of Venice remains then *Terra Incognita* outside Italy, and although in recent years have appeared important contributions by Piero Del Negro, Luciano Pezzolo, Guido Candiani, followed by Pietro Marchesi, Luca Porto, Alberto Prelli, Guido Ercole, Pier Luigi Tamburrini, Marco Morin and Riccardo Caimmi. Unfortunately, these works are scarcely available outside Italy. Recently, Mario Infelise and Anastasia Stouraiti had been the editors of an important contribution about the war in Morea of 1684–1699. In 2019 the celebration for the 400th birthday of Francesco Morosini has further increased knowledge of the matter. These works include research by Italian and foreign specialists focusing on the political and cultural scenario of the campaigns (for further information see the bibliography).

the matter a mystery just to elude it. Even contemporary sources show some difficulty in understanding Venetian warfare. Several commenters agreed that Venice entrusted its safety to the fleet, making its military forces strongly asymmetric, which were considered too skewed towards the navy compared to the land forces. From a broad perspective, a strong dichotomy seemed to exist between the navy, made up of officers and sailors who were mostly Venetian, and the army, composed of a high percentage of mercenaries recruited from all over Europe and commanded by foreign officers. The decision to rely on mercenaries was, in effect, a calculated price to guarantee political stability, avoiding the formation of a class of professional soldiers who could change the internal balance of the state. Differing from it would have meant questioning the political and social order. Moreover, the appointments of foreigners to military positions of prestige were useful to manage the network of diplomatic relations to which Venice had always attributed great importance.[7] In this perspective, contemporary commenters outlined the 'predominant' presence of foreign mercenaries.

This and other hasty statements undermined Venice's reputation as a military power in Italy.[8] However, more recent research has challenged this and other statements, such as the native Venetian presence in the army, which was not a minority as claimed by certain sources. Although throughout the seventeenth century defining the army as 'Venetian' was almost like defining Francisco Franco's forces in the civil war of 1936–39 as 'Spanish', officers and soldiers from the Venetian mainland and from the capital itself remained relevant throughout the century.[9] Even less numerous compared to the officers who participated in the Cretan War and surely less renowned, several experienced Venetian captains served during the War of the Holy League, mainly in the navy. Families such as Mocenigo, Valier, Zeno, Marcello, Corner, Dolfin, Molin, Contarini and others provided the Venetian officer corps with able seamen and soldiers through the war.[10] All this is even more remarkable

7 In this context, something exemplary is the enlistment of the Marquis Jacques de Grémonville in 1647, namely the brother of the French ambassador in Venice, with the rank of lieutenant general of the infantry.

8 Gregorio Leti, in *L'Italia regnante o vero Nova descritione dello stato presente di tutti prencipati e repubbliche d'Italia (Rome, 1675)*, p.319, deplores the employment of foreign officers, 'who subtract resources from the Country'.

9 Gregory Hanlon, *The Twilight of a Military Tradition, Italian Aristocrats and European Conflicts, 1560–1800* (London: UCL Press, 1998), pp.221–261.

10 The debate concerning the Venetian aristocracy's attitude to war has occupied the main part of scholars' contribution to the history of the Republic. In his excellent *La Difesa Militare della Terraferma Veneta nel Settecento*, pp.13–14, Sergio Perini provides an interesting explanation: 'With the persistence of standing garrisons, the question of socio-economic integration of the military class in the society was also raised. In particular, the phenomenon showed a worrying turn for the officers, inclined to establish relations and economic ties with the wealthy local class, especially the aristocratic families. Venice looked at the evolution of this ambiguous situation with the hope of encouraging the inclinations of the nobility of mainland in the profession of arms, facilitating the entry of the wealthy classes in the recently formed state system. On the other hand,

considering the high turnover applied to the Venetian aristocrats when they held public offices, which tenures rarely lasted more than three years. The centrality of the aristocracy in the Venetian 'military' is also attested by the fact that Venetian nobles could not bear arms for another state or prince on pain of their family's expulsion from the ruling councils.[11]

Possibly the leadership of Francesco Morosini modified, more than commonly accepted, the relations within the Venetian aristocracy and the career in the army and navy. In the campaigns of 1689 and 1693 Morosini was *Doge* and Captain General at the same time, and he could easily manage the complicated Venetian network without considering his unquestioned authority as commander. Moreover, the double meaning of the Captain General office, as well as other major military positions, implied the early disbursement of large sums. This can be explained by the fact that the Senate did not only prefer recognised leadership qualities when selecting commanders from among the candidates, but also considered family prestige, personal wealth and political faction.

46. Equestrian portrait of *Doge* Francesco Morosini by Giovanni Carboncino, dating to 1690 (Correr Museum, Venice). See image commentaries for more information.

Despite a reduced effort on the sea compared to the previous conflict of Crete, the Venetian fleet and army successfully improved several war tactics during the war of 1684–99 while the fleet, by using the galleys in a wide radius, barely paralysed Ottoman supplies in the Aegean Sea. The technique and methods used by the Venetian fleet to be unnoticed resemble those used by the German *U-boats* in the two World Wars. The massive use of amphibious operations and the special role played by irregular formations to keep the Ottomans alert on the secondary fronts, such as in Dalmatia and Albania, represent very innovative aspects with results comparable to those achieved by the northern European navies in the seventeenth century.

The War Economy

On an economic-financial level, the expenses of the bitter struggle fought on land and sea during the Cretan War had consumed the equivalent of 25

the Venetian nobility of the modern age did not consider as satisfying the career in the army and those who were most interested in military life converged in the war fleet.'

11 Hanlon, *The Twilight of a Military Tradition*, p.143.

years of tax revenues.[12] In 1665 alone, the deficit had amounted to one-third of total revenue, and in subsequent years the debt rose to unprecedented levels.[13] In 1668 the consequences of the war effort became unbearable. According to contemporary historians, in a single year the defence of Candia consumed more than four million *ducati*, a sum equal to all the ordinary annual revenues of the Republic.[14] The military and logistical effort for a war engaged several hundred kilometres from the lagoon required enormous resources. In 1668 the ambassador to the Holy See, Antonio Grimani, listed to the Pope the amount of money, men and materiel that the recent campaign had required. This comprised 975,000 *ducati* necessary to pay 8,700 soldiers, 2,000 pioneers and miners, 1,000 oarsmen, 221 artillerymen, 70 workers 'for different jobs', 41 guns, 2,879,000 lb of gunpowder, 730,000 lb of match and then weapons 'in great quantity', ironware, timber, fireworks, uniforms, bombs and other items.[15] A few years after the end of the conflict it was declared that the total cost had amounted to 125 million *ducati*, which on average would have represented an annual expenditure of 5,000,000 *ducati*· well above the average level of the available state budget.[16]

Since the Venetian government had resorted to all possible means to feed the resistance in Crete, the subsequent years were used to bring the budget back into surplus. Of the many measures introduced to find money, the public debt had proved to be the safest. There were many opponents of this method in the Senate, but in the end the advocates of the public debt prevailed. In some respects it was the lesser evil, since the increase in state debt and the resulting

12 Infelise, 'L'ultima crociata', p.12.

13 Luciano Pezzolo, 'Stato, Guerra e Finanza nella Repubblica di Venezia fra Medioevo e prima Età Moderna, in acts of the conference *Navies and State Formation*' (Volos, 9–12 September 2004), p.100, Table III.

14 Batista Nani, *Istoria della Repubblica Veneta*, in *Degl'Istorici delle Cose Veneziane, i quali hanno scritto per pubblico decreto*, IX (Venice, 1720), p.575.

15 Luciano Pezzolo, 'Una finanza in guerra, 1645–1669', in G. Ortalli, G. Gullino, E. Ivetic, *L'inestinguibile sogno del dominio. Francesco Morosini* (Venice: Istituto Veneto di Scienze, Lettere e Arti, 2021), pp.67–68.

16 *Ibid.*, p.69: 'A papal agent estimated an average expenditure of about 4,900,000 ducats for 1647. This figure would be in line with the budget of 1665, which indicates an expenditure of 5,250,000 ducats against an income of 3,740,000 ducats. However, it must be considered that the course of the conflict went through alternating phases, with pause periods interrupted by naval campaigns and, finally, the decisive attack by Ottoman troops on the walls of Candia. It is plausible, therefore, that the direct cost of the war (troops, fleet and supplies) could be around three million ducats. The Papal observer already cited as a witness indicates an expenditure of 300,000 ducats per month for the Armada and military apparatus in the Levant. Of course, from this purely conjectural figure, one would have to subtract the ordinary expenses of the military apparatus in peacetime, in order to obtain the actual increase in expenditure for the war. The calculation is not straightforward, especially since the years leading up to the war saw the Serenissima engaged in a vigorous policy of border protection, maintaining a military force that required a huge outlay. Is it plausible, therefore, to think that Venice was faced with an increase in military expenditure of about one third? The question mark is a must.'

interest payments went largely to the Venetians themselves. Moreover, the public debt mechanism had a long tradition in Venice. At the beginning of the Cretan War the state had offered bonds whose capital was not subject to repayment in pre-established time, namely it was a debt linked to the life of the holder, who, once deceased, rendered the bond null and void and thus also the obligation to repay the money. Later, bonds were issued that included even a single heir.[17] The yield was around five percent and was considered advantageous by both the state and the creditor. In the late 1670s the debt rose so high that state failure seemed likely. To avert this risk the government resorted to all the expedients, included the infamous 'sweepstakes' in which, through the payment of 10,000 *ducati*, 10 participants entered a draw to achieve aristocratic status, inscription in the golden book of nobility, and a path towards public office and political life.[18] Yet, even these measures failed to appease the state's urgent financial need, and perpetually converting interest into capital thus became necessary.

After some 15 years of peace, the prospects of a new war presented a new need for money and thus more debt. As in the past, the increasing of ordinary taxation and recourse to extraordinary fiscality were not sufficient to meet the costs, both because the resources collected were not sufficient to finance the entire war effort, and because the collection time did not allow the money to be available quickly. Public debt was therefore the most effective means of raising the resources to finance the war.[19] However, in 1683 the die was cast: the Ottoman defeat at Vienna; Pope Innocent XI's exhortations for a crusade; the pressures of Austrian and Polish ambassadors; the desire to avenge the loss of Crete, weighed too much on the scale of decisions. In March 1684 nothing could prevent the Republic from taking up arms. Of course, this required reigniting relationships between society and the army, which Venice preferred not to change. Furthermore, Venice sought to develop a strategy capable of defeating the enemy in the shortest possible time. Finally, and above all, strengthening the 'military' could be pursued only with the available financial resources, since Venice wanted to fight a war at a reasonable cost.

The Senate was aware that the Republic's situation was unfavourable at best. After the Cretan War the Republic invested considerable resources to revive

17 Pezzolo, 'Una finanza di guerra', p.81.

18 Sergio Perini, 'Venezia e la guerra di Morea' in *Archivio Veneto* n. 153 (Venise, 1999), p.67. Between 1685 and 1699, 38 new families had entered the Golden Book of Venetian nobility, despite the high cost of this social elevation, namely 100,000 *ducati* for the right to sit on the Grand Council new families. However, much less than during the Cretan War, when 80 families had bought the titles of nobility, which brought eight million *ducati* to the state.

19 Pierluigi Tamburrini, *L'organizzazione militare veneziana nella prima metà del Settecento* (Rome: SISM, 2014), pp.2–3. While in 1679 the budget still managed to close with a surplus of 250,000 *ducati*, at the end of armed neutrality during the War of the Spanish Succession the total debt reached 1,200,000 *ducati* – so much so that in 1714 the Republic was forced to halve the interest rate from four percent to two percent – and by the time of the Peace of Passarowitz in 1718 it had reached 3,723,000 *ducati*.

trade by reducing tariffs and lowering transaction taxes to encourage private companies' initiative. Moreover, the Senate simultaneously contended with the aggressive Dutch and English trade companies in the Mediterranean. In spite of these efforts the *Serenissima*'s financial framework remained dismal. Interest rates rose up to 14 percent of the borrowed money.

This affected state economic policy in the years to come. When the war against the Ottomans ended with the Peace of Carlowitz in 1699, and notwithstanding the conquest of the Peloponnese, the accumulated debt of Venice had reached new unprecedented levels, which heavily influenced the future military policy.[20] The Republic tried in every way to recover the money spent to finance a maritime war in such a distant theatre of operations, which involved very long lines of communication and, consequently, an enormous logistical effort. To meet the expense of recruiting men and the constant demand for ships, first the city's properties were offered for sale, then public offices and civil charges.

In the new century, the increasingly unfavourable economic situation would force the government to pursue a policy of 'armed neutrality' destined to sharpen the contradictions of a military organisation now launched towards an irreversible disarmament.

Venetian Geostrategy

The history of Venice is closely linked to the sea. On the sea Venice was born, and on the sea the Venetians made their fortune, achieving a political and economic power of great importance. The symbiosis between the city lagoon and the sea was considered so strong and involving that, as soon as the Venetians turned to the *Terraferma*, there were charges of an identity crisis, of betrayal, of moral and economic decline. The mainland, however, was not the competitor of the sea: the two elements complemented each other. The conquest of a large area in the Po Valley at the beginning of the fifteenth century was conceived as a function of strengthening the maritime interests.[21] Control of the mainland had been made necessary to prevent the formation of an opposing power in proximity of the lagoon and to protect the transit routes of goods arriving in Venice.

However, as a result the Republic had to share a border with many neighbours: to the south the Papal States and the Duchy of Mantua, from the north the Grisons, and in the remainder it was surrounded by the States of the House of Austria and Spain, namely the Duchy of Milan, the Bishopric of Trento, Tyrol and Carniola, and in some places even divided by small territories that also belonged to the Habsburgs of Austria, such as the

20 Éric Pinzelli, *Venise et la Morée: du triomphe à la désillusion (1684–1718)* (Université de Provence, 2003), p.284. The war expenses averaged two million *ducati* after 1688, so the conflict would have cost 36 million *ducati* in 16 years.

21 Pezzolo, 'Stato, Guerra e Finanza nella Repubblica di Venezia', p.68.

territories of Aquileja, Gorizia and Trieste. The Austro-Spanish encirclement was for Venice the worst fruit of the House of Habsburg's presence in Italy.

From the sixteenth century Venetian interests in the mainland increased significantly, as a result of the transformation of economic activities. In this period, the Venetian ruling class moved its interests to land ownership at the expense of trade. However, the maritime projection of the state was not weakened: the overseas territories were always defended with huge military and financial resources. A common view about the Venetian 'military' is its presumed weakness in field campaigns.[22] This poor attitude appears to rely on considerations related to its military policy – which took place mainly in the eighteenth century after the war against the Ottomans in 1714–18 – claiming it as well-identified in the previous century as the beginning of the demilitarisation and the renunciation of playing a role of territorial power in Europe. The fact that in less than a century from the heavy investment in armaments, fortifications and in the fleet, a phase of actual demilitarisation followed, has distracted historians from investigating the real objectives that Venice pursued in the last phase of the century and especially from the dynamics which led to these choices: to control its domains in the Mediterranean Levant with a fleet capable of carrying relatively numerous but efficient troops; to be protected in the Milanese and the Eastern Alps; to obtain all this at low cost. The image of Venice, which was powerful on the sea and weak in its terrestrial device, should therefore be reinterpreted in a different perspective, namely the substantial unity of the Venetian military structure, where all the land forces were regarded as garrisons or 'landing troops' without difference. This latter aspect became clear considering that the supreme military command remained invariantly committed to the *Capitano Generale da Mar* (Sea Captain General).

In addition to service aboard ships, until the war against the Austrian Habsburgs in 1615–1618, Venetian troops operated mainly for passive defence and internal security, as can be clearly deduced from their distribution in the fortified centres of the mainland and overseas. The elementary military functions minimised the need to increase the forces, which in the early seventeenth century barely reached 7,000 regular soldiers in all. Despite this, since the outbreak of the war against the Austrians, the army had quickly grown to a total of 26,000 soldiers of all specialities. Later on, the undertakings against North African corsairs and the successive international political crises acted as modifiers of these numbers, resulting in an alternating pattern of consistency quotas.

In spite of its unconventional military structure, Venice still appeared as one of the most remarkable European sea powers and certainly the first in Italy. The decision to maintain a standing army below 10,000 men found comfort assuming as a model the army of the United Provinces of the Netherlands.

22 In 1675, the historian Gregorio Leti, in *L'Italia regnante*, p.318, even offered a more drastic judgement. He argued with some truth, but also with harshness and undeserved criticism, that 'in Italy, the Republic (of Venice) is the poorest state in the profession of arms. Admittedly, the Venetians can be invincible on the sea ... but in campaign they value very little or nothing.'

47. Map of the Morea (Peloponnese) with its main fortresses, by Vincenzo Maria Coronelli (author's archive). See image commentaries for more information.

DI LEPANTO
DUCATUS ATHENIENSIS
PARS
GOLFO D
SICYONIA
ARGIA
ROMANIA MINOR
GOLFO DI NAPOLI
CHIPE-
DI ROMANIA.
LAGO
LACONIA
GOLFO DI CASTEL RAMPANO
GOLFO DI COLOCHINA
ENZA
LEPANTO
CERIGO
ATENE
MODON

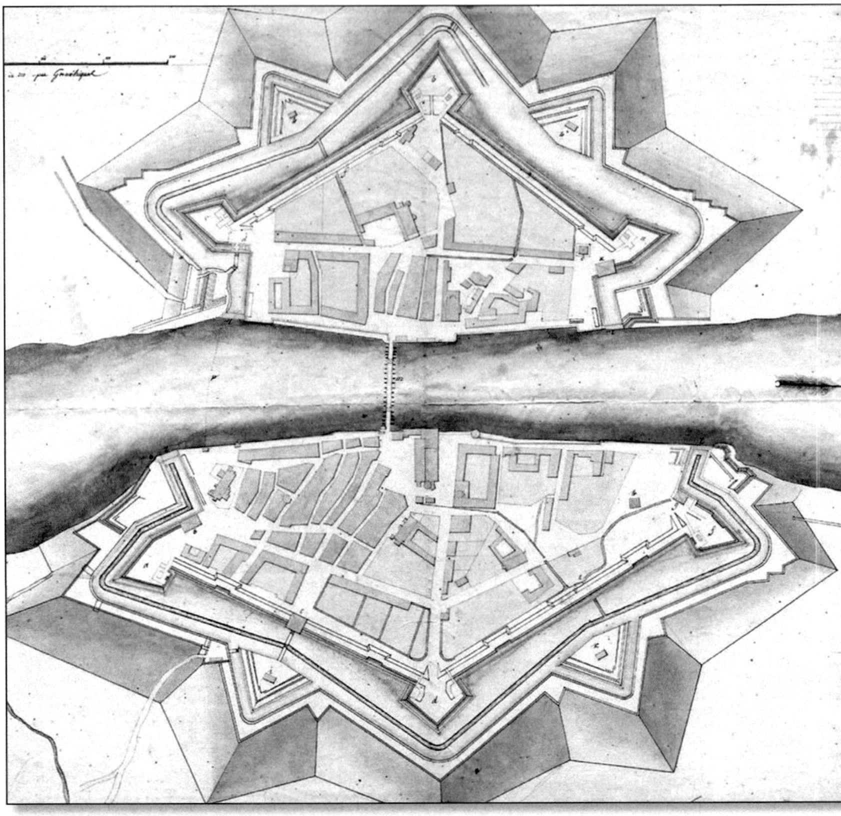

Right: 49. Plan of Legnago, in the early eighteenth-century plan. After Verona and Brescia, Legnago was the main Venetian fortress guarding the border with the Spanish *Estado de Milan*.

Below: 50. The fortified town of Rovigo, after the Willem and Johan Blaeu's *Atlas Maior* (1665). Rovigo was the main defensive square on the border with the Papal States, which faced on the other side of the Po the much better fortified and garrisoned Ferrara. Venice had always taken care to update the defence of Rovigo's main centre of Polesine. Rovigo could quarter up to 1,600 men. In January 1643, at the eve of the war against the Pope, the garrison numbered 1,522 infantrymen, including Italians, Corsicans, *oltramarini* and Greeks, 45 heavy horsemen and 152 light cavalrymen.

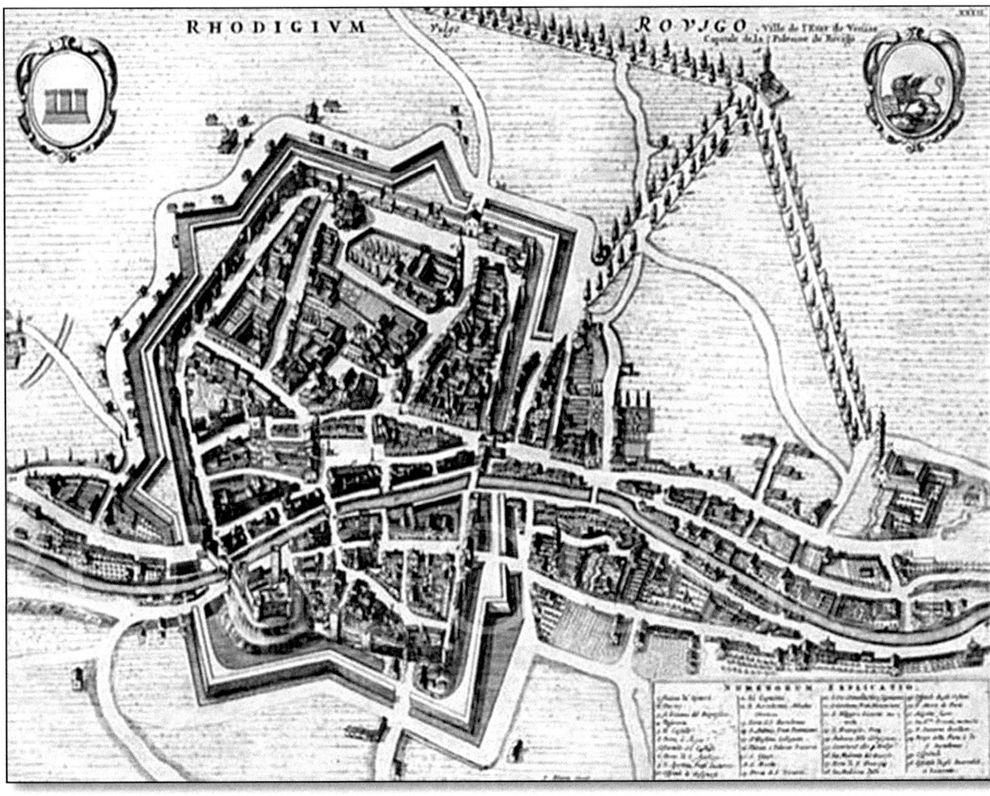

Plate A

Savoy-Piedmont, 1660–1670

1. *Gendarme* cavalryman in buff, 1669–70; 2. Infantry officer, 1660; 3. Guards Regiment, musketeer, 1668–69

(Illustration by Bruno Mugnai © Helion & Company 2023)

See Colour Plate Commentaries for further information

Plate B

Savoy-Piedmont, 1671–1684

1. *Savoie* Infantry Regiment, NCO, 1672–76; 2. *Savoie* Infantry Regiment; musketeer, 1672–76; 3. Guard Infantry Regiment, officer, 1684

(Illustration by Bruno Mugnai © Helion & Company 2023)

See Colour Plate Commentaries for further information

Plate C

Savoy-Piedmont

***Royal Piémont Cavalerie*, 1670–71**

(Illustration by Bruno Mugnai © Helion & Company 2023)

See Colour Plate Commentaries for further information

Plate D

Venice, 1680–1684

1. Galley commander, 1684–88; 2. Sailor, 1680s

(Illustration by Bruno Mugnai © Helion & Company 2023)

See Colour Plate Commentaries for further information

Plate E

Venice, *oltramarine* infantry, 1680–1690

1. *Schiavone* infantryman, 1686; 2. Albanian infantryman, 1685–90; 3. Morlach irregular, 1680s

(Illustration by Bruno Mugnai © Helion & Company 2023)

See Colour Plate Commentaries for further information

Plate F

Venice, cavalry and dragoons

1. Dragoon Regiment *Courbon*, dragoon, 1686; 2. German free company of *Carabini*, NCO, 1699

(Illustration by Bruno Mugnai © Helion & Company 2023)

See Colour Plate Commentaries for further information

Venice, 1694–1698

1. Artilleryman, 1694; 2. Artillery driver, 1694; 3. Infantry Regiment *Veneto Real*, musketeer, 1698

(Illustration by Bruno Mugnai © Helion & Company 2023)

See Colour Plate Commentaries for further information

Plate H

Venice's Italian allies, 1684–1690

1. Grand Duchy of Tuscany, Knight of the Order of St Stephen (Santo Stefano), 1684–88; 2. Grand Duchy of Tuscany, pikeman, 1686–88; 3. Papal States, *Guardie di Nostro Signore*, musketeer, 1690s

(Illustration by Bruno Mugnai © Helion & Company 2023)

See Colour Plate Commentaries for further information

51. Encampment scenes attributed to Francesco Simonini (1686–1753 or 1755), preserved in a private collection. See image commentaries for more information.

52. Verona in the late-seventeenth century (author's archive). Verona was among the first Italian cities rebuilt on the trace italienne model. In the last decades of the seventeenth century, Verona still quartered the largest garrison on the Venetian mainland.

Although Venice adapted to itself the military policy of the Dutch Republic in a rather incongruous way, all facts and events regarding both the Dutch army and fleet were held in high regard. Therefore, since the beginning of the seventeenth century, the government subscribed to the declaration of Maurice of Nassau, who considered a well-trained force of 8,500 foot soldiers and 1,500 cavalrymen, supported by a powerful fleet and by a modern network of fortresses, as able to stand up to any opponent.[23] In 1640 the Senate voted for a peacetime standing army of 9,000 professional soldiers, of which 2,200 in the Italian provinces – divided into 15 main towns and fortresses, but another 6,800 men were needed in Dalmatia, Corfu, Zakynthos, Cephalonia, Cerigo

23 Contarini's relation, cited in Ian Heath, *Armies of the Sixteenth Century* (Guernsey: Wargames Research Group, 1988), p.107. On this subject, Pezzolo in'Stato, Guerra e Finanza nella Repubblica di Venezia', pp.111–112, adds: 'The Dutch Republic was the country at the forefront of innovations in military practice in seventeenth-century Europe. This is not surprising: Dutch society is the most dynamic and the most ready to stimulate and incorporate technological innovations. The environment tends to reward entrepreneurship and the army is likely to be seen as a means of social advancement. The urban militia itself enjoys a prestige that is hard to find elsewhere. The members of the militia stood socially between the upper class of the patriciate and the simple wage earners; it was a strongly cohesive group that performed a function of controlling public order as well as defending the city. It is interesting to note that from the 1620s onwards, initially in Amsterdam and later in other cities, it was customary to post pictures depicting members of the militia. The military structure is thus a reflection of the environment and the socio-institutional system. A dynamic society, such as the Dutch one, produces far-reaching war innovations. The same can be said in the Venetian case. The medieval centuries of growth and expansion stimulate innovations and improvements in the military fleet as well as significant developments in the organisation of the army. From the seventeenth century onwards, the impetus faded and it became increasingly difficult to come across innovative attempts in the *Serenissima*'s military apparatus. The reciprocal influences between politics, economics and institutions had an impact on the military machine and limited its efficiency.'

(today Kithyra in Greece), Tinos and Crete. The government specified that all these troops could be transferred onto the fleet if necessary. In the mid century the Venetian permanent troops were completed with 1,600 cavalrymen, 400 artillerymen and another 200 including *bombardieri*, engineers and other specialists. Besides these soldiers and officers under contract the government could associate, if necessary, hired foreign troops and finally turn to the mobilisation of militias – the *ordinanze* or *cernide* in Italy, *craine* in Dalmatia, and *proli-stradioti* in Greece – with a physiologically heterogeneous level of efficiency, but they could increase the army by several thousand men.

For centuries, the fleet – commonly referred to as the *Armada* – had represented the Venetian main instrument of war. In fact, the navy had always been the main weapon against the greatest enemy of the Republic – the Ottoman Empire – but already in the early seventeenth century, war fronts had moved on land and this time the opponents were the troops of the Austrian Habsburgs. The war of 1615–18 had compelled Venice to come to grips with completely new strategic problems. This conflict represented a new challenge for the Republic, because the conflict's centre of gravity was not on the sea, but moved its forces to the Alpine borders, leaving the fleet with only the task of liquidating the pirates paid by Vienna. Now the attack came from the land, and above all the technological escalation generated by a conflict against a modern European army forced the government to reconsider its military policy. Further troubles for Venice arose during its involvement in the first War of Castro (1641–44), when the Venetian troops and galleys had to face the Papal threat in Emilia and in the Adriatic.

During the Cretan War the huge extension of the borders, and the expansion of the conflict, urged the Republic to face strategic decisions which could not be postponed, and which could not disregard a policy of heavy investment to increase the strength of the army. Infantry especially was the most needed to protect the fortresses, to attack the islands with amphibious landings, and to besiege the enemy strongholds in Bosnia and in Greece. In the Cretan War the whole armed force had reached unprecedented levels, scoring at various times more than 25,000 professional soldiers, 20,000 sailors, gunners and oarsmen, and about 30,000 militiamen from all the domains, including several horse and foot irregulars recruited in Dalmatia, Greece and Albania. Between 1659 and 1660 – when Venice planned the expedition to expel the Ottomans from Crete with a landing assault – contingents were recruited in every corner of Europe. In the summer of 1660, 11,200 infantrymen and 1,200 horses were assembled at Cerigo (Kythira), who landed in the following September in front of La Canea (today Chaniá). Six years later, in the last attempt to deprive the Ottomans of the major island's ports, 8,295 foot soldiers and 1,008 horses landed on Crete. The last three years of fighting at Candia demanded an even larger number of soldiers to support the resistance of the besieged city. Every week hundreds of lives were consumed in the fierce fighting, as in a furnace. Without counting the irregulars, in just two and a half years Venice enlisted thousands of professional soldiers, most of which came from without their borders.

There were now choices that the *Serenissima Repubblica* could not escape, and the fierce combat against the Ottomans would later require even more drastic changes. This exhausting conflict proved even more crucial in the evolution of the army and navy for the future Venetian geostrategy. If the great island represented the centre of gravity, this time the strategic duel was bound to take place on the seas. The scenario of war influenced the choices and so, during the whole seventeenth century, despite the gradual increase of military involvements, Venice continued to consider 'fleet' and 'army' as a single instrument. Seaborne assaults with landing troops continued to be perfectly coherent to the Venetian strategy, especially against targets far from its domains, combined with a huge net of garrisons in the mainland and overseas. The result was the creation of an entirely original instrument of war unlike any other European army: a result that was probably not the best possible one to defend the Republic, but surely the most appropriate way to face any political contingency and war emergency. In this context the aristocracy's atavistic conservationism contributed to slow the development of military armed forces in the modern meaning, but even more decisive was the attitude derived from the 'garrison system' to influence Venetian military policy.[24] Moreover, because Venetian political doctrine adhered to a principle of balanced power, this aspect contributed ultimately to maintain the land forces separately in the rigid classification of the troops according to their composition, origin and economic remuneration.

Like many Italian states in the seventeenth century, Venice also focused on strengthening its defensive system. The government followed the recommendations of military theorist General Annibale Porroni, who elaborated his ideas just before the War of the Holy League.[25] He emphasised that fortresses could compensate for manpower, especially for smaller states unable to deploy large contingents.[26] In Venice, the adherence to this

24 Del Negro, 'Il Leone in Campo', p.331.

25 Annibale Porroni, *Trattato Universale Militar Moderno* (Venice, 1676).

26 Tamburrini, *L'Organizzazione Militare Veneziana*, p.21.

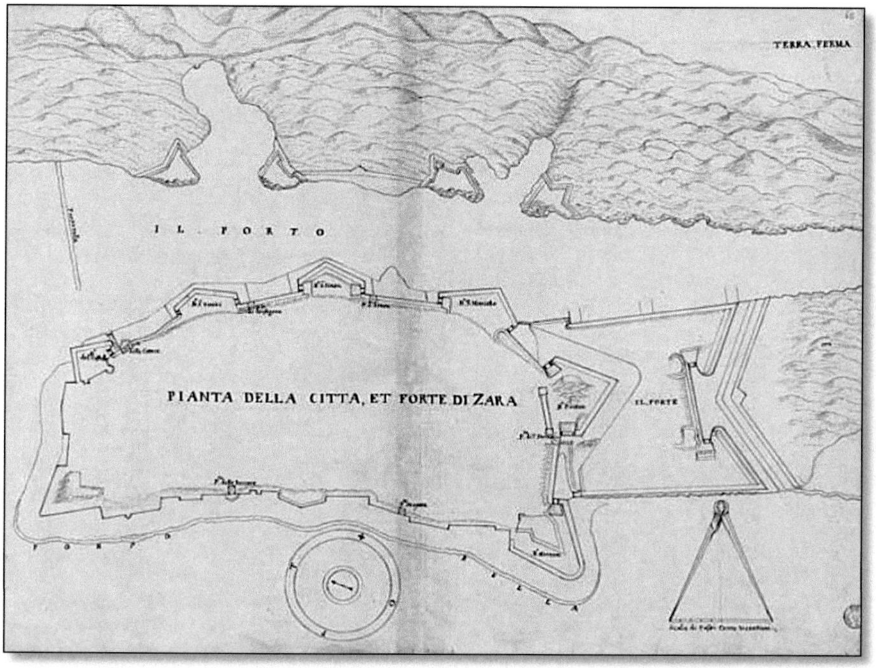

53. Plan of Zadar in the seventeenth century, by Agostino Alberti. (Author's archive)

philosophy resulted in a virtually uncontrolled proliferation of fortifications. These were 106 in 1683; increased to 134 in 1699 after the conquest of the Morea, and further rose to 143 in 1711. By the early eighteenth century, fortifications were divided into three categories of importance depending on their size. Despite the severe financial crisis caused by the war, after the Peace of Carlowitz (1699), the Venetians maintained 78 large and medium fortresses; 45 of these strongholds were located between Dalmatia and Albania and another 12 in Greece.[27] This total also included towers with a small arsenal and a garrison of a few soldiers.

Clearly, adequately maintaining this mass of fortifications proved difficult. Except for Palmanova and Verona, most of these places remained in poor condition. Furthermore, economic limitations continuously postponed restoration and modernisation. At the end of the seventeenth century, 32 garrisons were distributed between the major and minor fortresses and towns in Italy. Verona was among the first cities anywhere rebuilt on the *trace italienne* model, and other pioneering projects were raced out on the western Lombardy border, such as the fortresses of Legnago, Orzinuovi and Brescia.[28] The improvements, however, did not include a citadel and adequate barracks, leaving Verona's fortification incomplete.

The defensive line coincided with the main strongholds and provincial capitals. The highest concentration of mainland garrisons was located between the Tagliamento and Adige rivers, the pre-Alpine region, and the lagoon area. This latter zone joined the Mincio River to the west with a triangle of fortresses

27 ASVe *Inquisitori sopra l'Amministrazione dei Pubblici Ruoli*; f. 684–696.

28 Gregory Hanlon, *The Twilight of a Military Tradition. Italian Aristocrats and European Conflicts, 1560–1800* (London: UCL Press, 1998), p.147.

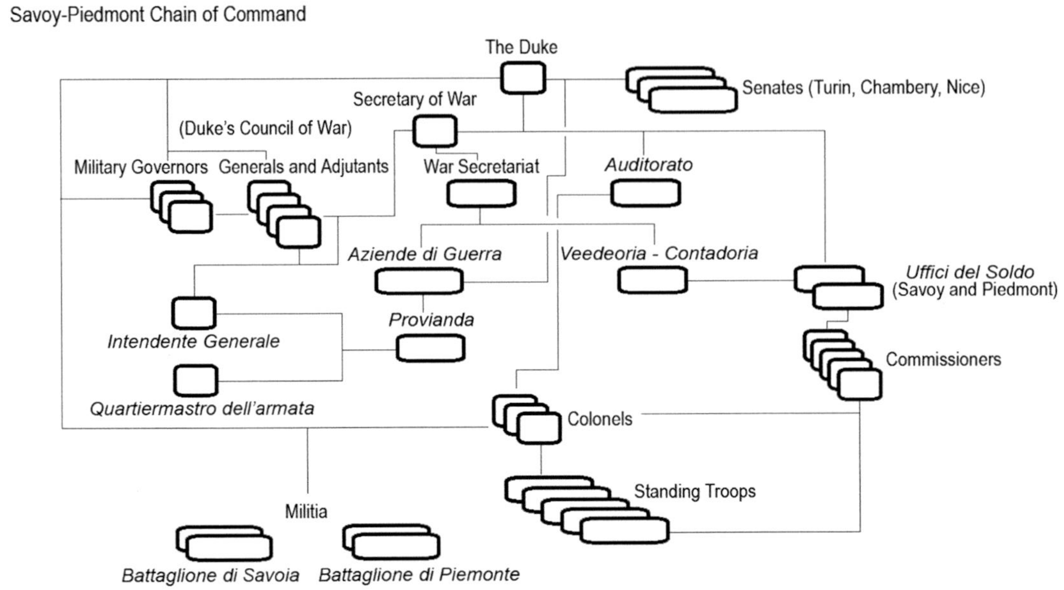

48. The chain of command of the Venetian army and navy

formed by Brescia, Bergamo, and Crema. In addition to Venice, four defensive systems centred in Verona, Legnago, Palmanova and Zadar could face the enemy approach from every direction. The Republic classified 14 additional places as second-class fortresses. However, the Venetian government simultaneously considered them to be of equal strategic importance to the main sites. Bergamo, Orzinuovi and Peschiera were deemed suitable for the principal defensive system, while Crema, Pontevico, Salò and Asola merely provided support especially to protect the lines of communication, as did Capodistria (today Koper in Slovenia) on the Adriatic. The fortified town of Rovigo guarded the southern frontier with the Papal States, but like Udine in Friuli, no longer held a strategic role, and the latter in particular served as a logistics base for the garrisons quartered on the border with Austria. All these fortresses guarded the Italian territories, or the *Stato da Terra*.

Although the Italian mainland could not be considered safe from external threats, the overseas domains prompted the major concerns. By 1684 the three *reggimenti* of the Adriatic, Ionian, and Aegean seas formed a network of 74 big and small garrisons in the overseas domains. Of these, 44 garrisons were distributed in Dalmatia. These strongholds were centred in the aforementioned Zadar, Novegradi (today Novigrad in Croatia), and the islands of Arbe and Pago (today Rab and Pag in Croatia). Both Zadar and Novegradi were advantageously positioned and provided with modern fortifications. Additionally, the latter received support from its inland defences in Obrovac and Bencovac. These fortresses surveyed the border with Ottoman Croatia, while Sebenico (Šibenik), with the modern fort of San Zuane, and Spalato (Split), with the forts of Botteselle and Grippe, formed the major coastal defences. In central Dalmatia, Clissa (today Klis in Croatia) guarded the mainland and was considered the most strategic holding in the region, since the fortress was considered as 'the gate to Bosnia.' These locations relayed communications with the minor coastal outposts such as Salona (Solin), Traù (Trogir), Brazza (Braz), Curzola (Korčula), and Lésina (Hvar). This last location served as the primary Dalmatian naval base and was capable of mooring 30 galleys. Situated further east of these island fortresses, strongholds in Makarska on the coast and Duare (today Zadvarje in Croatia) further inland completed the defences in Dalmatia. The fortified Dalmatian villages of Vergoraz and Naretna guarded the Venetian frontier with the Republic of Ragusa (today Dubrovnik). Naretna's location on the Naretva river blocked access from Herzegovina. On the southern coast of Ragusa the fortified villages of Budua (Budva), Risano (Risan), Perasto (Perast), and Teodo (Tivat) surrounded major Venetian towns and villages in Albania, such as Cattaro (today Kotor in Montenegro), Scutari (Shkodrës) and Butrinto, this latter included in the defensive system with Corfu (Kerkira). In the Ionian Sea, the 'regiment' of the Levant deployed 24 garrisons with Corfu as the main fortress. South of Corfu, strongholds on the islands of Passo (Paxo), Ithaca, Cephalonia (Argostoli), and Zakynthos formed the first line of defence against the Ottoman sailing ships coming from the Gulf of Corinth.[29] Outposts in Suda, Grabusa and Spinalonga close to Crete; Tine (Tinos) in the Cycladic islands; Cerigo (Kythira), and Cerigotto (Antikythira) marked the easternmost Venetian domains manned by garrisons of regular troops. In this area, Venice also extended its protection on the Cham-Albanian communities of Parga (Pargè) and surroundings.

The *Serenissima Repubblica*

In Venice, the republican form of government was a boast and a tradition to which the ruling class – the aristocracy – remained tenaciously faithful. All this had produced a form of government charged with the appellations of a monarchy: the *signoria*.[30] However, this system of government entailed maintaining the balance of power. The elected *Doge* represented the 'highest dignity' of the Republic, but he had to tailor his direction to that of the main institution. As a result, powers were shared with the Senate (or *Maggior Consiglio*, Major Council). As the Renaissance historian and diarist Marin Sanudo declared: 'He [the *Doge*] could do nothing without the Major Council and the Major Council could do nothing without him.' Thus, the true 'heart' of the political life of the *Serenissima Repubblica* was the *Senato*.[31]

29 In Epirus, in front of Corfu, Venice also extended its protectorate over the town of Parga, and garrisons were allowed there.

30 Venice claimed to be a Republic, but actually followed a mixed government model, combining elective monarchy in the *Doge*, aristocracy in the senate, and 'democracy' in the Major Council.

31 The Senate of the *Serenissima Repubblica di San Marco* had been instituted in 1229, the Venetian Senate and was originally composed of 60 members, soon increased to 60 additional members. At the beginning of the sixteenth century the Senate numbered 200 members. In the modern era, the Venetian Senate assumed the direction of several affairs, including political, legislative, administrative and ecclesiastical ones. These institutions were combined into the *Signoria*, which consisted of the *Doge*, the Minor Council and the three leaders of the Quarantia. The

54. Portrait of Count Girolamo Secco-Suardo, early eighteenth century, by Vittore Ghislandi, also known as Fra' Galgario (Carrara Museum, Bergamo). See image commentaries for more information.

This venerable institution comprised the representatives elected exclusively among the Patrice families comprised in the *libro d'oro* (Golden Book), the members of the Technical Magistrates, and the exclusive and secret *Consiglio dei Dieci* (Council of Tenths), in charge of foreign affairs. Alongside the *Maggior Consiglio* another council had been established, the *Minor Consiglio* (Minor Council) in order to further balance the *Doge*'s powers. This comprised six advisors to the *Doge*, and the *Quarantia* (the Fourths), which was a supreme civil and administrative tribunal. Other prominent members of the Venetian power were the *procuratori di San Marco*. They carried the state's highest responsibility after that of the *Doge* and took their office for life. They were assigned key functions, including expertise on public and ecclesiastical affairs. Usually, the *Doge* was elected among the *procuratori*. This complex network was reflected in the command structure of the army and navy and in the offices appointed to the administration and inspection of the troops, sailors, gunners, rowers, galleys and sail ships. In practice, the government exercised control over the 'military' in the same way as it did over every other sector of the state. In this regard it is interesting to note that the presence of a war department or council composed only of military professionals was always opposed, and even an actual military code was never instituted, preferring to judge officers and soldiers in the civil tribunals.[32]

In the Venetian power system the *Consiglio dei Savi* (Council of the Elders) had a special importance in both army and navy affairs. This council was the operative core of the Senate, organised in a collegial branch composed of elected magistrates. There were 16 *Savi* in all, and the five *Savi agli Ordini* or *da Mar* (Elders to the Orders or to the Sea) managed matters regarding trade and navy, including the war fleet. Together with them, another five *Savi di Terraferma* (Mainland Elders) had specific competences in the field army. Specifically, the first *Savio di Terraferma* was responsible for the regular army, while the second was the *Savio alle Ordinanze*, dealing with the militia, but also including sailors, gunners and oarsmen. The first *Savio di Terraferma* was also identified as *Savio alla Scrittura* (Elder to the writings): the Venetian variant of the war secretary. He supervised the standing troops, fortresses and artillery, and had the direction of a six-member 'conference' in charge of military affairs. All officers and soldiers were dependent on him and he

Signoria was then the actual core of the government, representing the continuity of the Republic as shown in the expression: 'The Doge is dead, but the Signoria is not.'

32 Sergio Perini, *La Difesa Militare della Terraferma Veneta nel Settecento* (Chioggia; La Libreria Editrice, 1998), p.81.

could even condemn them to death without appeal.[33] In peacetime the *Savio alle Scritture* directed the administrative affairs for the army, but in the case of war the Senate appointed further offices to better coordinate the military forces, considering the need to take urgent decisions in any upcoming campaign. The military policy and the strategic approach to the conflicts was decided within the *Consulta dei Savi*, which included all the members. Each *Savio* had to submit his strategic considerations to the Senate, including those relating to the continuation of a conflict, or, as happened in the winter 1683–84, debating resolution of the war.[34] The matter deliberated by each council of war had to be approved by the Senate even though it was often a more formal than substantial passage. In 1684 in the first *consulta di guerra* (council of war) of the conflict against the Ottomans, a Senate's representative participated in the meeting, strongly addressing the first actions of the war. According to the Republic's laws, the *Savis* lasted only six months in their office, followed by another six months of absence in which they could not participate in the council. This rule was not always respected, or in other cases, especially with regard to the *Savi di Terraferma*, they systematically alternated their assignments on a six-monthly basis for several years. This system guaranteed the balance of power, but made it difficult to maintain an accurate military policy with this continual change of offices. The *Savi* managed the work of the *inquisitori di stato* (State Inquisitors, namely inspectors, in charge of controlling the strength of the corps in a campaign, like the contemporary army commissioners), and the personnel employed to control the funds for the army, fleet and militia. Other commissioners were appointed to inspect cavalry, military chancellery, marine arsenal, equipment and supplies.

The Venetian military structure was the result of the particular political organisation of the state, where the principles of collegiality and polyarchy characterised the relations of power. This resulted in a proliferation of posts and offices that appear at least redundant compared to the size of the armed forces. The main Venetian military field commander was the aforementioned *capitano generale da mar*, which position represented the pinnacle of Venice's armed forces. The Senate appointed him only in the case of war and his service usually lasted three years. Although he was the commander of the fleet, the Captain General assumed the strategic direction of all the operations conducted in different war theatres overseas, therefore including those involving land troops. Like any other elected office in Venice, the Captain General was appointed from among the aristocracy and he was responsible directly to the *Doge*. As the supreme power of the state was conditioned by policy, also the military command resented the limitations imposed by the civil authorities. The constitution of the Venetian Republic, in which power

33 Alexandre-Toussaint Limojon de Saint-Didier, *La Ville et la République de Venise au XVIIe siècle. Histoire – Institutions – Moeurs et Costumes* (Paris, 1891).

34 In 1683 the *propositione* introduced by the *Savi* Michele Foscarini and Ascanio Giustiniani opposed the proposal elaborated by Pietro Valier to join the Holy League in the war against the Porte. See Michele Foscarini, *Degli Istorici delle Cose Venetiane* (Venice, 1722), vol. X, pp.152–153.

was theoretically shared in equal parts between all members of the aristocracy, attributed functions such as 'Prince-Commander' to the Captain General: it was a very special case in which the commander-in-chief was at the same time an exponent of the class power and servant of that same power.

In the opinion of authoritative contemporaries, the actual powers of the Captain General were not what was expected from a commander-in-chief. The control exercised by the government over all military matters was seen as a restriction on the autonomy of the Captain General, and he constantly had to manage Venetian policy. Possibly, in no other country in Europe did civil power so directly influence the armed forces. In the opening phase of the war of 1684–99 the prominent Senate leader, Pietro Valier, strongly influenced the Venetian strategic plan, suggesting the navy undertake the aggressive amphibious campaigns against the enemy fleet and ports, while the land forces were being employed to destroy or conquer strategic areas in Bosnia and Albania.[35] This strategy was soon discarded, but the duel with the Captain General lasted until Morosini's death in 1694. The next year the assault on Chios was firmly supported by Valier, and once the expedition had failed, the senator was able to cast the responsibility for the failure on opponents, considering that the unsuccessful action was caused by the fleet of galleys.[36]

However, the restrictions imposed by the government were not considered so limiting by other commentators. Among those who argued otherwise was Henry Watton, the King of England's ambassador to Venice. In 1620, he claimed that the Captain General exercised a 'kind of dictatorship'.[37] This claim was substantially reiterated in 1676 by a former diplomat, this time a French one, Abraham Nicolas Amelot de la Houssaye. According to him, 'the power of the Captain General is similar to that of a dictator or sovereign … and his authority is absolute.' Amelot was convinced that the authority of the Captain General had increased with the passage of centuries. He stated:

> Many times in the past, the Senate did not allow him to undertake a campaign without its consent, but because of the distance of the capital from the theatre of operations, this greatly delayed affairs and resolutions were only applied after precious time had been lost, and therefore afterwards the Captain General was left free to decide according to circumstances.[38]

35 Guido Candiani, *Dalla galea alla nave di linea. Le trasformazioni della marina veneziana (1572–1699)* (Novi Ligure: Città del silenzio, 2012), p.301.

36 *Ibid.*

37 Piero Del Negro, 'Francesco Morosini Capitano Generale da Mar', in G. Ortalli, G. Gullino, E. Ivetic (eds), *L'inestinguibile sogno del dominio. Francesco Morosini* (Venice: Istituto Vento di Scienze, Lettere a Arti, 2021), p.31.

38 Amelot de la Houssaye, Abraham Nicolas, *Histoire du gouvernement de Venise* (Paris, 1676), pp.121–122. The author adds: 'the power of the captain general is absolute on all commanders and officers, so much so that he seems to be a dictator or at least a sovereign. His authority extends not only to the fleet, but still on all ports, islands and fortresses, where everyone obeys his orders without question.'

With another statement, Amelot de la Houssaie partially corrected his opinion:

> Other times, the Senate did not allow [the Captain General] to undertake anything without having first received the order, but because the distance significantly slowed this type of affairs, and all decisions were taken when the opportunities had already vanished, he was free to do everything necessary according to the occurrences.[39]

In the course of the Cretan War it had become clear that it was unwise to expect to dictate strategic choices from Venice, and this allowed the commanders to gain more and more autonomy in decision-making, however this did not mean that the Captain General always had *carte blanche*. In fact, at the beginning of each campaign the Senate directed its preferences to the commander as to which objectives to consider. Even in this case, however, the final decisions rarely coincided with those expressed by the Senate. In 1688, while it was indicated from Venice that Crete was the preferred target to turn against, Morosini managed to make his argument prevail in favour of Negroponte, which however resulted in a complete failure.

Surely, the authority of the Captain General depended much on the influence and prestige with which he held the office. His authority could be relevant, assuming he served the Republic positively. It was not by chance that to further raise his dignity, the Senate instantly gave him the rank of *procuratore di San Marco*: naturally, his performance in campaigns conditioned this appointment.[40] Over the years, the influence of certain commanders had grown up, especially during the period in which the command was held by Lazzaro Mocenigo, in 1657, and Francesco Morosini, Captain General from 1658 to 1660, again from 1667 to 1669 and lastly from 1684 until 1689 and from 1693 until his death in 1694, the latter period shared with the office of *Doge*.

As supreme commander, the Captain General could require a war tribunal to examine the performance of his subordinates, as happened in the October of 1688, during the process against the commander of the galleasses, Domenico Querini. He was accused of failing to comply with the orders of the Captain General. In 1690 another trial was instigated against Captain Marco Pisani for the situation at Milos, which caused the death of the sail ships' squadron commander Pietro Valier. Not even the Captain Generals could escape from a trial. Apart the famous case concerning Morosini after the surrender of Candia in 1669, the process was standard every time a campaign closed with an unsuccessful outcome, as experienced by Domenico Mocenigo in 1692, after his fault in Crete, and three years later by Captain General Antonio Zeno, who died in jail before the opening of the trial.

39 *Ibid.*, p.123. According to the French diplomat, at the start of a conflict and often before beginning of the operations, the Senate, through the *Consiglio dei Savi*, conditioned effectively the strategic direction, issuing specific orders to the captain general.

40 The original number of *procuratori* had been established at nine, but the selling of the title during the Cretan War had increased the *procuratori* to 40. See Infelise, 'L'ultima crociata', p.12.

One of the major duties performed by the Captain General in campaigns was the presidency of the *consulta* (council of war), which usually took place aboard his galley. Decisions were usually taken in this 'little senate', which joined the *Capi da Mar* (the fleet senior commanders), the senior officers of the field army, and some advisors and specialists such as engineers. Finally, the commanders of the allied troops and fleet also participated in the councils of war during the campaigns. During the war of 1684–99 these councils turned into endless, sometimes unnecessary, discussions and quarrels with Allied commanders.

The problem was well known. According to a contemporary historian, 'These disagreements have always affected the Republic, but ordinary problems concerned among those who had to sit at the same table. And although the Senate continually recommended a general union, evil grew without remedy.'[41]

More than once, rivalry and suspicion existing between the allies caused delays to the beginning of operations, setbacks and failures, as macroscopically happened in 1688 at the siege of Negroponte. Matters of precedence of the complicated ceremony regulating diplomatic relations between the states were used whenever the prestige of an ally was undermined. Often the Senate and the Captain General complained of such miserable rivalry between the allies, in several cases getting the support of some Italian sovereign; however, even among Venetians, harmony did not always reign and sometimes incomprehensible conduct occurred, explainable only by the fear of offending the sensibilities of some important families. The result of these internal rivalries excluded from the army or the fleet figures who had shown excellent quality as commanders.[42] Such episodes offer a new insight that allows reconsideration of the opinion of some historians, taking with caution the supposed lack of dedication of the Venetian aristocracy to military careers.

Consequently, the Venetian councils of war could last for days, not only because of the diversity of tactical-strategic opinions, but for the rivalry among the participants. The auxiliaries were the first source of disputes. From 1684 to 1688, in every council of war, the Maltese and Tuscans did not fail to quarrel over matters of prestige and precedence. In certain cases the council of war could be extended to the *provveditori generali* (general superintendents), namely the governors of the provinces involved in the campaign, which made these meetings very crowded. Even if he retained a considerable power, the Captain General had to interact with the civil authorities in the Venetian domains, which were equally prestigious and more experienced, such as these officials, who were closely linked to local institutions and jealous of their prerogatives.

The *e* was the key figure of the Venetian administration in civil and military matters as well. There were two categories of *provveditore*: permanent ones

41 Andrea Valier, *Historia della guerra di Candia* (Venice, 1679), p.511.

42 Possibly the most resounding episode of exclusion happened during the Cretan War, when the valuable but politically disliked Antonio Barbaro was excluded from any position of command. See Bruno Mugnai, *The Cretan War, 1645–1671* (Warwick: Helion & Company, 2018), p.134.

and others appointed as *provveditori straordinari* (extraordinary *provveditori*). There was no clear hierarchy: some had jurisdiction over a single town or fortress, while others oversaw whole districts and operational theatres. Not until 1617 did the Senate place the Captain General above the *provveditori* in the council of war.[43] They were more usually Venetian patricians, who by virtue of their monopoly over the command of galleys had military experience and training. These directional and administrative charges had been instituted in 1467 during the first war against the Ottoman Empire, and in the early sixteenth century their office became a stable appointment. In 1684 there were 35 *provveditori*, each provided with specific functions. The three *provveditori generali all'Armata* managed the arsenal activity, namely the production of galleys and vessels. The number of ships built and maintained every year was deliberated by the Senate, but the *provveditori* represented the executive office with competences similar to a contemporary admiralty. They supervised the service of the officers of the fleet, including the recruitment of sailors, gunners, rowers and *fanti da Mar* (marine soldiers). In addition to dealing with logistical problems they played the delicate role of intermediaries between the military command, the fleet, and the government. The appointment lasted three years, but they could be reappointed after a year of absence. In peacetime the *provveditore generale all'Armata* held the most senior position in the fleet, and after the conflict began he automatically became the Captain General's vice admiral and lieutenant. As discussed before, each *provveditore* participated in turn in the military campaigns as a regular member of the council of war. Depending on the strategic context, another *provveditore* could be appointed with the title of *provveditore straordinario all'Armata*. When resident in Venice the *provveditori* presided, in turn, over the *Collegio da Mar* (Sea Council) composed of three *Savi* (advisers), a high counsellor and administrative personnel, the latter under the three *provveditori all'armar* (fleet administrators). The college included three other *provveditori*: the *provveditore all'Arsenale* (administrator for the Arsenal of Venice); the *provveditore sopra il biscotto* (administrator for the food supply for the navy); the *provveditore all'artiglieria* (administrator for the artillery). Other *provveditori* dealt with troops or personnel on campaign, such as the *provveditore alla cavalleria* (administrator of light cavalry), or the *provveditore al campo* (camp administrator), who managed organisation and discipline inside the encampments and quarters on campaign. Further offices as *provveditore* with military competences were the *provveditore generale in Terraferma* (administrator for the Mainland), who had competence over the militia, and the *provveditore sopra le fortezze* (administrator for the fortresses). The latter controlled and directed affairs concerning forts, fortified outposts and urban walls, as well as bridges and storage for food and ammunition. His action was considerable in keeping the extended Venetian defensive system as efficient as possible and therefore he had four adjutants. His office worked in coordination with the aforementioned *provveditore all'artiglieria* when a significant number of guns were inside the fortresses.

43 Hanlon, *The Twilight of a Military Tradition*, p.145.

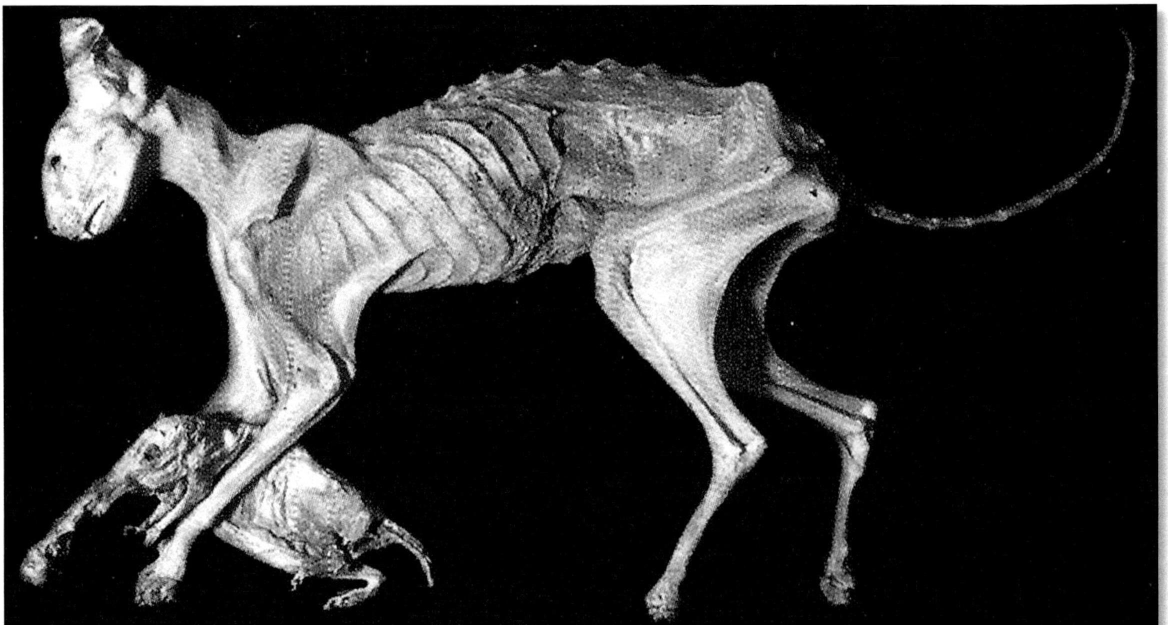

Above: 56. The funeral procession for Francesco Morosini's burial service, celebrated at Nauplia in 1694. The painting, attributed to Alessandro Piazza, is a useful source for the uniforms of the Venetian army. In the foreground there are artillerymen wearing blue coats with red facing, and drivers with pale yellow coats with black cuffs.

Facing page: 55. Pistol book (second half of the seventeenth century) and mummified cat, Museo Correr Venice, both belonging to Francesco Morosini. The pistol book is symptomatic of the uneasy climate existing in seventeenth-century fleets, theatre of mutinies and revolts, in one of which Morosini himself was involved in 1685. The image of the cat instead reveals a private aspect of the great captain-general. A mummified cat was found in a box on board the galleass on which Morosini spent the last days of his life. The animal was identified as *Nini*, the red cat to whom Morosini, who also had red hair, had become attached and always carried with him, even into battle.

Other *provveditori* played important roles in planning and supporting the campaigns in the eastern Mediterranean. During the wars against the Ottomans the *provveditori in Levante* (*Provveditori* in the eastern domains), such as Zadar, Corfu and Cephalonia often joined the councils of war and their opinion was considered as that of a senior officer. In peacetime naval forces and garrisons depended on the *provveditori generali*, who extended their jurisdiction over the local militia in wartime. The *provveditori* usually directed the troops in campaigns, as occurred several times during the war, for example in 1687 when Girolamo Corner, *provveditore in Dalmazia*, besieged and conquered Castelnuovo di Cattaro (today Herceg Novi in Montenegro). Their main role was economic-financial. In each province the *provveditore generale* dealt with military matters regarding supply and quartering of troops. This task was no means negligible, considering that soldiers and animals had to be conveniently quartered and fed. In peacetime the problems were minimal, but in wartime the Senate usually appointed another official with the designation of *provveditore straordinario* to help the titular officer or to replace him if his service had been disappointing. This was a position that exposed the *provveditori* as much to the wrath of the soldiers as to criticism from the Senate, but which also represented an excellent start in the career of a patrician. It was a task of great responsibility that, if successfully completed, could quickly lead to the top echelons of the State or, if not, would tarnish the name of the family. For every Venetian nobleman, being elected *provveditore* was a recognition of his qualities. Through dense correspondence with the Senate he had the task of moderating action and making the voice of the government heard. But the main burden that fell on their shoulders was to deal with the – often legitimate – protests of the troops: 'money and food', these being the invocations raised by the soldiers towards the government representatives.[44] Often the *provveditore* was thus caught between two fires: on the one hand, the soldiers calling for food, and on the other the population who protested against the harassment they suffered. The other major problem faced by the *provveditori* was the availability of money. Most of the documentation preserved in Venetian archives consists of letters asking the capital for bags of money to be sent to them. Naturally, they had to ensure that the distribution of the salaries took place without malfeasance and abuse. In each dispatch a situation was presented that, although sometimes described in gloomy colours to impress the government, was often in danger of getting out of hand for the Venetian authorities in the army. The anger of the soldiers towards those who should have paid them grew in proportion to the delay in payments, contributing to a very dangerous situation. It could even be that the *provveditori* sought loans from merchants in the area surrounding the camp, or pawned their own money, obviously expecting to be reimbursed on their return to Venice. These officials served in close contact not only with troops or crews, but also with the dangers of battle. Many *provveditori* were actual commanders, especially in the case of those with the fleet, or those assigned to the frontier regions. Numerous

44 Luciano Pezzolo, 'Istituzioni Militari Veneziane', in V. Ilari (ed.), *Le Armi di San Marco* (Rome: Società Italiana di Storia Militare, 2011), p.64.

Venetian nobles were personally involved in military campaigns in their role of *provveditore*, especially those of Greece and Dalmatia, who usually acted like a field commander.[45]

Although Venice had never pursued a military policy in the modern sense, the government managed to create a considerable number of men skilled in military matters.[46] In wartime the Senate appointed other officers in specific military functions, which tenures usually lasted three years. In the fleet, the *capitano straordinario delle navi* (Extraordinary Captain of the Sail Ships) was also appointed. He was tasked to direct the squadron known in Venice as the *Armata Grossa* (Great Fleet), while galleys and galleasses were joined in the *Armata Sottile* (Light Fleet), under the direct command of the Captain General. On campaign, the council of war included the aforementioned *provveditore all'armata*, the *cancelliere* (Chancellor, appointed by the Minor Council), the *commissario* (commissioner) and the *sopramasser* (in charge of administrative and logistical affairs). The council of war operated like a typical major staff of the baroque age, including further officers depending on the strategic scenario. Since the mid seventeenth century the *generale dello sbarco* (General of the Landing Forces) had become a particularly important figure, also appointed by the Senate. He held the command of landing troops during amphibious operations. Apart from rare exceptions,[47] this rank was always assigned to foreign mercenary officers, mostly Italian, and later German.[48] In the context of Venetian warfare, marked by intense amphibious warfare, this assignment became crucial. It is well known that Captain General Morosini usually followed the opinion expressed by the general of the landing troops Otto Wilhelm von Königsmarck, despite the fact that the latter was 20 years younger. As shown by the examination of the council of war reports from 1686 to 1688, Morosini held Königsmarck in the highest esteem, in whom he recognised '[a] subject who is here promoting the most desirable and fortunate successes to the increase of arms' and who had 'given in the part of valour and good intelligence to the craft of arms … full and distinguished essays.'[49] Morosini often relied on the opinion of the Swedish-German general both when he had

45 Lunardo Foscolo, who was *provveditore* of Dalmatia between 1645 and 1651, successfully led the campaigns against the Ottomans as field commander, See Mugnai, *The Cretan War*, pp.114–115.

46 Pezzolo, 'Istituzioni Militari Veneziane', p.65.

47 The last Venetian *Generale dello Sbarco* had been Count Ossalico Polcenigo in 1657, while another 'Venetian' officer, in charge from 1684, was the Imperial but Udine native *General Wachtmeister* Nicolò Strassoldo. The latter died of illness in January 1685 in Corfu.

48 Alberto Prelli, *L'esercito veneto nel primo'600* (Venice: Filippi, 1993), pp.41–42. This derived from the *Condottiere* who during the Renaissance assumed the functions of general commander of the Army in the mainland. They were enlisted from among foreign candidates belonging to prominent families, such as don Giovanni the Medici and Luigi d'Este, or were experienced veterans such as the Corsican Pompeo Giustiniani.

49 Del Negro, 'Francesco Morosini Capitano Generale da Mar', p.27. However, Morosini reproached his general because of 'a certain partiality' for German troops with little or no esteem for the Venetian regiments.

to designate senior officers of 'foreign' troops for special command tasks, and even when a Venetian aristocrat was submitted for a promotion.[50]

Considering that political power controlled every civil and military activity, even the senior officers were subject to the balance of power, which was typical of Venice. In fact, the Captain General had to share his authority in war theatres involving the Venetian overseas domains with the local *governatori delle armi* (governors of the troops), who directed the garrison and the militia of their respective provinces. Another prominent military figure was the *governatore generale delle armi* (General Governor of the troops), appointed by the Senate to lead the field army on the mainland. This supreme officer was chosen among the candidates – usually foreign – who were expert in western warfare techniques, and he extended his command to all the infantry and cavalry in the mainland war theatre. The last and highest general officer in Venetian service received the title of *maestro di campo generale* (General Field Captain), however it was a function more apparent than substantial, partly because Venice no longer had to confront opponents on the mainland, and this and the previous post remained vacant after 1645. Regardless of the presence of a commander in the *Terraferma*, every major Venetian town in Italy had two officials who dealt with the local forces: the *capitano delle armi* (army captain, or military governor), with military and administrative functions, and the *podestà* (mayor), with judicial and civil duties, but also dealing with the militia. Both these ranks maintained links with the Captain General and other senior commanders. Finally, throughout wartime temporary ranks could be established to lead the troops in campaign, such as the *sergente maggiore di battaglia*, in charge of commanding corps of infantry formed by two or more regiment-battalions. In wartime the government appointed further governors to join the army on campaign in charge of managing specific tasks, such as the *governatore dei forzati*, who managed matters for convicted oarsmen, or for the *oltramarine* infantry. The hospital service also depended on a newly established governor.

It was only in October 1686 that the Senate finally decided to take action against the epidemic that had been decimating the troops in the Morea. In mid February the *Magistrato alla Sanità* received a commission to send medicines, physicians, surgeons and other specialists who, if possible, were also fluent in German to facilitate the care of the foreign troops. This salutary decision came very late. However, during the winter of 1686–87 the epidemic had stopped on its own, at least for a while.[51]

50 ASVe, *Senato, Provveditori di Terra e Mar, Dispacci*, d. 89, from Nauplia, dated 9 September 1686. On that occasion Morosini followed Königsmarck's advice to promote Faustin da Riva to the position of *provveditore straordinario* as reward for good behaviour during the siege of Naufplia, replacing Daniele Dolfin, who had fallen ill.

51 Pinzelli, *Venise et la Morée*, p.143.

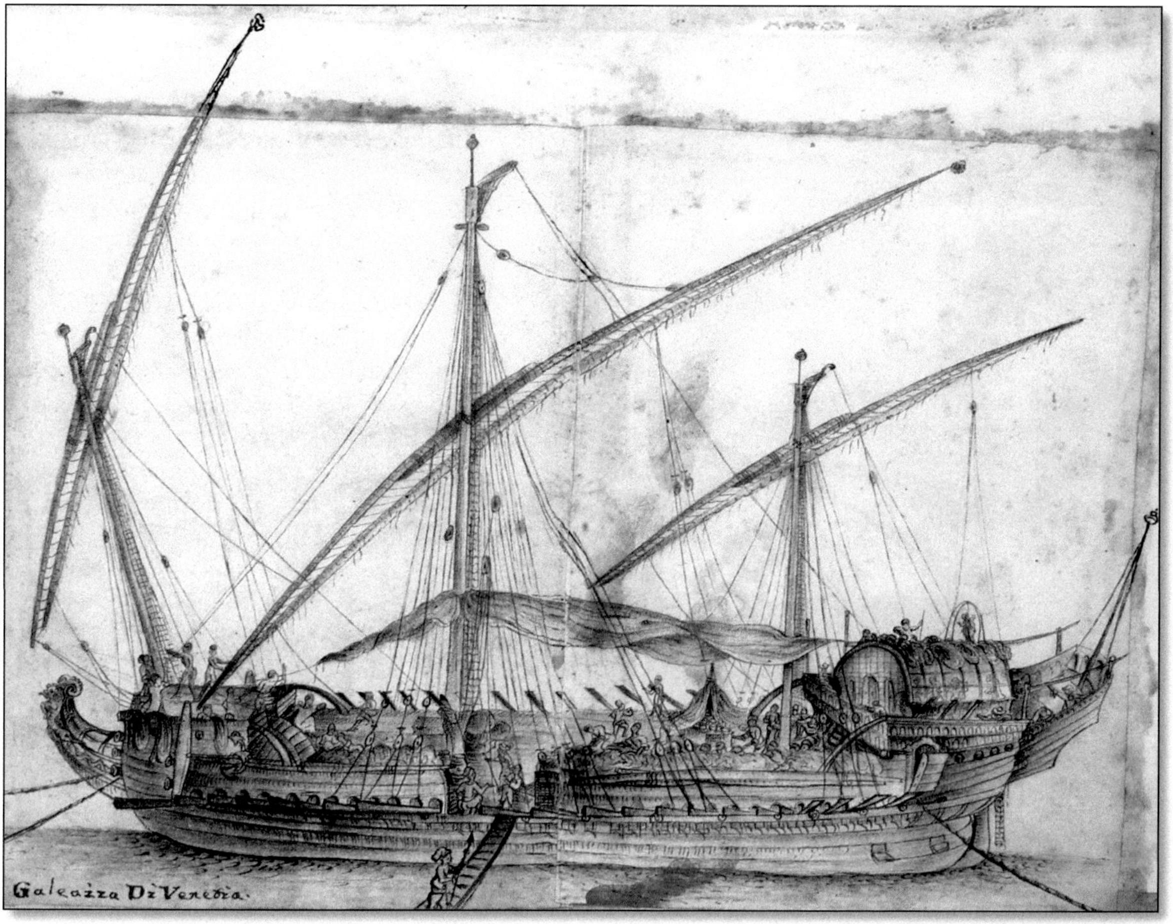

57. Venetian galleass, 1680s, copy after the Manfroni Manuscript (Florence, Biblioteca Nazionale Centrale).

The Venetian *Armata*

If the presence of foreigners in the army's senior ranks was customary, the fleet was exclusively assigned to the Venetian aristocracy. Service on the fleet was not just a duty but also a symbol of power, and a post of command into the *Armata* – a term that designated the Republic's entire war fleet – attained strong political value. In spite of the Venetians' loss of confidence on the sea in the last quarter of the century, the city's most important noble families still cultivated an exalted naval tradition that appeared in state symbols. Unless there was a very good reason for his exclusion, every young Venetian aristocrat began his apprenticeship as a sailor with the title of *Nobile sopra la Galea* (noble on the Galley) and had to complete at least three campaigns.[52]

At different times during the Cretan War the Venetian fleet successfully thwarted Ottoman strategy, and nearly collapsed the enemy siege operations

52 Apprenticeship in the fleet began very early for young Venetians, even for the era. At the Third Battle of the Dardanelles in 1656 the Muazzo brothers Andrea and Antonio, 12 and 13 years old respectively, participated as *Nobili sopra le Galee*.

58. Sea corselet, Brescia manufacture, 1680–85, belonged to the Martinengo family (Armeria Reale, Turin). Venetian galley commanders widely used corselets like the one in the picture. The breastplate is decorated with religious images and war trophies. The stunning decor suggests that this protection qualified the rank of the navy officers, identifying them from those of the army.

at Candia. After a series of formidable victories the fleet seemed to be on the verge of victory – or at least close to reaching an armistice with the Sultan – in 1657. In those years the Venetian fleet deployed captains, sailors, and gunners of extraordinary value. In Venetian naval history, and even among the best contemporary navies, this force was by far the most skilled. Thus, the Republic remained convinced that it possessed a powerful weapon that could easily prevail against the weak and neglected Ottoman fleet. This perspective certainly influenced the decision to enter the war in 1684.

However, the Venetian fleet that participated in the new conflict differed from the one 30 years earlier in several respects. Among the most important changes was the ongoing technical evolution, which rapidly compensated for the disadvantages that the large vessels faced in the Mediterranean against oared ships. Improving technique, and the increasing ability to exploit the wind rendered sailing ships increasingly independent from the oared fleet. This allowed the Venetians to adopt the linear tactics successfully introduced in the second half of the seventeenth century during the Anglo-Dutch wars. These developments profoundly affected the cooperation between the galleys and galleasses of the Venetian *Armata Sottile* (light fleet) and the tall sailing ships of the *Armata Grossa* (heavy fleet), which, however, achieved excellent exploits in the 1650s and 1660s. During 15 years of peace the Republic began a major transformation of the navy, which after 1675 culminated in a construction programme for large sailing ships divided into three classes. The government based this decision on the Cretan War experience. In the 1670s the *Serenissima* intended to abandon its armed merchant vessel policy, especially the hiring of very expensive vessels from northern Europe. The hiring of sail ships had been a considerable expenditure during the Cretan War, when the Republic paid a total of over 200 vessels and crews,[53] mostly Dutch, English and French, but also from the Hanseatic towns of Hamburg and Denmark. The practice of chartering established considerable links between the state and some important ship-owners, capable of mobilising up to a dozen ships at the same time, links which became useful for the obtaining of trained sea officers, and which easily brings to mind the experience of the great military entrepreneurs of the Thirty Years' War. Additionally the custom established

53 Guido Candiani, *I vascelli della Serenissima. Guerra, politica e costruzioni navali a Venezia in età moderna, 1650–1720* (Venice: Istituto Veneto di Scienze, 2009), p.172. 'Alongside these entrepreneurs, however, the Venetian authorities forged less demanding and more elastic relations with a series of captains-armourers of individual units, who acted on their own or, more often, in collaboration with one or more contractors.'

with this type of contract meant that when, in the 1670s, the Serenissima began to develop a component of state-owned warships called *navi pubbliche*, the administration of ship and crew was also delegated to the captain.[54] In this way the figure of the captain, instead of becoming an actual public official, remained in part a private contractor in the more or less temporary service of Venice, and the *Armata Grossa* continued to bear the mark of a profit-making military enterprise which remained with it until the fall of the Republic.[55] Although the commander of a public ship was less reputed than one of the oared fleet, his appointment had a considerable economic value, considering that a first-rate ship had a crew of 200 men, including offers. To each sail ship the government provided four *capi bombardieri*, four *capi* (chiefs) and 12 *sottocapi* (junior chiefs).[56] The state also supplied *mozzi* (cabin boys), chosen from among the orphaned or abandoned boys in the Venetian hospitals, or those who wandered through the city. These boys, between 6 and 20 per ship, were added to the sailors enlisted by the captain.

Ultimately, In Venice there had been no evolution in the professionalisation of the officers' staff and this continued to be composed of patricians, who held the office of *governatori* or *capitani* in the sailing fleet.[57] The former fulfilled a political function because, belonging to the ruling class of the Republic, they represented 'the presence of the state', and ensured its administrative function, helping to make 'national' the sail fleet; the latter, because they came from the little nobility or the lower ranks of officialdom, could not have access to command positions, and were dismissed at the end of each term of service, but nevertheless contributed technical competence to the conduct of the sail ship.[58]

The decision to strengthen the sailing fleet was essentially due to strategic considerations. Already in the spring of 1653, Dutch and English vessels engaged themselves in a fierce battle in front of Livorno. Twenty years later, the menace coming from European belligerents became a real threat in the Mediterranean too. In 1674 the French fleet landed soldiers to support the rebellion against Spain in Messina, attracting the Spanish and Dutch fleet close to the Ionian Sea; then in 1684 – even more worrying – the French navy

54 *Ibid.*, p.173. By stipulating a contract between the *provveditori all'armar* and the captain the state entrusted the ship's hull, equipment and artillery to the captain, while the latter undertook to collect and organise the crew in return for a monthly sum for each enlisted sailor.

55 *Ibid.*

56 ASVe, *Senato Mar*, f. 611, dated 1 September 1676. However, this establishment was rarely respected.

57 Venice did not have a large number of professional officers who made military life their final choice. However, at the beginning of the seventeenth century no European fleet had a corps of professional naval officers. The United Provinces appointed them only after 1625, whilst in England it was only in the 1650s that a modern corps of officers, paid by the government, was formed. See Luciano Pezzolo, 'Stato, Guerra e Finanza nella Repubblica di Venezia', in *Società e Storia*, 26, n. 102 (2003), p.87.

58 Francesco Zampieri, 'Angelo Emo e la riforma della marina veneziana', in V. Ilari (ed.), *Le Armi di San Marco* (Rome: Società Italiana di Storia Militare, 2011), p.145.

59. The naval battle of Livorno, attributed to Johannes Lingelbach (1622–1674), preserved in the Rijksmuseum Amsterdam. On 14 March 1653, a major battle was fought off Livorno by the Dutch and English fleets, during the war of 1652–1654. The two fleets contended for control of trade in the Mediterranean, right in front of an Italian port. The encounter ended in a Dutch victory.

bombarded Genoa and then landed infantry at Sampierdarena, to punish the Republic for siding with Spain. Moreover, the North African corsairs did not diminish their presence in the Mediterranean and their commanders introduced new tactics employing squadrons of sail ships to repulse enemies and better intercept the merchant sea trade.

The new scenario, at least, favoured a gradual strategic change from a fleet based on galleys and galleasses to one relying on sail ships. In the early phase of the Cretan War Venice paid the price of traditionalism in naval matters, as its fleet was almost exclusively composed of galleys and galleasses, namely oared units best suited for navigation in the Mediterranean.[59] The lessons learned during the war had demonstrated the Ottoman weakness when facing the North European sail ships in Venetian service. By the 1660s the Republic began to replace the costly and sometimes unreliable foreign units with new vessels provided by the Venetian Arsenal to form a larger *Armata Grossa*.[60] Then in the 1670s the Senate decided to proceed with a significant increase of sail warships through the construction of sail ships and the formation of a new class of trained commanders for this kind of vessel. The following year the initial anti-foreign trade policy was directed towards the Venice's archenemy, the Ottoman Empire, based on the report presented to the Senate by *bailo* (ambassador to the Ottoman Porte) Giacomo Querini after his return from Constantinople. Querini emphasised that the Sultan was without a warship fleet and suggested recovering supremacy in the eastern Mediterranean. The year 1675 marked the actual turning point for the Venetian navy. Over the years, five new vessels came from the Arsenal to drop anchor in Corfu. In 1683, on the eve of the war, Venice possessed seven warships and 12 others were under construction, ready to join the war fleet in less than five months.

Although the oar and sail fleets remained distinguished at a strategic level, these two components had cooperated tactically during the Cretan War,

59 Del Negro, 'Francesco Morosini Capitano Generale da Mar', p.32.

60 The first Venetian-built sail vessel was the *Giove Fulminante*, with 62 cannons, launched in May 1667.

but by the end of the seventeenth century they faced a more problematic integration.[61] On the eve of war in 1683 the light fleet outnumbered the heavy one, but within 10 years the heavy vessels overtook the galleys and galleasses. When deployed in a line, the sailing ships' firepower became too important for even the traditionally minded Venetian ruling class to overlook. In spite of the tremendous economic effort, the massive renovation programme continued throughout the seventeenth century.[62]

In peacetime the strength of the navy included the light fleet with 20 or 21 fully equipped and armed galleys; four galleys were permanently displayed in Corfu, Zakynthos and Cephalonia, joined by four more in summer; four or six were at anchor in Venice, while another four formed the Dalmatian squadron. In Venice there were always hulls in reserve for 40 new galleys, 20 of which were armed and ready to sail: a significant decrease in comparison with 20 years before, when 60 hulls were normally available.[63] During the Cretan War the galley fleet had deployed more than 50 galleys, a number never equalled in subsequent conflicts. For the first campaign the Venetians deployed 22 galleys, joined by two more from Dalmatia, two from Cephalonia and two from Zakynthos and Corfu.[64] In peacetime the *flotta sottile* (the light fleet of rowing ships) still comprised two galleasses with another four in reserve in Venice.

As occurred with the field army, the Senate and the Major Council appointed and elected all fleet commanders, from the Captain General to the simple *sopracomito* (a galley commander). Other important ranks included the *capitano delle navi* (the commander of the sailing vessels), the *capitano della guardia in Golfo* (Captain of the Gulf squadron, who directed the Adriatic galley squadron based in Venice) and the *capitano delle galeazze.* All of these tasks were assigned to experienced officers and formed the first step towards reaching the high rank of Captain General. In the last quarter of the seventeenth century the increased numbers of sailing vessels necessitated dividing them into two or more squadrons. Thus, new high-ranking positions, such as the *almirante delle navi* (Rear Admiral) and the *patron delle navi* (Lieutenant Admiral), could be appointed. All these ranks were collectively known as *capi da mar* (Chiefs of the Sea). Other personnel in charge of dealing with the army on campaign were represented by the simple *governatori*, who usually managed specific tasks or personnel, such as the *governatore dei forzati*, who was responsible on campaign for the convicted oarsmen.

---

61 On this topic, see also the excellent essay by Guido Candiani, *Vele, remi e cannoni: l'Impiego congiunto di navi, galee e galeazze nella flotta veneziana, 1572–1718*, in G. Candiani and L. Lo Basso (eds), 'Mutazioni e Permanenze nella Storia Navale del Mediterraneo, secc. XVI–XIX' (Milan: Franco Angeli, 2010), pp.116–162.

62 At first 1,200,000 *ducati* had been budgeted for the war, but by 1684 more than two million had been spent. Annual spending gradually grew from year to year and reached four million *ducati* in 1688; see Pezzolo, 'Stato, Guerra e Finanza nella Repubblica di Venezia', pp.95–96.

63 Mario Nani Mocenigo, *Storia della Marina Veneziana* (Rome, 1935), p.257.

64 Michele Foscarini, *Degli Istorici delle Cose Veneziane*, p.134; these figures are confirmed in the Archivio di Stato di Venezia (ASVe), *Senato Mar*, ff. 656, 1684.

60. Detail of the standard of the Francesco Morosini's galley during his mandate as *capitano generale da mar* between 1684 and 1694, preserved in Castello, Venice, Scuola Grande di San Marco (author's photo). Red background with golden yellow lion, edged with silver lilies and golden laces and embroidery.

Above them, the three aforementioned *provveditori all'armar* closely administrated the fleet. Every two months this trio received notes from the *Capi da Mar*, and the commissars in charge of inspecting the fleet's units, regarding the role and number of the crewmen and the state of armaments, oarsmen, ammunition, expenses, and other matters relating to the fleet's administration. Officials under the *savio alla scrittura* recruited sailors, rowers and gunners. They also appointed non-commissioned and subordinate officers.[65] At an intermediate level the galley commander's responsibilities for his ship resembled those of an infantry or cavalry captain for his company. Both the *sopracomito* and the *governatore* commanded a galleass, and each led a composite major staff consisting of a *comito*, *sottocomito*, *pilota*, *padrone* (the sailors' senior NCO), *capo dei provisionati* (infantry commander), *capo bombardiere* (artillery senior NCO), secretary, chaplain, and *eccellente* (physician). The presence of other ranks depended on the vessel's characteristics. For example the *sopramasser*, the maritime version of the quartermaster, served on the Captain General's galley. Other tasks and duties aboard the galleys and galleasses were appointed to other non-commissioned officers and specialists such as the *maestranze* (caulker, smith, carpenter), the *Titolati* (senior sailors), and the *agozzino* (executioner). The *scappoli* (the embarked infantry picket), and obviously the oarsmen, completed the galley and galleass crews. Through the work of officials the *Serenissima* constantly exerted control, not only over crews and ships but also over local inhabitants. All sailors aged 18 and over were registered into categories according to their respective characteristics so that, in case of need, fleet replacements could be found and loaded in a short

65 A function that corresponded to a secretary of war.

time. Sailing vessels included different functions and ranks, and the captain usually exercised his authority over a smaller number of subordinates, whose denominations were often borrowed from foreign naval terminology.

Although the fleet primarily consisted of Venetians, several nobles from the mainland served, but the Venetian field army's typical ethnic was less present at sea. Sailors and gunners were registered in the *ordinanze da mar* and came essentially from Venice and Chioggia, but apart from some pilots and seamen enlisted in northern Europe, the presence of other 'nationals' such as Greeks and Slavs was not irrelevant. Throughout the duration of the Ottoman Wars the cosmopolitan Venetian overseas domains were the second great recruitment pool for sailors and rowers. Slav or Greek captains only led galleys from Istria, Dalmatia, and the Ionian islands. In contrast, the sailing ships included larger numbers of commanders and other officers from the overseas domains. The same ethnic groups provided the majority of oarsmen for the galleys.[66] Considering that oarsmen represented 70 percent of the crew of the light fleet, their presence was always significant.[67] These men underwent very harsh treatment, although it was less brutal than some literature has suggested. Unlike the other Mediterranean fleets, the Venetians limited the use of slaves and convicts to fill the crew. This was far more common on the galleys of the Tuscan Order of St Stephen, the Pope, and Malta.[68] The oarsmen recruitment system was developed in Venice as early as the mid sixteenth century, with the establishment of an actual levy, the *Ordinanze da Mar*, in Venice and the mainland cities; in wartime, 10,000 rowers aged between 18 and 45 were recruited among the bachelors and children of large families. In the seventeenth century, however, this system was in crisis. Venetian galley commanders had little consideration towards the peasants enrolled in the mainland, and rioters almost always served in the fleet. By 1647 the ordinance levy was virtually abolished. After this year the overseas domains, especially from the Greek islands, became the main recruitment pool of oarsmen. In these territories high poverty rates compelled the population to accept the harshness and risks of the naval campaigns, enlisting as *buonevoglie*, and also, perhaps, because the Greek islanders exhibited greater aptitude for navigation.

66 While the officers and crew aboard galleys or galleasses granted preference to Venetian nobles, aristocratic membership was not a required prerequisite for the sail fleet. On this matter see Candiani, *I vascelli della Serenissima*, pp.123–124.

67 An ordinary galley required 200–220 oarsmen, and 300 for the *bastarda*: the captain general's galley. The galleasses could have up to 440 oarsmen.

68 The living conditions were harsh but not as much literature of the past has described, drawing more from novels than from sources. Slaves held in some Italian *bagni* (prisons) seem often to have been relatively well protected and cared for. Some individuals insisted on receiving the waters of baptism; others were engaged in commercial activities, making use of their skills as artisans. Indeed, in the early eighteenth century Pope Benedict XIII moved to clamp down on these small businessmen. Fortunately his edict proved to be short-lived and ineffective. See also Salvatore Bono, 'Schiavi musulmani sulle galere e nei bagni d'Italia dal XVI al XIX secolo', in R. Ragosta (ed.), *Le genti del mare Mediterraneo* (Rivista trimestrale di studi e documentazione dell'Istituto italiano per l'Africa e l'Oriente, 1982), vol. 37, pp.856–858, 861–863, 866–867.

The use of slaves was sporadically practised in Venice, usually to complete the benches, while the recruitment of convicts remained usual. The latter were typically offered a sentence reduction in exchange for one or two years aboard a galley or galleass, and a death sentence could be commuted to 10 years at the oar. The Venetians also employed prisoners of war, especially at the end of a campaign when the number of oarsmen became insufficient.[69]

Although contemporary sources rarely mention the oarsmen's condition, the Venetians and their allies reserved little regard for the Greek inhabitants under Ottoman rule. If necessary, they provided an important source of oarsmen recruits. In the summer of 1687 Morosini ordered 'repression against the communities of Mystras in the Peloponnese, accused of having favoured the Ottomans during the last campaign'. For this reason 768 young Greeks were forcibly recruited as oarsmen, 'chosen among the most vigorous'.[70] In other circumstances, Venetian commanders ordered actual campaigns to retrieve defectors who had found refuge in some remote corner of the Aegean Sea. Apparently, escaping the oar was far from easy and the commanders promised to protect communities from looting and deportations if they could facilitate their return. The harshness of life in the fleet did not prevent convicts from performing other tasks, perhaps against the promise of license or prize. More often they dug trenches or unloaded artillery from the galleys, but at other times they carried out more dangerous tasks, and these were not always accepted voluntarily. As the troops in the siege of Negroponte neared exhaustion in 1688, the Venetian Army also enlisted volunteer oarsmen and assigned them to infantry regiments to serve in the terrible campaign.

Compared to northern European fleets, the *Serenissima* faced a significant technological gap in matter of sail ships. After much delay, the first vessel entirely built and armed by the Venetian Arsenal, *Giove Fulminante* (Lightning Jupiter) with 62 cannons, set sail in September 1667.[71] However,

---

69 There are relatively few studies concerning the living conditions and the death rate of the oarsmen in seventeenth-century Mediterranean fleets. Some Tuscan archival sources from the late century show with good detail the incidence of mortality among the crews. Out of 920 oarsmen employed in the galleys of the Order of St Stephen, after 10 years of service, 508 men died. The mortality rate was six percent annually. The causes of death are not documented, but only 78 were those who died on the sea. It must be noted that, in Tuscany, the percentage of convicts and slaves was much higher than in Venice, where each galley had to include at least six *buonevoglie*, volunteers. Among the latter the casualties were only 33, compared with 248 deaths among the slaves and 225 among the convicts. It is possible, however, that different treatment conditions were decisive in survival expectancy. ASFi, *Archivio Mediceo del Principato*, '*Galee di Santo Stefano*', f 21, 1679, and '*Forzati del Bagno di Livorno*', f. 223. Concerning the presence of slaves in the fleet of the Republic, often concealed by the Venetians, see Luca Lo Basso, *Uomini da Remo. Galee e galeotti del Mediterraneo in età moderna* (Milan: Selene, 2004), pp.161–170.

70 Giacomo Diedo, *Storia della Repubblica di Venezia* (Venice, 1751), Vol. III, pp.399–400. The punishment was not only limited to this, since even 600 Greek 'children' were taken aboard the fleet as servants, and even 1,000 girls were held to be 'put in the freedom of sailors and soldiers'.

71 Recent investigations suggest that the existence of an original Venetian tradition of large sailing vessels started in the fifteenth century. See also Guido Ercole, *Vascelli e fregate della Serenissima.*

Venice never passively suffered this technological gap. While acquiring large vessels and hiring crews abroad, the government began to plan the production of sailing vessels divided into three homogeneous classes as early as 1660. During the Cretan War the Arsenal never stopped experimenting with new armament solutions for sail ships, galleys, and galleasses, but in the 1670s, with the conclusion of the war, only eight sail ships remained in service. Despite the delayed development of large vessels the Venetian war fleet could have been still considered one of the largest in the world and probably the first in the Mediterranean.

The coexistence of galleys and ships in the Venetian fleet has been interpreted in different ways. Today, scholars no longer consider old theories valid. Instead, they describe the passages from rowing to sailing – and then steam – like a kind of Darwinian evolution applied to navigation. This traditional view originated from an alleged Mediterranean backwardness compared to the northern European naval scenario, where sailing vessels occupied an undisputed primacy in the war fleets. The actual situation was very different. The Mediterranean, with its irregular winds, presented serious problems for large vessels, at least until ship and sailing technology overcame these limitations. Even the Venetian Arsenal's seemingly backward vessel designs withstand the light of recent investigations which, on the contrary, demonstrate a scenario of fruitful experiments in all fields of shipbuilding and armament production.

Oared ships had always proved excellent tools for naval wars in the Mediterranean. The oar offered agility, quality, and handling. These characteristics proved essential for campaigns along the coast, thus Venetian commanders hesitated to abandon a weapon that had always been considered useful for naval warfare. Moreover, a galley's armament was considerable – especially in the forecastle where mounted pieces could shoot at a greater distance than the artillery of other vessels. Even more significant, the galleass's huge bow guns could strike targets beyond 1,000 metres. Finally the galley, with its shallow draught, was an excellent landing craft that was fully enhanced by Francesco Morosini during the Cretan War. As the main architect of a spectacular series of amphibious actions, Morosini conquered the Peloponnese in only three campaigns.

Although commanders tried to use the greatest possible care, the life of the oarsmen was pushed to the limit of endurance. Besides risks arising from combat, they were living in a small space and were constantly exposed to the elements and tormented by parasites, which according to many witnesses were present on every galley. Each bench housed three oarsmen who shared a lined leather mattress on which they sat and slept, and two water barrels. Each bank was held accountable, and punishing fellow oarsmen from a deserter's bench proved a simple way to impose discipline and prevent desertions.

Navi di Linea della Marina veneziana. 1652–1797 (Trento: Gruppo Modellistico Trentino di studio e ricerca storica, 2011), pp.11–14.

Left: 61. Officer and private of the *Alabardieri* (Lifeguard Halberdiers), in 1694. See image commentaries for more information.

Below: 62. The 'ordinary uniform' of the *Alabardieri* is described in the documents preserved in the Venice State Archive. See image commentaries for more information.

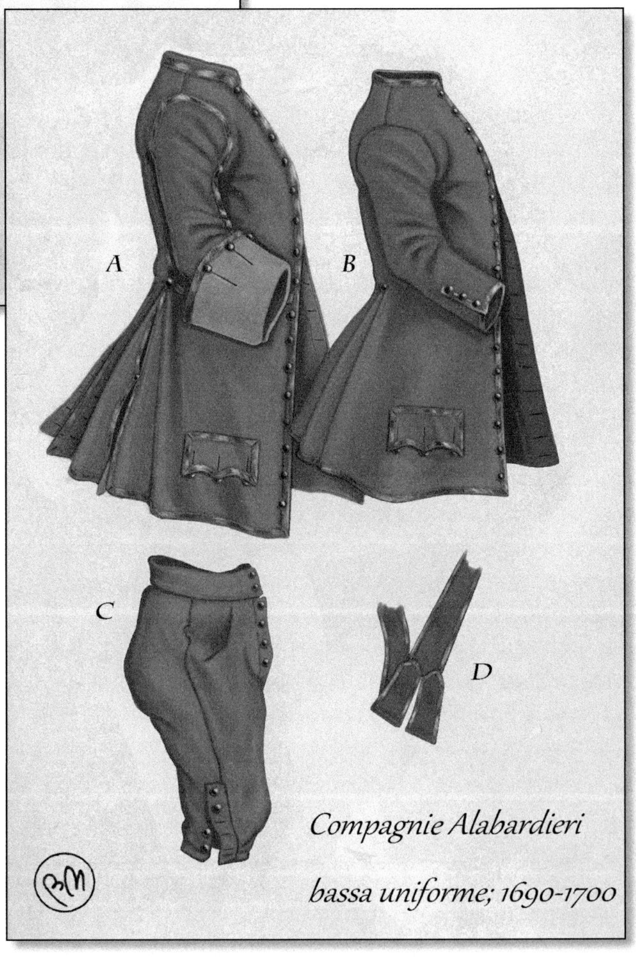

The Field Army

After a period of disengagement and demilitarisation between 1670 and 1684, the War of the Holy League increased Venice's military forces again, with the deployment of landing corps composed of thousands of men. However, the numbers reached in the final years of the Cretan War were never equalled, and rarely totalled more than 16,000 professional soldiers at the same time. On the eve of the war against the Porte the standing garrisons in the *Stato da Terra* totalled 2,240 foot and 1,400 horse, while the defensive 'regiments' of the *Stato da Mar* numbered 6,670 regular infantrymen,[72] with some quotas of irregular light cavalry. Only the major fortified places had strong garrisons. In 1683 the standing garrison of Zadar numbered 300 infantrymen, while a mere 24 soldiers manned Pago, a little outpost in the Adriatic Sea.[73]

In January 1684, in the weeks before its entry into the Holy League, the Republic undertook the raising of a land force of 9,300 men.[74] In June, for the first action of the war – the siege of Santa Maura, today Levkas, Lefkada island, in Greece – the force available totalled just 8,000 Italian, German, Maltese, Croatian and Albanian infantrymen and four and a half cavalry companies.[75] One year later, for the upcoming campaign in the Peloponnese, more than 12,000 men were gathered in Corfu but the actual fighting force totalled 9,500 soldiers.[76] In May 1686 the strength increased to 13,060 foot and 1,240 horse, including auxiliaries from Milan; however, the troops available for the upcoming campaign were 8,953 foot and 1,130 horse, since the remaining force constituted the garrisons of Zakynthos and Corfu.[77] As the campaign progressed, *capitano generale da mar* Morosini sketched out plans to modernise the army entrusted to him, along the lines of the foreign standing armies set up in the second half of the seventeenth century. Some changes were cosmetic, such as the introduction of uniforms for the different regiments, but more fundamentally, he distributed the 9,000 regular infantrymen into regiments based on their national origin. The largest group, the Italian infantry, was organised into six regiments, totalling 6,200 men.[78] In 1687, at the siege of Nauplia (today Naufplio in Greece), the land force totalled 14,000 infantrymen and 800 horsemen.[79] In 1688 the Venetian effort

---

72 ASVe, *Senato Mar*, f. 650 (1684).

73 Luciano Pezzolo, 'Stato, Guerra e Finanza nella Repubblica di Venezia', p.94.

74 Pinzelli, *Venise et la Morée*, p.52.

75 BNM., ms. It. VII 2592 (12484), *Diario anonimo della guerra di Morea* (1684–1687), f. 38. This figure does not include an artillery company, a grenadier company, and the Greek infantry from Cephalonia, Corfu and Zakynthos, which increased the strength to 10,300 foot and 100 horse.

76 Diedo, *Storia della Repubblica di Venezia*, Vol. III, p.369.

77 ASVe, *Senato dispacci Provveditori di terra e di Mare, Dispacci*, b. 1249, d. 36, dated 27 May 1686. In detail they were 3,234 from Brunswick, 2,202 Saxons, 2,154 from Milan, 220 Neapolitans(?), and 4,638 *oltramarini*, Italians, Corsicans and German *Oltramontani*.

78 Del Negro, 'Il Leone in Campo', p.329.

79 ASVe, *Senato dispacci Provveditori di terra e di Mare, Dispacci*, b. 1249 (1687), f. 1, ff. 390.

63. Count Otto Wilhelm von Königsmarck (1639–1688), portrayed by David Klöcker Ehrenstrahl, Nationalmuseum, Stockholm). See image commentaries for more information.

produced the considerable field strength of 15,874 men,[80] deployed at the costly siege of Negroponte of Euboea (today Chalkis, in Greece), but this force included a significant percentage of sailors and even armed oarsmen, employed as additional besieging manpower in the final phase of the campaign.[81] One year later the outbreak of the War of the League of Augsburg (1688–97) represented the turning point not only for the Imperial offensive against the Porte, but also for the Venetian strategy in Greece, due to the growing difficulty of enlisting further German mercenaries. For the campaigns of 1689 Francesco Morosini could deploy just 11,248 soldiers from the mainland and overseas domains,[82] while on the Bosnian border the professional force consisted of 4,000 men supported by local militia and irregulars.[83] Between 1690 and the end of the war, every year Venice mobilised about 18,000–25,000 soldiers and militiamen, necessary not only for the war theatres in Greece and Dalmatia, but also to secure the unsafe Italian western border, threatened by the passage of the armies that faced each other in the War of the League of Augsburg.

Infantry

In the early seventeenth century, troops began to be classified by nationality. The infantry was divided into three broad categories: Italians, in other words the subjects of the *Stato da Terra*, or recruits from the Italian peninsula with the permission of local governments; the *oltramontani* (from beyond the Alps) which included the *Alemanni* (Germans), Swiss, Grisons, Dutch and the French as a separate category; and finally, the *oltramarini*, namely the subjects of the eastern Adriatic domains and Greek islands.[84] In Venetian sources, the *oltramarini* are occasionally referred to as *nazionali*, while Italians and *oltramontani*, when they were not hired contingents or auxiliary corps, were designated *truppe particolari* (particular troops), *provvisionate* (salaried), or even *marcoline*. Overall, infantry units were organised by employment, and although the *oltramontani*, especially the Swiss, despised service aboard the fleet, all troops played a dual role of ground infantry and amphibious landing force. The intricate Venetian military organisation necessitated further

80 *Ibid.* (1688), f. 1, ff. 401–412

81 Diedo, *Storia della Repubblica di Venezia*, Vol. III, p.407.

82 ASVe, *Savio alla Scrittura*, f. 1, ff. 478. As for the dragoons of the *Estado de Milan*, see in *Wars and Soldiers in the Early Reign of Louis XIV*, *Volume 4 – The Armies of Spain 1639–1688* (Warwick: Helion & Company, 2021), pp.241–242.

83 ASVe, *Savio alla Scrittura*, f. 1, ff. 479.

84 See Piero Del Negro, 'Venezia e gli Oltramarini nelle guerre di Candia e di Morea', in *Mito e Antimito di Venezia nel bacino adriatico, secoli XV–XIX*; Rome, 1997, p.324.

64. Portrait of the *oltramontane* Colonel Bartolomeo Manganoni, from Bergamo, by Fra' Galgario, alias Vittore Ghislandi, 1693 (Musèe des Beaux Arts of Narbonne). See image commentaries for more information.

distinction between new units and corps formed by the *provveditori*, and those formed by other commanders in the course of a campaign. These corps commonly joined mixed companies of *oltramarini*, but some also joined Italians and *oltramontani*. In such cases, these units were ad hoc fighting corps, classified as *battaglioni* (battalions), a word identifying a seventeenth-century battle formation. The Venetians used this term interchangeably, since this allowed a more flexible use of the infantry.

Enlistment provided further and particular divisions among troops. The first category consisted of corps recruited directly by the government under licensed colonels. In such cases, the commander with his captains or professional recruitment agents directly enlisted soldiers. As indicated in their contract, these recruits were gathered in the *Stato da Terra*, where they received weapons and equipment and were usually assigned to Venetian officers. Soldiers from the exterior could also be assigned to the garrisons, marching from the mainland to Dalmatia, or sailing to Greece. Regardless of their origin, enlistment in the army entailed that soldiers were naturalised as Venetian subjects. This recruitment method included all the Italian troops, the *oltramarini*, and some of the foreign troops like the Swiss, the Grisons, and the French before 1669. The struggle for Crete profoundly changed the Venetian military. The original structures of the army transformed into an organisation directed by professional officers paid by the government. The new models initiated changes regarding traditional recruitment methods. During this period, infantry became specifically defined and divided according to the men's province of origin: national Italians (subjects of the Republic), foreign Italians (including Corsicans), Germans, Swiss-Grisons, and *oltramarini*.

Since the sixteenth century, Venice frequently resorted to hiring foreign mercenaries – comparable to modern contractors – already organised, equipped, and ready for battle. This process continued seamlessly in the new century.[85] Agreements signed with the cantonal authorities regulated

85 Between 1616 and 1644 Venice hired 27 infantry regiments through various capitulations. Almost half of these – 13 regiments – came from Switzerland, five regiments were hired from the Netherlands, four were *Alemanni* (Germans), three from the Grisons, one from France, and one was an English regiment under Colonel Patton. The latter appeared only in the battle order of 1620. The emergency caused by the Cretan War pushed the Republic to seek further troops outside of Germany and Switzerland. This also happened in 1645 when Venice hired two

Venetian contracts with Swiss and Grisons. Until the advent of Louis XIV, however, the 'market of soldiers' from Germany and France flourished, especially since negotiations could be directly conducted with the colonels-entrepreneurs. Given their complete autonomy, these 'warlords' recruited the soldiers, managed their equipment, and handled any other concerns. Until the 1640s the formation of a regiment was akin to a commercial enterprise, with many colonels acting as specialised entrepreneurs. The commander's fame, especially when he had served in Flanders, Germany, or Hungary, conditioned the contract in terms of number of men, and naturally his salary. Thus, many of the colonels in Venetian service could be considered veterans, and they were granted privileges. Eventually, specific agreements with the local governments replaced private, direct negotiations. Once assured of payment, whole officered regiments were transferred to Venice. Institutional relations slowed the acquisition of troops, and after 1688 the League of Augsburg diminished the availability of mercenary soldiers of this 'free market'. Nevertheless, mercenary regiments raised by private colonels did not disappear in the Venetian army.

The second category consisted of corps hired from foreign states, usually from Germany. These soldiers already served under a major staff, completely equipped and ready for deployment. In these instance, service conditions were very different, because their governments could require their return when the campaign finished. Furthermore, these corps could become very expensive when contracts called for an amount of money to be paid for each dead recruit. Additionally, their governments established a series of compensation payments to protect troops against unexpected events, namely delayed salaries once the corps entered a campaign.

Troops of the Italian allies represent the last component of the Venetian army. Italian contingents are usually registered in the sources as *truppe ausiliarie* (auxiliary troops). Similar to hired contingents, they were maintained by their states of origin, and in most cases carried out the important role of landing troops in accordance to Venetian strategy. The participation of allied infantry in Levantine campaigns remained contingent upon their state of origin's foreign policy. Consequently, these policies often changed and depended upon their state's rapport with Venice. Like the mercenary hired corps, special agreements were negotiated before providing these soldiers, and could be deployed to different war theatres or on the respective fleet. This was the case of the Papal, Tuscan, and Maltese infantry. Unlike the other two categories, auxiliary soldiers spared the Republic from the cost of recruitment and equipment, and in some cases their maintenance in winter quarters, since they returned to their country at the end of a campaign. This was a half-advantage, considering that the Papal and Tuscan contingents rarely continued a campaign beyond the first week of September, and only the Maltese stayed longer. Consequently the terms of

French regiments under the colonels Dumesnil and Beaucastel, and two years later the Walloon regiment of the Count of Longueval. See Mugnai, *The Cretan War*, p.246.

formal alliances did not always bring significant savings, and these benefits maintained a degree of uncertainty.[86]

Until the mid seventeenth century the *compagnia* (company) formed the basic administrative as well as the tactical infantry unit. A small unit of companies were commanded by a single captain or lieutenant to form larger corps, and larger units of five, 10, or more companies formed the *reggimento* (regiment). These large units were usually organised for operational purposes on campaign. As in other contemporary armies, the term 'regiment' was an elusive concept that was occasionally defined as companies gathered for a single campaign. Since soldiers were quickly quartered in the garrisons and on the fleet, the 'regiments' usually dissolved. In several cases until the second half of the century, actual regiments exclusively consisted of foreign corps recruited or hired outside the Venetian state. Temporary aggregations of companies endured and proved practical, especially for Venetian national troops who often formed the bulk of the landing force.

Regardless of origin or conditions of recruitment, most Venetian regiments committed to a few years of service. In several cases the government decided on reductions and then, in addition to the units already regimented, the Senate maintained a number of independent companies from the licensed or reformed larger units. This system continued into the Cretan War. During this conflict infantry units were referred to as *reggimenti a piedi* (regiments of foot) for the first time. However, as discussed earlier, these units were still temporary aggregations of companies under a single commander for tactical purposes, but the presence of foreign mercenaries, organised in regiment-sized corps, introduced new principles to the Venetian military organisation. The formation of regiments in the modern sense, namely an administrative unit that joins several companies together, dates back to late 1680s. It is probable that the emergence of a permanent regiment-size unit was favoured by the financial crisis experienced by the Republic towards the end of the century. The scarcity of resources may have favoured an option that was de facto a forced choice, given the ever-increasing prices needed to enlist mercenaries. Or else, this transitional phase was dictated by the political design to ensure the Republic had a standing army that would allow it to assimilate the nobility, and include them in the career of arms as had already happened with the fleet. However, this process was very slow. The practice of merging infantry companies in temporary regiments even continued until the last years of the seventeenth century. Yet, the wide distribution of infantry in garrisons and the fleet did not favour the birth of permanent regiments. This dispersion of forces prompted the government to continue

86 In this regard the Maltese contribution should be noted, especially given the resulting disputes regarding contribution precedents and battle order. Despite these constraints, Malta remained a faithful ally until the end of the war and contributed galley squadrons and effective landing infantry regiments. In the spring of 1684, together with the Maltese, the Holy See was the first Italian state to send an auxiliary contingent to support Venice, shortly followed by Tuscany, Parma, and Piacenza. One year later the King of Spain provided auxiliary troops from Milan and Naples. In 1687 Genoa joined the allies, but only contributed galley squadrons.

the traditional scheme. It is no wonder then that a French officer in Venetian service, Monsieur de la Haye, wrote that the infantry was usually shared in *compagnie franche* (free companies) for garrison duties in peacetime and in war.[87] A muster roll dating to 1701 concerning the *Terraferma* listed 13 infantry regiments, together with still 135 free companies, amounting to 5,636 and 5,955 men respectively.[88]

Until the eve of the new war against the Porte, and even during the early campaigns, the Venetian government primarily continued its archaic system. Distrust of the Venetian nobility – especially regarding relationships with foreign military units and their novel methods – and the political culture of the city-state, which preferred not to entrust power to a single individual, encouraged the continuation of these obsolete military methods. Overcoming these tendencies happened slowly, yet the war provided a catalyst for change. In May 1684 Nascimben Gatti and Andrea Mirabello, who had already been promoted to regular colonels, became captains of Italian infantry regiments. In the same month, newly appointed Colonel Pietro Gabrieli took command of a German regiment, while Pasqual Maron led another French regiment.[89] Additionally, patents issued to Angelo della Decima and Giovan Battista Metaxa made each a colonel of two Greek 'regiments' from Cephalonia. Two years later, on the initiative of Captain General Francesco Morosini, the Italian infantry organised into six regiments totalling 6,200 men under the command of six colonels, two of which were already promoted in 1684.[90] The following year, the order of battle from Kalamata indicates five 'battalions' under colonels Maron, Graziani, Geremia, Catti, and Corbon.[91] These Venetian documents permit historians to tie the initiation of the infantry's structural transformation to that period. From 1687 onwards the Venetian infantry was identified by the regimental name of the colonel, which changed frequently or appeared classified under a different nationality.[92] *Oltramarine*

87 'Tout leur soldates que generalment est dans les garrisons de la Dalmatie … & ils n'entretiennent aucune armée sur pied, que celle de mer … Les Venitiéns n'enassemblent jamais de corps considerables & les distinguent en compagnie franches qu'ilentretiennent separéments … divisant ainsi l'authorité en plusiers mains qu'un seul auroit à la teste d'un regiment.' De la Haye, *La Politique Civile et Militairedes Venitiéns* (Cologne, 1669). The historian Gregorio Leti even offers a more drastic judgement. In 1675 he argued with some truth, but also with harshness and undeserved criticism, that 'In Italy, the Republic [of Venice] is the poorest state in the profession of arms. Admittedly, the Venetians can be invincible on the sea … but in campaign they value very little or nothing.' Leti, *L'Italia regnante o vero Nova descritione dello stato presente di tutti prencipati e repubbliche d'Italia*: Rome, 1675, p.318.

88 Del Negro, 'Francesco Morosini Capitano Generale da Mar', p.34.

89 Cited in Alessandro Locatelli, *Racconto historico della veneta guerra in Levante diretta dal valore del Serenissimo Principe Francesco Morosini …* (Venice, 1691), p.27.

90 Italian infantry regiments *Moron, Catti, Maraba, Jeremiae, Graziani e Magnani*.

91 Vincenzo Coronelli, *Memorie Istoriografiche della Morea riacquistata dalle Armi Venete* (Venice), 1687, p.30.

92 The inventory of the *Inquisitori sopra l'amministrazione dei pubblici ruoli* in ASVe contains the oldest documents concerning the regimental history of the Venetian infantry: the regiments

units continued to be, more or less, temporarily assembled until the final stages of the conflict. The first records of a standing infantry regiment of *schiavoni* date back to March 1687, when a regiment was formed in Dalmatia under Colonel Mitrovich. One month later this unit, along with other troops, embarked for Negroponte.

Although Venetian policy was inspired by more modern principles, with the war of 1684–99 the scenario of the Cretan War reappeared, as it was the international market that allowed Venice to arm a contingent capable of facing the Ottoman enemy on campaign. Whether he was formerly a Senate-appointed officer or a mercenary contractor, after 1690 the rank of colonel acquired a relatively significant military position. The growing importance of colonels is not matched by a definitive regulation of units and notwithstanding adaptation to modern organisational forms, the number of soldiers within the regiments varied by tens of men. In 1662 the Senate had established the Italian infantry regiments to eight companies,[93] each composed of:

1 *capitano* (captain)
1 *tenente*
1 ensign
1 sergeant
1 fourier (quartermaster)
1 *governatore* (muster writer)
6 corporals
2 or 4 musicians
84 infantrymen

In 1684 the number of companies of each regiment was increased to 10, but exceptions remained a constant feature. For a long time regiments varied from 6 to 14 companies and more, such as the *Veneto Real* regiment in 1698, which had 15 companies.[94]

Even before the war of 1684–99, the ratio of muskets to pikes was very unbalanced in favour of firearms, marking continuity from the end of the previous war against the Porte. The soldiers' dual nature as amphibious infantry and field troops rendered pikes impractical and ill-preferred. In 1684 at Santa Maura, the company of Captain Furietti fielded 54 musketeers, six grenadiers, and only 18 pikemen.[95] A year later, in the encounter on the plain of Kalamata in the Peloponnese, pikemen represented less than 30

of colonels *Bartolamio Manganone, Zorzi Mauromatti,* and *Corponese.* The first regiment was initially classified as *oltramontane,* but later the regiment was amalgamated with Italian companies and national recruits 'from the territory of Salò'. Even the *Mauromatti* regiment is registered in 1696 as *oltramontane,* but in 1705 it becomes an 'Italian' regiment.

93 ASVe, *Savio alla Scrittura,* 1685, f. 2, ff. 28.

94 *Ibid.,* 1698, f.4, ff. 819.

95 *Ibid.,* 1684, f 1, ff. 67.

65. *Schiavoni* (Slav) infantrymen at the siege of Modone, 1686. Copy after the Manfroni Manuscript. See image commentaries for more information.

percent of the infantry, including foreign units.[96] In 1686, well before the rest of Europe,[97] the Venetian infantry suspended the use of pikes in the Levant. Only some foreign or auxiliary units used them for the next few years. A regulation published in 1694 and dedicated to the *Savio alla Scrittura* Giovanni Francesco Morosini clearly states the definitive abandonment of the pike; it only reports the use of muskets with bayonets, and hand grenades. Even the detailed regulations for landing infantry,[98] published in Venice in 1697, does not mention pikes. This suggests the definitive abandonment of these weapons in the first years of the war. The war of 1684–99 also marks a transition from organisational models imported from France, whose mercenary officers had dominated the last phase of the Cretan War, to German models. In the *oltramontane* regiments, however, company numbers and strength continued to vary, becoming a persistent feature. For instance, the firearm-equipped *oltramarini* lacked a defined, established, company

96 Anonymous, *Relatione di tutti i progressi fatti dalle Armi Venete e Alleate nella recente guerra nel Levante, con un ragguaglio dei fatti accaduti in Dalmazia, fino all'anno MDCLXXXIX* (Florence, 1690), p.225.

97 The main Allied army of the Holy League, the Habsburg Imperialists, ceased to employ the pike on the Hungarian front in 1689, on the initiative of Markgraf Ludwig von Baden.

98 Antonio Sala, *La Pratica in Teorica del Soldato istruito in Mare* (Venice, 1697).

strength. In contrast, Greek infantry of the Ionian islands were organised into companies of 100 men.

A staff composed of colonels, lieutenant colonels, and *sargente maggiore* (majors) usually managed the Venetian infantry on the field, while the *provveditori* served as liaison with the government. However, state control over these units frequently alternated. In the corps directly recruited by the government, the Senate approved the appointment of officers, the Republic issued weapons and equipment, and service was indefinite, theoretically for a lifetime. Regarding the foreign recruits, certain obligations existed to ensure that soldiers could return to their natural sovereign. Dissolution of these units, however, required the full consent of the Senate.

During the conflict of 1684–99, Venice continuously looked for soldiers throughout Europe with little regard for their origin. Historically, Venice never considered the soldiers' faith to be of any particular importance. Already during the Cretan War, the Pope and the Italian allies deplored the presence of the Reformed Dutch, German, and Swiss; but Venice saw no reason to interrupt this flow of recruits. Until the end of the century Venice continued to recruit foreign troops using every available channel of supply. In 1686, with the French deserters from Monferrato, Venice formed a regiment of 800 soldiers. Similarly, in 1695, with the French deserters from Catinat's army, the government formed another regiment for the Morea. Intermediaries based in Livorno and Civitavecchia often prowled Genoese borders and managed the recruitment of Corsicans.[99] Like other Italian states, Genoa could not escape the Pope's pressure to help Venice in the war against the Ottomans. Moreover, the presence of Corsicans in Venice dates back to the previous century, and recruitment agreements were revised in 1646, 1648, and 1662. Still, the limits imposed by Genoa did not provide sufficient soldiers for Venice. Thus, the clandestine traffic of Corsican recruits continued until 1669. Between 1691–92 the Genoese government fixed the number of recruits to 1,000 , so as 'not to deprive the island of a remarkable amount of young people'.[100] This forced Venice to resort again to illegal recruitment from Corsican 'soldier contractors'. A regiment recruited in Corsica was sent to Greece in 1692, and another followed the next year.

In 1686 an agreement for an infantry regiment of 1,000 'volunteers' was concluded with the Viceroy of Naples.[101] This unit was in addition to the Spanish contingent already made available to Venice the previous year, but unlike the latter, soldiers and officers entered Venetian service as *truppa regolata* of Italian infantry.[102] The genesis of the regiment is followed step

99 For a focused study on the Corsican recruitment for Venice see Federico Palaeologo Oriundi, *I corsi della fanteria Italiana della Serenissima Repubblica di Venezia* (Venice, 1912). Although the book is a very dated text, this essay contains many interesting records, despite the author proposing several wrong conclusions.

100 ASVe, Senato, Rettori, f. 119.

101 ASV, *Segreteria*, 1026, *Avvisi*, *Avvisi di Napoli*, 3 February 1686.

102 Concerning the contingent for Venice, see Volume 4 of this series, *The Armies of Spain, 1659–1688*.

by step from the signature of the capitulation signed in Naples between the representatives of the Republic and the Viceroy Gaspar Méndez de Haro, Marquis del Carpio, who submitted the appointment of the colonel, don Vespasiano Scipione Giovine. On 26 February, about 20 days after the agreement, the colonel informed both governments that in Naples alone 300 recruits had been enlisted, 'all from chosen people', 'and within a month the regiment will be ready to leave for Venice'.[103] Certainly anxious to make a good impression, the colonel had taken care of every detail, including buying the cloth for the uniforms from some Neapolitan dealers. Days later, news arrived from Venice that there were no ships available large enough to transport the regiment to Greece, and therefore the sailing would be made by tartane. Finally, on 12 March, the recruits left Naples heading to Bari, where the Venetian ships waited for them.[104] In 1696 a regiment of dragoons raised by Colonel Vandreis joined the Venetian army in Greece until its dissolution in 1699.

In 1685 another particular contingent from the Kingdom of Naples was taken in Venetian service. The Senate collected auxiliaries haphazardly in its war theatres, such as the gang of Abruzzi bandits serving in exchange of pardon, who formed a loose unit of soldiers of fortune under the Neapolitan outlaw Luca della Rocca. Hired in 1685 with the consent of the Spanish-Neapolitan authorities, the gang was sent for three years to Dalmatia. Employed in acts of sabotage and plunder in enemy territory, these brigands provided an excellent service, at least judging from the reports of the Venetian officers.[105]

Although a foreign contingent could be raised in a relatively short time, sources of troops remained insufficient, and Venice was forced to turn to *Stato da Terra* conscripts to fill the gaps caused by the war's many campaigns. Because Venetian subjects were incorporated in the militia and the fleet, enlistments occurred also in the Republic's allied states,[106] but decrees also commonly recruited from the Venetian mainland. In the last years of the Cretan War the government enlisted 'volunteers' from the militia with the *decimazione* system, namely one recruit from every 10 militiamen.[107] A rank list from a seventeenth-century Venetian infantry company shows that 90

103 ASV, *Segreteria*, 1026, *Avvisi*, *Avvisi di Napoli*, 26 February 1686.

104 *Ibid.*, 12 March 1686.

105 Nicola Beregani, *Historia delle Guerre d'Europa dalla comparsa dell'Armi Ottomane in Ungheria* (Venice, 1698),

Vol. I, p.34. In 1691, Della Rocca deserted the Venetian army and consigned the island of Grabusa to the Ottomans.

106 Since 1684, and renewed until the end of the war, patents for the enlistment of soldiers in their states were granted by the dukes of Mantua and Modena, the Republic of Lucca and the Papal State.

107 It was an extreme and very unpopular decision, but the urgency of finding men to defend Crete did overshadow the traditional caution towards political subjects. Since 1660, the government resorted increasingly to recruits from the provinces of Lombardy, Veneto and Friuli, initially a few hundred, then 3,000 recruits in 1665. See Girolamo Brusoni, *Historia dell'Ultima Guerra tra Veneziani e Turchi* (Venice, 1673), Libro XVII, p.277.

percent of the soldiers came from central and Northern Italy. Furthermore, half of the recruits from the northern states were *Stato da Terra* subjects.[108] The remaining 10 percent came from Southern Italy and the surrounding islands, or lack specification.

Greek islands and overseas territories constituted another useful recruitment pool. Already in 1605–07, during the Spanish mobilisation for the invasion of the Milanese, Venice gathered 9,200 *milizie extraordinarie* from Greece, Albania and Dalmatia.[109] The enlistment of soldiers from the overseas domains increased after 1650. This occurred after some Balkan communities joined the Republic's side. Additionally, agreements with local leaders permitted the recruitment of Greeks from the Mani Peninsula and mercenaries from Montenegro. These were mostly irregular soldiers but provided a useful force. Moreover these mercenaries, like the *oltramarine* infantrymen, offered a significant economic advantage. Their salary was based on the money circulating in overseas provinces, which was worth less than the currency used on the mainland. During the war of 1684–99 the *oltramarini* and other irregulars represented up to a third of the Venetian infantry in Greece, and more than half in Dalmatia and Albania. An essential prerequisite was the Christian faith, given that an Orthodox priest, who was responsible for their spiritual assistance, accompanied them on campaign. Corfu was the main recruitment centre. From there the recruits sailed to the Lido of Venice, where they were examined, and if accepted assigned to the companies.

The overseas communities provided troops for frontier defences in the wars against the Porte. In this task they served like the coeval Austrian *Militärgrenze*. Though Venice deployed large corps of *oltramarine* soldiers, they performed with various results and could not always be used on campaign, given their unequal quality. Furthermore, the soldiers' various nationalities created a mosaic of infantry with different languages. Given their intended tactical purposes, and in some respects their military experience and training, Greek infantry troops were considered similar to corresponding Italian soldiers. In the early stages of the war *oltramarini* primarily referred to Greeks, and it was only later that this term included all soldiers recruited in overseas possessions. In this context, on 30 April 1685, Captain General Francesco Morosini prepared the first Peloponnesian campaign. In Corfu he organised his infantry troops by ethnicity, distinguishing 'four nations': Italians, Corsicans, *oltramarini* – ethnic Greeks – and '*crovati con albanesi e*

108 Rank list of the Italian infantry company under Captain Rovarelli, in 1687, compiled by the *governatore* Francesco Brascuglia in Palmanova, preserved in the Archiepiscopal Library of Udine; in Alberto Prelli, *Sotto le Bandiere di San Marco, le armate della Serenissima nel '600* (Bassano del Grappa: Itinera Progetti, 2013), p.143.

109 Stathis Birtachas, 'Stradioti, Cappelletti, Compagnie or Milizie Greche: Greek Mounted and Foot Mercenary Companies in the Venetian State (1400–1700)', in G. Teotokis and A. Yldiz (eds), *A Military History of the Mediterranean Sea. Aspects of War, Diplomacy and Military Elites* (Leiden-Boston: Brill, 2018), p.336.

cimariotti'.[110] Since the salary paid to the Greek officers doubled that of Croats and other officers native to the eastern Adriatic, the Venetian commanders clearly considered Greek captains on par with Italians;[111] Morosini reiterated this preference for the *oltramarini* several times, as when in 1687 he wrote that 'Oltramarine levies are in my opinion always the best, and more profitable than all the others.'[112] The Captain General had probably managed to amend his Greek soldiers from the intemperance of the previous campaign. It had in fact happened that at Santa Maura the 2,000 soldiers from the Ionian islands had started by looting their compatriots: in a single day they confiscated 20,000 head of cattle and Morosini, who needed the support of the locals, did his best to return the loot.[113]

Since limited regimental records exist, the history of these units during the war of 1684–99 becomes far more fragmented than that of other Venetian regiments.[114] Under the orders of Ioannis Ghica, the governor of the *oltramarini*, Morosini deployed a 'regiment' of Greek infantry during the first campaigns in the Peloponnese until the siege of Negroponte in 1688.[115] Especially since Greek subjects often served in the navy and the militia, records from the end of the conflict present difficulties in distinguishing these troops from other units recruited in the *Stato da Mar*. In the first years of the war, approximately one quarter of the Venetian infantry were Greeks.

In 1699 this composition dramatically decreased. Not even the Venetian conquest of the Peloponnese led to increased numbers of Greek infantrymen. According to the major Venetian contemporary historians, the new subjects of the Republic proved wary 'and prejudiced' towards the new rulers: 'reluctant to learn instructions and addicted to indolence, they fled their post … and had a great fear of weapons.'[116] In reality, the region's permeable border with the Ottoman Empire and the threat of pirates from the North African coast made it difficult to adopt a military policy similar to the rest of the *Stato da Mar*. Additionally, the fear of a return to Ottoman rule discouraged the population from taking an active role in the army.

---

110 The division based on ethnicity was previously proposed by Camillo Gonzaga, commander-in-chief in Candia in the early stages of the war of 1645–69. At that time the garrison included French, Italian, Corsican and *oltramarine* soldiers. See Del Negro, 'Il Leone in Campo', p.321.

111 Copy of the *Terminazione* by Francesco Morosini, in ASVe, *Archivio Proprio*, b. 40, c. 130.

112 ASVe, *Senato, Dispacci, Provveditori da Terra e da Mar*, b. 626, n. 125, dated 11 October 1687.

113 Pinzelli, *Venise et la Morée*, p.89.

114 Del Negro, 'Il Leone in Campo', p.386. Two 'regiments' from Cephalonia under the colonels Della Decima and Metaxa were recruited in 1684, but possibly they were later scattered in free companies.

115 Diedo, *Storia della Repubblica di Venezia*, Vol. III, p.402.

116 Samuele Romanin, *Storia documentata di Venezia* (Venice, 1853), vol. VIII, p.493. This historian also highlights the scarcity of the Peloponnese population, a mere 86,488 inhabitants not including Corinth and the Mani Peninsula. At the beginning of the eighteenth century, because of reforms introduced to promote immigration, the number of inhabitants increased to 116,000.

In some instances, volunteer aggregates reinforced the corps during campaigns. One such occurrence happened in 1686 when a 'company' from Ternis, close to Nauplia, left the Ottoman fortress to enter the Venetian service.[117] Venice also resorted to the Greeks as labourers for the field fortifications and, of course, for the information service.[118] However, the limits of the Republic's policy in the *Stato da Mar* emerged above all with regard to the Greeks. This for historians remains a key issue in all the wars fought by the Venetians. Though Morosini never missed an opportunity to praise the Greeks, always trying to protect and gratify them, and the Senate aimed to 'support [the Greeks] for a universal revolt against the Turk', the government was never touched by the idea that, if this goal was to be achieved, it would be necessary to abandon a 'colonial policy' for another that favoured the autonomy of the region, creating a federated and allied state.[119]

Mercenaries recruited on the Mani Peninsula provide a different example of the Greek presence in the Venetian army. This fierce population from the Peloponnesian eastern 'finger' had nearly acquired complete autonomy from the Porte. The coast offered few landing areas, but despite the presence of three coastal forts manned by the Ottomans, land access to the peninsula was easily defendable. Thus, geography sealed the region from external invasion. The *mainotti* became 'partisans' against the Ottomans and the Porte's other Greek subjects. They had established a political relationship with the Venetian government since the Cretan War, and during the conflict several hundred mercenaries left the Mani Peninsula for service in the Venetian fleet or to defend Candia. In 1684 a Maniote privateer named Stai Maneta held the office of vice-commander of the landing force under Strassoldo. In September the *consulta* discussed the possibility of raising the Mani Peninsula against the Ottomans, or at least gaining the support of the inhabitants, hoping that these could increase the number of soldiers for Venice.[120] With this goal in mind, Venetian emissaries sought negotiations with Limberakis Gerakaris (1645–1710), known as *Liberachi*, a leader of the Mani clans and a personality who became a key figure in the Peloponnese scenario. This influential Greek chief assured the Republic that he could provide more than

117 Beregani, *Historia delle Guerre d'Europa*, p.88.

118 Pinzelli, *Venise et la Morée*, p.102: 'The Greeks served as informers for the Venetians and sometimes for both sides at the same time. During the Holy League War, and in the following years, not only the Venetian commanders but also all local representatives maintained a correspondence with informers, often churchmen, in Greece, the Archipelago and even Constantinople. Furthermore, the fleet captains of all origins arriving in the ports of the Serenissima were systematically interrogated. Their reports, called *costituti*, formed a considerable part of the additional documents attached to dispatches addressed to the Senate. Few historians have examined this aspect to date.'

119 Del Negro, 'Francesco Morosini', pp.32–33.

120 Camillo Contarini, *Istoria della Guerra di Leopoldo Primo Imperadore e de'Principi collegati contro il Turco* (Venice, 1710), p.431. According to the author, Morosini had kept contacts with two characters, Paolo Macri and Nicolò Dossarà, and this time he intended to succeed in freeing the Mani Peninsula and placing it under Venetian control, as he had envisaged since 1658. See also Alessandro Locatelli, *Racconto Historico della Guerra in Levante* (Cologne, 1691), Vol. II, p.163.

66. To the left, a Croat light cavalryman or *cappelleto*; to the right, a *schiavone* infantryman, drawings of Luca Carlevaris, early eighteenth century (Collection of the British Museum, London). Balkan warfare was centred on the raid, which was usually launched as far as 50–60 km afield. Raiding parties generally comprised 40–50 horsemen and the same number on foot, but on occasion a large number of these small corps, under a *serdar*, would unite to make expeditions on particular targets such as fortified villages. The Morlachs made it a rule a never to engage in a fight unless there was a good chance of success.

4,000 soldiers in exchange for a colonel's salary for himself and the same pay as Greek 'national' soldiers for his men. These assurances never became a reality, and just half of this number arrived in Corfu for the campaign of 1686. Nevertheless, Liberachi proved to be a skilful captain, and his men showed excellent quality as light infantry. They managed to operate in small groups inside enemy territory, and their ability to blend in among the natives provided the main army with accurate reconnaissance regarding Ottoman forces. Additionally, Liberachi and his men proved useful for amphibious operations. In the summer of 1686, 1,500 Mainots along with another 8,000 regular soldiers landed near Cape Matapan, which forced the Ottomans to abandon the siege at the fort of Chielafà.[121] In spite of these successes, recurring financial crises plagued the relationship between the Greeks of Mani and their leader. In 1689 the Senate sought to cut expenses and ended its contract with the Mani mercenaries. Enticed by Ottoman offers, Liberachi eventually joined the opposing camp.[122] This incident occurred amidst a crucial moment in Venetian military policy, namely during the gradual and increased use of soldiers recruited from eastern Adriatic populations.

Venice employed Croatian notables as military officers and even occasionally as *provveditori*, alongside Greeks of the Ionian Islands. The fierce Croatian-Dalmatian and Albanian villagers needed few pretexts to engage in a war of skirmishing and rapine against Ottoman Bosnia, and several sources underline the ferocious nature of the endless border war. Croats, *Cimerioti*, and Morlachs formed bands of guerrillas led by their own chiefs. Their feuding culture accustomed men to carry firearms everywhere, for their own protection from domestic and foreign enemies. Coupled with their tendency to live by thievery and raiding, this meant that some chiefs had little faith in them. Girolamo Dolfin, who had succeed Girolamo Corner as *provveditore* in Dalmatia, observed that 'they are Christian when they will, and Muslim at their pleasure' and certainly Muslim chiefs could sometimes

121 *Ibid.*, p.386.

122 Less than a century later, Giacomo Nani compiled a handwritten complaint on the Venetian Republic's mistakes in its relations withe the *Stato da Mar*. Despite the unscrupulous behaviour of the Greek warlord, according to the Venetian patrician the Republic lost a unique opportunity by not adequately rewarding Liberachi in the early stages of the war: 'Nani warned with unusual passion that a new era opened for the ultramarine peoples and an embryonic national consciousness was born.' He recounted that the Ottomans never managed to erase 'the Greeks' innate principle of pride and the support of a Greek prince would have been infinitely useful to Venice in exchange for assigning him states and domains.' A means of solving one of the major problems in managing overseas provinces involved the separation between Catholics and Orthodox. Nani explicitly refers to patriotism as one of the most important debates of his time, wondering: 'who knows what the term is to begin the awakening of a nation?' And again: 'Liberachi could be Spartacus, the Roman Sartorio, he could be Masaniello of Naples, but the Venetians wanted to do everything for themselves and gain for themselves. They did not see that, before he agreed to pieces of the Empire of the Turks, they ate it one bite at a time.' Giacomo Nani, *Memorie manoscritte per servire alla istoria militare marittima della Repubblica*, III, cc. 78–80, in *Biblioteca Civica di Padova*; C.M. 139 III.

67. *Crovato* horseman, by Francesco Simonini (1686–1753), early eighteenth century (private collection). See image commentaries for more information.

be found fighting for Venice, and Christian irregulars for the Porte.[123]

Beyond Dalmatia and Venetian Albania, the Ionian islanders in Corfu, Zakynthos and Cephalonia manned galleys and served in garrisons. One strategy employed by Venice was to stir the Christian population of the Balkan Peninsula to revolt. This was a ferocious little war of irregular ambushing, raiding and seizing villages from the enemy, all tasks for which the Croatian and Morlach light horsemen were suited. These irregulars preferred surprise attack and ambushes to pitched battle against Ottoman forces, which resembled their own. These troops also accompanied units of the regular army mounting expeditions to seize fortified towns in Ottoman Bosnia, as occurred at Castelnuovo di Cattaro in 1687 and Knin in 1688. However, the selected targets were rarely farther than a few days' march. The Republic levied a 10 percent tax on the booty the Croats, Albanians and Morlachs acquired from the Muslims and Christians on the other side of the border.[124]

In the 1690s, increasing numbers of Croatians, Dalmatians, and Albanians filled the Venetian infantry's ranks. Hitherto, troops from these regions were designated *schiavoni*, *crovati*, *cimeriotti*, *perastini*, and other terms. With their growing numbers they became fully-fledged frontiersmen of the *Serenissima*.[125] In terms of numbers, the Albanians were the least numerous component of the *Stato da Mar*. They came from the small territories held by Venice: Scutari, Cattaro, Butrinto and also from

123 Tea Mayhew, 'Soldiers, Widows and Families: Social and Political Status of the Professional Warriors of the Venetian Republic (1645–1718)', in B. I. Waaldijk (ed.), *Professions and social identity: new European historical research on work, gender and society* (Pisa, 2006), p.98.

124 Catherine Wendy Bracewell, 'Uskoks in Venetian Dalmatia before the Ottoman War of 1714–18', in G. Rothenberg, B. Király, P. Sugar (eds), *East Central European society and war in the pre-revolutionary eighteenth century* (Boulder, Colorado: 1982), p.432.

125 Ennio Concina, *Le trionfanti et invittissime armate venete* (Venice: Filippi, 1972), pp.29–30. *Crovati*, *sciavoni*, Dalmatians, slavs: a series of largely interchangeable terms, at least in general, and classifiable as *oltramarine*. For example, the *oltramarini regolati del Peloponnesiaco* formed the lifeguard of Francesco Morosini, the Captain General of the Sea. According to Concina, they were 'a mixture of Dalmatians and Croats, Cimariotti, Morlacchi, Kaiduci, and Montenegrins'. Further research has supplied new knowledge, revealing that this unit was mainly composed of Greeks from the Ionian islands.

68. Albanian light infantryman, after a painted chest of the late seventeenth or early eighteenth century (private collection, Venice). See image commentaries for more information.

the Chameraria mountains,[126] but despite their small numbers the ethnic Albanians provided a significant number of soldiers to Venice.[127] Their presence in the field army is confirmed since the first campaigns, when a 'regiment' was formed with the free companies under Pietro Cechina. In 1689 a large contingent of 1,500 Albanian foot soldiers formed the bulk of the garrison in charge of defending the fortifications of Acrocorinth.[128] In the next decade Albanian irregulars continued to serve in the Morea, organised in bands called in sources *partitanti*.[129]

During the war, the soldiers from the overseas domain comprised up to a third of the Venetian infantry and were employed on all fronts against the Ottomans. As discussed before, organising these units took longer and was more unstable than Italian regiments. Tactical requirements dictated that these companies formed ethnic 'regiments'. The 'field colonels' were appointed by the Captain General or his lieutenant, and not by the government, and this provides evidence about the temporariness of these corps. In the summer of 1697, in anticipation of landing in Patras, the *generale dello sbarco* Count Otto Wilhelm von Königsmarck gathered the companies of *schiavoni* in a single 'battalion'. On the other hand, smaller numbers of Albanians remained divided into autonomous companies.[130] In March 1698 Gasparo Bragadin gave a report to the Senate regarding the *oltramarini* in the Morea. At the time, this term referred to all soldiers from

126 This term used today mostly by Albanians for parts of the coastal region of Epirus in southern Albania and Greece, traditionally associated with an Albanian-speaking population called Chams.

127 Lucia Nadin, *Venice ad Albania. History of Encounters and Secular Ties* (Venice: Regione Vento, 2014), p.77: 'Albanians were perceived as 'different', as 'the other', and could not be fully integrated artisan or merchant, but rather belonged to an antithetical world: that of war. Therefore, the Albanians also were the soldiers and the mercenaries par excellence.'

128 Érik Luc Guillaume Pinzelli, *La défense de l'isthme de Corinthe durant la période vénitienne (1687–1715)* (Université de Provence, Aix-Marseille – Premier Département d'histoire, 1996–1997), p.64.

129 Pietro Garzoni, in Biblioteca Querini Stampalia, classe IV, cod. n. 168 (424), *Diario del Senato tenuto da P. G. dal 1693 sino al 1732*, f. 25, 4–9 September 1694.

130 Beregani, *Historia delle Guerre d'Europa*, vol. II p.296. Ceclina, the valiant commander of the Albanian infantry, was killed in action during the campaign leading to the conquest of Patras in 1687.

the overseas domains. In his report, Bragadin indicated that these troops were gathered in 'two corps' under the command of Colonel Bossina, with Vito Luposovich as deputy commander, and Helia Damianovich, with Lindorichi as his substitute.[131] Even after the war, six temporary regiments of *kaiduci, panduri, crovati*, or *schiavoni* manned the *Stato da Mar*. Considering that in some cases these units comprised two or four companies, it is difficult to consider them as actual regiments.[132]

Nevertheless, the reservoir of recruits from the Adriatic provinces proved very useful to Venetian strategy. Specifically, their relatively lower salary offered economic advantages. Additionally, these troops served many tactical roles: landing troops, light infantry, and scouts in sieges or in the open field. During the siege of Santa Maura (Lefkas), the first major action of the war, the *oltramarine* soldiers were the first to enter the breach in the curtain. In doing so they lost one of their commanders, Captain Pietro Bissich.[133] On the eve of the 1686 campaign the Venetian battle order counted 1,200 *schiavoni*, divided into 17 small corps under the command of *sergente maggiore* Lauro d'Andria. A note specifies that they always occupied the vanguard position in the battle order.[134] During all subsequent actions in the Peloponnese the reports always mention that Croatians, Dalmatians, and Albanians were gathered into 'corps' or at the most, 'battalions' of 300–400 men. Their service was positive, since these troops distinguished themselves in all the Greek campaigns until the Battle of Argos. In the latter engagement the *oltramarini* formed the reserve of the Venetian army and performed the decisive counter assault. The campaign of 1688 registers the highest presence of these troops: 2,500 men under the command of their *governatore* Antonio Medin.[135] By the end of the bloody campaign these troops had lost almost half their number from casualties and disease.

Obviously, the *oltramarini* from Adriatic provinces also fought on the domestic front during the conflict and participated alongside Italian and auxiliary units in actions against the Ottomans in Bosnia and Albania. In 1688 during the conquest of Knin, the main Ottoman fortress in western Bosnia, the Venetian army employed Albanian soldiers and *schiavoni* from Dervis. *Oltramarini* of all ethnic groups participated in the inconclusive campaign of Crete in 1692 and Chios in 1695. In the last stages of the war, a 'regiment' appears in the battle order for the Venetian army on the border with Boeotia, a position held until the Peace of Carlowitz.

131 Locatelli, *Racconto Historico*, part II, p.172. The *provveditore* warned the Senate about the precarious state of the corps, diminished by desertions and not regularly paid. Thefts and other 'excesses' against the population necessitated a reaction from the command, and a few soldiers were executed. Additionally, fears that this commander would defect with his men, as Liberachi did, persuaded the commander to restrict punishments.

132 Del Negro, 'Il leone in campo', p.324.

133 Diedo, *Storia della Repubblica di Venezia*, vol. III, p.372.

134 Beregani, *Historia delle Guerre d'Europa*, vol. II p.2.

135 Diedo, *Storia della Repubblica di Venezia*, vol. III, p.407; in the last assault against the city, the *oltramarini* were given the position of honour.

69. An alleged portrait of Stojan Kankovič Mitrovič (1636–1687), chief of the Morlachs, by an anonymous artist (private collection). See image commentaries for more information.

Managing the army, especially the formation of temporary aggregations with mixed ethnicities, granted more variety to the Venetian *koine*. On campaign, since different companies assembled into temporary regiments and battalions, new mixed corps could be formed at a moment's notice. Sometimes this amalgamation also occurred with non-*oltramarine* national troops. In 1696, for example, three companies of *crovati* under Captain Pietro Marinovich joined the Italian regiment of Colonel Nicola Corponese, but a closer inspection reveals that many components of these companies were not Venetian subjects.[136] As often happened in other seventeenth-century armies, the Venetian military was a repository of men with various origins. Recruits from Ragusa (Dubrovnik), Trebigne (today Trebinje in Bosnia), the Mani Peninsula, 'Germans from the Empire', and even 'Turks become Christian' served as *oltramarini* alongside soldiers born in Dalmatia, Venetian Albania, and other Italians from Udine, Treviso and Bassano.[137]

In the early stages of the conflict, the *Serenissima* recruited 1,000 Montenegrin mercenaries alongside Venetian subjects from the Adriatic provinces.[138] These mercenaries, almost always self-organised and equipped by their leaders, were substantially 'soldiers of fortune' attracted by the prospect of looting. The *provveditori* of Dalmatia and Cattaro considered the Montenegrins' lack of discipline to be a major problem. Both Venetian officials complained that these soldiers habitually dispersed in search of booty, which in turn halted military actions in enemy territory. Additionally,

136 ASVe, *Inventario degli Inquisitori sopra l'amministrazione dei Pubblici Ruoli*; f. 511, c 715.

137 Prelli, *Sotto le Bandiere di San Marco,* p.109.

138 The Venetians had important ties and considerable support among the Montenegrins, with solid ground established previously during the Cretan War. In 1684, Venice strongly considered placing Montenegro under its own protection. In 1685 Montenegrin Metropolitan Rufim Boljević, 'the most loyal friend of Venice' as said by the Venetians themselves, had died, and after a brief tenure Vasilije Veljekrajski was replaced by Visarion Borilović Bajica. Borilović ascended to the throne as a protégé of his relative Patriarch of Peć Arsenije III Čarnojević. Previously a great supporter of Venice, after establishing contact with the Emperor's representatives in 1688, Arsenije became an important ally of the Habsburgs in the Balkans. The Venetian Senate was worried that under Arsenije's influence the Montenegrins would lean more towards the Austrians, and thus kept at distance Borilović as well. The course of the war did not always coincide with Venetian interests, and thus this two-sided politics resulted in an indecisive and irregular shape of the war in Montenegro.

when Ottoman resistance appeared more resolute, compelling these units to fight became difficult.

Similarly, despite 30 years of service in the Venetian overseas domains, the *morlacchi* (Morlachs or Vlachs) failed to arouse much admiration in their actions against the Ottomans. Morlach warfare was centred on raids, which were usually launched as far as 50 km afield. In the summer to autumn of 1683, before the Venetian adherence to the Holy League, the Morlachs from the territories of Zadar, Split and Klis had looted the neighbouring villages in the *paşalik* of Bosnia. It was not uncommon for these turbulent communities to make a private war against the Porte. Venice turned to them to raise semi-permanent forces at best, but the Morlachs became hated by the populations upon whom they preyed, and cohabitation was often difficult. Unpaid bands of Morlachs did not hesitate to plunder the villages on the Dalmatian islands, forcing the Senate to order severe disciplinary measures against the chiefs and their gangs. The *provveditore generale* of Dalmatia, Lorenzo Donado, was ordered 'to curb the ferocious inclination of the Morlachs with strict prohibitions, and to attempt to arrest some of their leaders' while the Venetian diplomacy did its best to face the Porte in an attempt to disassociate the Republic from these incidents. These events happened in a very delicate period, since the Republic had not yet made a decision about joining the anti-Ottoman alliance. However, in the long run the government could not ignore the fact that such disapproval risked alienating the loyalty of the populations settled on the frontier.[139]

In the first months of the war, the Morlach leader Stojan Janković enthusiastically offered his help to Venice. After some success against the Ottoman outposts on the border in 1684, the Morlachs performed very poorly during the raid against Castelnuovo and Signa in the spring of 1685. In this encounter, already overloaded with booty, they immediately routed after receiving news of the enemy cavalry's arrival. Thus, the Morlachs' poor reputation in the open field discouraged their use alongside regular forces. Instead they were allocated to militia duty, border surveillance, and sabotage in enemy territory. Yet their lack of military discipline rarely prevented them from defending fortified places. A turning point came with the appointment of Ardennes-born Count Claude de Saint-Paul Longueville as *governatore delle armi* of Dalmatia, in 1686. Selecting a class of authoritative and motivated officers, Saint-Paul was able to achieve good results.[140] Under him the irregulars performed with good results in the Makarsca region of Herzegovina. On the other hand this required diligence and an investment

139 Pinzelli, *Venise et la Morée*, p.49.

140 Locatelli, in *Racconto Historico*, p.113, describes Saint-Paul as 'an officer experienced in the Wars of Germany, having long been in the service of the General States of the Netherlands and participated in more than 60 sieges during his long career. He had been Lieutenant General to the King of Denmark and the Elector Palatine.' The initiative of Saint-Paul continued the path traced by *provveditore* Girolamo Cornaro in 1685, who had appointed – with the title of *Serdari* – four commanders from the Zadar province in charge of the troops. Note the similarity to the Ottoman term *serdar*, which means territorial commander.

of financial resources, and unfortunately the government's devotion to these units fluctuated, which ultimately produced poor results. In the winter of 1689 a campaign under the *provveditore generale* of Dalmatia, Alessandro Molin, failed after crossing the border. At the first encounter the Morlachs immediately fled after their first contact with the Ottomans, and the Venetian cavalry in reserve was quickly overrun. The government considered such failures proof that, without the help of regular infantry transported by the fleet, the Morlachs could not guarantee a successful campaign.

It has been rightly noted that the Adriatic regions were 'suitable to be held by a marine power who would counteract a powerful continental army … The winning card in the hands of Venice … against any Ottoman offensive was the combination of a small but well-equipped mercenary army, coupled with an almost unquestioned superiority … on the sea.'[141]

In hindsight, organising a militia on the border like the Habsburgs' *Militärgrenze* remained a possibility, but the opportunity eluded the government thanks to a lack of foresight and a shortage of economic resources. Moreover, a combination of further factors dissuaded the Senate from developing a regular militia on the borders. In fact, considering that the Venetians perceived the Morlachs as a mass of unruly marauders, the Albanians – *Perastini* and *Cimeriotti* – enjoyed a more positive reputation. Opposed to the Morlachs, the small but aggressive community that settled in Venetian Albania provided a core of determined and sufficiently disciplined warriors. Albanian soldiers fought like the other nationals during the Peloponnesian campaigns. About 600 infantrymen distinguished themselves during the siege of Nauplia in July 1686, where they remained in garrison until the following year. At that same time recurring fever epidemics, which afflicted all military campaigns in those regions, decimated their ranks.[142]

Cavalry and Dragoons

At the eve of the war Venice possessed a modest standing army, aside from the fleet. Yet, since the *Serenissima* had gradually reduced its cavalry in the mid seventeenth century, with the exception of irregular units consisting of *crovati* (Croats) and other subjects from the eastern Adriatic shores, the Venetian army significantly lacked mounted troops. The Cretan War increasingly focused on defending Candia, and this objective inhibited the need for a modern equipped and trained mounted force. Additionally, cavalry was the most expensive component in any European army, since a mounted trooper could cost roughly three times as much as a single infantryman.

Although the *oltramarine* light cavalry could efficiently fulfil tasks such as reconnaissance and surveillance along the rugged Dalmatian and Albanian

141 Eckhard Eickhoff, *Venezia, Vienna e i Turchi. Bufera nel Sud-Est Europeo, 1645–1700* (Milan: Rusconi, 1991), pp.87–94.

142 As happened for the Greeks, after 1685 many Albanians who were serving the Ottomans switched to the Venetian side, expanding the pool of recruits. In June 1686, during the early stages of the Siege of Corone, 500 Albanians of *Greek rite* were incorporated into the besiegers' army; Beregani, *Historia dell`e Guerre d'Europa*, Vol. II, p.11.

70. Venetian *corazze*: trumpeter and officer, regiment *Giona*, 1696–1700 (author's reconstruction after contemporary paintings) . See image commentaries for more information.

frontiers, the Greek theatre of war necessitated a large number of mounted soldiers to counter the unquestionably fearsome Ottoman cavalry. Among the countermeasures introduced to face this threat, the infantry widely used Frisian horses to defend against enemy *sipahis*. Nevertheless, carrying large numbers of horses to Greece remained an unresolved problem, considering that raising transport vessels presented further obstacles. Moreover, the Venetian experience in the Cretan War highlighted the horses' difficulty acclimatising to the Aegean and the consequent need to provide large numbers of reserves. According to reports, most of the horses became useless in a short time, or, as the officer of the Tuscan contingent, Captain Romolo Navarette, recounted: 'became only useful for the troops' dinner.'[143] Venice tried to remedy the problem by fielding Greek horses, but these were only of modest size and therefore less suitable for heavy cavalry. Similarly, as experienced and noted by Venice's Austrian allies, horses captured from the Ottomans were 'not accustomed to firearms, undisciplined in close order, and defective for charging.'[144] However, both Morosini and Königsmarck obviously considered mounted troops essential. Thus, the *Peloponnesiacus* urged the Senate several times to make agreements with the Papal States and the Kingdom of Naples to purchase local horses, considered more resilient than those bred in the Venetian mainland.[145] During the Cretan War Francesco Morosini had used the cavalry for a new tactical role, never hesitating to board horses on the galleys during his aggressive and spectacular amphibious campaigns between 1654 and 1660. Despite the effectiveness of these operations, in addition to Morosini's successful repetitions after 1684, cavalry represented an extremely modest proportion of the Venetian armies. Except for the semi-regular light cavalry, soldiers on horseback represented on average of between eight and 10 percent of the army strength; a particularly low figure when compared not only with the cavalry of the major warring armies but also to that of other Italian states.[146] On the Venetian side there was an awareness that the Ottoman cavalry was numerically superior, but on the other hand there was the conviction that the infantry could easily sustain a combat in the open field. Moreover, as was experienced during the Cretan War, the transportation of horses during amphibious operations was always a major problem. Hence the need for cavalry was reduced to very modest numbers, and in this regard Morosini even judged

143 Archivio di Stato di Firenze (ASFi), *Archivio Mediceo del Principato, Spedizione di Soldatesche in Levante dal 1684 fino al 1688*; f. 220.

144 K.u.K. Kriegsarchiv, *Feldzüge des Prinzen Eugen von Savoyen* (Vienna, 1876), vol. I, p.324.

145 ASVe, *Senato Mar*, Reg. 224.

146 David Chandler, *The Art of Warfare in the Age of Marlborough* (New York, NY: Hippocrene Books, 1976), p.30. Between the late seventeenth and early eighteenth centuries, cavalry represented about 30 percent of the French army, the same percentage as Austria-Hungary, Spain, and the German states. In England the cavalry was 27 percent; Russia 20 percent; Prussia and Denmark 40 percent, Sweden and the Ottoman Empire 45 percent. According to the same source, Italian states, especially Savoy-Piedmont, deployed a cavalry percentage of 27 percent.

71. Venetian cavalry standard dated to the late 1600s to early 1700s (Cleveland Museum). Golden Marcian lion advancing right, on an azure background, holding an open book with a customary inscription; crimson red silk faded outline with fringe. Overall: 87.2×87.2 cm.

300 horsemen to be sufficient to support 12,000 infantrymen.[147]

In the 1650s the heavy cavalry companies were combined into a single regiment of 800 men, later diminished to 500 in 1669.[148] Quartered in Verona, in 1684 the 12 companies still in service formed the regiment of *corazze* (cuirassiers). Each company comprised 40 soldiers and officers, and during peacetime, the staff was reduced to one colonel, one lieutenant, one adjutant, some administrative personnel, and two or three musicians, namely kettle drummers and trumpeters. For many years these horsemen provided border surveillance and armed escort for officials and ranked personalities on the Venetian mainland. The ranks of the heavy cavalry included some Venetian recruits and others from the Italian states, but most troops were Germans and 'Spaniards' of Milan who entered Venetian service through the many, often obscure, recruitment channels of the late seventeenth century.

After the new war began, the regiment was mobilised. But just a half-company left Verona for the Lido of Venice. During the first campaign, which culminated in the conquest of Santa Maura and Preveza, Morosini employed the *corazze* to escort the commanders.[149] Despite the lack of evidence regarding combat losses, it is known that the campaign decimated most of the horses, and large numbers of the cuirassiers contracted diseases. By the end of September 1684 widespread illnesses necessitated that all of these *corazze* return to Corfu for quarantine. This campaign marked the heavy cavalry's last action in Greece, 'having experienced that the cost of the cuirassiers in the Morea is considerable for the Public Treasury'.[150] Nevertheless, two heavy cavalry companies joined the Venetian field force in Dalmatia, where they participated at the conquest of Knin in 1688. In the same year, the whole regiment was transferred to Dalmatia.

As hostilities resumed between France and Spain in 1690, belligerents constantly travelled in Northern Italy. Thus the *Serenissima* deemed it necessary to form a second heavy cavalry regiment. Whereas the pre-

147 ASVe, *Senato, Provveditori di Terra e di Mar, Dispacci*, b. 1070, d. 12: 'With a corps of 10 or 12,000 soldiers and 300 horses, with the necessary provisions, it would not have been difficult to take the Castle of Lepanto, and then assault Corinth.'

148 The heavy cavalry company of 1648 formed two *corazze* (cuirassier) regiments: one Italian and one German.

149 Beregani, *Historia delle Guerre d'Europa*, Vol. I, p.179.

150 ASVe, *Savio alla Scrittura*; f. 28 (1685).

existing unit was divided between Palmanova, Zadar and Split, this new unit would be quartered in Verona. In 1696 the treaties of Pinerolo and Turin diminished the dangers along the border, and the two regiments, respectively under Colonels Lodovico San Bonifacio and Marquis Gerolamo Giona, were reduced to half strength.[151] At the end of the century the heavy cavalry companies in Dalmatia were often recorded as *carabini*. This kind of heavy cavalry was introduced in Venice in imitation of the Imperial *Karabinier* or the French *carabiniers*. These troops were trained to the use firearms on horseback, which became the specialty of the elite heavy cavalry.[152] At the end of the war against the Porte, the squadron of *carabini oltramontani* remained in Zadar under the command of Colonel Carlo Giussani. With a strength of 100 soldiers, NCOs and officers, this unit, also registered as an independent *oltramontana* company, formed the lifeguard for the *Provveditore Generale* in Dalmatia; it served there until its dissolution in 1705, when the rank and file joined the *Massa* dragoon regiment.

After the use of heavy cavalrymen was discontinued in the Morean campaigns, dragoons gradually replaced them. Relatively new in Italy, this type of cavalry was already introduced to the Venetian army in the 1620s, modelled after the dragoons of their Archducal opponent during the Uskok War (1615–17). The dragoons formed independent companies, which were combined into a regiment for strictly administrative purposes as campaigns coincided. Although sources occasionally mention a regiment of Venetian dragoons, the companies continued to operate tactically as independent formations until 1685. Gradual changes in the numbers of Venetian dragoons further confirm this attitude. For the 1684 campaign the Venetian 'cavalry corps' consisted of the aforementioned half squadron of cuirassier and 16 dragoon companies under the command of Marquis Nicolò Grimaldi de Courbon, an officer from Avignon who had already served the Habsburg Emperor, and was reputed as a 'colonel of great valour, having gave proof of his intrepidity and courage at Neistat' (Neustadt an der Donau).[153] In 1685 the

151 Both regiments returned to surveillance of the western border, which was often violated by belligerents in the subsequent War of the Spanish Succession. Under the reform of General Steinau in 1706 the regiments combined into a single unit.

152 In 1692, chronicler and writer Doroteo Alimari compared the different disciplines and uses of armour and weaponry, including the rapid changes related thereto: 'The cuirassiers [are] equipped with a corselet, pistols, and heavy sword. Their function was to provide morale, support, and furor by engaging battle with sword in hand while charging in close order without breaking their formation. Now of this type of horseman remains only a name, since these duties are rarely performed, no longer arming themselves with the cold weapons, but in their place they use the carbine, so that essentially there is little distinction from the carabineers except the name.' Cited by Prelli, *Sotto le bandiere della Serenissima*, p.94.

153 Beregani, *Historia delle Guerre d'Europa,* Vol. I, p.251. The Marquis de Courbon, having left his family at a very young age, had experienced various adventures before entering the Imperial army in 1672. He had served 15 years in the cavalry, distinguished himself at the Battle of Kalhenberg in the regiment *Castell*, then during the first siege of Buda the following summer. Like other foreign aristocrats, Courbon had entered Venetian service as a volunteer.

Above and facing page: 72. Venetian dragoons in 1686, probably regiment *Courbon*; copies after the Manfroni Manuscript. They wore a French dragoon-style uniform comprising red coat with yellow facing and lining, and slouch hat with a red St Mark lion on the frontal side.

Marquis received the patents to enlist a regiment of 'German' dragoons with a strength of five companies of 100 men each. The recruits were assembled in San Nicolò al Lido. When Courbon embarked in June with four companies already on board, he had to leave behind his associate Baron de Colombier, the regiment's sergeant major, in order to assemble the missing 30 men of the last company.[154]

For the first campaign of the war, the total number of dragoons rose to about 600 men and increased to 800 in 1686. Like the cuirassiers, the dragoons also had to struggle against the loss of horses. During the siege of Nauplia in 1686 the dragoon squadron 'had very weakened horses from their assiduous employment and the scarcity of fodder. The horses remained almost completely disabled, and it was necessary to permit refreshing them on the island of Hydra.'[155] However, the dragoons' horses were less expensive, and indigenous horses could also be employed for some duties. The Marquis de Courbon managed these affairs. He displayed remarkable organisational skills by creating an efficient supply network of remounts, gathering horses each spring and delivering them to the recruits, personally leading them from the

154 Biblioteca del Museo Correr BMC, Venice, ms. Donà dalle Rose n. 428, dossier n. 1, '*Copia 1684, 23 decembre in Pregadi* and ASVE, *Senato da mar*, Reg. 151 (1685), f. 47 (15 March), 136 (27 May), and 205 (21 July).

155 Beregani, *Historia delle Guerre d'Europa*, Vol. II, p.40.

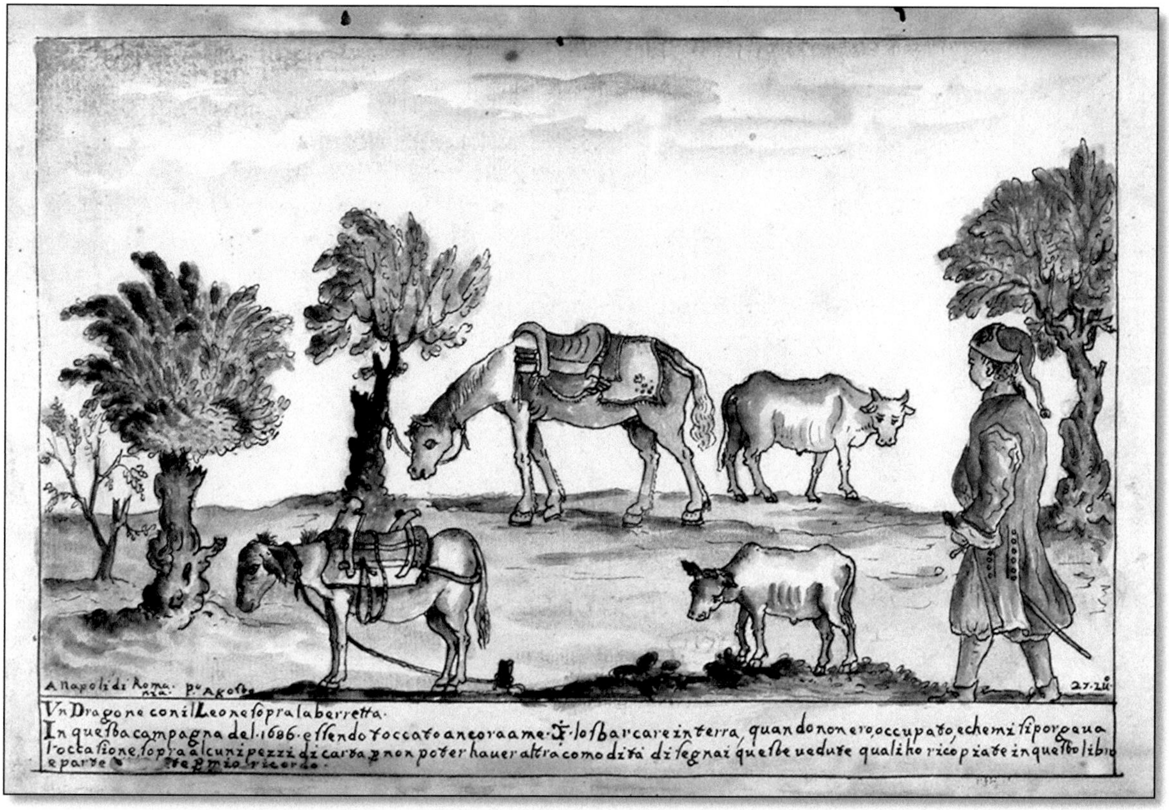

Venetian Lido to Greece.[156] The dragoons participated in all major actions in the Peloponnese until the end of the war. In the summer of 1685, the Marquis de Courbon and 200 dragoons escorted the long-awaited supplies to the Venetian camp. At Calamata, two 'little squadrons' were deployed to the left wing of the Venetian army, and they were involved in the battle fought on 1 September 1685. *Sergente Maggiore di Battaglia* Giovanni Magnano commanded them during this engagement, 'with the fire of muskets that left many enemies extinct on the ground'.[157] In May 1686 the dragoons fought against the Ottoman relief corps at Navarino Nuovo. Deployed at the forefront of the Venetian defensive line, a sudden onslaught of Ottoman *sipahis* overwhelmed and jeopardised the dragoons. Given their service, the Venetians generally regarded the dragoons as satisfactory; however, during the siege of Modone in June 1686, records indicate an increased number of desertions.

The able pen of the historian Nicola Beregani also provides valuable information about the soldiers' actual provenance:

> The dragoons … are mostly hired from the boundaries of Geneva, and in the provinces adjacent to France, accustomed to ordinary pillaging and desertion. Although well paid, they fled daily from the Campo … but the Greek peasants

156 *Ibid.*, Vol. II, p.2.

157 Beregani, *Historia delle Guerre d'Europa*, p.295.

> arrested them, sentenced some to punishment, and others remained in chains and were sent to the oar on the galleys.[158]

Despite these drawbacks the dragoons and their colonel performed valorous actions which earned them distinction during the siege at Nauplia in 1686, where they repulsed several enemy sorties. In July 1687 the horses' chronically poor state did not prevent de Courbon from leading his dragoons in a charge during the battle fought in front of Patras: '[the dragoons,] their swords still hot for the *sipahìs*' blood, charged against the enemies, killing many of them in a cruel massacre by sword and bayonet.'[159] The allied camp mourned the loss of the brave and able de Courbon after he died from disease during the siege of Negroponte. By the end of the campaign, further casualties had taken their toll. The entire dragoon corps had been reduced to little more than 500 men.[160]

In the 1690s new regiments were raised for Greece and Dalmatia. In 1696 there were six regiments in the Morea, quartered between Argos, Mistra and Nixi. The organisation mirrored the heavy cavalry, with a minimum of five companies forming a regiment. Yet the strength of a single company was established at 50 men. The overall strength, however, varied considerably. In the spring of 1696 regiment *Fenicio* (formerly *Courbon*), comprised seven companies with 230 dragoons; regiment *Vandreis* had three companies with just 96 men; regiment *Strel* five with 216; regiment *Gualtieri* six with 249; regiment *Onigo* five with 209; regiment *Lasso* four with 209. There were also two dismounted free companies with 127 dragoons and a further 160 men from regiment *Massa*, which was quartered in Dalmatia.[161] Overall there were in Greece 1,496 dragoons. One year later this force had decreased to 1,447 divided into five regiments.[162] As in the heavy cavalry, officers and soldiers belonged to various nationalities. Among the officers there were Germans, French, Corsicans and Italians from various states. Dragoons from regiments *Onigo*, *Gualtieri* and *Strel* participated at the Battle of Argos on 6 August 1695, playing a decisive role in the Venetian victory.

Between 1699 and 1700 the dragoons in the Morea were finally joined into two regiments under the command of Colonels Brandis and Municasa. A third dragoon regiment served in Dalmatia under Colonel Giovanni Massa.

For centuries Venetian light cavalry was identified with the *cappelletti* horsemen, named for the small cloth headdress typical of Venetian subjects in Dalmatia and Croatia. The position of *provveditore* for the light horses and administrator of the Dalmatian people was established in the second half

158 *Ibid.*, p.30.

159 *Ibid.*, p.295; Beregani continues: 'Courbon, who surveilled the flank, realised the excessive furor of his [dragoons], which had advanced out of control in hopes of plundering the Turkish camp, and then ordered Lieutenant Cungy to recall them.'

160 Pfister, *Der Krieg von Morea*, p.148.

161 ASVe, *Senato, Dispacci, Provveditori di Terra e di Mar*, b. 847, d. 40 (15 July 1696), and b. 1131, d. 37 (September 1696).

162 Ethniki Bibliothiki tis Ellados (National Library of Greece), Nani manuscript, n. 3917, f. 130.

of the sixteenth century. The *provveditore*'s subordinates included *cappelletti* and *stradioti* horsemen, the latter of Albanian or Greek ethnicity. In the seventeenth century the term *cappelletto* eventually identified all lightly armed cavalry troops from the Balkans and was sometimes associated with the term *crovati a cavallo* (Croats on horseback). The term *stradiota* had disappeared before the middle of the century, and was replaced by *cimeriotto* to designate soldiers of Albanian origin. In peacetime the Republic maintained 1,500 light cavalrymen in service. These troops were organised into companies of 50 men each and largely assigned to garrisons in Dalmatia, Albania and the Venetian mainland, especially in Palmanova where they even served as invaluable military police for capturing deserters. These troops often performed this task with excessive zeal and rarely reported that their prisoners were alive.[163] If cuirassiers and dragoons derived from various nationalities, the light cavalry were even more diverse. In 1690 a garrison company in Split was generally comprised of Croatian soldiers and Slavs but also included Italians, Hungarians, Greeks, Albanians, and even a couple of Turkish Christian converts.[164]

The Republic conceded a salary to the commanders that also included a reimbursement for their horse, since these animals were a soldier's private property. This aspect had repercussions beyond their salary. Certainly, company commanders ran the horse market, and similar to other infantry and cavalry practices of other seventeenth-century armies, they derived profits. However, the strong link between the peoples of these regions prevented the abuses that normally occurred in these cases. Documents preserved in the Venice State Archive that relate *Inquisitori* affairs rarely report cases of embezzlement. On many occasions the officers allowed their men to sell the horses to other soldiers or to use salary deductions to pay off the debt incurred from purchasing a horse – a business risk far from insignificant, considering the possibility of losing the creditor or the animal in combat. The cavalry's wide variety of dress and weapons makes its semi-regular condition clearly apparent. Towards the last quarter of the seventeenth century some *cappelletti* units, and especially *cimeriotti*, used spears and round or square shields like their Ottoman enemies, but ultimately firearms spread much more quickly in their ranks than amongst the Ottomans. Based on their personal experience, the officers further varied their arsenal and tactics by adopting fighting disciplines that they considered more congenial and effective.

In the war against the Porte, Venetian commanders employed the Albanian and Croatian light cavalry in the difficult Greek campaigns. In late May 1686, anticipating the upcoming Peloponnesian campaign, 500 *schiavoni* on horseback awaited in Santa Maura (Lefkada) for other contingents to arrive. Croats and Albanians fought at Corone, Modone and Navarrino Nuovo. These troops also provided reconnaissance outside the besiegers' contravallation line. Other mounted light troops participated in the 1687

163 Prelli, *Le Milizie venete in Palma* (Udine: Chiandetti, 1988), p.127.

164 *Ibid.*

and 1688 campaigns, in addition to later campaigns that led to the conquest of Malvasia (Monemvasia) in 1690. During the 1696–98 campaigns, light cavalry from Dalmatia and Albania opposed Ottoman incursions into Attica. Obviously, Dalmatia and Albania served as the light cavalrymen's principal war theatre, where they were present in virtually all major encounters until the end of the conflict. They provided irreplaceable border surveillance and reconnaissance along the paths of those otherwise inaccessible districts.

Like the dragoons, the light cavalry records listed them as 'regiments' by the end of the war. In 1695 the *cappelletti* horsemen in the Morea were joined in a single regiment under Colonel Antonio Medin. In the spring of 1696 the regiment numbered seven companies with 313 men.[165] The Venetian commanders trusted the loyalty of the Croats, and usually assigned them sensitive tasks such as the role of gendarmes and close protection of the highest officials. In 1696 four companies of Medin's regiment were the only ones to remain active throughout the winter as lifeguards. These were the company of Captain Tomaso Medin assigned to Captain General Alessandro Molin, that of Lieutenant Colonel Michiel Slade to *provveditore* Agostino Sagredo, that of Lieutenant colonel Marco Medin to General Steinau, and that of Captain Felippo Pedemonti to the *provveditore straordinatio* Filippo Donà.[166]

In 1699 a general review of the mounted troops now included six 'regiments' of Croats garrisoned in Palmanova, Segna, Zadar, Split, Trogir, Novegradi, Klis, Traù, and Knin. The same document relates the presence of two *cimeriotti* regiments quartered in Cattaro, Perasto, and other nearby locations. However, their regimental strength was often unequal. The *cimeriotti* numbered a mere 245 and 229 officers, NCOs and troops, and only the regiment in Palmanova fielded anything near 500 men.[167]

Artillery and Specialists

Alongside the navy, Venice maintained proficiency in artillery. In fact, when compared to other sectors of the Venetian armed forces, the artillery received more resources regarding the technological development of armaments and staff training.[168] Even before the Cretan War, an event that marks a crucial step in the *Serenissima*'s military policy, the *Provveditore Generale in Terraferma* proudly stated that the Venetian artillery was 'the best equipped among those of any prince of Europe'. To urge the government to take action, his report also added that maintenance involved the consumption of '1,000 provisions, powder, bales, carriages, and other accessories'.[169] Actually, the detailed correspondence between the *provveditori* and the government clearly demonstrates the artillery corps' importance. An examination of administrative acts in relation to finances serves as a barometer for every

165 Ethniki Bibliothiki tis Ellados (National Library of Greece), Nani manuscript, n. 3917, f. 130.

166 ASVe, *Senato, Dispacci, Provveditori di Terra e di Mar*, b. 847, d. 46 (25 October 1696).

167 ASVe, *Inventario degli Inquisitori sopra l'amministrazione dei Pubblici Ruoli*; f 718.

168 Concerning the Venetian artillery, see also the 'focus on' contents in two parts published in *History and Uniforms,* Issue 0 (October 2015), pp.32–38, and Issue 1 (November 2015), pp.44–47.

169 ASVe, *Savio alla Scrittura*, b. 1 cc. 178–179.

political decision. In the late sixteenth century the government assumed direct administrative control of the artillery, which included military personnel, foundries, and workers involved in armament production. In the next century the artillery corps assumed an organisation that it maintained until the last years of the Holy League War. Each mainland and overseas province instituted its own company to man the fortress guns. More than a professional military corps, these were militias of salaried reservists who served as sedentary gunners and rarely participated in military campaigns far from their homes. Membership of this specialised force coincided with the typical peculiarities of artillerymen in all European armies. Their military career occurred entirely within the corps, and rarely did the artillerymen allow an infantry or cavalry officer to directly issue orders to them without graduating from an artillery school. In the Venetian domains the *scuole* recruited and trained artillerymen for forts and garrisons, which on the eve of the war against the Ottomans added up to 17 in the mainland, five in Dalmatia, four in the Ionian Greek islands, and one in Albania.[170] By the mid seventeenth century 121 officers and NCOs with 4,549 *bombardieri* were enrolled as *bombardieri provisionati* (salaried artillerymen).[171] These corps, also indicated in the sources as *compagnie bombardieri per il pubblico servizio* (artillery companies for the public service), trained recruits to serve 'in the fortress as in any other place where needed'.[172] From these schools were drawn officers and gunners for the artillery on campaign, which from the time of the Cretan War began to be increasingly distinguished from the bombardiers. In 1679, school reforms were issued for creating the *bombisti*, a middle class between sedentary garrison personnel and artillery troops for the army or fleet, especially for the mortars. This new type of artillerymen could provide reinforcements and replacements for the overseas campaigns.

At the beginning of the war of 1684–99, the usual shortage of soldiers in the garrisons did not correspond with the number of guns. In the late seventeenth century 183 cannons and mortars were deployed to the forts surrounding Kotor, a considerable figure if compared with the very small number of artillery personnel registered in the overseas garrisons: 221 *bombardieri* (artillerymen), 34 miners, and 31 other specialists. Other strategic strongholds had similar numbers. Corfu possessed an arsenal of 363 guns and mortars; Sebenico 143; Zadar 120; Suda 92; Spalato 87.[173] Overall, remarkable numbers of heavy artillery pieces in the Venetian arsenal remained a constant throughout the years. In the 1680s the arsenal held

170 In Italy there were schools in Brescia, Bergamo, Crema, Orzinuovi, Pontevico, Asola, Peschiera, Verona, Legnago, Padova, Treviso, Rovigo, Palma, Marano, Vicenza, Bassano, and Udine; in Dalmatia: Spalato, Zadar, Clissa, Novegradi, and Koper; in Albania Kotor; and in the Greek islands: Corfu, Cephalonia, Zakynthos, and Tinos. Together with Venice and Chioggia, the latter also provided gunners for the fleet, destined only to man the guns aboard the galleys and sail ships.

171 ASVe, *Savio alla Scrittura*, b. 1 cc. 189–190. The number considerably varied over the years, up to a maximum of 5,097 *scolari* with 720 *provisionati* in 1679.

172 ASVe, *Provveditori sopra le Artiglierie*; f. 48, ff. 2–4.

173 *Ibid.*

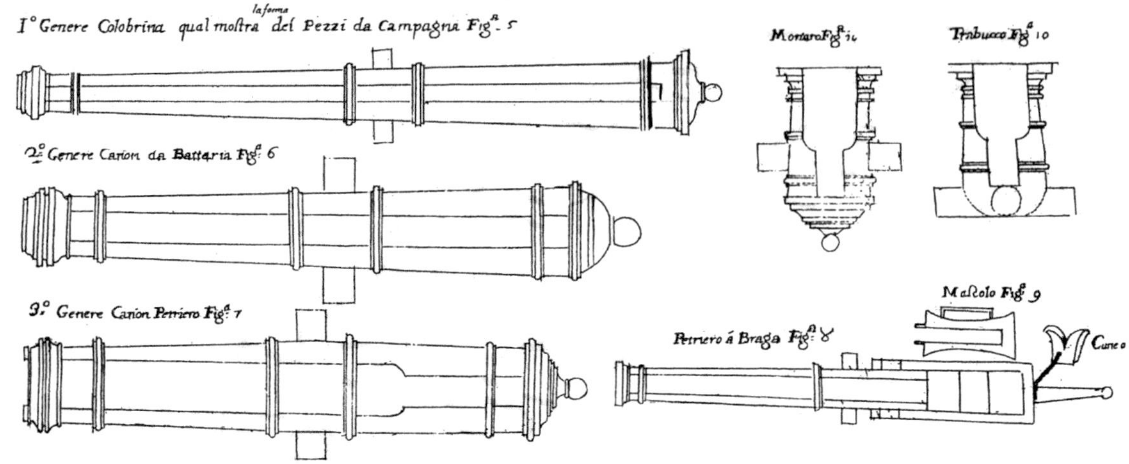

73. Illustration after Tommaso Moretti's *Trattato dell'Artiglieria* (Venice, 1672). This fine work presents the main calibre of the bronze guns produced in the Venetian foundries and employed by both the Navy and the Army. In Venice, the classification of guns and mortars within the general categories continued to be based on the simple definition of the poundage of the ball they employed. Thus a *cannone* of 30 corresponded to a *mezzo cannone*, a *colubrina* of 14 to a *mezza colubrine*.

2,461 guns, mostly bronze, and after the capture of the Ottoman arsenals in the Peloponnese during the Holy League War, this number further increased.

From 1684 to 1692, Venice pursued an offensive war in Bosnia and Greece, and this required an appropriate and modern artillery train for sieges and open field battles. As a result, the Republic's armies resorted to higher proportions of field artillery compared to the previous war. Additionally, Venetian commanders exploited the presence of the fleet. Naval artillery proved an effective support for both sieges and landings. The mutual use of naval cannons and mortars inhibited the formation of large batteries for campaigns. Until 1689 the Venetians rarely used more than 30 guns and mortars at once in any major siege. When a greater number of guns was needed, however, the fleet provided supplemental firepower. On more than one occasion, such as Negroponte in 1688 and Malvasia in 1690, naval artillery was landed and mounted on carriages. Thus the contribution of the naval artillery makes it difficult to identify and count the actual numbers of field and siege artillery, and it caused further confusion regarding ranks and responsibilities. One famous case concerned an explosion of the Ottoman ammunition depot in the Athenian Parthenon, which destroyed a considerable part of the famous monument. Accusations from all the European courts prompted the Senate to order an investigation. Though the incident was later clarified, the navy and army accused each other of being responsible for this debacle.

A roll dated to the 1690s shows the composition of an artillery company on campaign. The company staff included:

1 *capitano*
1 *primo tenente*
1 *secondo tenente*
1 *capo dei sergenti*
3 *sergenti*
1 *capo d'armi*
1 *capo conduttore*
1 *furiere*

3 corporals
2 drummers
2 *garzoni di marangone* (carpenter adjutants)
2 *garzoni di maniscalco* (smith adjutants)
2 *garzoni per il maestro dei letti per il cannone* (carriage maker adjutants)
2 *garzoni per il mastro sellaio* (saddle maker adjutants)
2 *sottofurieri*
21 artillerymen of the first class
56 private artillerymen, and 104 other gunners and drivers[174]

The war of 1684–99 significantly contributed to the development of artillery in campaigns. Yet by the end of the conflict its progress halted. The resumption of basic tasks related to the static defence of the scattered Venetian fortresses and strongholds resulted in the gradual decay in efficiency of the artillery organisation. After the war the artillery comprised eight companies totalling 1,623 men; by the early eighteenth century this number was decreased to six companies at half strength.

Despite this ambivalent scenario, the development of technical matters had a major centre in Venice. Together with Amsterdam, in the seventeenth century Venice was the largest centre of book production in the world.[175] This resulted in large numbers of treatises dedicated to military matters, which naturally included the artillery. Many contained detailed information on manufacturing methods, classification, ammunition, and field use in accordance with the calibres and their standardisation. A 1669 artillery treatise by Tommaso Moretti[176] presents Venetian artillery classification and the barrels manufactured in the Venetian arsenals during the final years of the Cretan War. The experience accumulated in this conflict accelerated the process of calibre rationalisation and the division of artillery into three classes according to their use. On the eve of the new war against the Ottomans these categories included field artillery, siege or position artillery, and naval artillery. After Moretti, other theorists like Sigismondo Alberghetti and his major rival, Antonio Muttoni, Count of San Felice, developed weapons and projectiles throughout the years of the war against the Porte from 1684 to 1699.

Before the 1680s, field gun classifications ranged from the *smeriglio* to the *sagro* (or *quarto di colubrina*). With a calibre of ½ lb to 1 lb, the *smeriglio* was equivalent to the wall musket. This weapon was sometimes mounted

174 ASVe, *Senato mar*, Reg. 188.

175 Venetian military theoretical production remained of absolute value to that of the rest of Europe and the other Italian states comparable to the Serenissima in terms of extension, population and armed forces. What the Republic lacked, as Piero del Negro points out, was the almost absolute lack of a military debate in the light of day, hence 'on the one hand, the karstic nature of some certainly valuable writings and, on the other, the almost always reduced breadth of printed reflections on military art.' See Del Negro, *Il Leone in campo*, p.341.

176 Before entering the *Serenissima*'s service as an *Ingegnero,* Moretti had served in the Imperial army and accumulated considerable artillery experience according to the doctrine of the major European armies.

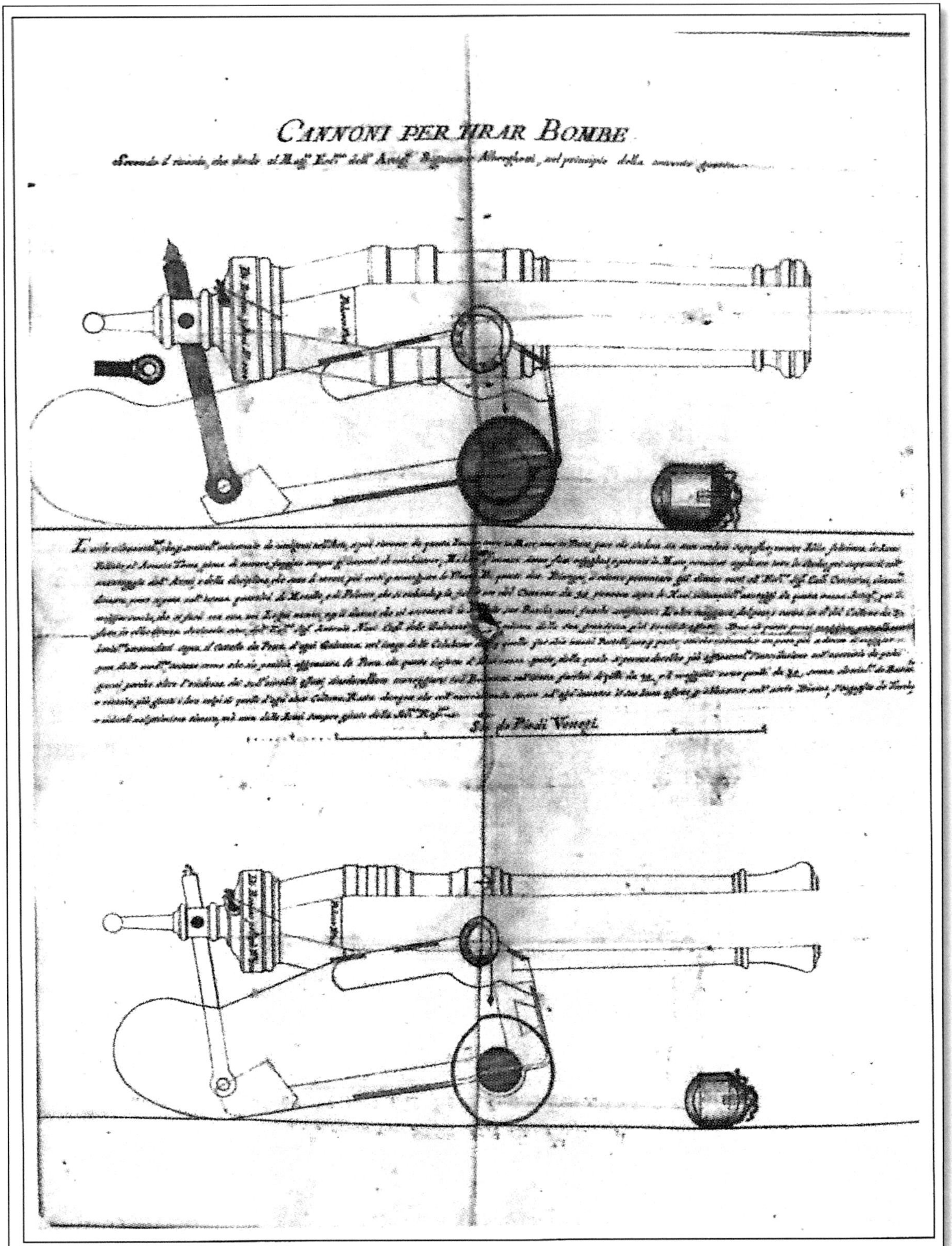

74. Gun for firing bombs, after the project drawings of the renowned artillery technician and caster Sigismondo Alberghetti. See image commentaries for more information.

on ships, but was mostly used in fortresses and occasionally in sieges as a precision weapon against single targets. The Ottomans experimented with this latter application with some success. Actual field guns included the 2, 3, and 4 lb *falconetti*, the 6 lb *falcone* or *mezzo sagro*, and the 8, 10 and 12 lb *sagro* or *quarto di colubrine*. Different lengths added further variety to these pieces, classified as *Ordinarij*, *Straordinarij*, and *Bastardij*.

Siege artillery included the larger guns, with the 16 or 18 lb *quarto di cannone*, followed by the 20 lb *mezzo cannone*, the 30, 40, 50, and 60 lb *cannone*, the 120 lb *doppio cannone*, and finally the 130, 150, or 200 lb *basilisco*. Mortars and *trabucchi* were used alongside these guns. This latter classification substantially resembles the other siege artillery and is only distinguished by the location of the handles: the mortars had them mid barrel while the *trabucchi* had them near the base. Aside from their use alongside siege artillery, mortars that fired new explosive shells – known as French mortars – were also successfully used by the fleet in the war's early campaigns. The calibres of mortars and *trabucchi* ranged from small 50 lb pieces up to the larger 500 lb. The *petrieri* with calibres ranging from 2 to 14 lb ended the list of guns. These were mostly used by the fleet but, when mounted on an iron carriage, they were also useful in coastal towers and small forts. In the mid seventeenth century some Venetian artillery officers deemed that 50 and 30 lb culverins were 'too heavy, long, and hard to manage, consuming much powder' for campaigning.[177] As a result, the 20 lb became the higher calibre field weapon used in the 1684–99 war, which unlike the former required 'less powder and a small crew to serve as well as to train'.

75. Venetian Engineer, 1680s (author's reconstruction).

At the end of the century the classification of Venetian field artillery still included 21 different kinds of gun, divided in eight classes: *falconetto*, *falcone*, *passavolante*, *sagro*, *aspide*, *cannone*, *colubrine*, and *petriere*. An arsenal that clearly bucked the trend compared to the rest of Europe.

The use of specialised personnel for construction and demolition of defensive works had long been a part of the artillery corps. In his 1669 treaty, Camillo Di Piccoli suggested that 'a well proportioned corps of engineers with hoes and shovels, well supplied with good ropes, wooden planks, axons, pontoon, accessories for bridges, and other instruments and weapons like

177 Camillo Zonta, *C. Z. capitan d'Artiglieria, opera non ancora d'altro autore trattata* (Venice, 1640), part II, p.3.

76. *Bombardieri Provisionati*, Kephalonia 1688–99 (author's reconstruction). The Venetian garrison artillerymen received red uniforms in the early eighteenth century, as confirmed in the Manfroni Manuscript, which refers the Kepahlonia artillerymen, either Venetians or Greeks, as uniformed in *vermiglio* (vermillion red). Possibly they already wore red coats in the last year of the previous century, perhaps those previously issued to the infantry.

iron balls, lights, nails, leather …'[178] should precede the artillery train. Also the presence of professionals in siege warfare, as well as pitching bridges and other engineering works, was firmly rooted in the Venetian army. During the Cretan War numerous engineers from the Netherlands served in Venice and other places in the Republic. In turn they taught a nucleus of talented specialists in the implementation of external defence works and explosives technology. Even excellent engineers arrived from France, such as the Besseti de Verneda family, already serving in Candia. In 1684 the son of Jean Besseti de Verneda participated as an engineer in the Greek campaigns and subsequently at the sieges of Corone, Chielafà, and Passava. Otto Wilhelm von Königsmarck also brought with him engineers from Sweden: Pierre Romagnal, and above all the skilled Major Tomas Boger, with a company of 200 miners.[179] Both were immediately enlisted. Among the Italian engineers, Giovanni Bassignani gained a good reputation during his service in the Morea.

The lack of engineers was one of Morosini's main concerns after 1687. Further aid came from the auxiliaries. Rinaldo de la Rue appears positively in the campaign reports.[180] He entered Venetian service in 1687 after serving as a *venturiere* in the Tuscan knightly Order of St Stephen. De la Rue distinguished himself at the siege of Negroponte in 1688. Despite the negative outcome of the campaign, he managed to break into one of the Ottoman 'towers' of the curtain, personally completing his audacious plan using explosives and protective gabions. Like many others, he died of illness before the end of the siege.

The engineer corps remained part of the artillery, and in addition to specialists included a small aliquot of other technical staff and adjutants. Venetian commanders resorted to the national infantry or, more often, the galley rowers when manpower was needed for digging. Foreign mercenaries were exempt from digging work, and the commanders only resorted to recruiting locals during the expedition in Crete in 1692. However, 'given that the villagers around Chaniá feared the reaction of the Turks though the shipment had failed',[181] the attempt had little success.

Guns and mortars were normally cast in the *Arsenale* of Venice. The most ancient Venetian guns lacked 'dolphin' handles, and are easily recognised by the absence of decorations. A few guns show relief decorations, but only the lion of Saint Mark appears on the barrel. Bronze artillery production for the army and fleet was managed by the *Arsenale*. The casting of bronze took place in the arsenal foundry and in other places in the immediate vicinity.

178 Camillo Di Piccoli, *Il Capo interrogativo al suo scholaro, ovvero breve esame di Bombardiere e Bombista…* (Venezia, 1678), p.12.

179 ASVe, *Senato da mar*, Reg. 152, dated 28 March 1686.

180 Rinaldo de la Rue is also known by other names: Rinaldo Buchett or Bouchet. This engineer was a protégé of the Grand Duke of Tuscany Cosimo III, and a friend of the Tuscan ambassador in Venice, Matteo del Teglia. De la Rue had come to the Levant after being invited by the Count of San Felice. Some chroniclers attributed to him the shot of 26 September 1687 against the Parthenon. Thanks to Érik Pinzelli for this notice.

181 Diedo, *Storia della Repubblica di Venezia*, Vol. III, p.452.

The most important one was the foundry of the Alberghetti family, whilst the carriages were built inside the Venetian arsenal, in the *carreri* (carters' workshops) located next to the artillery storage. There was also a 'workshop for models and compasses' where prototypes of machines, equipment and ships produced in the arsenal were designed.[182]

The arsenal not only produced cannons and ships but was also regarded as the 'Heart of the State'. This Venetian institution converged military production with all of its related activities. During the war of 1684–99 the Venetian arsenal worked at full strength and produced galleys, sailing vessels, and other minor ships. The escalated construction of sailing ships forced the Venetian authorities to modify the building where they were produced. This increased production also necessitated 13 new structures to launch the ships, and above all *squeri* (covered shipyards) to better refit the vessels. Internal manpower completed all these works: carpenters and craftsmen as well as casters and specialists in the production of gunpowder and flintlocks for muskets. Thousands of workers and technicians operated concurrently on different stages in the production chain, much like a modern factory. During the last quarter of the seventeenth century the average number of workers totalled 3,500–4,000 employees, a considerable figure especially given that about 100,000 people resided in Venice. Men primarily worked in the arsenal; however, female workers manufactured the sails. These women were placed in a separate building controlled by senior female employers. Several pickets and posts in the arsenal were manned by the *sciavoni* or *schiavoni* (Slavs), light infantry recruited in Dalmatia. Due to language barriers, this military police corps could barely establish relationships with the labour force. Other minor naval arsenals were active in Zadar, Lésina, Cattaro, Zakynthos and Corfu. The latter location also produced gun carriages.

Foreign Hired Troops

Increased percentages of Italian troops within the Venetian infantry during the last years of the Cretan War, and the subsequent conflict against the Porte of 1684–99, favoured the birth of a less fragmented military structure. The army included Italians recruited outside the Venetian domains who had been naturalised as Venetian subjects after entering the service of the *Serenissima*. Additionally mercenaries recruited from abroad, especially from Germany, joined the ranks. For much of the seventeenth century Swiss cantons provided the main source of foreign recruits,[183] though the Swiss and Grison presence considerably diminished by the mid 1650s. During the war of 1684–99, however, Switzerland supplied a single regiment of 2,000 soldiers, recruited in 1686 from the Lucerne and Schwyz cantons. This unit endured a very short but troubled history. The flow of recruits halted during the following winter as mountain passes closed, but in early June 1687,

182 Antonelli, *Guida per l'Arsenale di Venezia* (Venice, 1829).

183 Eleven Swiss infantry regiments, plus another Grison regiment, entered Venetian service from the 1640s onwards. Reasonable estimates regarding the actual ethnic origin of Venetian troops indicate that Germans and Swiss comprised at least half of the *Serenissima*'s infantry.

1,000 Swiss arrived in Venice and were quartered at the Lido; the Venetian commissioners discovered, however, that many recruits did not qualify to serve as soldiers and as a result of their journey many arrived critically sick and required hospitalisation. The cantonal authorities lethargically dispatched recruits to Venice until late summer, and just over half of this figure were ready to embark for the Levant in September 1687. However, the commissioners then discovered recruits 'still novices' and even two women.'[184] As a result, only 800 recruits were shipped to Corinth in late September. Unfortunately, after entering the Saronic Gulf, Algerian pirates attacked the fleet and captured some transports, including those carrying the Swiss, and after this episode their destiny was lost in the North African slave markets.[185] Under the Walloon Colonel Count de Lannoy, a 300-man regiment was finally assembled in Greece;[186] ultimately, these soldiers sacrificed themselves in the siege of Negroponte, where they remained involved in the desperate attempts to break the Ottoman resistance during the terrible days of the siege between 14 July and 24 September 1688. The regiment was disbanded in the winter, and the survivors joined the *oltramontane* regiments.

The decreasing numbers of Swiss troops from the 1660s onwards coincided with an increased *Alemanni* (German) presence, fuelled by both the Catholic and Protestant States of Germany.[187] German soldiers gained great renown in the seventeenth century, especially after achieving the great victory under the walls of Vienna. Given their experience against the Ottomans, popular clichés and many contemporaries, including the Venetian government, regarded these mercenaries as elite infantry. Moreover, the Venetians viewed German troops and their officers as essential assets to any army that wished to wage successful campaigns against the Porte. This perception added to their value.[188] Colonel-entrepreneurs also acted as intermediaries between the Republic and the German princes. On behalf of the *Serenissima*, these

184 ASVe, *Inquistori*, f 560, 1687.

185 Diedo, *Storia della Repubblica di Venezia*,Vol. III, p.461.

186 Pfister, Franz, *Der Krieg von Morea in den Jahren 1687 und 1688* (Kassel,1845), p.147.

187 The custom of enlisting whole foreign regiments already existed in Venice. In 1616 Count Johann Ernst of Nassau recruited 3,000 Dutch, including 600 Englishmen under Lieutenant Sir John de Vere. A second Dutch regiment of 3,000 footmen transferred to Venetian service in 1617 under the Palatine nobleman Georg Ludwig von Löwenstein. That same year Colonel Vassenhoven with 1,000 soldiers from the Netherlands arrived in the lagoon. Further foreign regiments came from Germany and the Netherlands between 1625 and 1630. In 1625 the Senate sent the Duke of Candalle, recently appointed to the Republic's service, to Valtellina with his French regiment of 1,500 men. In 1647 another French regiment, under Colonel Count Achilles de Romorantin, entered Venetian service after signing an agreement requiring the recruitment of 20 companies, totalling 4,000 foot soldiers. In 1646 the cantonal authorities of Zurich and Bern agreed the levy of 2,000 men in 10 companies. The search for soldiers pushed the *Serenissima* to seek recruits in several places, as happened in 1647 with the Walloon regiment under Colonel Longueval. See John Hale and Michael Mallet, *The Military Organization of a Renaissance State* (Cambridge: Cambridge University Press, 1984), p.504.

188 Diedo, *Storia della Repubblica di Venezia*, Vol. III, p.360.

77. Venetian grenadier, *c.* 1690 (author's illustration), reconstruction after a wooden figure of a private collection in Verona. All the figures appear as well detailed, although in this case the grenadier has only the grenade bag without an ammunition pouch. Grenadier bearskin hat with red bag; red coat with white lace and buttonholes, red stockings, white metal buttons; natural leather belt, straps and bandolier with brass fittings.

'professionals of war' obtained licenses from local rulers to enlist soldiers in the German states. Upon completing recruitment, these officers commanded the regiment, and like the other infantry they became Venetian subjects. Between 1686 and 1687, recruitment licenses were negotiated in Swabia and Salzburg for the formation of three *Alemanni* regiments. Later these amalgamated into one regiment, which remained in service until 1706. Other licenses authorised enlistment in the Rhineland and the Tyrol.[189] Additionally, the recruitment of a further three German regiments was negotiated between 1690 and 1693 with colonel-entrepreneurs in Westphalia and Rhineland.[190] Representatives of important families with direct contact to the Habsburg Imperial court, such as Styrum and Trauttmansdorf, commanded two of these regiments. The relationships were very useful to the government, because agreements with mercenary colonels guaranteed and continued the Venetian policy on military matters: a characteristic feature of exercised power in the seventeenth century.[191] The search for mercenary soldiers spanned to Flanders: in 1687 the Elector Prince-Archbishop of Cologne issued a license for a Walloon regiment of eight companies under Colonel Cleuter of Liège.[192] According to authoritative research, between 1684 and 1697 Venice recruited about 18,500 German soldiers, of whom 14,000 were battle casualties and victims of epidemics.[193]

In addition to these foreigners, Venice resorted to renting in Germany entire corps 'ready to use', which further varied the already composite army. In the second half of the seventeenth century, private negotiations and direct

189 Negotiations for these contingents were conducted with the court of Vienna; see Diedo, *Storia della Repubblica di Venezia*,Vol. III, p.376.

190 German infantry regiment *Stader*, later *Carrara*, see Appendix II in part 2 of this work.

191 Appointment to prestigious military positions proved useful in managing a diplomatic network, to which Venice always attributed great importance. For example, in 1647 Marquis Jacques de Grémonville, the brother of the French ambassador in Venice was enlisted with the rank of lieutenant general.

192 The regiment is recorded in the Order of Battle at the siege of Negroponte; see Pfister, *Der Krieg von Morea*, p.146.

193 Peter Wilson, *War, State and Society in Württemberg* (Cambridge: Cambridge University Press, 2010), p.77.

78. Possibly a Venetian grenadier, copy after the Manfroni Manuscript, 1684–88. See image commentaries for more information.

recruitment gave way to specific contracts with foreign princes who made available contingents of their troops. These agreements transferred to Venice whole regiments complete with a major staff, equipment, and uniforms. From the Republic's perspective, this option guaranteed fewer organisational problems, and while implying higher costs, avoided unpleasant incidents such as that which occurred with the Swiss recruits in 1687. The Republic's link with some German princes, established during the Cretan War, proved useful when another war against the Ottomans arose in 1684. Among these Duke Ernst August of Brunswick-Lüneburg Celle – the future Elector of Hannover – signed two *convenzioni* for renting three infantry regiments in 1684 and a fourth in 1688.[194] With him, in 1685, the Prince-Elector Johann Georg III of Saxony agreed the rent of three infantry regiments. Then in 1687 and 1688 new contracts were signed with Prince Regent Carl Friedrich of Württemberg, who became the leading supplier of mercenaries to the Republic when replaced the Braunschweig and Saxon contingents with his troops.[195] Growing engagements in the Levant persuaded the Senate to rent further troops. A capitulation for one infantry regiment was signed in 1687 with Hessen Kassel, and another with Braunschweig-Wolfenbüttel in the same year. Venice highly esteemed the contribution of the German troops, not only for their discipline, but also because the government could establish useful contacts with experienced captains. Alongside the German mercenaries Venice also hired a 500-man infantry battalion in Sweden,[196] which in January

194 Duke Ernst August had already provided 2,400 soldiers in four regiments to Venice in 1668 during the siege of Candia.

195 The Prince Regent monopolised the German mercenary market. This business proved very lucrative, and when he was unable to meet the demands of the market, he unhesitatingly resorted to troops from his neighbours. For instance, in 1687 Württemberg hired 10 infantry companies from Hessen-Darmstadt and joined them with the troops destined for Venice. The substantial gains that derived from these trades led to actual business associations. One such relationship formed in 1687 between the *Landgrafschaft* of Hessen-Darmstadt and the Duke of Sachsen-Meiningen. These partnerships provided Venice with a regiment of nine Hessian companies and one Saxon company. After a new agreement with the Republic in May 1695, Carl Friedrich asked the Duke of Mecklenburg to transfer 100 soldiers in order to raise a regiment of 1,000 infantrymen.

196 BMC, ms. *Donà dalle Rose*, 428, n. 1, *Contenuto in Ducale dell'Eccellentissimo* Senato. Unlike Königsmarck, these soldiers did not make a good impression. They were commanded by the Count of Oxenstierna, and once they arrived in the mainland the officers wanted to take up

1686 preceded the arrival of Count Otto Wilhelm von Königsmarck, the valiant *generale dello sbarco* who directed all major actions in the Peloponnese from 1685 to 1688 under Francesco Morosini: a dualism that produced a successful military collaboration.[197]

However, institutional relations made obtaining contingents an arduous process. Especially after 1688, the outbreak of the War of the League of Augsburg (1688–1697) significantly diminished sources of mercenaries, due to the involvement of the German *Reich* in the war against France. The new scenario forced the Republic to pay higher costs, not to mention engaging in exhausting negotiations for replacements and other financial details. Such circumstances usually compelled the Republic to rent these units. The *Vertrag* signed between the Republic and Carl Friedrich of Württemberg, on 20 November 1687, illuminates the conditions of service negotiated by the Venetian government with the German state. The contract established that the two regiments raised in the Duchy had to be comprised of wealthy men aged 20 to 50. Each regiment deployed two field battalions including one grenadier and four musketeer companies 'to employ exclusively in Greece against the Ottomans'. Weapons, equipment, and uniforms were issued in Württemberg 'in the shortest possible time' and the complete contingent awaited in the Venetian Lido before the end of April 1688 to be reviewed by the Venetian commissars. The Republic paid 50 *Reichsthaler* for each recruit; half of this sum after signing the contract and the other half after inspection, less if any men were missing in the review. The salary for officers, NCOs and private soldiers had to be paid each month in Verona. After two years the troops returned to the Lido 'to be fully catered for by the Republic until then, and here in addition to a bi-monthly salary passed to a Württemberg commissar'.[198]

The French invasion of the Palatinate in the autumn of 1688 – and the resulting war – forced the Senate to resort to smaller armies of the immediate Imperial states. Their rulers considered agreements with Venice as not only a source of income, but also sources of great prestige for their houses, since they participated in the war against the Porte. Between 1687 and the Peace of Carlowitz of 1699, the Republic signed capitulations with the Duke of Brunswick, the Landgrave of Hessen-Cassel, the Margrave of Brandenburg-Bayreuth, the Count of Waldeck-Pyrmont, the Prince-Count of Hohenlohe, and the Prince-Bishops of Würzburg and of Salzburg for one or more infantry regiments.[199]

---

quarters in Verona and asked for pay the senators considered excessive. After rejecting the requests, the senators ordered the battalion to go to the Lido, the embarkation point for the Levant. The soldiers served until 1688 without arousing any admiration from the Venetian side.

197 After Königsmarck, the German liaison brought to Venice able commanders such as Adam Heinrich von Steinau, and above all the saviour of Corfu, Matthias von der Schulenburg.

198 Leo Ignaz von Stadlinger: *Geschichte des Württembergischen Kriegswesens* (Stuttgart, 1856), p.326.

199 The Prince-Archbishop of Salzburg also helped the Republic by sending aid in the form of money and ammunition, such as 60,000 pounds of gunpowder in 1687.

The Senate expressed some doubts about the forces coming from small states, which could not always provide sufficient expertise and a skilled officer corps for service in the Morea. Moreover, German mercenaries were not very seaworthy and therefore it was often problematic to deploy them as landing troops, when for Venetian strategy this type of infantry had always been fundamental. Even transfers aboard ships turned into real suffering for these recruits, who fell ill in greater numbers. Of the 759 German recruits who left by ship from Venice in April 1694, on their arrival in Nauplia 27 days later there had been 68 deaths and another 131 soldiers were classified as sick.[200]

Nevertheless, some of the infantry coming from these small states gained a good reputation thanks to skilled commanders such as the Danish *Sergente Maggiore di Battaglia* Karl von Sparr,[201] commander of the Bayreuth contingent.

Like the ready-to-use German mercenaries, the hiring of a mounted contingent was negotiated between Venice and the Duchy of Savoy. Duke Carlo Emanuele II had already supplied an infantry corps to the Republic in the Cretan War from 1660 to 1669, while permitting the recruitment of volunteers in Piedmont and Savoy. In March 1685 his son Vittorio Amedeo offered one regiment of cavalry and one of dragoons to be employed against the Ottomans. The terms of the *conventione* were established in the minutest detail. The cavalry regiment, under Don Gabriele of Savoy, had two companies of 50 horsemen with captain, lieutenant, ensign, *marechal de logis* and three brigadiers. Each company had a trumpet and a smith, and the first company also included one kettledrum. A further two companies had the same staff but only 45 horsemen. The dragoon regiment had six companies with two of 47 dragoons and four of 44.[202] The contract contained a number of particularly onerous guarantees concerning the replacement of horses and men, as well as the possible ransom of prisoners, all at the expense of the Republic. However, at the last moment the agreement was not signed, ending the participation of the Duke of Savoy in the war even before it began.[203] One year later, a new offer of troops was sent to Venice. This time the Duke offered 2,000 *barbetti* (mountaineers), including Waldensian captives, but the Senate 'kindly declined the proposal'.[204]

During the war acts of sedition were quite rare, but those that occurred came from the mercenaries. In 1685, troops aboard a convoy led by Iseppo

200 ASVe, *Senato, Dispacci, Provveditori di Terra e di Mar*, b. 1129, d. 9.

201 Sparr was the main collaborator of Captain General Girolamo Corner, and for a while seemed to revive the fruitful cooperation between Morosini and Königsmarck, but the Venetian captain general died of 'malignant fevers' in 1690, while Sparr was killed in action the next year.

202 ASTo, *Materie Ecclesiastiche*, Cat. I, *Negoziati*, 7 March 1685.

203 The reason for the non-participation of the ducal contingent is unclear, but past experience concerning the use of mounted troops in the context of amphibious warfare probably had an influence in the final decision. However, French diplomacy could have persuaded the Duke not to grant aid to the Venetians engaged in a war on the side of their enemy, the Habsburgs of Austria.

204 Beregani, *Historia delle Guerre d'Europa*, vol. II, p.84.

Morosini mutinied off the coast of Ragusa. The agitators killed four people, and tried to seize the 100,000 *zecchini* and capture the aged commander by keeping him in his cabin, but he managed to escape by climbing out of a window and reaching the deck by climbing onto the aft superstructure. According to the report, the mutineers rose to the shouts of *Viva Franza!* and *Viva Luigi!*, which leaves little doubt as to their nationality.[205] The mutiny was severely repressed, and in the following years no other sedition occurred. In 1691, however, the Republic faced two serious rebellions when mutinies occurred aboard Bartolomeo Contarini's flagship and on the *Madonna del Rosario*. When the latter reached Dulcigno, Captain Pinetti's *oltramontane* company tried to seize the ship, but the mutiny failed. Thirteen of those responsible were tried: two of them were hanged, the others sentenced to prison. On Contarini's ship a large number of French mercenaries took up arms; the mutineers rushed into the commander's cabin and Contarini was wounded, but managed to escape. The crew managed to counter-attack and defeat the rebels, who lost 75 men, and the few survivors ended up at the oars of the galleys.[206] The expectation of seizing money or the desire to regain freedom were not always the causes of rebellion. In some phases of the war it was economic hardship that favoured mutiny. In September 1696 the situation had become catastrophic: the coffers were empty and the payment of salaries was late, causing the mutiny of the regiment of Salzburg.[207]

Auxiliaries

As discussed before, the troops of the Italian allies represent the last component of the Venetian army. Allied support during the Cretan War provided the Senate with decades of experience in the military affairs of the Italian states. However, compared to the past conflict, in the war of 1684–99, forces sent by the Italian *ausiliari* (as they are usually named in Venetian government correspondence) were greatly reduced. In the last phase of the war only Malta regularly contributed with ships and soldiers to strengthen the ranks. Other states such as the Grand Duchy of Tuscany from 1684 to 1688, the Duchy of Parma and Piacenza from 1684 to 1689, and the Republic of Genoa in 1687 sent aid to Dalmatia and Greece to support the Holy League. Genoa, however, provided exclusively naval support in the period 1687–1690, while Parma, Mantua and Lucca contributed only with patents of recruitment.

Part of the troops' maintenance costs fell on the Venetian government. These included providing winter quarters in Corfu for the Spanish-Milanese troops and in Dalmatia for the Parma and Piacenza regiment. Obviously, such varied contingents yielded unequal results. Except for the Maltese infantry, most of these troops found war theatres such as the Peloponnese to be very exhausting. Venetian commanders considered the allied infantry better suited to support sieges rather than open field battles. Additionally,

205 ASVe, *Senato, Dispacci, Provveditori di Terra e di Mar*, b. 880, dispatch dated 6 December 1685.

206 *Ibid.*, b. 847, d. 44 (18 September 1691).

207 Pinzelli, *Venise et la Morée*, p.426.

poor sanitary conditions severely affected these troops, who were 'little accustomed to the rigours of the Levant'.[208]

However, the opportunity to clear the Mediterranean of the Ottoman presence, and the prestige acquired by the Italian princes for participating in the Holy League, overshadowed the war's difficulties and costs. The auxiliary presence began auspiciously, and each victory fed a rebirth of the crusading spirit which attracted volunteers from all social classes. This climate fostered a baroque mythography that exalted the Christian faith and transformed it into a heroic quest. Such religious fervour radiated beyond the boundaries of Italy. Additionally, forms of communication profoundly changed. Novels, treatises, and paintings began to escape the narrow confines of the courts and include broader numbers of people. This, in turn, formed an actual public opinion that propagated a desire to fight. Thus the war against the Porte drew in large ranks of young Italian and foreign aristocrats who arrived in Venice to enter service as *venturiere* (adventurer) volunteers. These were aristocrat cadets driven by heroic exaltation who, in terms of primogeniture, lacked substance. They considered the Venetian conflict as an opportunity to acquire useful military experience that, upon returning home, would merit them prestigious assignments under their monarch. The war acted as a magnet, not only to increase the ranks of adventurers in Venetian service, but also to increase the ranks of the Knights of Malta and the less famous, but equally resolute and aggressive, Knights of St Stephen of Tuscany. Overall, the Italian auxiliaries contributed 12,000–14,000 soldiers, sailors and oarsmen, but on average they deployed not more than 4,000 men, with a peak of 5,000–6,000 infantrymen, sailors and oarsmen in 1688.

The *Milizia delle Ordinanze*

The establishment of the Venetian militia dated to the Renaissance. Under the influence of Nicolò Machiavelli, even in Laguna the government joined the concept that the states had to provide for themselves by 'turning to their weapons', believing that there may not be better and more trusted soldiers than their own subjects. Machiavelli's influence is evident since in Venice, as in Florence, the militia took the name of *Ordinanze* (ordinances). This term was long applied to the militia as a whole, while the appellative *cernide* qualified the militiamen in the mainland, *proli* and *stradioti* in Greece, and *craine* in the eastern Adriatic, the latter introduced definitively in 1570.[209] In

208 A comment then currently used in contemporary relations, see for example *Relazione in forma di Diario dell'Assedio e Conquista di Modone e Navarino Nuovo*, 22 giugno 1685, Collezione Querini-Stampalia, Venice; ff. 36–40.

209 In 1593 the rules called *Ordinationi et Regole in materia di Ordinanze* were issued, and except for a few changes, this document continued to be adopted for almost two centuries. The militia carried out their tasks admirably in the war against the Habsburgs in 1615–18, despite not being professional soldiers. The basic unit of the ordinances was the *centuria*, formed by 100 men. The required obligations were represented by five annual *mostre* (reviews) and a preliminary

order to coordinate military affairs, the overseas provinces were divided into two and later three 'regiments', each presided over by the local *provveditore*: Dalmatia and Albania, based in Zadar; *Levante*, with residence in Corfu; the Morea (Peloponnese) after 1687, based in Nauplia. The fourth 'regiment' was the Venetian *Terraferma*, also known as *Riparto d'Italia*.

The clear distinction between the militia and the regular army, composed of mercenaries, is clear at the financial level since militia affairs were attended by a *savio all'Ordinanze*, distinct from the official who was in charge of economic issues for the regular army, the aforementioned *savio alle Scritture*. Similarly there was a commander-in-chief of the militia, with the rank of *governatore delle Ordinanze* (Governor of the Ordinances).

Though the relationship between civil society and the 'military' had always been a sensitive nerve of Venetian policy, contemporary commentators exaggerated about Venetian citizens' alleged mistrust of military service. However, the decisions regarding the militia were often hesitant and conditioned by conflicting factors in the government. First, there was certainly the desire not to turn the civilians to regular and continuous military exercises, but only those basic exercises necessary for the formation of a force, so taking the people away from their labours as little as possible. This especially concerned the mainland population, because the citizens of Venice and Chioggia were excluded from service in the *cernide*, both cities being already involved in the *ordinanze da mar*.

In addition to these precautions, the government was also pressed by the need not to endanger the consensus between the 'dominant city' and the periphery. At the end of the century there was still a very vivid memory of the severe measures introduced in the Italian provinces during the Cretan War, regarding service in the *cernide*. The militia was mobilised for the first time in 1645 to face possible Ottoman raids in Friuli. Then it was called again to provide a constant service in arms during 1657–58, when the government doubled the number of men in the companies. In 1668, to find new recruits to send to besieged Candia, the government was forced to resort to the 'hated measure of Decimation', drawing lots to 'volunteer' one militiamen in 10 as a replacement for the regular infantry which defended the city. This decision was greatly opposed in the Senate and provoked many disagreements; some disorder took place in the mainland campaigns, however this method to find troops to be sent into the Cretan furnace remained until the end of hostilities.

The mobilisation of the militia again became a matter of Venetian policy in 1684, on the eve of the new war against the Porte. The mobilisation of regular troops, that anywhere in the states of the *Ancien Régime* also maintained public order, required the presence of an armed force that would replace them in that duty. However, the service was very decayed after the Cretan War. As in many other Italian states of the time, the militia was the receptacle of problems and inequalities deriving from civil society. The

---

training of one week. The age limits were initially set from 16 to 40, but the family heads were released from the service and the government avoided mobilising more than one man per family. Seasonal workers were also excluded, because 'due to poverty they change home every year'.

introduction of a fee to enable the avoidance of service had the effect of transferring the whole weight of military obligations on the poorest people. Further, several drawbacks occurred in the provinces close to the border. The most frequent abuses concerned the case of militiamen who had entered the Venetian Ordinances to enjoy the privileges accorded to the *cernide*, but avoided the regular service and exercises by declaring their domicile in the neighbouring state.[210] The efficiency of the companies was also unequal and conditioned to different circumstances. Cases were common, in which the officers complained about the presence in the ranks of an aged replacement in place of the son or even the nephew. Apart from a few exceptions, these troops were poorly trained and badly equipped.

In the 1650s and 1660s, on paper the militia numbered 20,000 men in the mainland with an additional 18,000 in the Archipelago and in Dalmatia: substantial numbers required by the emergency of the long war against the Porte. Over the years, especially in Dalmatia, the militia was constantly involved in the defence of the border, often alongside the regular troops. Even in the eastern provinces of the mainland the government mobilised the local *cernide* whenever the presence of the Ottoman army was reported at the border with Austrian Croatia: the gateway through which they could break into Friuli, as had already happened in 1499.

79. Foot militiaman of the *Reggimento Offerto dalla Città di Padova*, c. 1690. See image commentaries for more information.

In 1684 the government acted with greater caution and foresight regarding the militias, establishing more modern criteria focusing on the formation of infantry regiments in every major centre of the mainland. Therefore, in order to find recruits to replace the troops destined for the Levant, the government instituted the so-called *allettanze* (alluring) in the mainland in order to form corps of 3,000 soldiers organised into foot regiments. Each year after the summer of 1684, the Senate issued to the communities the order to raise the contingents. The terms employed already expressly stated the end and purpose as being 'meritorious

210 In the 'Book of Ordinances' were recorded the names of the militiamen, and the individual's age, hair colour, height and any distinguishing physical marks.

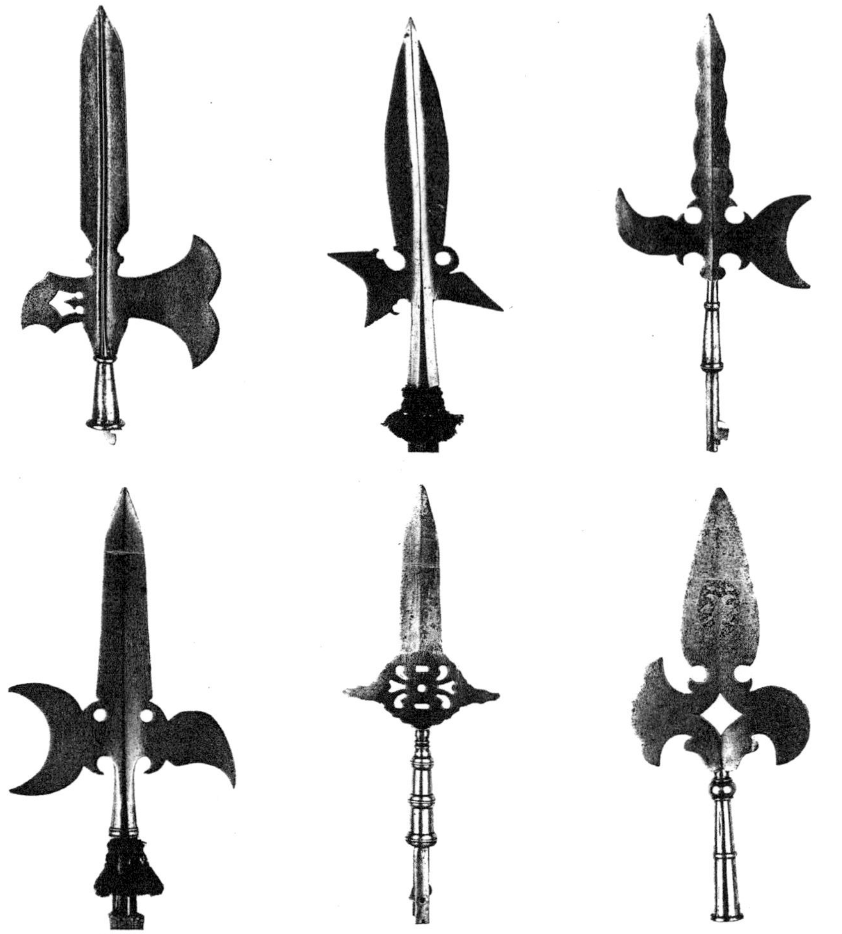

80. Infantry halberds or *sergentine*, Venetian manufacture, late seventeenth century (Armeria Palazzo Ducale, Venice). The third weapon on the lower right carries a two-headed eagle embossed at the centre of the blade, which probably alludes either to the heraldry of the Mocenigo family or to a German infantry unit.

service for the public'.[211] The ordinance prescribed that every urban centre was beneficed by conceding to civilians not only the traditional privileges already recognised to the militiamen – a hunting license; suspension of debt processes; permitting the carrying of a sword – but also other more tangible rewards, such as the exemption from extraordinary taxes, which always coincided with military spending. The admission age was established as a minimum of 18 years to a maximum of 35 for privates, while that for officers was elevated up to 45 years. The service lasted at least three years, renewable for another three up to a maximum of 12 years and was carried out according to a schedule that had to make available in a reasonable time at least one third of each regiment. The constitutive project also included the appointment of special staff; ranks could be purchased, but the major functions were elected in every city, subject to ratification by the *provveditore* and finally by the Senate. The first *allettanze* were formed in Padua, Vicenza, Verona and Udine; in subsequent years, regiments were raised in Treviso, Bergamo and

211 Giacomo Diedo, *Storia della Repubblica di Venezia. Dalla Sua Fondazione Sino l'Anno MDCCXLVII* (Venice, 1751), p.401.

Crema; then Brescia in 1686, and Pordenone, Legnago, Peschiera, Rovigo and Cologna Veneta in 1691. Obviously the regiment's strength depended on the density of the population, thus in February 1685 the city of Padua managed to present 'around 845 men' divided into companies of 100 privates, NCOs and musicians. The territory of Crema, the small Venetian enclave in Lombardy, fielded only three companies in 1690, while Cologna Veneta had only one company in 1691.[212] These units were tasked primarily with internal surveillance in the towns and in the countryside, and after 1690 also with providing garrisons to the forts on the western border threatened by the passage of belligerent armies during the War of the League of Augsburg. Apart from some minor accidents on the frontiers with foreign soldiers who had strayed into Venetian territory, the mainland's *cernide* were never involved in fighting. Halfway between regular troops and militia a corps of *Benemeriti*, deserving soldiers above 60 years of age, performed guard duties in Venice.

The same caution shown towards the subjects of the mainland was not adopted in the overseas provinces. The Dalmatian *craine*, as the rest of the eastern Adriatic militia, followed a pattern similar to the *cernide* regarding the appointment of the officers, but did not enjoy the same privileges and above all were mobilised in large numbers regardless of the economic environment. On the other side of the Adriatic, the caution employed by the mainland's *provveditori* was for their overseas colleagues a negligible concern. The Dalmatian *craine* supported the first encounters of the new war against the Porte as early as the autumn of 1683, when several fights took place at Obravac and Duare between the Bosnian-Ottoman frontiersmen and the militia of Split and Klis. The *craine* was involved not only whenever the Venetian domains were under enemy pressure, but also in operations across the border, as happened during the unsuccessful expedition against Duare in 1684 and for the siege of Vlorë in 1690. The military scenario in the Levant was very different from that of the Italian mainland. In fact, the overseas communities had faced constant Ottoman pressure on the borders and therefore the level of mobilisation was physically higher in those regions.

The social structure of the communities in the Adriatic, organised in clans or 'extended families', was much more functional than elsewhere, because in the case of mobilisation the chiefs were identified as the natural military leaders. This feature was reflected more often by Dalmatian and Albanian populations that, on several occasions, were the only guards and defenders of the border with Ottoman Bosnia. Although it was normal to expect a level of unequal efficiency between the militiamen, and normally the Venetian commanders were aware of the limitations of these troops in an open field, the *craine*, if well commanded, could be used in the defence of fortified towns like the regular troops. The Dalmatian militiamen fought fiercely in 1684 at Traù, and in 1687 at Castelnuovo and especially at Sinj, rejecting all Ottoman attempts to seize the fortress. In the course of the war, militiamen of eastern Adriatic provinces benefited also from the guidance of prepared officers such

212 ASVe, *Senato, Provveditori di terra e di Mar, Dispacci*, b. 1098, d. 12, dated 1 July 1691.

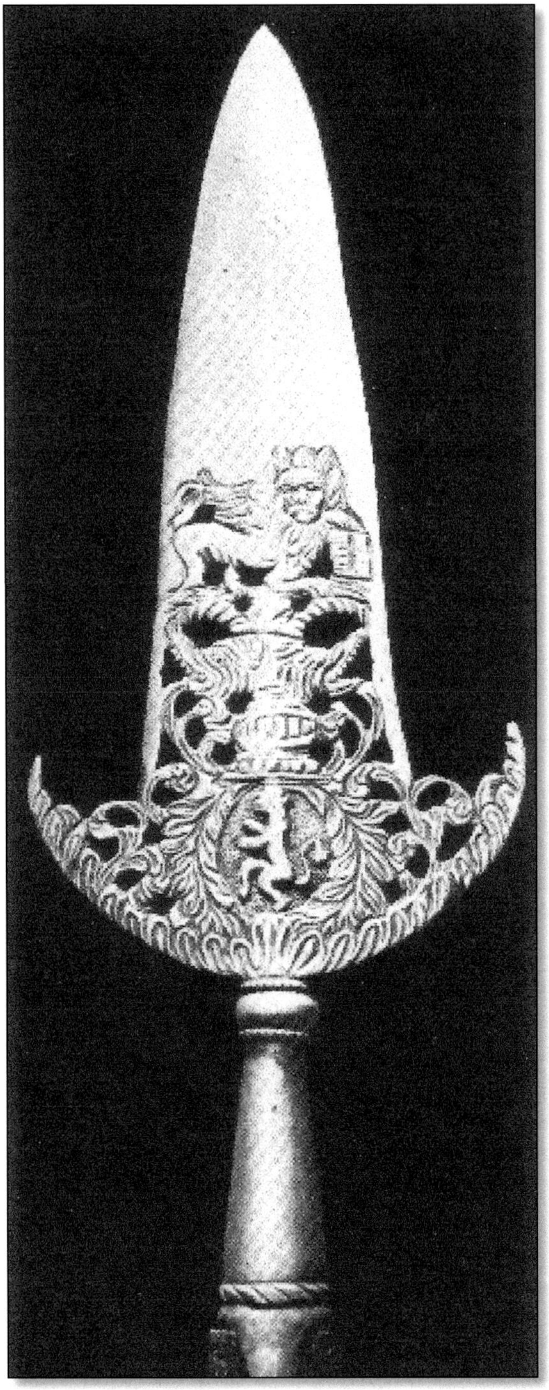

Left and below: 81. Partisans, Venetian manufacture, late seventeenth century. (Armeria Palazzo Ducale, Venice)

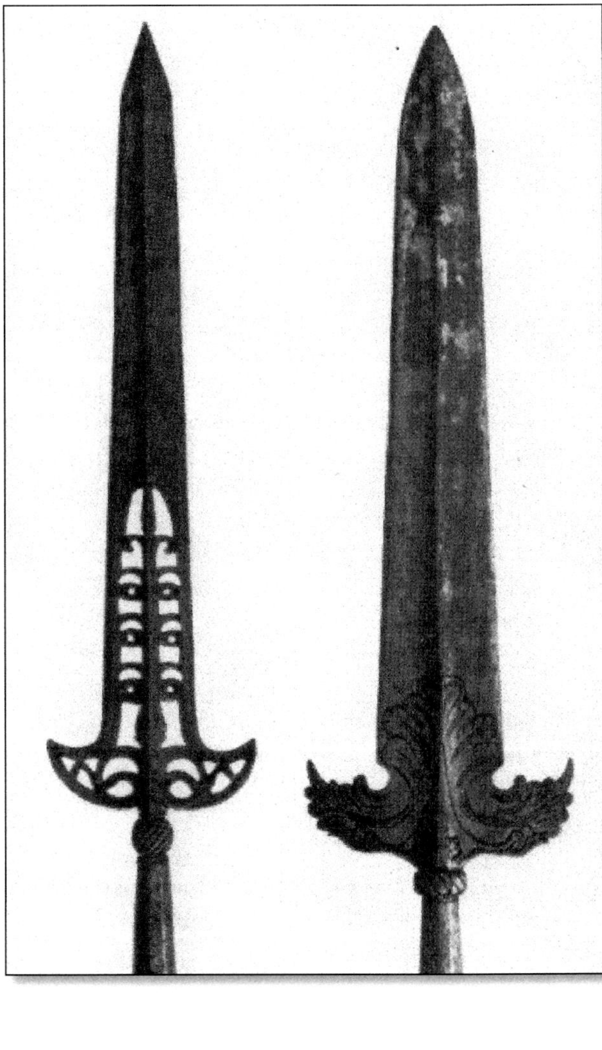

as Count Francesco Possidiaria, appointed as commander of the Dalmatian *craine* in 1685. In 1686 he continued the reorganisation of the militia, cooperating with Girolamo Corner when the latter held the position of *provveditore straordinario* in the province. In the last years of the seventeenth century the Dalmatian, Croatian and Albanian *ordinanze* could put in arms a force of 24,000 militiamen on foot and 1,500–2,000 on horseback, with arsenals and depots in Zadar, Split, Klis and Kotor.[213]

82. *Schiavona* broadsword, late seventeenth century manufacture from Venice or Brescia (private collection). In the 1680s this weapon became the typical sidearm of the Venetian infantry, which was distributed in the overseas domains as well as on the Italian mainland.

Normally, access to the ranks of the *oltramarine* troops was affected by the passage of volunteers directly from the *craine*. Even in the Greek islands the local militia represented an institution already established, well organised and usually effective. Since the Greeks had a long tradition of service in the Venetian army, they retained the traditional denomination of *stradioti* when they served as mounted frontiersman. Whether in the problematic form of farmer-soldiers or involved exclusively with their military duties, the *stradioti* continued to serve in the garrison of the Ionian islands until Venetian rule dissolved in 1797, receiving a salary and being dispatched outside their territory.[214] However, between the end of the seventeenth century and the beginning of the eighteenth, the Greek mounted militia declined when Venice reorganised the service on the border and limited numbers and privileges. Furthermore, either the number of ethnic Greeks decreased or the companies became exclusively Albanian or Croatian, or acquired diverse ethnic identity. Nonetheless, the officers were frequently Greeks who retained links with Venetian authority. The number of men in each company rarely exceeded 20–40 horsemen, while the 'regular' strength was 50–60.[215]

Corfu, Cephalonia and Zakynthos provided on several occasions not only militia units in support of the army on campaign, but also regular soldiers to form boarded pickets on the fleet and to serve as pioneers for the sieges that one after another invested the Ottoman fortresses of the Peloponnese. In the spring of 1684, during the first campaign of the war, the militia of the Greek islands were mustered between 8 and 12 June by the *provveditore straordinario* Domenico Mocenigo, fielding a total of 6,000 footmen 'all well equipped'.[216]

213 ASVe, *Senato, Provveditori di Terra e di Mar, Dispacci*, b. 1082, d. 7, 24 May 1686.

214 Birtachas, 'Stradioti, Cappelletti, Compagnie or Milizie Greche', p.334.

215 *Ibid.*

216 Foscarini, *Degli Historici delle cose Venetiane*, p.160.

The conquest of Santa Maura (Lefkas), involved 1,500 volunteers from the nearby Greek villages under Anastasio Animo; their contagious enthusiasm also persuaded 150 Orthodox priests led by the Bishop of Kefalonia to join the Venetian troops.[217]

Relations between the Venetian government and the militia of the Greek regions conquered in the war against the Porte were decidedly ambivalent, and in the end the results remained below expectations. For coastal defence Venice turned to the Greeks of the Peloponnese, although this clashed with the population's aversion to arms, and the fear of a sudden reversal of the conflict's fortunes.[218] It was only during the imminent danger of an enemy invasion that the Peloponnesian Greeks served more regularly, but many preferred to pay a tax that exempted them from presenting themselves for the call to arms. Despite the general unwillingness of the population to engage in armed service, in the 1690s the Venetian government started the experiment of compulsory conscription in the *cernide greche* entrusted to the four provincial *provveditori*, with 23 captains and as many sergeants in charge of the arduous training of the reluctant militiamen.[219]

Venturieri and Volunteers

Like other states engaged in the war against the Porte, even Venice welcomed volunteers both from their own domains and abroad.[220] The chronicles give much prominence to the presence of volunteers even in the early stages of the war, when the fleet departing to Corfu embarked along with the troops dozens of young people from prominent Venetian families, such as Bembo, Vendramino, Foscari and Pasqualigo.[221] Most served aboard the fleet, but together with other young aristocrats from the mainland, many took part in field operations as 'demi lances' in the infantry regiments.

The reasons that lay behind the phenomenon of volunteers were manifold. Generally, they were cadets whom primogeniture had deprived of the inheritance rights to their father's properties, and who were faced with the choice between an ecclesiastical and a military career. In the seventeenth century there were no schools or military institutions in the modern sense. People who wanted to learn the profession of arms, in order to ascend to the

217 *Ibid.*

218 Sergio Perini, 'I provvedimenti veneziani in Morea (1687–1714)', in G. Ortalli, G. Gullino, E. Ivetic (eds), *L'inestinguibile sogno del dominio. Francesco Morosini* (Venice: Istituto Veneto di Scienze, Lettere e Arti, 2021), p.133.

219 *Ibid.*, p.134.

220 The presence of volunteers was indeed a tradition started already during the Cretan War and boasted illustrious and glorious examples. One of the most notable cases was represented by Lazzaro Mocenigo: in 1656 he fought as a simple *governatore di nave* (governor of a sail ship) under Lorenzo Marcello during the extraordinary campaign which ended with the great victory in the Third Battle of the Dardanelles, fought on 20 June between the Ottoman and Venetian fleets.

221 Foscarini, *Degli Historici delle cose Venetiane*, p.149.

officer ranks, presented themselves as volunteers to participate in a military campaign. Service inside the army, perhaps as an adjutant or simply as an ensign would long remain 'the forge of the commanders', according to a typical definition of the period. In fact, as can be seen from the biographical notes of volunteers serving the *Serenissima*, careers unfolded through very similar contexts, which allows us to form a homogenous range of cases. However, the biographies leave silent or avoid reporting the economic conditions of many gentries of the time, which was the actual motivation that pushed many young aristocrats into the profession of arms. Economic difficulties and adverse conditions encountered in their countries of origin caused volunteers to seek in the army a position suited to the rank of their family. However there were not only economic reasons pushing these volunteers to risk their lives in the service of Venice or the Emperor of Austria: there was the desire for glory and adventure typical of the young generation of all eras, and the meagre prospects of life as a cadet pushed these young people to risk their lives in battle.

A powerful motivational lever was certainly religious faith and the spirit of crusade that pervaded every conflict against the Ottoman Empire. The war was not only fought on the battlefields: it was relived from afar like a collective participation, which marked the emergence of new forms of culture thanks to the first information tools in full development, such as the countless printed gazettes and monitors published everywhere. The victory of Vienna or the conquest of Athens aroused throughout Europe an enthusiasm that is not improper to define as massive, and which became a powerful magnet that attracted many young aristocrats to choose to undertake an uncertain but still glorious military career. These took place through a script unchanged: the volunteer left the home town comforted by the applause of the most conspicuous citizens; his letters passed from hand to hand and the progress in his career flattered municipal pride. *Avvisi*, poems, and ceremonies emphasised his achievements, or lamented his death in battle. The volunteer, in turn, did not interrupt the relationship with his city of origin, arranging to be joined by family, friends and fellow citizens, thus perpetuating the phenomenon. It is difficult to determine the number of volunteers, but evidence from the sources are such that it can be regarded as relevant. The presence of these adventurers appears higher in the early stages of the war, and then decreases with the unwinding of the Venetian offensive after 1689. A characteristic feature of the volunteer in the Venetian army and navy was that, like other belligerent powers, the government received not only Venetian and other young Italian aristocrats but also foreigners, creating a truly unique case in the Italian military history of the seventeenth century. In 1684, together with the Venetian volunteers and others from Ferrara, Tuscany, Milan and Rome awaiting to embark for Corfu, is recorded the presence of a Swedish *venturiere*.[222] The following year, at the siege of Calamata, there were also 'the Chancellor of Denmark's son, an English Milord and two Marquises of Fenelon'.[223] The presence of prominent personalities had been qualified in 1685

222 Beregani: *Historia delle Guerre d'Europa*; Vol. I, p.156. The author refers to him as 'Baron Walter'.

223 *Ibid*., p.392.

by the presence of a cadet from the House of Savoy, the Prince don Filippo, who fought in all major actions of the campaign; his exposure to the dangers of war, and especially to the Greek climate, caused his transfer in August to Zakynthos for convalescence. Although they were volunteers, the respect and attention normally reserved for 'quality people' were always maintained. This caused some inconvenience in the internal organisation, however the presence of volunteers was of huge propaganda value for the Republic of Venice and of course it was very useful in the maintenance of that network of relationships that have always distinguished the foreign policy of the *Serenissima*. In this regard, the presence in Greece of such a volunteer as Prince Louis Philippe de Turenne represented an added value of great importance, not only because the young French aristocrat distinguished himself with considerable valuable acts, but also as his enterprises gave wide resonance to Venice's war effort, pushing other volunteers to join the Venetian army. He served for several campaigns alongside the volunteers before returning to the favour of Louis XIV, who appointed him lieutenant general.[224]

However, the presence of these volunteers became a problem, especially when they were supported by important figures. One of these was Count Alessandro de Vimes, who had volunteered to serve the Republic in May 1685 and the Senate had agreed without specifying his rank. Already a *Feldmarshall-Lieutenant* of Emperor Leopold I, and above all an old man, he was to occupy a more important post than the young Prince of Brunswick in the council of war, an event that could raise endless disputes of precedence. However, when Vimes arrived at the camp he was instructed to direct the repair of the breaches at Corone. With this order, Morosini removed him from the theatre of operations for a very specific purpose, and temporarily eliminated this problem.[225]

In the field of artillery Venice also found qualified recruits. Among them one of the most discussed was certainly Antonio Muttoni, Count of San Felice, a Veronese ennobled by Louis XIV who had just returned to his homeland after a career in the army of the King of France, participating in the bombardments

---

224 Louis Philippe de Turenne, eldest son of Godefroy Maurice, Duke of Bouillon, arrived in Venice in April 1686, apparently by a whim of fortune. Having been allowed by Louis XIV to fight in the Polish army the previous year, Louis and his cousins, the princes of Conti, had in fact entered the Imperial army under the Duke of Lorraine, a fierce enemy of the French king. After falling completely out of favour with the scandal of the Conti letters, the young prince found himself banished from France. Destitute, he turned to the Republic of Venice, which willingly accepted to host him and 20 members of his retinue. The Senate, which knew the situation in which the prince found himself, immediately voted to offer him a *rinfresco* and a prize of 150 *ducati*. He died at Enghien on 4 August 1692 from wounds received at the Battle of Steinkerque. Pinzelli, *Venise et la Morée*, p.120.

225 *ASVe, Senato, Dispacci, Provveditori di Terra e Mar, b. 1070*, n. 83; ASVe, *Senato da mar*, Reg. 152 (1686), f. 136. According to Contarini, *Istoria della Guerra*, vol. I, p.458, the Count of Vimes had been promoted to *sergente maggiore di battaglia*.

of Genoa and Algiers.[226] In 1685 the *provveditore all'artiglieria* gave him the task of melting down mortars similar to those used by the French artillery. Once the tests carried out in March in Brescia and Vicenza appeared to be conclusive, Muttoni was immediately sent to Greece in order to improve the siege artillery. However, he achieved unflattering results and was harshly criticised by Morosini and Königsmarck, though managed to stay in service thanks to the support of his influential friendship in Venice.

The high turnover required by the military campaigns, resulting in the availability of available officer places, allowed some couragious and lucky volunteers to take over the command of companies and regiments. Everything was functional for the Venetian army, which had always looked abroad to recruit officers of all levels. Of course this caused inconvenience and unpleasant episodes, due both to the lack of controls on the origin of the volunteers, as well as the imponderables of human inclination. The most negative case involving a foreign *venturiere* happened in November 1685 off the coast of Ragusa (today Dubrovnik), which put in danger the life of the General Captain Francesco Morosini. On the Captain General's galley had been boarded 120 infantry soldiers under the Captain De Wilmotz, 'a Calvinist from Provence, and person with any faith' who, as relates the historian Beregani, had been promoted to that rank after his arrival the previous year in Venice as volunteer 'even though honoured by Morosini with more decorous treatments'.[227] The officer had developed a plan including the mutiny of the company and the seizure of the military treasure, and first of all the kidnapping of the Venetian commander to ensure their flight to Algiers. With him, even two subordinates were part of the conspiracy: the Dutch officers Louis Temesmans and Simon Van Mayr. During the night the three men tried to penetrate the Captain General's room, but the courageous resistance of the servants and Morosini's grandson foiled the kidnapping. De Wilmotz was killed almost immediately while the other conspirators, after a fierce resistance aboard the galley, were eventually overwhelmed by sailors and other soldiers from the nearby galleys: 'the battle lasted for three hours, until many grenades launched through a window of the room, where the rebels were barricaded … forced them to retreat in the bow castle, and finally they were overwhelmed by the *oltramarine* soldiers.' The mutineers' destiny was terrible. Both Dutch officers were chained and thrown into the sea, while the body of De Wilmotz was torn to pieces and hung on the galley's mainmast.[228]

226 Garzoni, *Istoria della Repubblica di Venezia*, vol. I, p.128; and Foscarini, *Historia della Republica Veneta*, p.259. In his youth Muttoni had been banished from the territories of the Republic 'for some youthful background'.

227 Beregani, *Historia delle Guerre d'Europa*, Vol. I, pp.394–395.

228 *Ibid.*

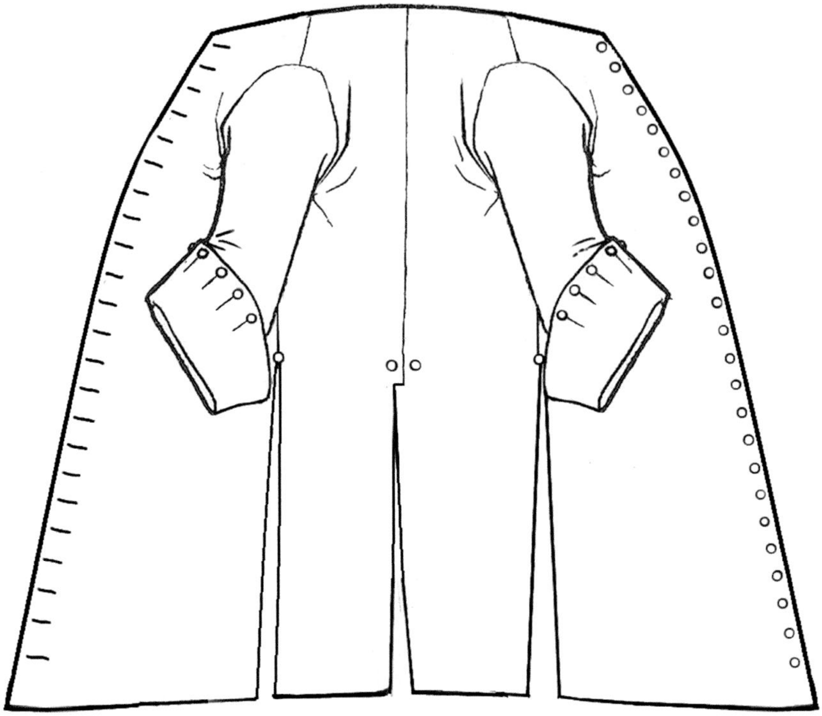

Above: 83. Venetian coat pattern for infantry, 1685. (Author's reconstruction)

Below: 84. Officer's *velada* coat and private infantrymen *camisiola* waistcoat, *c.* 1690, after the collection of wooden figures preserved in Verona

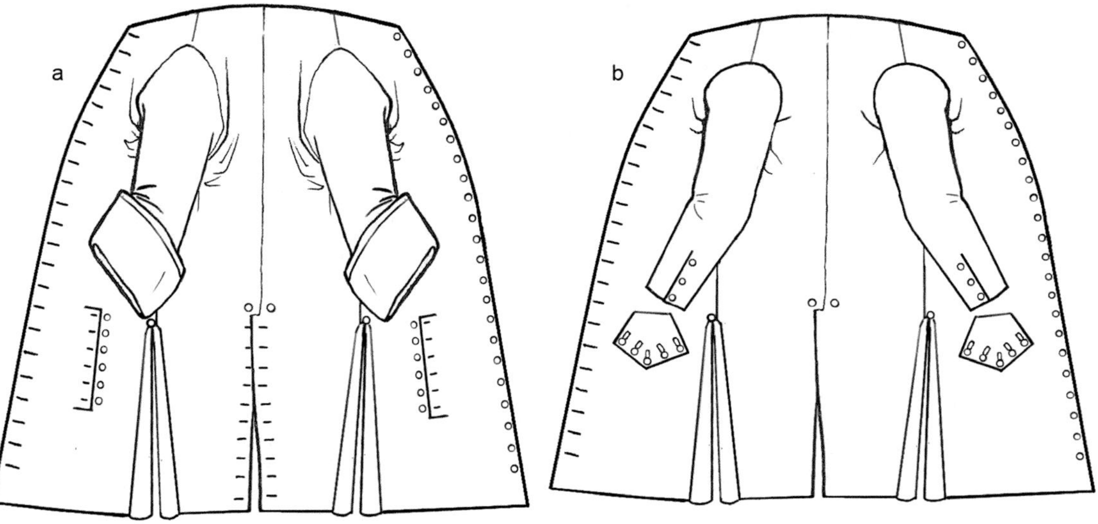

85. Venetian infantry wearing red, blue and light grey coats at the siege of Corone in 1686. Note in the centre a full red ensign with the golden lion of St Mark. (Correr Museum, Venice)

Uniforms and Equipment

The oldest evidence of Venetian 'uniforms' dates from the Cretan War. This is a painting portraying infantrymen wearing red doublet and breeches, and black broad-brimmed hat, dating to 1656. The officer, drummer and NCOs wear clothing of similar patterns but of different colours. It remains unclear whether the figures portrayed represent an Italian regiment or one of the many foreign mercenary units in Venetian service.[229] Nonetheless, this painting demonstrates that uniformed clothing was considered standard practice in the 1650s. Moreover, when Antonio Grimani listed to the Pope the amount of money, men and material that the 1668 campaign had required, he specifically mentioned the *uniformi* as a regular expenditure for the soldiers.[230] This is quite surprising considering the many archaic aspects of the Venetian military, but this policy stemmed from precise reasons, namely state control over supplies destined for the fleet and the army. Standardisation became a necessary measure to safeguard the treasury from abuse and malpractices.

Although no specific act had been issued by the government on the subject of military clothing before 1690, with the exception of the ordinance on the distribution of overcoats in winter to the garrisons on the *Terraferma*, some pictures show infantrymen wearing red, blue or light grey clothing in 1686. One of the first documents regarding infantry uniforms dates to October 1690. It is a contract for the purchase of red wool cloth for 4,000 *velade* (coats), and 'moss colour' *bragoni* (breeches) for issue to the Italian infantry, signed on behalf of the government by *Savio alla Scrittura* Gabriele

229 Red coats were traditionally worn also by Swiss mercenaries. In 1668,Venice hired four infantry regiments of Brunswick-Lüneburg Celle, mostly uniformed in red.

230 Pezzolo, 'Una finanza in guerra, 1645–1669', p.68.

Zorzi and the private supplier Bortolo Davia.[231] Two years later, Zorzi wrote that 4,811 'coats of uniform' had been sent to Greece over the last 24 months. He commented that it 'could be better to vary the colour for each regiment ... to dress the soldiers in the best way as an evident sign of order and attention.'[232] The documents produced by the *Savio alla Scrittura* reveal that the government regularly supplied all items for the infantry uniform, including *velada* and cloth *bragoni*, shirt, cravat, and headgear.[233] All these official records suggest that regular distribution of uniforms was a pre-established practice, and above all the adoption of red and blue as the colours for the coats. A contract signed in March 1695 reiterates that 'for the manufacturing of 3,000 uniforms, according to the decrees of the Senate on 28 October [1694] and 24 February [1695], 2,000 coats will be of red cloth, 1,000 of blue, with moss-colour breeches.'[234] The document also specifies the use of tin buttons. In 1695, similar sources always mention red or 'turquoise' cloth for manufacturing *velade* and red cloth for the breeches.[235] Alternatively, other contracts mention breeches of natural leather in the German style, or of red cloth.[236] Contemporary iconography concerning the first campaigns confirms these colours. Infantrymen wearing red and azure-blue coats appear in a series of paintings of the war of 1684–99 by Francesco Morosini, now preserved in the Correr Museum in Venice.[237] In these works, officers are dressed in the baroque style of that age, and in line with the practice of the period, NCOs wear different coloured coats. It is difficult to determine whether the coats have cuffs in a colour different to the base fabric; the lack of evidence in the original documents excludes this hypothesis. Among the peculiarities of these images, grenadiers cannot be identified, which suggests that in those years elite soldiers did not have special headgear. Drawings from the Fabroni manuscript also portray Venetian infantrymen in red alongside allied infantry during the Siege of Modone, in 1686.[238] Although the drawings are just sketches, all of the images confirm the use of red coats without facing which distinguishes them from the uniforms of foreign infantry. Official documents and reports, such as records of captured deserters, provide further interesting information about infantry uniforms. In November 1686 a deserter from Duare in Dalmatia was taken back to the garrison, and a sergeant described his clothing as 'red cloth coat, white doublet, and white canvas breeches'.[239]

231 ASVe, *Senato Mar*, f. 688; 9 October 1690.

232 *Ibid.*, f. 698; 15 aprile 1692.

233 This did not include weapons but only the *pendon con sua tasca*: the bandolier and ammunition bag. One uniform totalled 70.10 *Lire*. *ASVe, Senato Mar*, f. 698; 9 March 1691.

234 *Ibid., Registro* 161; dated 12 March 1695; the moss-colour is deep brown-grey.

235 *Ibid., Senato Mar*, f. 724; 16 November 1695.

236 *Ibid.*, f. 698; 9 March 1691. See also the paintings illustrating the Siege of Corone in 1685 and Old Navarino in 1686.

237 *Ibid.*

238 Biblioteca Nazionale Centrale, Florence, 199 – Fondo Rossi-Cassigoli, *Manoscritto Fabroni.*

239 ASVe, *Senato Mar, Rapporti,* 1686, ff. 39–40.

Details regarding the uniform's cuffs remain elusive. A collection of wooden figures, possibly parts of a table game, provide a clue. Now preserved in a private collection in Verona, the wooden characters portray Venetian soldiers dating between 1685 and 1695. They are partially painted, wearing a red or azure coat, and some even include fine details such as button laces, which suggests their manufacturing from real models. Their coats, similar to a waistcoat, fit very tightly and lack cuffs.[240]

Venetian documents concerning infantry equipment in the early years of the war also discuss the soldiers' armament. In December 1685 the Senate decreed that the *Arsenale* should discontinue the production of infantry swords, and private soldiers were to be issued a bayonet. The decree specified that sword production would continue only if the number of bayonets proved insufficient to encounter the troops' needs. Additionally it required that the sword model was the *schiavona*. Some evidence regarding pikemen can be indirectly traced in arsenal inventories and military commanders' assessments; an analysis of these documents implies that Venetian pikemen had abandoned corselets and helmets for some time. The fact that no pieces of Venetian pikeman armour dated after the early seventeenth century survive further supports this supposition. According to a Venetian officer these protections were 'useless … for the minimum defence against the musket's ball'. General Fabio Gallo's regulation book clearly expressed this sentiment as early as 1620. Venetian infantry definitively abandoned the pike in 1686.

The outdated appearance of Venetian infantry became a typical characteristic during the last years of the war. Economic shortages forced the government to continually recycle armaments and equipment, therefore the Venetian army's equipment and uniforms strictly followed the *Serenissima*'s financial policy. Having completed the naval offensive and burdened by its incurred costs, the Republic found itself at a crossroads in the 1690s. By 1689 communications from the *Savio alle Scritture* emphasised the 'heavy contributions' consumed by army and fleet, and suggested some solutions to save 'everything possible'.[241] Moreover, the pike's abandonment around 1686 was not universally accepted in Western Europe. Therefore, the infantry stationed in the mainland were not always issued with bayonets, and the sword remained an individual accessory weapon. This ambivalence in armament lasted until the end of the war, and also survived into the following century.[242] The government tried to save resources by reusing infantry equipment and renounced the beautiful but

240 See Alberto Prelli, *Sotto le bandiere di San Marco. Le armate della Serenissima nel '600* (Bassano del Grappa: Itinera Progetti, 2012), illustrations 7–10 by Pietro Compagni.

241 ASVe, *Senato, mar, Rapporti*, 1689, ff. 12–13.

242 On 15 May 1702, the *Governatore delle Armi in Terraferma*, Du Hamel, wrote to the Senate: 'I would say anything over the soldiers' weapons … troops arrived from the *Levante*, which I found in good conditions, not knowing the reason why they have only the bayonet without swords, perhaps they were not useful against the Turks, but I believe that here, we could use them again with excellent service, still maintaining the bayonet', in: ASVe, *Senato, Provveditori di Terra e Mar, Dispacci*, b. 1248, d. 21.

also more expensive red or blue uniforms for more affordable items. These items derived from a variety of sources, including weapons and equipment from deserters of other Italian and foreign armies, which were sent to the arsenals or sold to other countries. Documents dating after 1696 contain some evidence relating to this change. Alongside the red and blue *velade* manufactured for the overseas front, increasing numbers of uniforms were tailored in undyed cloth. In addition to these official records, which rarely reveal which units received the different coloured uniforms, iconography indicates that, between the end of the seventeenth century and the beginning of the eighteenth, light grey became as common as the basic red or blue coats for the 'national' infantry.[243] A reasonable hypothesis is that the Italian regiments or at least the units created after 1694 received the new grey coats. Documentary evidence partly supports this conjecture, since immediately after the end of the war the regiments *Sala Veneto Real* (VI-12), *Marchesini* (VI-14), *Soardo* (VI-15), *Michiel* (VI-16), *Paradisi* (VI-17) and *Rossi* (VI-19) wore white coats with red or blue cuffs, while a more recent regiment, *Giuseppe Battaglia* (VI-28), received a light grey coat. Another Italian veteran regiment – *Degli Oddi* (VI-22) – still dressed in red, was distinguished by blue facing. The mixed Italian and *oltramontane* regiment of Colonel Francesco Bernardini (VI-30), formed in 1696, wore the same uniform. In 1700 a blue coat distinguished four *oltramontane* and two Corsican regiments, each identified by different coloured cuffs: red for the *oltramontane* and white for the latter.[244] The adoption of a less expensive fabric provided savings that allowed new items to be issued to the soldiers. The first document that mentions *sottovelade* or *camisole* (waistcoats) dates to November 1695 and summarises the costs incurred for the manufacture of 1,500 Italian regimental uniforms, consisting of red or blue *velade*, cloth breeches, shoes, and *sottovelada* of cloth as for the *velada*.[245] Adopting waistcoats was anything but a luxury. As experienced by other contemporary armies, these garments restricted the use of arbitrary informal clothing, the latter making it difficult to identify deserters. Contemporary documents use *camisiola* to identify the waistcoat, a term evidently borrowed from the German *Kamisol*. Presumably the waistcoat was introduced in imitation of the same clothing worn by German mercenaries. Towards the end of the century the Venetian infantry uniform seemed well on its way towards the German model. Therefore, from this date onwards, the common soldiers probably wore a tie with the knot behind their neck to distinguish themselves from non-commissioned officers, who instead wore the reverse,

243 ASVe, *Senato Mar*, Reg. 161.

244 A wide variety of Venetian infantry uniforms continued, at least up to 1706, and frequent changes occurred over few years. The regiment *Degli Oddi* in 1701dressed in white with red facings, five years later, it was dressed in red with blue cuffs, while on the same date the regiment *Veneto Real* changed from red to blue cuffs. In 1705, the *oltramontane* and Corsican regiments were dressed with white or blue coats; in 1706, only the *Bernardini* regiment, at this point completely Italian, maintained the original red uniform with blue cuffs.

245 ASVe, *Senato Mar*, f. 724, *16 IXmbre 1695*.

a practice from the Imperial army and other German states. The only resistance to adopting the most fashionable shapes and patterns appeared in the headgear. Within the Venetian army, the black felt cap maintained a form far from the tricorn, except that most of the edges were adorned with piping, usually white. Only the grenadier headgear followed the latest trends, and again it appeared very similar to the German models. The use of grenadier bearskin caps, similar to those used by the infantry of the Catholic countries, reaffirms a German influence.

This work continues in Part 2

Image Commentaries

Chapter 1

1. Capitan Spaventa, after a series of prints illustrating the characters of the Commedia dell'Arte, 1670–80 (author's archive). The image of Italians as a people with poor military qualities had already been established at the dawn of the modern era, following the collapse of the peninsula's political system as a result of the Italian Wars. Starting from these years, a disparaging interpretation emerged against which other literary testimonies would proudly attempt to react. These consisted of galleries of 'illustrious soldiers' and 'egregious exploits' to profile Italian officers, especially after the mid seventeenth century. Among the most famous works: Galeazzo Gualdo Priorato (1606–1678), military professional and historian, who wrote several works such as *Scena d'huomini illustri d'Italia conosciuti da lui singolari per Nascita, per Virtù e per Fortuna*, printed in 1659; the Domenican friar Raffaele Maria Filamondo (1649–1706), author of *Il genio bellicoso di Napoli. Memorie historiche d'alcuni capitani celebri napoletani, c'han militato per la fede, per lo Re, per la patria nel secolo corrente*, printed in 1694; the Count Giacomo Sanvitale (1668–1753), Jesuit and professor of mathematics and letters who in 1742 wrote *Scelta di azioni egregie operate in guerra da generali, e da soldati Italiani nel secolo ultimamente trascorso decimo settimo di nostra salute.*

2. Work of an anonymous artist, possibly a portrait of Prince Alessandro Farnese (1635–1689), general commander in the army of the Spanish monarchy (author's archive). A list of families boasting many men-at-arms in the sixteenth and seventeenth centuries can be reconstructed examining the career of Italian aristocrats who served as officers in their country or outside. The marquises of Saluzzo hold the first position with 96 names, followed by the Gonzaga with 94, the Orsini with 91, the Malatesta with 80 and the Savoye with 79. But great and small families from all over Italy belong to this remarkable military tradition: Biandrate, Borromeo, Bourbon del Monte, Brancaccio, Broglia, Caracciolo, Carafa, Colonna, Doria, Farnese, Fieschi, Incisa, Martinengo, Montecuccoli, Pallavicino, Piccolomini, Pignatelli, Savelli, Savorgnan, Spinola, Strozzi, Trivulzio, Visconti and many others. 'For every general who served abroad' – writes historian Enrico Stumpo – 'there were at least ten colonels; for every colonel, hundreds of other officers; for every officer, thousands of simple soldiers, recruited everywhere.' However, their history today is almost completely ignored.

4. The city-fortress of Palmanova, after the Civitates Orbis Terrarum of Braun and Hogenberg (1623). The fortress, located in the Republic of Venice near the border with the Austrian territory of Trieste, was one of the finest examples of the *trace italienne*. Bastioned fortresses were of fundamental importance for the Italian states. Raimondo Montecuccoli explained that fortresses were 'effective means to public tranquillity by securing the strength of the regents, the obedience of their subjects, good order inside, and resistance to violence outside.'

5. Genoese light infantry in an imaginative reconstruction by Italo Cenni (1874–1956). Watercolour of the Vinkhuijzen Collection of Military Uniforms preserved in the New York Public Library. Although much military literature evades this matter, in the second half of the seventeenth century, some Italian armies and communities successfully reintroduced the tactic of skirmishing. Infantrymen were thrown forwards and trained to fight in open order. Moving quickly and making use of cover, they fired on the enemy line, annoying and goading it, and all the time distracting it from the infantry battalions in close order coming up behind. Venice, Genoa and also the Waldensians of Piedmont turned to light infantry tactics, achieving many successes in Greece, the Balkans, Liguria and Alps.

6. War scene with cavalry, oil painting by Pandolfo Reschi (1643–1699) preserved in a private collection. Despite the flourishing of the 'battle scenes' genre in the second half of the seventeenth century, the Italian military was essentially a static defence force with a few exceptions. This contributed considerably to decreasing the efficiency of the troops. Among the consequences generated by this scenario emerges a little considered aspect, namely the progressive ageing of soldiers and officers, who, in the absence of a physical turnover due to military campaigns, remained in service until the end of their lives. Although the first records regarding the generalities of soldiers date back to the first half of the eighteenth century, the scenario must not have been very different from the one existing 50 years earlier. More or less throughout Italy, many soldiers were found continuing to serve despite their very advanced age. For example, in 1745 in the Tuscan garrison of Portoferraio, on the island of Elba, a soldier with a declared age of 96 years(!) was still serving after having spent 67 years as soldier.

8. Frontispiece of Antonio Maurizio Valperga's Indirizzo del Nuovo Soldato (1650). The author was a leading military theoretician and architect who still awaits full recognition. Probably born in Turin in 1605 or 1606, Valperga became the disciple of military architect Carlo di Castellamonte as early as 1626 and entered the service of the Duke of Savoy as an engineer in 1634. In the 1640s he entered the service of France and was sent by Mazzarino to Orbetello following the French conquest in 1646. Captured by the Spanish, he was imprisoned at Naples in the fortress of Castel Sant'Elmo. He remained a prisoner until 1659 and during this time published two works on military technique. Returning to freedom, he was still in the service of Mazzarino who entrusted him with the project (later passed to Guarino Guarini) for the

Church of Sainte-Anne la Royale in Paris, in which the cardinal intended to be buried. Valperga was again in Turin in 1663, where he became a renowned technician and thanks to his earnings began the construction of his own residence in Turin and another in Grugliasco. However, he did not interrupt his travels which, as a military engineer, took him not only to France but also to Flanders, Munich and Malta. He died in Turin in 1688.

Chapter 2

9. Alessandro II Pico della Mirandola (1631–1691), portrait attributed to Biagio Falcieri, City Museum of Mirandola. The Duchy of Mirandola and Concordia had no standing troops, only a militia estimated in the 1690s by Henrich Ludwig Gude (*Staat von Parma und Piacenza, Mirandula, und Concordia…*), at about 4,000 infantrymen. However, in 1669 the small state of Emilia contributed together with the Pope, Mantua, Modena and Parma to raise a contingent of 3,000 soldiers, sailors and volunteers to relieve Candia, under siege by the Ottomans. The Duke was appointed as a commander-in-chief. Part of the contingent joined the garrison a few weeks before the surrender, but Alessandro II arrived in Crete late and did not take part in the fighting, which, as his biographers report, he longed for. Despite the unfortunate outcome of the expedition, an extensive and interesting chronicle of the journey to Crete was written by the Duke's surgeon, Giovanni Francesco Piccinini.

10. A view of Piombino in 1700 (author's archive). The small fief ruled by Buoncompagni-Ludovisi was another Spanish facility on the route from Catalonia to Naples, but differently from the *Estado de los Presidios*, Piombino was an independent state with domains on the Tuscan mainland and on the island of Elba. Since the Middle Ages, every vassal exercised power, at least formally, by mandate and investiture by the emperor as his feudal lord. The same instrument of Imperial investiture was used to legalise city lordships and principalities, thus emphasising the formal and direct bond with the Empire.

11. The city of Messina, in a print by Vincenzo Maria Coronelli (1690). In 1674, Louis XIV had taken advantage of an anti-Spanish insurrection in Messina to send an expeditionary force to Sicily. France's move surprised and worried Venice, which decided to rearm a substantial number of ships while professing its neutrality. However, although it was recognised that the strengthening French presence in the Mediterranean posed a serious danger to the *Serenissima*'s trade network, the fear of offending Louis XIV prevented a more aggressive policy. Indeed, when the Emperor asked the Senate to allow Spanish ships to embark the troops he had gathered in Trieste to send them to Sicily, Venice resolutely refused transit in the Adriatic. 'Louis XIV had made it known through his ambassador that any aid granted to the Habsburgs of Austria and Spain would be considered an action of war against France' (P. Duparc (editor), *Recueil des Instructions donne aux ambassedeurs et ministres de France depuis les traités de Westphalie jusq'a la Revolution Française*, XXVI, *Venise*, (Paris, 1958).

15. The Sala del Collegio of Venice, in the seventeenth century. Foreign ambassadors to Venice were received in this hall, where the doge and his councillors presided over the audiences. There was a severe etiquette, explained in a letter of 21 November 1670 by English resident John Dodington: 'I entered the *sala*, which has a double door … both were open and so remained during the whole time of my audience. This ceremonial is only applied to representatives of crowned heads. Florence enters with both doors open, but immediately afterwards they are closed, Modena enters with one door only open and then closed, so that no one else can enter the College.'

17. The territory of the Republic of Cospaia in a seventeenth-century map (author's archive). The Republic came into being in 1441 after the treaty between Pope Eugene IV and Florence, which provided for the cession of the territory between Sansepolcro and Città di Castello to the Florentines as a compensation for a money loan. Each of the parties established a commission to delineate the new borders, but there was no mutual co-ordination, nor were any verifications carried out on the location. Here, a small hill village was surrounded by two streams with the same name, Rio, and each commission took the one closest to its border as a reference: hence the territory of Cospaia, about three square kilometres populated by a few hundred people, remained without a ruler. None of the parties asked for a revision of the treaty, and the territory of Cospaia began to govern itself according to egalitarian principles three centuries before the French revolution. With any ruler, army, and foreign interference, the Republic survived until 1826, and enjoyed considerable prosperity thanks to tobacco cultivation and trade, but also contraband.

Chapter 3

20. Carlo Emanuele II, Duke of Savoy (1634–1675), portrayed by unidentified artist, c. 1660 (private collection). He was the son of Vittorio Amedeo I and Christine of France. His maternal grandparents were Henry IV of France and his second wife Marie de' Medici. In 1637 Christine of France assumed the regency, confronting the pro-Spanish faction reborn under the princes Tommaso and Maurizio. The period of civil war between the *madamisti* and *principisti* (1638–1642) practically wiped out all attempts to implement an independent foreign policy. In 1638 at the death of his older brother Francesco Giacinto, Carlo Emanuele became duke of Savoy at the age of four. Even after reaching adulthood in 1648, he invited his mother to continue to rule. Only after her death in 1663 did he actually assume power. After his premature death at 41, his wife became the second *Madama Reale* in the history of the Duchy. The period between the regency of Maria Giovanna of Nemours and the reign of Vittorio Amedeo II marks a particularly important period in Savoy-Piedmont military history, because it saw the introduction of innovations that were to remain unchanged until the nineteenth century. Despite his failures in the military field, Carlo Emanuele II is considered the founder of the military tradition of Savoy-Piedmont, and consequently of post-unification Italy.

21. Youthful portrait of Vittorio Amedeo as Prince of Piedmont, approximately 1675–76, by Pierre Mignard, Museum of Palazzo Madama, Turin. Vittorio Amedeo II was born on 14 May 1666, and was a little over nine years old when his father died. He was a delicate boy. During his childhood it had been feared that he would never live to grow up; according to tradition he owed his life to a village doctor the Duchess called in, who, having vetoed various drugs prescribed by the Court physicians, ordered his little ducal patient to be brought up on the very simplest fare, and thus saved his life. He was very precocious, and showed signs of gravity and strength of character really unusual in so young a boy. When Vittorio Amedeo came of age he developed a 'chameleon-like attitude' that became a distinctive trait for the rest of his life.

22. The fortification of Turin after the enlargement of the north-west sector in the 1670s, in a French print dated 1690 (Bibliothèque Nationale de France, Paris). After the improvements, Turin's curtain and ramparts formed a block with a remarkable pentagonal citadel, built by the famous architect Francesco Paciotto (1521–1591), designed in the so-called *di rinforzo* style, namely a defence projected for forcing a besieger to concentrate on a specific point. The citadel disposed of five ramparts, of which two guarded the city, known as *Duca* and *Duchessa*, and the other three toward the countryside, bearing the name of *San Lazzaro*, *San Maurizio* and *Beato Amedeo*. In 1572 two ravelins were also added with two galleries of countermines, enlarged and extended several more times until the end of the century. Substantial enlargement occurred in the 1670s, with the construction of a new curtain with two ramparts in the north-west side between the citadel and *la Consolata*.

26. 'The Boar Hunting', by Jean Miel, 1660–61 (Collection of the Venaria Reale, Turin). The series included scenes of court's life of the Savoy house. The figures are dressed in French style, and blue coats are predominant in the clothing of high-ranked people. Most recent historiography has produced a more objective picture of the Savoy court in the seventeenth century, previously regarded as provincial and stubbornly closed to novelties from outside. Although Turin appeared to be a less attractive and lively city compared to other Italian metropolises, its role as the capital of an undisputed regional power was sufficient to place it among the most important centres of the Peninsula. Important witnesses of the role of Turin's court were many gentlemen who, especially from the late seventeenth century, chose the Savoy capital as a training stop on their grand tour.

28. Carlo Emanuele Giacinto di Simiana, Marquis of Pianezza (1608–1677) in a print after Gualdo Priorato's Historia di Leopoldo Cesare (1670). Born after his father's death, he was educated by his mother according to the principles of an ascetic and rigid Catholicism. This contributed to giving Carlo Emanuele Giacinto a closed, gloomy character, and a tendency to loneliness that would mark him deeply in his later years. His first political assignment was in 1632, when he was sent by Vittorio Amedeo I as extraordinary ambassador to Emperor Ferdinand II, to agree on the cession of the part of Monferrato obtained with the Treaty of Cherasco. Returning home, he was called to serve on the ducal council. He then began his military career, serving under Marquis Guido Villa. On the death of Duke Vittorio Amedeo I in 1637 Duchess Christine, regent for her son, assigned Pianezza increasingly important tasks. This initially met with opposition from France, but when civil war broke out between the *madamisti* and *principisti* in 1638, Pianezza and his family sided firmly with the former. After the arrest of Filippo d'Agliè, Christine's favourite, on 30 September 1640, and his deportation to France, Pianezza became the actual prime minister of the state, holding this role for over 25 years. He supported the severe policy against the Waldensians in 1655. In the 1660s the resumption of diplomatic relations between Venice and Turin was one of his major achievements. When Christine died in 1663, he tried to adapt to the policy of Carlo Emanuele II. In May 1667, having obtained permission to leave the court, he retired into a convent. His post passed to his son Carlo Giovanni Battista.

34. Vittorio Amedeo visits the port of Nice, 1689; oil painting of unknown artist (Umberto II and Maria José of Savoy Foundation, Geneva). Note the *guard du corps* in foreground carrying a carbine. The companies of the *Garde du Corps* are the best documented units of the Savoy-Piedmont army regarding uniforms and equipment. Notwithstanding the lack of iconographic sources concerning the Duchy's army, the *Garde du Corps* appear in several contemporary paintings illustrating Victor Amadeus in his early phase of government.

36. *Gardes du Corps*, 1685–89. When engaged in official duty or as escort for the ruling family, the household troops wore a 'high uniform' consisting in broad-brimmed hat with silver piping and white plume, scarlet coat with silver lace, scarlet waistcoat and breeches; a wide red cloak and an azure bandolier with golden edgings completed the uniform. On campaign the *Gardes du Corps* replaced the red coat with one of leather. (Author's illustration after Ciro Paoletti's *William III's Italian Ally. Piedmont and the War of the League of Augsburg*, Helion & Company, 2019)

43. Exhibition of the Holy Shroud in Piazza Castello, Turin 1684, by Pieter Bolckmann (Collection of the Castello di Racconigi, Cuneo). Two regiments of dragoons in the foreground, one dressed in blue and the other in red, attend the ritual religious ceremony that took place every year. They are probably the dragoon regiment *Madama Reale*, which existed between 1683 and 1685, and the one of *Sua Altezza Reale*. Note in the background officers and soldiers of the *Guardie*, including grenadiers wearing red slouch caps. The infantry still comprises pikemen.

45. Savoyard cavalry, 1670–1690, in a painting of an anonymous artist (the Italian Army's Cavalry Museum of Pinerolo). This painting represents a mystery that is difficult to solve. The caption states that the scene represnts the formation of the *Savoie* cavalry regiment in 1692. However, the cavalrymen deployed in the background are dressed in blue, whereas in 1692 the regiment wore a grey coat with red facing. Moreover, some of the figures are dressed in a style at least 20 years earlier. As if this were not enough, the two horsemen in the foreground, two *Gardes du Corps*, seem to have been added at a later date, since their *justaucorps* are apparently from the 1730s–40s.

Chapter 4

46. Equestrian portrait of *Doge* Francesco Morosini by Giovanni Carboncino, dating to 1690 (Correr Museum, Venice). After his extraordinary performances from 1684 to 1687 the great Venetian commander did not always have equally capable substitutes, and except for Girolamo Corner, the captain-generals who succeeded him achieved poor results. During the war against the Porte, the succession of the commanders in chief comprised Girolamo Corner (1689); Domenico Mocenigo (1690–92); Francesco Morosini (1693); Antonio Zeno (1694–95); Alessandro Molin (1695–97); Giacomo Corner (1698–99). The oblivion that has fallen on the military history of the *Serenissima* has contributed to relegating Morosini to a secondary position among the great captains of the second half of the seventeenth century. However, his successes were no less striking than the ones achieved by skilled commanders such as Condé, Turenne or Montecuccoli, to the extent that Morosini would rightfully enter the Pantheon of the great generals of his age.

47. Map of the Morea (Peloponnese) with its main fortresses, by Vincenzo Maria Coronelli (author's archive). After the conquest, the territory was divided in four provinces; Acaia in the north-west, Romania in the north-east, Messenia in the south-west, and Laconia in the south-east. For the Venetians, the newly conquered 'kingdom' appeared to be in very poor condition: sparse population, poverty and backwardness were to blame for bad Ottoman administration as a long negative experience. Immediately, the Senate favoured a policy of colonisation. Not only soldiers, engineers and sailors made their way to the Morea, but also impoverished aristocrats, lawyers, artisans and farmers. A dispatch dated 7 September 1686 states that 'many labourers with their families arrive in the new territories to build churches and palaces … this kingdom being the most fertile among those the Sultan has in Europe, abounding in waxes, silks and many other goods.' Despite this idyllic scenario, Venice encountered many difficulties when it tried to raise a defence force in the newly conquered territories. In each province of the Morea a militia system was raised, but poor funds and lack of cooperation from inhabitants left this domain without an effective defence, forcing the Venetian commanders to maintain strong garrisons. Coeval commenters stated that the Greeks of these provinces were a 'very coward' population, who in the aftermath of the conquest of the Peloponnese reacted with fear whenever they were shown weapons or asked to serve in the militia.

51. Encampment scenes attributed to Francesco Simonini (1686–1753 or 1755), preserved in a private collection. The artist obtained considerable success in Venice, when he worked for Johann Matthias von der Schulenburg, the commander-in-chief of the Venetian army from 1716 to 1733. Both paintings clearly show Venetian troops, however the figures wear a style unrelated to the painter's period of activity. Although many subjects seem to derive from Mannerist models, some details are very representative, and can be dated between 1680 and 1690. In the first painting there are some officers wearing leather coats and breast armour with fronts and backs. Behind them, a red and yellow square flag charged with the Lion of St Mark indicates the presence of infantry. On the left side, trumpeters with sleeveless coats are calling for the assembly of the troops. In the second painting, another officer wearing leather coat and cuirass greets a senior commander, who has a similar leather coat but without sleeves.

54. Portrait of Count Girolamo Secco-Suardo, early eighteenth century, by Vittore Ghislandi, also known as Fra' Galgario (Carrara Museum, Bergamo). The Venetian aristocracy held the control of the state, and the command of the fleet, however the ranks of nobility and the officer posts were less impermeable for the lower class compared to other Italian states. Noble status could be purchased to accede to office in the Republic, and after 10 years of service in the army or fleet the NCOs could accede to higher ranks after an examination, and if their service was positive they could climb up to the rank of colonel or ship commander.

57. Venetian galleass, 1680s, copy after the Manfroni Manuscript (Florence, Biblioteca Nazionale Centrale). The galleass was a Venetian invention introduced at the Battle of Lepanto in 1571, and other fleets, including the Ottomans, later imitated them. It differed from a galley in size, and because of the presence of two castles, forward and aft, which significantly increased its firepower. Galleasses could have 32 to 46 oar banks and were able to carry up to 900 men, of which oarsmen represented three-fifths. Armament consisted of 22 artillery pieces, including a pair of 50- and 430-pounders. Four of these large pieces were culverins, longer and more powerful than ordinary guns. In total there were six culverins greater than 14 lb, plus additional 14-, 6-, 20-, and 30-pounders with eight *petrieri* (a gun that shot stone projectiles) of smaller calibres. Eight guns were placed on the aft: two culverins ranging from 14- to 30-pounders together with four 6-pounders. Like the galleys, the Venetian galleass had a red hull, while the ship of the squadron commander was painted in black. Slower and more difficult to handle than the galleys, galleasses performed very poorly during the 1684–99 war. After 1698 they were used for transport and escort duties and in the following century were finally excluded from the war fleet.

61. Officer and private of the *Alabardieri* (Lifeguard Halberdiers), in 1694. The origin of this corps dates back to the early 1500s. The unit was a palace guard corps, employed to escort the *Doge* and other important personalities in Venice or in the Domains. The corps had a size of one company with 24–30 halberdiers, and also included 14 musicians, 18 *staffieri* (footmen) and one captain with one lieutenant. In the painting preserved in the Correr Museum in Venice, the halberdiers are portrayed in Nauplia while they are escorting the burial service of Francesco Morosini. On that occasion, the guards wore the 'high uniform' consisting of gold laced doublet, breeches and stockings of yellow cloth, azure-blue waistcoat for private halberdiers, and yellow for officers and musicians. The officer's sash is of azure silk with golden edgings. Black headgear with white plumes for officers, and red-azure-white for privates. Note the false sleeves on the back of the private's doublet.

62. The 'ordinary uniform' of the *Alabardieri* is described in the documents preserved in the Venice State Archive. This uniform was tailored of red velvet with yellow facing and lining, golden laces and buttons, and was less aulic compared to the previous one, although it was completed by a large plumed hat in black felt piped with yellow. Uniforms included azure-blue stockings for private halberdiers and red for musicians and officers. A) *velada* (coat); B) *camisiola* (waistcoat); C) *braghe* (breeches); d) detail of sword bandolier for both uniforms of red velvet with golden edging.

63. Count Otto Wilhelm von Königsmarck (1639–1688), portrayed by David Klöcker Ehrenstrahl, Nationalmuseum, Stockholm). The second 'architect' of the glorious Venetian victories was born in Minden, Westphalia, son of General Count Hans Kristofer, originally from Brandenburg, who entered Swedish service in 1631. Like his father, Otto Wilhelm entered the Swedish army, but in 1674 moved to France where he reached the rank of *lieutenant-général* during the campaigns in the Netherlands, the Rhine and Franche-Comté. After the Peace of Nijmegen, Swedish King Carl XI appointed Königsmarck field marshal and gave him a position of authority, appointing him governor-general of Swedish Pomerania. After negotiations with the Venetian Senate for his appointment, the Count arrived in Venice in February 1686 accompanied by his wife Katarina Charlotta de la Gardie (1655–1697), a woman of equally determined character, who followed her husband on all the Greek campaigns until 1688. In July 1686, after the conquest of Modone, it was a sensation that the Countess immediately entered the city, despite the rubble still to be removed and the rotting corpses. Not even the Marquise de Courbon, who had accompanied her husband during this campaign, 'despite much he had insisted on remaining in Venice', restrained herself from entering the city, competing with the Countess as if they had been at the court of a European capital. The Countess was temperamental, but the Marquise no less so, 'one of the Amazons of our times', as the chroniclers of the time reported. As a result, an unhealthy atmosphere of jealousy and competition developed between these two women and their husbands.

64. Portrait of the *oltramontane* Colonel Bartolomeo Manganoni, from Bergamo, by Fra' Galgario, alias Vittore Ghislandi, 1693 (Musèe des Beaux Arts of Narbonne). In October 1685 Manganoni received a commission to recruit 3,000 infantrymen 'from beyond the Alps' to be divided into 10 companies. The regiment, formed with mercenaries from Germany and the

Grisons, was formed in 1686 and remained in service until 1702: a remarkable longevity for the Venetian army of those years. During the war against the Porte the regiment served in Dalmatia and Albania. The red coat and gold embroidery are coherent with the Venetian trend for military uniforms in the 1680s, whilst the yellow cuffs are less common for the infantry, but in the late seventeenth century the officers could dress as they wish.

65. *Schiavoni* (Slav) infantrymen at the siege of Modone, 1686. Copy after the Manfroni Manuscript. The author has depicted all the soldiers with clothing and red hats. The text describes the weapons *alla turchesca*, comprising musket, sabre and 'iron mace'. To distinguish themselves from the Ottomans, the Venetian light infantrymen applied a white cross of paper on the headdress. Like their opponents, they did not use drums for war signals, but whistles. Note the NCO with a halberd, and the unique arrangement of muskets in the space outside the encampment.

67. *Crovato* horseman, by Francesco Simonini (1686–1753), early eighteenth century (private collection). Venetian-Slavic light cavalrymen were also called *cappelletti* after their headdress, which usually was a small cap manufactured of red cloth or felt. Relations between Venice and the populations of the overseas domains did not always run harmoniously, however, a strong bond developed between the *Dominante* and these remote peripheries. In 1698 the communities in Dalmatia bordering the regions under the Austrians declared in a letter sent to the *provveditore*, that they preferred 'to die free with Venice, than to live as slaves under the Germans'.

68. Albanian light infantryman, after a painted chest of the late seventeenth or early eighteenth century (private collection, Venice). Albanian soldiers in Venetian service mainly came from Kotor and the Chimerya mountains. This irregular wears a white plumed cap of red cloth and the typical *fustanella* skirt over a pair of trousers buttoned on the sides. The dark blue short *koret* jacket with squared collar and buttoned sleeves is an uncommon feature. The *fustanella* was a common garment of the male population settled in the Adriatic and Ionian regions of Albania and Greece.

69. An alleged portrait of Stojan Kankovič Mitrovič (1636–1687), by an anonymous artist (private collection). After the death of the legendary Stiepan Sorič, in the 1660s Mitrovič replaced him as leading chief of the Morlachs who had joined the Venetian side after 1645. At 15 years old Mitrovič began service during the Cretan War as an irregular, together with his father. In 1659, the now experienced young warrior was chosen as the leader of the Morlachs of Žegar. In this role he constantly took part in the raids and encounters against the Ottomans on the border between Dalmatia and Bosnia. He became famous for defeating numerous Ottoman contingents and killing several enemy commanders. In 1666, near Obrovac on the Cetina River, Mitrovič was captured by the Ottomans and spent 14 months as a slave in Constantinople before managing to escape and return home. In 1681 he became the 'principal leader of the Morlacs', with a monthly salary of 25 *ducati* (ducats). In 1683 his brother and second in command Ilija conducted several actions against the Ottomans, despite war between Venice and the Porte having not been declared. For this the brothers were imprisoned, but in 1684 they returned to lead their irregulars alongside the Venetian troops in Dalmatia. In 1687, at the siege of Castelnuovo di Cattaro (Herçeg Novi), Mitrovič participated with his troops and plundered the Ottoman villages of Tomislavgrad, Livno and Glamoč. In this last encounter he was killed on 23 August 1687. The Venetians wrote of him that he had 'a heart bigger than his brain', but despite the ambivalent judgements, Mitrovič became famous among the Christian Slavic peoples of the Balkans.

70. Venetian *corazze*: trumpeter and officer, regiment Giona, 1696–1700. Venetian heavy cavalrymen wore leather coat with waistcoats and cuffs of red for regiment *San Bonifacio* and blue for *Giona*. Officers worn white coats with cuffs of the distinctive colours, and azure sash around the waist with golden edgings and fringes. The trumpeter wears the livery of the company commander, captain Fulvio Porcia: straw-yellow headgear with blue and yellow plumes; sleeveless coat of azure-blue laced of gold and gilded buttons, over a natural leather coat. (Author's reconstruction after contemporary paintings)

74. Gun for firing bombs, after the project drawings of the renowned artillery technician and caster Sigismondo Alberghetti. During the battle of Mythilini, fought on September 1698, the Venetian fleet used this type of gun which was capable of firing explosive projectiles. Throughout the war against the Porte experiments were being made in all directions. There was a very lively controversy between the renowned Antonio Muttoni, Count of San Felice and Alberghetti who, during his stay in England in 1683–1685, had registered a concession from the Senate for the production of 120 mortars, with an exclusive right for 20 years. However, as the latter bitterly affirmed towards the end of his life, 'nothing was considered good for the public service in artillery matters, if it was not proposed by Muttoni', since the Count enjoyed the support of Captain-General and later *Doge* Francesco Morosini.

75. Venetian Engineer, 1680s (author's reconstruction). In the seventeenth century the term 'engineer' identified a specialist with different skills including fortification design, preparation of batteries for the artillery siege, use of explosives, and the direction of mine works. This activity occurred in a theoretical framework and in practical terms. Thus, it was an intermediate level between a craftsman with the rank of a warrant officer and a technician with the expertise of an artillery officer. During the war against the Porte in Greece and in the Balkans, Venice contributed to developing the engineer in the modern sense, as fundamental figures in the larger military framework. Thus, in siege tactics, engineers obtained the role of a specialist.

78. Possibly a Venetian *grenatier*, copy after the Manfroni Manuscript, 1684–88. Note the ribbon on the shoulder as distinctive for elite troops, as used in the French infantry, but with the grenadier fur cap of evidently German provenance. This extraordinary series of 265 drawings of the Rossi-Cassigoli collection, now preserved in the *Biblioteca Nazionale Centrale* of Florence, represents a vivid and fully illustrated source on the Ottoman wars in the Mediterranean during the last quarter of the seventeenth century. The Manfroni Manuscript is also an inestimable source of knowledge for the dress and equipment of the Italian navy and army in this period. The series starts approximately in 1669 and finishes in 1688, when the Tuscan fleet interrupted its participation in the war as a Venetian auxiliary.

79. Foot militiaman of the *Reggimento Offerto dalla Città di Padova*, c. 1690. The earliest records concerning the uniform for the *cernide* date back to the early eighteenth century, when the conflict between Austrian Habsburgs and French–Spanish Bourbons in Northern Italy forced the government to mobilise the Mainland's militia regiments. However, it is likely that uniforms and equipment received after 1701 were the same as those received years earlier, when units of this semi-permanent type were created on the Italian mainland. Despite the discipline of the Venetian militia often leaving much to be desired, the punishment reserved for those who did not present at reviews or tried to avoid exercise and mobilisation could be very severe. The first recall involved a financial penalty, the second three rope stretches, and a further relapse up to 18 months at the oar of a galley.

Colour Plate Commentaries

Plate A – Savoy-Piedmont, 1660–1670

1. *Gendarme* cavalryman in buff, 1670

This figure is from a painting preserved in the Cavalry Museum of the Italian Army in Pinerolo. Dating to the last decades of the seventeenth century, it depicts cavalrymen dressed in blue on parade. They are in all probability mounted gendarmes, who originated the first regular cavalry regiment of Savoy-Piedmont. This reconstruction is equipped in accordance with the items preserved in military storage for cavalry before 1690. Contemporary accounts also relate that the *Gendarmi* in active service wore a sleeveless leather coat like the coeval French *Cavalerie Légère*.

2. Infantry officer, 1660–62

This figure comes from a painting of Jean Miel, dating to the early 1660s. Wearing a fashionable *justaucorps* and broad-brimmed hat with plumes, he is hardly distinguishable from a contemporary French officer.

3. Guards Regiment, musketeer, 1669–70

Nineteenth-century iconography shows the Savoyard foot guards still wearing azure-blue coats with red facings and linings sin 1659. Although there is little iconographic evidence before 1684, the orders issued by Duke Charles Emmanuel in 1671 concerning the Guards' uniform seem to confirm pre-existing clothing that already identified the regiment with these colours.

Plate B – Savoy-Piedmont, 1671–1684

1. *Savoie* Infantry Regiment, NCO, 1672–76

2. *Savoie* Infantry Regiment, musketeer, 1672–76

Both these figures come from the painting attributed to Giovani Battista Abret in the early 1670s. The soldiers depicted are barely identifiable but some details could have been taken from life, since the musketeer and NCO wear clothing of different colours, a detail that does not seem accidental.

3. Guard Infantry Regiment, officer, 1684

An order issued by Duke Vittorio Amedeo prescribed scarlet-red coats for all the Guards Regiment's officers. This figure comes from the painting illustrating the exhibition of the Holy Syndon in 1684.

Plate C – Savoy-Piedmont

Royal Piémont Cavalerie, 1670–71

The former cavalry regiment of Prince Vittorio Amedeo was sold to France in 1671. The agreements stipulated that all officers had to be subjects of the Duke of Savoy and the regiment retained its original name. This regiment had been formed with volunteers from the mounted *gendarmi* of the Piedmontese Militia in 1670. In the 1670s and possibly before, the *gendarmi* wore an azure-blue coat or at least clothing related to the heraldic colour of the House of Savoy, namely azure. It is also confirmed that once in the French army, the regiment retained these colours until the following century.

Plate D – Venice, 1680–1684

1. Galley commander, 1684–88

This figure is a reconstruction from contemporary prints and items, like the elaborate *corsaletto da mar* possibly belonging to Pietro Antonio Martinengo and now preserved in the *Armeria Reale* of Turin. Armour remained popular among the Venetian aristocracy, and such defensive weapons were manufactured in considerable quantity in Brescia. In action, the broad-brimmed hat was usually replaced by a 'lobster' helmet.

2. Sailor, 1680s

This figure comes from the Manfroni Manuscript, illustrating sailors and crewmen of the Venetian and Allied fleet during the campaigns against the Porte in the Mediterranean. Contemporary accounts relate that at the beginning of a campaign the Venetian galleys crews, oarsmen included, received new clothing, consisting of short *velada* and slouch cap of carmine-red cloth. Such mass production inevitably meant they were not of a high standard and were liable to wear and damage in a very short time.

Plate E – Venice, *oltramarine* infantry, 1680–1690

1. *Schiavone* infantryman, 1680s

The first documents relating to the clothing issued to the *schiavoni* date back to 1695, when an order for purchasing red clothes is recorded. However, this colour had been definitely adopted as distinctive by the overseas native infantry in the second half of the 1680s. This is confirmed in the Manfroni Manuscript, where in 1686 the *schiavoni* are represented wearing short red coats.

2. Albanian infantryman with rampart musket, 1685–90
Legends and fantastic tales circulated about the countries where the Albanian soldiers came from. One account from the end of the seventeenth century claimed that the inhabitants of Chymeria lived on Mountains infested by vultures and other large birds of prey that could kidnap a lamb and even a child. This figure came from a seventeenth-century painting by David Selaniki illustrating a crucifixion, now preserved in the Museum of the Orthodox Cathedral of Tirana. Descriptions of Albanian soldiers in Venetian service describe them as noticeably strong, mostly tall and well-built. They usually shaved their head, but every adult male had a moustache. The *fustanella* skirt of white cotton worn over tight trousers was typical male dress of the communities settled in the coastal areas of Greece as well as Albania.

3. Morlach irregular, 1680s
Morlachs consisted predominantly of South Slavs but included a small number of Aromanian nomads coming from modern Romania, who had been established in the Balkans since the Middle Ages. Their dress varied considerably from one place to another; however, their weaponry was uniform and usually included knives and sabres, while the leaders were often armed with hammer axes or war maces. They wore a wide selection of hats, comprising fur hats, tall caps of fulled wool, and even coloured turbans. A contemporary traveller described the Morlachs and other Balkan communities like 'the Iroquois of these countries' because of their social structure and warfare.

Plate F – Venice, Cavalry and Dragoons

1. Dragoon Regiment *Courbon*, dragoon, 1686
Iconographic sources relating to the campaign in Greece show the dragoons wearing red coats with yellow cuffs and linings, and French-style forage caps with the Venetian lion embroidered on the front.

2. German free company of *Carabini*; NCO, 1699
The Venetians were chronically lacking in heavy cavalry, and this type of cavalry was an uncommon utility in their armies from the early stages of the war of 1684–99. Cuirassiers are sporadically mentioned in Dalmatia, and it was in this territory that a couple of companies of mounted *carabini* were formed with veterans from the German horse companies dissolved at the end of the war against the Porte. One of these was the lifeguard of Colonel Carlo Giussani, cavalry commander in Dalmatia. Like the German infantrymen, this carabineer wore a blue coat with red cuffs. The polished, bare metal armour with black stripes, and the lobster helm, are today preserved in a private Italian collection.

Plate G – Venice, 1694–1698

1. Artilleryman, 1694

2. Artillery driver, 1694

Both figures are based on the painting attributed to Alessandro Piazza, depicting the funeral of Francesco Morosini in Nauplia. Until the early 1680s the predominant influence in Venetian military dress came from France, but after the alliance with the Habsburgs and the substantial increase in contingents from Germany, the 'Imperial' style quickly prevailed throughout the army.

3. Infantry Regiment *Veneto Real*, Musketeer, 1698

The Austrian–German style is the appearance for this musketeer belonging to the Venetian landing infantry. The cravat tied behind the neck is typical of the Imperial infantry from the late seventeenth century, identifying private soldiers from NCOs. In the 1690s Italian infantry had coats of white or red, while *oltramontani* and Corsicans were dressed in blue with facings of different colours. This musketeer carries a modern flintlock which replaces the heavy and uncomfortable matchlock; however, the latter weapon continued to be issued to the infantry in the mainland garrisons until the following century.

Plate H – Venice's Italian allies, 1684–1690

1. Grand Duchy of Tuscany, knight of the Order of St Stephen (Santo Stefano), 1684–88

This figure comes from a painting portraying a knight of the Order of St Stephen in the 1680s, possibly the Count Camilli Guidi, commander of the Grand Duke's contingent in the Morea. He wears breast armour carrying the red cross of the Order of St Stephen, over a leather coat with embroidered cuffs. He also wears the azure sash with golden edging also issued to the Venetian officers.

2. Grand Duchy of Tuscany, pikeman, 1686–88

In the Manfroni Manuscript, the Tuscan infantry is depicted wearing grey coat faced of red, grey breeches and stockings. Pikes still formed the weaponry of one third of the Tuscan infantry contingent, as related in the contemporary sources. In the *Anonima Relatione* of the 1688 campaign, the Tuscan pikemen are described as wearing a cuirass and bourgonet of white metal.

3. Papal States, *Guardie di Nostro Signore*, musketeer, 1690s

This figure is based on the painting depicting the Papal infantry dating to 1690. The four Papal infantry companies wore a dark blue coat with cuffs, lining and stockings of a distinctive colour: red for the first company, 'citron yellow' for the second, grey for the third, 'cinnamon green' for the fourth.

Bibliography

Archival Sources

Archivio dell'Ufficio Storico dello Stato Maggiore dell'Esercito (AUSSME), Rome

Archivio di Stato di Torino (ASTo), *Sezione I & II, Materie Militari, Ufficio Generale del Soldo e Imprese Militari; Ordini e Regolamenti; Sezione III & IV, Ufficio Generale del Soldo, Ordini Generali Misti; Regolamenti Militari*

Biblioteca Nazionale di Torino (BNT)

Biblioteca Reale di Torino (BRT)

Archivio di Stato di Venezia (ASVe), *Senato Mar, dispacci di Provveditori di Terra e di Mar; Savi alle Scritture; Provveditore sopra le artiglierie*

Biblioteca Museo Correr (BMC), Venice

Biblioteca Nazionale Marciana (BNM), Venice

Biblioteca Querini-Stampalia (BQS), Venice

Archivio di Stato di Genova (ASGe), *Archivio Segreto; Guerra e Marina*

Biblioteca Civica Berio (BCB), Genoa

Archivio di Stato di Roma (ASRo), *Soldatesche e Galere; Congregazioni Particolari Deputate 1600–1760; Congregazioni Particolari*

Archivio Segreto Vaticano (ASV), Rome, *Commissariato Armi; Segreteria di Stato, Soldati*

Biblioteca della Camera Apostolica, Rome (BCA)

Archivio di Stato di Firenze (ASFi), *Mediceo del Principato, Spedizione di sodatesche in Levante; Depositeria Generale, Miscellanea Medicea, Scrittoio delle Fortezze e Fabbriche*

Archivio di Stato di Pisa (ASPi), *Ordine dei Cavalieri di Santo Stefano, Ruoli*

Archivio di Stato di Parma (ASPr), *Governo Farnesiano, Milizie; Memorabilia civitas Parmae, 1688–1708*

Archivio di Stato di Modena (ASMo) *Militaria Estense*

Archivio di Stato di Lucca (ASLu), *Camarlingo Generale*

Archivio di Stato di Mantova (ASMn), *Archivio Gonzaga*

Archivio di Stato della Valletta (ASVa), *Registri delle Camere del Tesoro*

Archives of the Order of Malta (AOM), *Correspondence*

Archivio del Gran Priorato di Venezia e Lombardia del Sovrano Militare Ordine di Malta (ASMOMVe), Venice, *Armamenti, Squadra, Commercio, Corsari, Prede, Schiavi (1430–1699); Marittimi e Commerciali (1684–1700)*

Coeval Works

Biblioteca Naciónal de España, Madrid, *Carta Escrita del Rev. N. al Ill.no continuando la novedades que resultan de las hostilidades, entre la Serenissima Republica di Genova, y el serenissimo*

Ducque de Saboya, y con mas distinta relacion del encuentro de Castel Vecchio (1675); 31. Leg. 2, n. 18.

(Anonymous), *Relazione del Glorioso acquisto della Fortezza di Coron, Capitale del Regno di Morea, fatto sotto il prudente Valoroso Commando dell'Eccellentiss. Signor Cavalier e Procurator Francesco Morosini Capitano Generale da Mar, il giorno 11 Agosto 1685* (Venice, 1685)

(Anonymous), *Esatta Notizia del Peloponneso, volgarmente Penisola della Morea, divisa in otto province.* (Venice, 1687)

(Anonymous), *Diario dell'Assedio di Negroponte assieme a un Giornale delle campagne in Dalmazia* (Venice, 1699)

Alimari, Doroteo, *Instruttioni militari appropriati all'uso moderno di guerreggiare. Opera nuova utile e necessaria a' professori dell'onorata disciplina della milizia* (Nurnberg–Venice, 1692)

Beregani, Nicola, *Historia delle Guerre d'Europa dalla comparsa dell'Armi Ottomane in Ungheria*, Vols I–II (Venice, 1698)

Bizozeri, Simpliciano, *La Sagra Lega contro la Potenza Ottomana* (Milan, 1690)

Bosio, Giacomo, *Dell'Istoria della Sacra Religione et Ill.ma Militia di San Giovanni Gierosolimitano*, Vol. III (Naples, 1684)

Burgo, Giovanni Battista, *Viaggio di cinque anni in Asia, Africa, e Europa*, volls I-IV (Milan, 1688)

Contarini, Camillo, *Istoria della Guerra di Leopoldo I Imperadore e de' Principi Collegati contro il Turco, dall'anno 1683 fino alla Pace*, vols. I–II (Venice, 1710)

Coronelli, Pietro Maria, *Memorie Istorio Grafiche delli Regni di Morea e Negroponte*, vols I–II (Venice, 1687)

Dal Pozzo, Bartolomeo, *Historia della Sacra Religione Militare di San Giovanni Gerosolimitano detta di Malta* (Venice, 1715)

Amelot De La Houssaye, Abraham Nicolas, *Histoire du Gouvernement de Venise*, vol. II (Amsterdam, 1705)

Fontana, Fulvio, *I Pregi della Toscana nell'Imprese più segnalate de' Cavalieri di Santo Stefano* (Florence, 1701)

Foscarini, Michele, *Historia della Republica Veneta* (Venice, 1696)

Garzoni, Pietro, *Istoria della Repubblica di Venezia in tempo della Sacra Lega contra Maometto IV e tre suoi Successori*, Vols I–II (Venice, 1712)

Giustinian, Bernardo, *Historie Cronologiche dell'Origine degli Ordini Militari e di tutte le Legioni Cavalleresche* (Venice, 1692)

Gualdo-Priorato, Galeazzo, *Relatione della Città di Genova e suo Dominio* (Cologne, 1668)

Gualdo-Priorato, Galeazzo, *Relatione della Città di Fiorenza, e del Gran Ducato di Toscana sotto il Regnante Gran Duca Ferdinando II, con tutte le Cose più degne e curiose da sapersi* (Cologne, 1668)

Gualdo-Priorato, Galeazzo, *Relatione della Signoria di Luca e suo Dominio* (Cologne, 1668)

Gude, Heinrich Ludwig, *Staat von Parma und Piacenza, Mirandula und Concordia, Massa und Carrara, Monaco, Doria, St. Piedro, Sesto St. Angelo und dei Fieschi* (1708)

Gude, Heinrich Ludwig, *Staat von Mantua und Monferrat* (1708)

Gude, Heinrich Ludwig, *Der Staat von Florenz, Modena und Reggio* (1708)

Gude, Heinrich Ludwig, *Staat der Republique von Genoua, Lucca und Marino* (1708)

Léonard, Jean, *Histoire des conquêtes des Vénitiens depuis 1684 jusques à présent* (Bruxelles, 1688)

Leti, Gregorio, *Itinerario della Corte di Roma o Vero Teatro Historico, cronologico e politico della Sede Apostolica, Dataria e Cancelleria Romana* (Valenza, 1675), vols I–II.

Locatelli, Alessandro, *Racconto historico della veneta guerra in Levante* (Cologne, 1691)

Marzioli, Francesco, *Precetti Militari* (Bologna, 1678)

Mainenti, Michelangelo (capitano), *Esercizii militari della fanteria secondo l'uso moderno dimostrati* (Venice, 1694)

Moretti, Tommaso, *Trattato dell'Artiglieria* (Venice, 1665)

Muazzo, Antonio, *Guerra coi i Turchi*, Biblioteca Nazionale Marciana, Manoscritti Italiani VII, n. 172 (8187)

Piccinini, Gianfrancesco (ed.), *Il Viaggio di Alessandro II Pico all'Isola di Candia* (Guastalla: Centro Internazionale di Cultura 'Pico della Mirandola', 2009)

Sala, Antonio, *La Prattica in Teorica del Soldato Instruito in Mare* (Venice, 1697)

Siri, Vittorio, *Il Mercurio, overo Historia de' Correnti Tempi*, vols IV–XV (Florence, 1667–82)

Vezzani, Antonio, *L'Esercizio Accademico della Picca* (Parma, 1688)

Viviani della Robbia, Luigi, *Compendio Civile, Economico e Militare della Toscana* (Florence, 1734)

Viceti, Francesco Maria, *Compendioso Racconto De principali Successi della Guerra mossa l'anno 1672 Alla Repubblica di Genova Dal Duca di Savoia Collo stabilimento della Pace nell'Anno 1673 Descritta Dà Francesco M:a Viceti* (Archivio Storico del Comune di Genova, Manoscritti, Ricci, 136, after 1673)

General Documentary Sources

Ales, Stefano, *Insegne militari preunitarie italiane, 1671–1870* (Rome: USSME, 2001)

Botta, Carlo, *Storia d'Italia continuata da quella del Guicciardini*, vols VII–VIII (Paris, 1738)

Cessi, Roberto, *Storia della Repubblica di Venezia* (Florence: Giunti, 1981)

Cont, Alessandro, *Corte Britannica e Stati Italiani, Rapporti politici, diplomatici e culturali (1685–1688)* (Rome: Società Dante Alighieri, 2019), Biblioteca della 'Nuova Rivista Storica' n. 55

Cont, Alessandro, 'L'uomo di corte italiano: identità e comportamenti nobiliari tra XVII e XVIII secolo', in *Rivista Storica Italiana* – a. CXXVI – Fascicolo I, April 2014, pp.94–119

Cremonini, Cinzia and Riccardo Musso (eds), *I feudi imperiali in Italia tra XVI e XVIII secolo* (Rome: Bulzoni, 2010)

Donati, Claudio, 'The Italian Nobilities in the Seventeenth and Eighteenth Centuries', in *The European Nobilities in the Seventeenth and Eighteenth Centuries' Vol. I: Western Europe*, (London–New York: Longman, 1995), pp.237–268

Martin, John; Romano, Dennis (editors), *Venice Reconsidered. The History and Civilization of an Italian City-State, 1297–1797* (Baltimore MA: Johns Hopkins University Press, 2000)

Muratori, Ludovico Antonio, *Annali d'Italia e altre Opere Varie*, vols IV–V (Milan, 1837)

Pezzolo, Luciano, 'Stato, Guerra e Finanza nella Repubblica di Venezia fra Medioevo e prima Età Moderna, in acts of the conference *Navies and State Formation* (Volos, 9–12 September 2004), pp.67–112

Pezzolo, Luciano, *'Violenza, costi di protezione e declino commerciale nell'Italia del Seicento'* in *Rivista di Storia Economica*, vol. 23, (2007), pp.111–124

Pezzolo, Lucino, *'Le spese degli stati italiani, 1350–1700: modelli a confronto' in El alimento del estado y la salud de la república: Orígenes, desarrollo y estructura del gasto público en Europa (siglos XIII–XVII)* (Madrid, Instituto de Estudios Fiscales, 2014), pp.381–402

Raviola, Blythe, 'The Imperial System in Early Modern Northern Italy: A Web of Dukedoms, Fiefs and Enclaves along the Po', in P. H. Wilson and R. J. W. Ewans (eds), *The Holy Roman Empire, 1495–1806: A European Perspective* (Leiden–Boston, MS: Brill, 2012), pp.217–238.

Setton, Kenneth M., *Venice, Austria, and the Turks in the Seventeenth Century* (Philadelphia: The American Philosophical Society, 1991)

Sodini, Carla, *Scrivere e compilare. Galeazzo Gualdo Priorato e le sue relazioni di Stati e città*, (Lucca: Pacini Fazzi, 2004)

Spagnoletti, Angelantonio, *Principi italiani e Spagna nell'età barocca* (Milan: Bruno Mondadori, 1996)

Military History

Bercé, Yves-Marie, 'Les guerres dans l'Italie du XVII siécle', in Y. M. Berce, G. Delille, J. M. Sallmann, J. C. Waquet (eds), with a preface of A. Corvisier, *L'Italie au XVIIe siècle* (Paris: C.D.U.-S.E.D.E.S., 1989), pp.313–331

Del Negro, Piero, 'La storia militare dell'Italia moderna nello specchio della Storiografia del Novecento', in *Istituzioni militari in Italia fra Medioevo ed Età Moderna*, Cheiron, 23 (1995), pp.11–33

Donati, Claudio, 'Il 'Militare' nella Storia dell'Italia Moderna dal Rinascimento all'Età Napoleonica', in C. Donati (editor), *Eserciti e carriere militari nell'Italia moderna* (Milan: Unicopli, 1998), pp.7–39

Donati, Claudio, 'Strutture militari degli Stati italiani nella prima età moderna: una rassegna degli studi recenti', in: *Società italiana di Studi Militari. Quaderno 2000*, P. Del Negro (ed.), *La storiografia militare in Italia e in Francia negli ultimi vent'anni. Due esperienze a confronto.* (Venice, 27–28 aprile 2001), Napoli, E.S.I., 2003, pp.45–62

Donati, Claudio, Militärstrukturen der italienischen Staaten in der frühen Neuzeit: ein Forschungsbericht jüngster Studien, in *Militär und Gesellschaft in der Frühen Neuzeit*, 7 (2003), n. 2, pp.145–167

Hanlon, Gregory, *The Twilight of a Military Tradition. Italian Aristocrats and European Conflicts, 1560–1800* (London: UCL Press, 1998)

Ilari, Virgilio, *Storia del servizio militare in Italia (1506–1870)*, vol. I, *Dall' ordinanza fiorentina di Machiavelli alla costituzione dell'esercito italiano*, Collana del Centro Militare di Studi Strategici (Rome: Rivista Militare, 1990)

Labanca, Nicola (ed.), *Storie di guerre ed eserciti. Gli studi di storia militare italiana negli ultimi venticinque anni* (Milan: Unicopli, 2011)

Lo Basso, Luca, 'Schiavi, forzati e buonevoglie. La gestione dei rematori delle galere dell'Ordine di Santo Stefano e della Repubblica di Venezia. Modelli a confronto' , in *L'Ordine di Santo Stefano e il mare* (Pisa: Edizioni ETS, 2001), pp.171–232

Paoletti, Ciro, *Gli italiani in armi. Cinque secoli di storia militare nazionale 1494–1997* (Rome: USSME, 2001)

Pezzolo, Luciano, 'La 'rivoluzione militare': una prospettiva italiana 1400–1700', in A. Dattero and S. Levati (eds) *Militari in età moderna. La centralità di un tema di confine* (Milan: Cisalpino, 2006), pp.15–62

Pieri, Piero, 'L'evoluzione dell'arte militare nei secoli XV, XVI e XVII e la guerra nel secolo XVIII', in *Nuove questioni di storia moderna*, vol. I (Milan: Marzorati, 1964), pp.1123–1179

Pieri, Piero, 'La storia militare', *in La storiografia italiana negli ultimi venti anni*, vol. II (Milan: Marzorati, 1970)

Stumpo, Enrico, 'La crisi del Seicento in Italia', in M. Firpo and N. Tranfaglia (eds), *La storia. I grandi problemi dal Medioevo all'Età Contemporanea* (Turin: UTET, 1986), vol. V, pp.313–337

Williams, Phillip, 'Mare Nostrum? Reform, Recruitment and the Business of Crusade in the Fleets of the Seventeenth Century Mediterranean', in *Storia Economica, XIX* (Edizioni Scientifiche Italiane, 2016), n. 1, pp.77–102

Savoy-Piedmont

Barberis, Walter, *Le armi del Principe. La tradizione militare sabauda* (Turin: Einaudi, 1988)

Bianchi, Paola, 'La riorganizzazione militare del Ducato di Savoia e i rapporti del Piemonte con la Francia e la Spagna. Da Emanuele Filiberto a Carlo Emanuele II' in García Hernán, E. and Maffi, D. (eds), *Guerra y sociedad en la monarquía hispánica: política, estrategia y cultura en la*

Europa moderna (1500–1700), (Madrid: Fundación MAPFRE, Laberinto; Consejo Superior de Investigaciones Científicas, CSIC, 2006), vol. I, pp.189–216

Bianchi, Paola, 'La corte dei Savoia: disciplinamento del servizio e delle fedeltà' in W. Barberis (ed.), *I Savoia. I secoli d'oro di una dinastia europea* (Turin: Einaudi, 2007), pp.135–176

Bianchi, Paola, 'Immagine e realtà dell'eccezione militare del Piemonte' in P. Bianchi (ed.), *Il Piemonte come eccezione? Riflessioni sulla 'Piedmontese exception'* (Turin: Centro Studi Piemontesi, 2008), pp.57–78

Bianchi, Paola, 'Al servizio degli alemanni. Militari piemontesi nell'Impero e negli stati tedeschi fra Sei e Settecento', in P. Bianchi, D. Maffi, E. Stumpo (eds) *Italiani al servizio straniero in età moderna* (Milan, Franco Angeli, 2008)

Bianchi, Paola, *Sotto diverse bandiere: l'internazionale militare nello Stato sabaudo d'antico regime* (Milan: Franco Angeli, 2012)

Bianchi, Paola, *Educare a corte: paggeria ed Accademia Reale fra Sei e Settecento*, in A. Merlotti (ed.), *Paggi e paggerie nelle corti italiane. Educare al comando* (Florence: Olschki, 2021), pp.45–70

Brancaccio, Nicola, *L'esercito del vecchio Piemonte, 1560-1859. Sunti storici dei principali corpi* (Rome, 1922)

Brancaccio, Nicola, *L'esercito del vecchio Piemonte. Gli ordinamenti. Parte I (1560–1814)* (Rome, 1923)

Duboin, Felice Amato, *Raccolta per ordine di materie delle leggi cioè editti, patenti, manifesti, ecc. emanate negli stati di terraferma sino all'8 dicembre 1798 dai sovrani della Real Casa di Savoja*, vols XXVII–XXVIII (Turin, 1848)

Fiora, Paolo, *Bandiere in Piemonte* (Turin: Centro Studi dell'Accademia di San Marciano, 1971)

Gerbaix de Sonnaz, C. A., *Bandiere, Stendardi e Vessilli di Savoia* (Turin, 1896–1911)

Giuliani, Giuseppe, 'Formazione e Struttura dell'Esercito Sabaudo nel XVII secolo e nel XVIII secolo' in *Studi Storico-Militari* (Rome: USSME, 2009), pp.5–56

Guerrini, Domenico, *La Brigata dei Granatieri di Sardegna. Memorie storiche* (Turin, 1902)

Paoletti, Ciro, *Dal Ducato all'Unità. Tre secoli e mezzo di storia militare piemontese* (Rome: USSME, 2011)

Paoletti, Ciro, *William III's Italian Ally. Piedmont and the War of the League of Augsburg 1683–1697* (Warwick: Helion & Company, 2019)

Ricchiardi, Enrico, *Bandiere della Fanteria Nazionale Sabauda (1690–1773)*, Vol. XVII-2 (Turin: Centro Studi Piemontesi, 1988)

Ricchiardi, Enrico, *Bandiere della Fanteria Straniera al soldo dei Savoia (1690–1773)*, Vol. XVIII-2 (Turin: Centro Studi Piemontesi, 1989)

Ricchiardi, Enrico, *Il Costume Militare Sabaudo*, Vol. I (Turin: Centro Studi Piemontesi, 1989)

Saluzzo, Alessandro di, *Histoire Militaire du Piémont*, Vols IV–V (Turin, 1818)

Salvi, Costantino, *Carlo Emanuele II e la guerra contro Genova dell'anno 1672* (Rome, 1933)

Sconfienza, Roberto, 'Sulla prima uniforme e lo stemma del Reggimento Dragoni di Piemonte', in *Armi Antiche. Bollettino dell'Accademia di San Marciano*, 1995 (1998), pp.75–81

Stumpo, Enrico, *Finanza e Stato moderno nel Piemonte del Seicento* (Rome: Istituto storico italiano per l'età moderna e contemporanea, 1979)

Stumpo, Enrico, 'Guerra ed economia: spese e guadagni militari nel Piemonte del Seicento', in *Studi Storici*, XXVII (1986), pp.371–395

Symcox, Geoffrey, *Victor Amadeus II. Absolutism in the Savoyard State*, 1675–1730 (Berkely–Los Angeles, CA: University of California Press, 1983)

Venice

Beltrame, Carlo and Marco Morin, *I Cannoni di Venezia. Artiglierie della Serenissima da fortezze e relitti* (Florence: All'Insegna del Giglio, 2013)

Birtachas, Stathis, 'Stradioti, Cappelletti, Compagnie or Milizie Greche: Greek Mounted and Foot Mercenary Companies in the Venetian State (1400–1700)', in G. Teotokis and A. Yldiz (eds), *A Military History of the Mediterranean Sea. Aspects of War, Diplomacy and Military Elites* (Leiden–Boston: Brill, 2018), pp.325–346

Candiani, Guido, 'L'evoluzione della flotta veneziana durante la prima guerra di Mora', in *Venezia e il Mediterraneo. La Guerra di Morea* (Venice, Fondazione Querini Stampalia – Dipartimento di Studi Storici Università di Venezia, 2001), pp.1–4

Candiani, Guido, *I vascelli della Serenissima. Guerra, politica e costruzioni navali a Venezia in età moderna, 1650–1720* (Venice: Istituto Veneto di Scienze, 2009)

Candiani, Guido, 'Vele, remi e cannoni: l'Impiego congiunto di navi, galee e galeazze nella flotta veneziana, 1572–1718', in G. Candiani and L. Lo Basso (eds), *Mutazioni e Permanenze nella Storia Navale del Mediterraneo, secc. XVI–XIX* (Milan: Franco Angeli, 2010) pp.116–162

Candiani, Guido, *Dalla galea alla nave di linea. Le trasformazioni della marina veneziana (1572–1699)* (Novi Ligure: Città del silenzio, 2012)

Camporota, Bonaventura, *Vita di Francesco Morosini Peloponnesiaco, Doge di Venezia* (Napoli 1865)

Casini, Matteo, 'Immagini dei Capitani Generali da Mar a Venezia in età barocca', *in* M. Fantoni (ed.), *Il 'Perfetto Capitano'. Immagini e realtà (secoli XV-XVII)* (Rome: Bulzoni, 2001), pp.219–270

Casoni, Giovanni, 'Nota sulle Truppe Marittime e Terrestri della Repubblica di Venezia', in *Venezia e le sue Lagune* (Venice, 1847), vol. I, n 2, pp.251–262

Del Negro, Piero, 'Il Leone in Campo: Venezia e gli Oltramarini nelle Guerre di Candia e di Morea', in S. Graciotti (ed.), *Mito e Antimito di Venezia nel Bacino Adriatico (secoli XV–XIX)* (Rome: Il Calamo, 2001, pp.323–344

Levi-Weiss, Dora, 'Le relazioni fra Venezia e la Turchia dal 1670 al 1684 e la formazione della Sacra Lega', in *Archivio Veneto* (1926), pp.97–155

Mayhew, Tea, 'Soldiers, Widows and Families: Social and Political Status of the Professional Warriors of the Venetian Republic (1645–1718)', in B. Waaldijk (ed.) *Professions and social identity: new European historical research on work, gender and society*, Vol. IV, (Pisa, 2006), pp.89–101

Morton Paton, James, 'A Florentine officer in the Morea in 1687', in *American Journal of Archaeology*, XXXVIII (1934), pp.59–66

Morton Paton, James, *The Venetians in Athens 1687–1688, from the Istoria of Cristoforo Ivanovich* (Harvard–Cambridge, 1940)

Nani-Mocenigo, Mario, *Storia della marina veneziana* (Rome, 1935)

Ongaro, Giulio, 'Il lavoro militare fra XVI e XVII sec.: contadini-soldato nella Repubblica di Venezia tra subordinazione e agency', in *L'empreinte domestique du travail*, Mélanges de l'École française de Rome – Italie et Méditerranée modernes et contemporaines , n. 131-1 (2019), pp.5–30

Panopoulos, Angeliki G. and Kostas G. Tsiknakis, 'Historical Research on the District of Agyos Georgios in the Second Period of the Venetian Rule', in S. Kourakou-Dragona (ed.), *Nemea Beloved Land of Zeus and Dionysos* (Athens: Foinikas Publications, 2011), pp.115–215

Pezzolo, Luciano, 'L'archibugio e l'aratro. Considerazioni e problemi per una storia delle milizie rurali venete nei secoli XVI e XVII', in *Studi Veneziani vol. 7 (1983)*, pp.59–80

Pezzolo, Luciano, 'Esercito e Stato nella prima età moderna: alcune considerazioni preliminari per una ricerca sulla Repubblica di Venezia', in *Studi Veneziani*, vol. 14 (1987), pp.303–322

Pezzolo, Luciano, *'Fonti e problemi per la storia dell'esercito veneziano nella prima età moderna'*, in L. Antonelli and C. Donati (eds), *Al di là delle fonti militari* (Catanzaro: Rubbettino, 2004) pp.32–40

Pezzolo, Luciano, 'Stato, Guerra e Finanza nella Repubblica di Venezia fra Medioevo e Prima Età Moderna', in R. Cancila (ed.), *Mediterraneo in armi (sec. XV–XVIII) – Quaderni di Mediterranea* (Palermo, 2007), pp.67–112

Pezzolo, Luciano, 'Una finanza in guerra, 1645–1669', in G. Ortalli, G. Gullino, E. Ivetic (eds), *L'inestinguibile sogno del dominio. Francesco Morosini* (Venice: Istituto Veneto di Scienze, Lettere e Arti, 2021), pp.65–112

Pinzelli, Éric Guillaume Luc, *La défense de l'isthme de Corinthe durant la période vénitienne (1687–1715)* (Marseille: Université de Provence, Aix-Marseille I, Département d'histoire 1996–1997)

Pinzelli, Éric Guillaume Luc, *Venise et la Morée: du triomphe à la désillusion (1684–1718)* (Marseille: Université de Provence, Aix-Marseille I, Département d'histoire, 2003)

Robuschi, Luigi, *La strategia di Francesco Morosini nella guerra di Morea (1684–1699) e il suo contributo alla nascita delle truppe da sbarco* (Centro Alti Studi per la Difesa – 8° Corso Superiore di Stato Maggiore Interforze, 2005–2006)

Schwenke, Alexander, *Geschichte der hannoverschen Truppen in Griechenland 1685–1689, zugleich als Beitrag zur Geschichte der Türkenkriege. Nach archivalischen Quellen* (Hannover, 1854)

Stouraiti, Anastasia, 'Printing Empire: Visual Culture and the Imperial Archive in Seventeenth-Century Venice', in *The Historical Journal* (April 2016), pp.1–34

Tamburrini, Pierluigi, *L'organizzazione militare veneziana nella prima metà del Settecento* (Rome: SISM, 2014)

(Various Authors), *Francesco Morosini, 1619–1694: l'uomo, il doge, il condottiero* (Rome–Venice: Poligrafico e Zecca dello Stato italiano, 2020)

(Various Authors), *Francesco Morosini in guerra a Candia e in Morea* (Exhibition Guide and Catalogue; Venice: Ente Editoriale per il Corpo della Guardia di Finanza, 2020)

Papal States

Bailly, R., 'La garnison pontificale du Palais des Papes aux XVIIe et XVIIIe siècles', in *Mémoires de l'Académie de Vaucluse*, (1954), pp.66–77

Brunelli, Giampiero, 'Poteri e Privilegi. L'istituzione degli ordinamenti delle milizie nello Stato Pontificio tra Cinque e Seicento', in *Cheiron*, XII (1995), n. 23, pp.105–129

Brunelli, Giampiero, *Soldati del papa. Politica militare e nobiltà nello Stato della Chiesa (1560–1644)* (Rome: Carocci, 2003)

Brunelli, Giampiero, 'Al vertice dell'istituzione militare pontificia: il Generale di santa Chiesa (sec. XVI–XVII)', in A. Jamme and O. Poncet (eds), *Offices et papauté (XIVe–XVIIe siècle)* (Rome: Publications de l'École Française de Rome, 2013), pp.483–499

Da Mosto, Andrea, 'Milizie dello Stato Romano dal 1600 al 1797', in *Memorie Storico Militari*, n. 22 (Città di Castello, 1914), pp.193–579

Giangolini, Luca, *Le Armi del Papa. L'esercito pontificio tra burocrazia curiale e nobiltà. 1645–1740* (Rome: Università La Sapienza, 2018)

Guglielmotti, Alberto, *La squadra ausiliaria della marina romana a Candia ed alla Morea* (Rome, 1883)

Ilari, Virgilio, 'L'esercito pontificio nel XVIII secolo fino alle Riforme del 1792–93', in *Studi Storico Militari 1985*, USSME (Rome 1986), pp.555–664

Ilari Virgilio, 'Gli antenati della Gendarmeria pontificia: il Battaglione de' Corsi e poi Dei soldati in luogo de' Còrsi (1603–1678)', in *Memorie Storico Militari 1983*; USSME (Rome 1984), pp.751–800

Lutz, Georg, 'L'esercito pontificio nel 1667. Camera apostolica, bilancio militare dello Stato della Chiesa e nepotismo nel primo evo moderno', in *Miscellanea in onore di Monsignor Martino Giusti Prefetto dell'Archivio Segreto Vaticano*, II (Città del Vaticano, Archivio Vaticano, 1978), pp.39–95

Paoletti, Ciro, 'La frontiera padana dello Stato Pontificio nel secolo XVII', in C. Sodini (ed.), *Frontiere e fortificazioni di frontiera* (Florence: EDIFIR, 2001), pp.127–134

Paoletti, Ciro, *Le Armi e le Chiavi – Storia militare degli Stati Pontifici nell'età moderna e contemporanea* (Rome: Commissione Italiana di Storia Militare, 2020)

Savestre, B., 'Les Corses au service du Pape' in *Les Troupes Corse et l'histoire militaire de la Corse*, 'Carnet de la Sabretache' - nouvelle série – n. 20 (Special Issue, 1973), pp.22–29

Genoa

Assereto, Giovanni, *La metamorfosi della Repubblica. Saggi di storia genovese tra il XVI e il XIX secolo* (Savona: Daner, 1999)

Beri Emiliano, *Genova e il suo regno. Ordinamenti militari, poteri locali e controllo del territorio in Corsica fra insurrezioni e guerre civili (1729–1768)* (Genoa: Università degli Studi di Genova, 2009–2010)

Dellepiane, Riccardo, *Mura e fortificazioni di Genova* (Genoa: Nuova Editrice Genovese, 1984)

Ferrante, Riccardo, 'La nazione dei genovesi dall'antico regime alla Restaurazione', in A. De Benedictis, I. Fosi, and L. Mannori (eds), *Nazioni d'Italia. Identità politiche e appartenenze regionali fra Settecento e Ottocento* (Rome: Viella – Società Italiana per la Storia dell'Età Moderna – Società per gli Studi di Storia delle Istituzioni, 2012), pp.346–374

Giacomone Piana, Paolo and Riccardo Dellepiane, *Militarium* (Genoa: Brigati, 2004)

Kirk, Thomas Allison, *Genoa and the Sea: Policy And Power In An Early Modern Maritime Republic, 1559–1684* (Baltimore MD: Johns Hopkins University Press, 2005)

Musso, Riccardo, 'Compagnie scelte e ordinarie nello Stato di Terraferma', in *Liguria*, LIII-1 /2, (1986), pp.4–36

Repetti, Giovanni, *L'ochio drito della Repubblica. Amministrazione e vita quotidiana della fortezza genovese del Priamàr di Savona nei secoli XVII e XVIII* (Savona: Elio Ferraris, 1998)

Ornano, Marquis de, *La Corse Militaire* (Paris, 1904)

Ricci, Jean-Baptiste, *Gênes e le maintien de l'ordre aux XVIIe et XVIIIe siècles (1568–1729)*: *les effectifs* (Bastia: Université de Corse, Mémoire de DEA, 1998)

Zanini, Andrea, 'Soldati corsi e famegli. La forza pubblica della Repubblica di Genova nel XVIII secolo', in L. Antonelli and C. Donati (eds), *Corpi armati e ordine pubblico in Italia (XVI–XIX sec.)*, pp.141–180

Tuscany

Angiolini, Franco, *I cavalieri e il principe. L'ordine di Santo Stefano e la società toscana in Età Moderna* (Florence: Edifir, 1996), pp.1–45

Angiolini, Franco, 'Le Bande medicee tra ordine e disordine', in L. Antonelli and C. Donati (eds), *Corpi armati e ordine pubblico in Italia (XVI–XIX sec.)* (Soveria Mannelli CZ: Rubbettino, 2003), pp.9–47

Bonifacio, Gaetano, *Campagne dei cavalieri di S. Stefano in Levante,1684–1688* (Livorno, 1938)

Capponi, Niccolò, *L'organizzazione militare del Granducato di Toscana sotto Ferdinando II de' Medici* (Padova, Università degli Studi, 1998)

Diaz, Furio, *il Granducato di Toscana. I Medici* (Turin: Utet, 1976)

Ferretti, Jolanda, 'L'organizzazione militare in Toscana durante il governo di Alessandro e Cosimo I de'Medici', in *Rivista storica degli archivi toscani*, I (1929), pp.58–275

Gurrieri, Gino, *I cavalieri di Santo Stefano* (Pisa: Nistri-Lischi, 1960)

Hibbert, Christopher, *The House of Medici. Its Rise and Fall* (New York: HarperCollins, 1980)

Labanca, Nicola, 'Le Panoplie del Granduca', in *Ricerche Storiche*, XXV n. 2 (May–August, 1995), pp.295–364

Mugnai, Bruno, 'Il crepuscolo dell'Ercole Tirreno: l'esercito degli ultimi Medici', in *Rivista Medicea* n. 5 (February 2010), pp.40–53

Pezzolo, Luciano, '*Note sulla finanza dello Stato Fiorentino, 1350–1700*', in A. Fornasin and C. Povolo, *Per Furio. Studi in onore di Furio Bianco* (Udine, FORUM, 2014), pp.293–305

Waquet, Jean Claude, *Le Grand Duché de Toscane sous le derniers Medici*, (Rome: Ecole Française de Rome, 1990)

Parma and Piacenza

Hanlon, Gregory, 'Parma during the era of Duke Odoardo, 'the Great' (1630–1650)', in G. Bertini (ed.), *Storia di Parma* vol. IV (Parma: Monte Universitaria, 2014), pp.2–33

Zannoni, Mario and Massimo Fiorentino, *L'esercito Farnesiano dal 1694 al 1731* (Parma: Palatina Editrice, 1981)

Modena

Bonacini, Pierpaolo, 'Per il gran bene della pubblica tranquillità e sicurezza … Giustizia e disciplina militare negli Stati estensi di Antico Regime (secoli XVI–XVII)', in *Historia et Ius*, n. 16 (2019), pp.3–70

Menziani, Alberto, 'L'esercito estense ed austro-estense (1598–1859)', in A. Spaggiari and G. Trenti (eds), *Lo Stato di Modena. Una capitale, una dinastia, una civiltà nella storia d'Europa* (Modena, 1998), Saggi 66 – Ministero per i Beni e le Attività Culturali – Direzione Generale per gli Archivi, pp.699–718

Signorotto, Gianvittorio, 'Modena e il mito della sovranità eroica', in E. Fumagalli and G. Signorotto (eds) *La corte estense nel primo Seicento Diplomazia e mecenatismo artistico* (Rome: Viella, 2012), pp.11–50

Mantua and Guastalla

Giuseppe Coniglio, *I Gonzaga* (Milan: Dall'Oglio, 1967)

Raviola, Blythe Alice, *Il Monferrato gonzaghesco: istituzioni ed élites di un micro-stato (1536–1708)*, (Florence: Olschki, 2003)

Sulpizi, Giorgio, 'L'organizzazione militare del ducato di Guastalla' in *Archivio Storico degli Antichi Stati Guastallesi* (Guastalla: Associazione Guastallese di Storia Patria, 2000), pp.97–162

Lucca

Nelli, Sergio: 'Indicazioni archivistiche circa la presenza militare in Lucca', in *Le fonti per la storia militare italiana in Età Contemporanea* (Rome: Ministero per i Beni Culturali e Ambientali – Ufficio Centrale per i Beni Archivistici, 1993), pp.267–296

Tommasi, Girolamo and Carlo Minutoli, *Sommario della Storia di Lucca* (Florence, 1847)

Malta

Blouet, Brian W., *The Story of Malta* (London: Faber and Faber, 1967)

Del Negro, Piero, 'L'Ordine di Malta e Venezia nelle storie veneziane del Seicento sulla Guerra di Candia' in *Studi Veneziani*, LX (2010), pp.1179–195

Devrım Atauz, Ayşe, *Trade, Piracy, and Naval Warfare in the Central Mediterranean: The Maritime History and Archaeology of Malta* (Middle East Technical University; M.A., Bilkent University, 2004)

Grech, Ivan, 'Dealing with Manpower Shortages in the Mediterranean: the Order of St John's Labour Force problems during the Long Seventeenth Century', in C. Vassallo and S. Mercieca (eds), *The Port of Malta* (Malta, 2018), pp.75–96

Grech, Ivan, 'The Dread of Violence and the Lure of Conflict. Contrasting Attitudes to Warfare: The Case of the Hospitaller Order of St John', in B. Borstner, S. Gartner, S. Deschler-Erb, C. Dalli, I. M. D'Aprile (eds), *Historicizing Religion. Critical Approaches to Contemporary Concerns* (Pisa: Pisa University Press 2010), pp.145–157

Mori Ubaldini, Ubaldino, *La Marina del sovrano militare Ordine di San Giovanni di Gerusalemme, di Rodi e di Malta* (Rome: Regionale Editrice, 1971)

Restifo, Giuseppe, 'I Cavalieri di Malta', in *Mediterranean Studies* (2014), pp.1–11

Messina

Barbagallo, Salvatore, *La guerra di Messina 1674–1678: 'Chiprotegge li ribelli d'altri principi, invita i propri a ribellarsi'* (Naples: Guida, 2017)

Gazzara, Piero, 'La rivolta antispagnola di Messina e la battaglia di Lombardello (1674)', in F. Imbasi (ed.), *Sicilia Millenaria. Dalla microstoria alla dimensione moderna* (Messina: Università degli Studi, 2019), vol. I, pp.173–196

Laloy, Émile, *L'expédition de Sicile et la politique française en Italie (1674–1678)*, vols I–III (Paris, 1929)

Ribot, Luis, *La Monarquía de España y la guerra de Mesina, 1674–1678* (Madrid: Actas, 2002)